Josephus, Paul, and the
Fate of Early Christianity

Josephus, Paul, and the Fate of Early Christianity

History and Silence in the First Century

F. B. A. Asiedu

LEXINGTON BOOKS/FORTRESS ACADEMIC
Lanham • Boulder • New York • London

Published by Lexington Books/Fortress Academic
Lexington Books is an imprint of The Rowman & Littlefield Publishing Group, Inc.
4501 Forbes Boulevard, Suite 200, Lanham, Maryland 20706
www.rowman.com

6 Tinworth Street, London SE11 5AL

Copyright © 2019 by The Rowman & Littlefield Publishing Group, Inc.

All rights reserved. No part of this book may be reproduced in any form or by any electronic or mechanical means, including information storage and retrieval systems, without written permission from the publisher, except by a reviewer who may quote passages in a review.

British Library Cataloguing in Publication Information Available

Library of Congress Cataloging-in-Publication Data

Names: Asiedu, F. B. A., author.
Title: Josephus, Paul, and the fate of early Christianity : history and silence in the first century / F.B.A. Asiedu.
Description: Lanham, MD : Lexington Books-Fortress Academic, 2019. | Includes bibliographical references and index.
Identifiers: LCCN 2018057328 (print) | LCCN 2019004684 (ebook) | ISBN 9781978701335 (electronic) | ISBN 9781978701328 (cloth) | ISBN 9781978701342 (pbk) Subjects: LCSH: Christianity—Origin—Historiography. | Josephus, Flavius. | Church history—Primitive and early church, ca. 30-600—Historiography. | Paul, the Apostle, Saint—Historiography.
Classification: LCC BR138 (ebook) | LCC BR138 .A85 2019 (print) | DDC 270.1—dc23
LC record available at https://lccn.loc.gov/2018057328

In memory of my father
B. B. Asiedu
1932–2014

Contents

Acknowledgments		ix
A Note on Translations		xi
Abbreviations		xiii
Chronology		xvii
Introduction		1
1	Josephus, Paul, and the Early Christians: Before and after 62 CE	21
2	Reading Josephus's Silences: Writing Paul Out of the Jewish Archives of the First Century	65
3	Josephus and Martial in Flavian Rome: The Rhetoric of Silence and the Language of Derision	129
4	Martial, Tacitus, Pliny, and Friends: On Fear, Suspicion, Exile, and Death in Domitian's Rome	197
5	Paul, the Jewish Past, and the Roman Contexts of First Clement	263
Epilogue		319
Bibliography		325
Index		341
About the Author		351

Acknowledgments

The argument that I have developed here received its first public expression in a lecture that I presented some years ago at Emory University in January 2010 during which I discussed briefly Josephus's silence about the fire that destroyed much of Rome in July 64 CE. This book is an expansive account of what I hinted at in that lecture about other silences and omissions in Josephus's writings and their significance for Jewish and early Christian history in the first century. The scholarship on Josephus is extensive, and I have been saved from many errors by the prodigious output of so many scholars. I should like to express my indebtedness to John M. G. Barclay, Christopher Begg, the late Per Bilde, Shaye J. D. Cohen, the late Louis H. Feldman, Martin Goodman, Steve Mason, Tessa Rajak, Daniel R. Schwartz, Seth Schwartz, Paul Spilsbury, and Jan Willem van Henten, among others, without whom the task I set myself would have been impossible.

I simply cannot imagine doing anything worthwhile on Josephus without Louis Feldman in particular. Given Feldman's encyclopedic knowledge of Josephus, I very much expected to find in his extensive writings some reasons as to why Josephus's testimony about the early Christian movement is so minimal and that he never mentions Paul. As such I have had to proceed without the benefit of his wide learning and insight on this and other related topics. Still, I would like to register at the outset that he is the one who has taught me, through his writings, how I should approach Josephus; and whose arguments have helped me formulate my own.

I should first like to express my deepest appreciation and thanks to Neil Elliott of Fortress Academic who reached out to me to make this publication possible.

I would also like to express special thanks to Professor Joel Marcus of Duke University, who encouraged the project, and to Professor David Mor-gan, Chair of the Department of Religious Studies at Duke University, who has extended to me over the last several years the status of a visiting scholar without which my research and writing would have been greatly hampered.

Thanks also to John M. G. Barclay, Daniel Boyarin, Martin Goodman, and Daniel R. Schwartz for responding to my queries about chapter 1; to Darrell L. Bock, for reading through the penultimate versions of chapters 1 and 2; and, also to Phillip Cary, Allen Kerkeslager, and J. Jayakiran Sebastian for feedback on chapter 1. And again to Allen Kerkeslager for help on Josephus chronology.

Other friends have had to endure various renditions of the arguments in this book, and for their patience in listening I am grateful. I should like to mention Rishi Goyal and Leonard Wills who have endured the most.

My thanks also to my nephews Nana Kwame, Kwadwo, Nana Baah, Panyin, and Kakra, whose curiosity and interest about "the Silent Historian" (as they dubbed Josephus) has been encouraging.

Shortly after I began writing the first draft of the book, I received news about the death of my father. That event interrupted my writing for a few months. Much of the writing of the first draft took place in what turned out to be a year of mourning. My father had been aware that I was writing a book that would be dedicated to him; and so it is to his memory that the book is dedicated.

A Note on Translations

I have quoted liberally from primary sources in translation, since so many of the sources in the words of the historical witnesses are not well known. I have also preferred extensive quotation to mere paraphrase because one often loses the voice and tone of the historical actors in paraphrase especially when dealing with material that is inherently self-reflexive. My hope is that by quoting so extensively we can hear the voices (even in translation) of the historical actors as they write for (and speak to) their readers. In so doing I also sacrifice rhetorical effect for extensive documentation. I, therefore, beg the indulgence of the reader when I quote so extensively and so often from the sources.

I have been eclectic in my choice of translations, sometimes preferring much older translations to more recent ones. I have done this, in part, so that this would be accessible to a wide readership since most of the older translations are available in the public domain. So, for example, I adopt, in the case of Martial's Epigrams, the translations from Bohn's Classical Library. Most of the other translations I have cited from the Loeb Classical Library.

Abbreviations

AGJU	Arbeiten zur Literatur und Geschichte des antiken Judentums und des Urchristentums
AJPh	*American Journal of Philology*
AJSR	*Association for Jewish Studies Review*
ALGJ	Arbeiten zur Literatur und Geschichte des hellenistischen Judentums
ANRW	*Aufstieg und Niedergand der romischen Welt*
APF	*Archiv fur Papyrusforschung*
AUSS	*Andrews University Seminary Studies*
BETL	Bibliotheca Ephemeridum Theologicarum Lovaniensium
BJRL	*Bulletin of the John Rylands Library*
BJS	Brown Judaic Studies
BO	Biblica et Orientalia
BR	*Biblical Research*
BZNW	Beitrage zur Zeitschrift fur die Neutestamentliche Wissenschaft
CBNT	Coniectanea Biblica New Testament Series
CBQ	*Catholic Biblical Quarterly*
CBQMS	The Catholic Biblical Quarterly Monograph Series
CJ	*Conservative Judaism*
CPh	*Classical Philology*

CPJ	*Corpus Papyrorum Judaicarum*
CQ	*Classical Quarterly*
CRINT	Compendia Rerum Iudaicarum ad Novum Testamentum
CSCT	Columbia Studies in the Classical Tradition
DBS	*Dictionnaire de la Bible,* Supplement
DSD	Dead Sea Discoveries
ETL	*Ephemerides Theologicae Lovanienses*
FRLANT	Forschungen zur Religion und Literatur des Alten und Neuen Testaments
FSRKA	Frankfurter Studien zur Religion und Kultur der Antike
GBLS	Greifswalder Beitrage zur Literatur und Stilforschung
HDR	Harvard Dissertations in Religion
HSM	Harvard Semitic Monographs
HTR	*Harvard Theological Review*
HUCA	*Hebrew Union College Annual*
HUT	Hermeneutische Untersuchungen zur Theologie
HZ	*Historische Zeitschrift*
JAOS	*Journal of the American Oriental Society*
JBL	*Journal of Biblical Literature*
JJS	*Journal of Jewish Studies*
JNSL	*Journal of Northwest Semitic Languages*
JQR	*Jewish Quarterly Review*
JRS	*Journal of Roman Studies*
JSJ	*Journal for the Study of Judaism*
JSNT	*Journal for the Study of the New Testament*
JSOTSup	Journal for the Study of the Old Testament Supplement Series
JSPSup	Journal for the Study of the Pseudepigrapha Supplement Series
JTS	*Journal of Theological Studies*
LCL	Loeb Classical Library
LEC	Library of Early Christianity
LXX	The Septuagint

MT	Masoretic Text
NT	*Novum Testamentum*
NTOA	Novum Testamentum et Orbis Antiquus
NTS	*New Testament Studies*
PAAJR	*Proceedings of the American Academy of Jewish Research*
Pauly-W.RE	Pauly-Wissowa, *Real-Encyclopadie der klassischen Altertums-wissenschaft*
RB	*Revue biblique*
RQ	*Revue de Qumran*
RSR	*Recherches de Science Religieuse*
SANT	Studien zum Alten und Neuen Testament
SBLDS	Society of Biblical Literature Dissertation Series
SBLMS	Society of Biblical Literature Monograph Series
SBLSCS	Society of Biblical Literature Septuagint and Cognate Studies
SCI	*Studia Classica Israelica*
SHR	Studies in the History of Religions
SJLA	Studies in Judaism in Late Antiquity
SLSR	Sage Library of Social Research
SNTSMS	Society for New Testament Studies Monograph Series
SPB	Studia Post-Biblica
ST	*Studia Theologica*
SupNT	Supplements to Novum Testamentum
TAPA	*Transactions of the American Philological Association*
TLZ	*Theologische Literaturzeitung*
TSAJ	Texte und Studien zum antiken Judentum
TV	*Texte und Untersuchungen zur Geschichte der altchristlichen Literatur*
VC	*Vigiliae Christianae*
VT	*Vetus Testamentum*
WMANT	Wissenschaftliche Monographien zum Alten und Neuen Testament
WUNT	Wissenschaftliche Untersuchungen zum Neuen Testament

TAW	*Zeitschrift fur die alttestamentliche Wissenschaft*
ZRGG	*Zeitschrift fur Religions- und Geistesgeschichte*

Chronology

4 BCE	Death of Herod the Great / Division of his territory
6 CE	Deposition of Herod Archelaus / Roman annexation of Judaea
14 CE	Tiberius Emperor
26 CE	Pontius Pilate prefect of Judaea
c. 30 CE	Crucifixion/Death of Jesus of Nazareth
32/33 CE	Paul's Conversion and Call as Apostle
37 CE	Gaius Caligula Emperor / Birth of Josephus
38 CE	Riots in Alexandria; subsequently Philo leads embassy to Gaius
39 CE	Death of Herod Antipas, ruler of Galilee and Perea
41 CE	Gaius Caligula assassinated; Claudius Emperor
44 CE	Death of Agrippa I; Herod Agrippa II remains in Rome
46–48 CE	Tiberius Julius Alexander (Philo's nephew) procurator of Judaea
48 CE	Death of Herod of Chalcis; Herod Agrippa II made ruler of Chalcis
52–59/60 CE	Antonius Felix procurator of Judaea / Drusilla meets Paul
54 CE	Nero Emperor
59/60–62 CE	Porcius Festus procurator of Judaea
59/60 CE	Herod Agrippa II and Berenice meet Paul

62 CE	Death/Murder of James the Brother of Jesus
62–64 CE	Lucceius Albinus procurator of Judaea
63/64 CE	Josephus leads embassy to Rome
64 CE	July: Great Fire of Rome
64–66 CE	Gessius Florus procurator of Judaea
66 CE	Beginning of Jewish War
67 CE	Fall of Jotapata in Galilee / Josephus Captured
68 CE	Death of Nero
69 CE	Year of the Four Emperors: Galba, Otho, Vitellius, Vespasian
70 CE	Siege of Jerusalem / The Destruction of Temple
71 CE	Josephus in Rome / Triumphal Parade
75 CE	Dedication of Temple of Peace in Rome
75–79 CE	Josephus writes *Jewish War*
79 CE	Death of Vespasian / Titus Emperor
81 CE	Death of Titus / Domitian Emperor
93 CE	Death of Agricola, Tacitus's Father-in-Law
93/94 CE	Josephus completes *Antiquities*
94/95 CE	Josephus completes *Life*
96 CE	September: Assassination of Domitian; Nerva Emperor
97 CE	Josephus probably writes *Against Apion*
98 CE	First Clement: Letter from church of Rome to church in Corinth
98 CE	Tacitus completes *Agricola*; Death of Nerva; Trajan Emperor
100 CE	Pliny delivers Panegyric on Trajan

Introduction

What does a historian owe his readers? What does he owe posterity? What does he owe to the world, if he knows that the archives of his city have been destroyed? What stories can he choose not to tell, especially if he knows that his history may be the only one available with any claim to representing or at least making known so much of what has been lost from living memory and from the archives?

These are some of the questions we should ask when we read the works of the historian Flavius Josephus (37–c. 100 CE), the priest from Jerusalem, commander of Jewish forces in Galilee in the War against the Romans, who surrendered to the Romans in 67 CE, and later took up residence in the city of Rome after the destruction of Jerusalem in 70 CE under the patronage of the Emperor Vespasian and his sons Titus and Domitian.

About Jewish life in the first century, we owe so much to Josephus, and yet there are so many gaps in Josephus's narratives and so much we would like to know about his native Jerusalem and Judaea that Josephus simply does not bother to tell his readers. Especially for the period from the appointment of the High Priest Josephus Caiaphas (18 CE) to the deposition of the High Priest Ananus son of Ananus shortly before the arrival of Albinus as the new procurator/governor of Judaea in 62 CE, Josephus can be annoyingly taciturn about some major figures in Jewish life.

Why, for example, does he not give an account of the High Priest Caiaphas, the longest serving high priest of the first century? Why does he not discuss the origins of Gamaliel the Elder, the great leader of the Pharisees, and the nature of his school, an institution generally considered to have been the most influential in first-century Jerusalem? Why does he say so little about the Christian Jews whom he certainly knew, since he mentions the judicial murder of James the brother of Jesus in 62 CE at the instigation of the High Priest Ananus son of Ananus?

Which brings me to Josephus and Paul the apostle: why does he say nothing about Paul, the former Pharisee, who was his older contemporary, and was almost certainly known to Josephus's father Matthias, if we are to believe Josephus that Matthias was one of the leading men of Jerusalem? It could be that for all their connectedness, Josephus and his father knew nothing about Paul. However, such a claim is an argument from silence simply because Josephus does not mention Paul in his writings. But the fact that Josephus does not mention Paul is not proof that he did not know Paul or anything about Paul just as the fact that he does not mention Tacitus, Pliny the Younger, or Martial is not proof that he did not know them, or know of them, in Rome.

Admittedly, Josephus lived in Rome when Tacitus, Pliny, and Martial were also resident in the city. The case with Paul is different. When Josephus was born in 37 CE, Paul was no longer a resident in the city. He was in the early stages of his mission to the Gentiles. By his own accounts in Galatians, Romans, and First and Second Corinthians, he returned to Jerusalem on a few occasions subsequently during Josephus's formative years. So there was never a period of time when both Paul and Josephus were permanently resident in the city. But that cannot be said for Josephus's father, Matthias, who was Paul's exact contemporary and was one of the leading men of Jerusalem when Paul was coming of age in the city. Matthias was also a priest, and as such would have been aware by personal knowledge, report, or subsequent rumor and gossip among the priests of Jerusalem what took place in the Temple precincts, especially if there were any riots, disturbances, or contentious disputes. In his letters Paul alludes to his personal involvement in such troubles in Jerusalem. Paul is mentioned in a number of episodes of this nature in the Acts of the Apostles. Therefore, unless Matthias was somehow hermetically sealed off from anything that involved Paul during his time in Jerusalem, Matthias would have had some knowledge of Paul who is variously linked to officials of the Temple and the Sanhedrin by the writer of Acts.

Interestingly, Paul is specifically linked to Gamaliel the Elder and to Caiaphas the High Priest in Acts: the former as his teacher, and the latter as his coconspirator or supporter in his persecution of the earliest Christians. Whatever we make of the merits of Acts as a historical narrative, the references in Acts cannot be dismissed as inconsequential for our assessment of Josephus's knowledge or ignorance of Paul and the earliest Christians.

The idea that Josephus did not know Paul or anything about Paul also requires a certain diffidence about Josephus's own claims about how he and his family were enmeshed in social life in Jerusalem, as I have already intimated. So we must at least consider the likelihood that Josephus's silences are not accidental. There is simply no reason or logic, for example, as to why Josephus would not describe the activities of someone like Caiaphas if he was so concerned about preserving Jewish memory about the past and about the institutions of the past that had disappeared on account of the destruction of the Temple in Jerusalem. There is no reason why Caiaphas should be reduced to just the time of his appointment in 18 CE and the time of his deposition in 37 CE (or 36 CE?) since the High Priest was the most important religious and political leader within Jewish life, next only to the King, as Herod the Great and his successors styled themselves.

What of Gamaliel the Elder? Josephus claimed to have affiliated himself with the Pharisees when he entered public life. If he did, he would be doing so in an environment shaped by Gamaliel the Elder and his "school." So why does Josephus leave this important aspect of Jerusalemite society and Jewish history out of his *Antiquities of the Jews*? Why does he do this when he repeatedly comments about the influence the Pharisees exerted on Judaean society in general and Jerusalem in particular?

If, in fact, Josephus deliberately left out any account of Caiaphas and Gamaliel from his writings, then we may be entitled to ask whether these omissions have something to do with how both Caiaphas and Gamaliel feature in the story of the Christian Jews about whom he is also so generally silent. This, in turn, may have some bearing on why he does not report on Paul the former Pharisee turned follower of Jesus and apostle for the gospel of Jesus Christ. So, if we find nothing about Paul in Josephus, it is not because Josephus did not know anything about Paul. It could be that he did not want to provide an account or any account that required an acknowledgment of the Christian Jews as a legitimate group within Judaism. In this respect, he treated Paul and the earliest Christians as *minim* or heretics, beyond the boundaries of legitimate Jewish life.

His reference to James the brother of Jesus may well have been forced upon him because he could not discuss the short but portentous reign of the High Priest Ananus son of Ananus in 62 CE without mentioning his role in the death of James, an event that shocked most of Jerusalem society. The reference to James, of course, implicates Josephus in his silences and omissions, because Josephus had personal knowledge of James in Jerusalem, and not by report, just as he knew personally the High Priest Ananus son of Ananus, and writes about his activities not only in the year 62 CE but up to and including the War.[1] Josephus, in fact, praised Ananus, who was murdered by Idumeans during the War, eulogizing him in Book 4 of the *Jewish War*. When he wrote that tribute in the *Jewish War* (between 75 and 79 CE), years before he attested to Ananus's role in the murder of James in the *Antiquities* (93/94 CE), he was writing with full knowledge that Ananus had, in fact, instigated the murder of James in 62 CE.

In the *Antiquities*, Josephus wrote eulogies for a number of the major biblical characters.[2] Still, his encomium of Ananus son of Ananus, which Steve Mason simply describes as "moving,"[3] stands out as one of the most impassioned in his writings about any person historical or contemporary. Josephus presents Ananus in all his singularity as the one and only person who could have saved Jerusalem and the Jewish nation. He writes:

> I should not be wrong in saying that the capture of the city began with the death of Ananus; and that the overthrow of the walls and the downfall of the Jewish state dated from the day on which the Jews beheld their high priest, the captain of their salvation, butchered in the center of their city. A man on every ground revered and of the highest integrity, Ananus, with all the distinction of his birth, his rank and the honours to which he had attained, still delighted to treat the very humblest as his equals. Unique in his love of liberty and an enthusiast for democracy, he on all occasions put the public welfare above his private interests. To maintain peace was his supreme object. He knew that the Roman power was irresistible, but, when driven to provide for a state of war, he endeavoured to secure that, if the Jews would not come to terms, the struggle should at least be skillfully conducted. In a word, had Ananus lived, they would undoubtedly either have arranged terms–for he was an effective speaker, whose words carried weight with the people, and was already gaining control even over those who thwarted him–or else, had hostilities continued, they would have greatly retarded the victory of the Romans under such a general.[4]

Henry St. John Thackeray suggested that it was modeled after the encomium of Pericles in Thucydides's *History* 2.65.[5] The references to Ananus's integrity, his love of liberty, of democracy, and his concern for the general welfare of the people, to say nothing of the influence he wielded among the people of Jerusalem, confirm the impression. It is difficult to think that Josephus felt so deeply about Ananus without having any personal sentiments about James the brother of Jesus and the group of Christian Jews to which James belonged in Jerusalem before his murder in 62 CE.

Interestingly, the description of Ananus as the champion or captain of their salvation (*hegemona tes idias soterias auton*) resonates with New Testament language about Jesus Christ and his followers in the Epistle to the Hebrews: that the captain of their salvation (*archegon tes soterias auton*), Jesus Christ, was made perfect through suffering (Hebrews 2:10). Later in Hebrews 12:2, Jesus is described as the author and finisher (or perfecter) of their faith. Paul, of course, writes incessantly that Jesus Christ died for the salvation of the world.

The writer of the Epistle to the Hebrews bears witness to the early Christian movement as a patently Jewish reality, much as the writer of the Acts of the Apostles does in describing a movement that began in Judaea and spread through the Roman world. Throughout this work I shall have very little to say about Acts.[6] But, it needs to be kept in the background.

I should like to stress at this point, what is universally acknowledged, that the writer of Acts ends his work at about 61 or 62 CE. Josephus was born in 37 CE. By his own account he did not enter public life until in his nineteenth year, c. 55/56 CE. Josephus's language is very specific. He uses the verb *politeuesthai*, literally, "to live as a citizen." However, for someone who was already a citizen of Jerusalem it has the connotation of doing political things, if you like. That is, to participate in the politics of the city (*polis*), to which he returned after his experiment in asceticism with a teacher named Bannus. It was not simply that he came of age, but that he began to participate in the political life of the city of Jerusalem.[7] So, if Josephus would not have been a public figure until 55/56 CE, then the period of his public/political life that coincides with Acts is precisely the six or seven years between 55/56 CE and 62 CE. Curiously, this falls within the seven-year period, from age nineteen to twenty-six, that Josephus also elides from his autobiography (*Life* 12).

This important omission, deliberate in every way on Josephus's part, prevents his readers from knowing just how he conducted himself among the Pharisees and the leading men of Jerusalem. It prevents us from knowing what Josephus knew, did, with whom he did it, and so on, as a political figure. The only detail that he provides in his writings is that he knew in 62 CE the events surrounding the murder of James the brother of Jesus. That incident, interestingly enough, is not recorded by Acts, which seems completely unaware of it. Since James features in the earlier part of Acts, and makes his final appearance in Acts 21:18 in the presence of Paul and the writer of Acts, who accompanied Paul to see James, his death would have been an important detail to add, if in fact the writer was writing after the event.

To those who might ask why Acts does not mention Josephus, the answer is relatively simple. In 55/56 CE, when Josephus claims to have begun his public career, the story told by Acts enters its final phase. The eighteen- to nineteen-year-old Josephus would not have attracted much attention in Jerusalem unless he was specifically tasked to do something exceptionally important at a time when his own father was still very active. Nevertheless, that eighteen to nineteen-year old would have been aware of what was going on in public life, if that is when he made his entry into the larger world of Jerusalem's political and social culture much of it centered around the Temple and the priests associated with it. Those early years of his public life (55–59 CE) would have coincided with the last few chapters of Acts that are centered on Paul's arrest in Jerusalem. It would, therefore, have been easier for Josephus to know about Paul's arrest than for the writer of Acts, to have known about Josephus, even if the author of Acts was in Jerusalem at the time.

Consequently, we cannot insist or maintain with any historical credibility that under no circumstances could Josephus or his father have known anything then or subsequently about the arrest of Paul in Jerusalem in the period between 55 and 59 CE. Thus, the burden of proof is upon those who insist that under no circumstances could Josephus or his father have known anything about Paul, not on those who surmise or conjecture, based on Josephus's own language about his involvement in Jerusalem politics, that Josephus and his father must have known something about Paul. We simply cannot presume as a matter of historical verity that the eighteen- to twenty-two-year-old Josephus (c. 55–59 CE), who was affiliated with the Pharisees in Jerusalem, who was a priest and the son of a priest, and whose father was among the leading men of Jerusalem, would not have known about the arrest of Paul in Jerusalem that involved leaders of the Temple and eventually led to Paul being sent to the procurator Felix in Caesarea Maritima, according to Acts. It is against this presumption that we shall have to proceed, knowing as well that it is Josephus who deliberately chose not to provide the details that would have allowed his readers to know what he did and what he knew during those early years of his public and political life in Jerusalem.

Anyone with even the slightest interest in matters concerning the history of the first century in the few decades before and the three decades after the destruction of Jerusalem and its Temple in 70 CE ought to be interested in Josephus's silences and omissions, and of his silence about Paul. The structure of the question about Paul is similar to one that could be posed about the Rabbinic tradition and the exclusion of Josephus from the Mishnah (redacted in the early third century) and in any of the traditions of the Talmud (Palestinian and Babylonian) that claim to go back to the first century. In spite of the indispensable nature of Josephus's writings for our understanding of the first century, Josephus is nowhere mentioned in the Mishnah or the traditions in the Talmud dealing with matters of the first century. This prompts the question whether he was deliberately excluded. The Mishnah and the Talmud, then, appeared do to Josephus what Josephus seems to do to Paul. The irony, of course, is that while Josephus is not mentioned in the Talmud, there are a few allusions to a character in the Talmud who looks like Paul.

Although there are many references in the Mishnah about the sages of Tiberias and Sepphoris, there is not a single reference to anything related to Josephus, even though Josephus was well known to the generation that lived from the time of the destruction of Jerusalem through the end of the first century in Tiberias, Sepphoris, and other places in Galilee. Based on the silence of the traditions in the Talmud about Josephus one might be tempted to say that the rabbis knew nothing of Josephus.[8] Yet, Josephus had done everything to ensure that those in Galilee, among others, would have a proper view of his motives, acts, and choices during the War with the Romans and its aftermath when he settled in Rome. Not too long after the War he produced what we presume to be an Aramaic version of his *Jewish War* especially for the benefit of those in Northern Mesopotamia, a work that is not extant. We must presume it had a readership in the Jewish communities of Northern Mesopotamia, including the Kingdom of Adiabene, since the Adiabene Royals had contributed to the War and also suffered a tragic fate. The subsequent Greek version of the *Jewish War* must also have attracted attention in the cities and towns of Galilee that had escaped the depredations of the War.[9] Much later Josephus would write his *Life* primarily to counter the criticism and aspersions of Justus of Tiberias who had been active during the War and who questioned in his own work about the War aspects of Josephus's account in the *Jewish War*. As late as the ninth century Bishop Photius of Constantinople commented on both Josephus and Justus in his *Bibliotheca* (C. 33). Photius did not have a copy of Justus's work on the War but he had another work that he described as his "Chronology of the Kings of Judah" (a history from Moses to Agrippa II, the seventh ruler from the family of Herod).

To think that after all these efforts made by Josephus and Justus of Tiberias as writers of Jewish history and as participants in the most recent events no one in Tiberias or Sepphoris in the period between 70 and 100 CE would have known of Josephus and his *Jewish War* is beyond belief. To suggest that the rabbis who began to consolidate their authority as the most legitimate transmitters of Jewish tradition, some of whom were connected to Tiberias and Sepphoris, had no memory of Josephus, also strains credulity. Yet this view has the status of a universal consensus. Martin Goodman avers:

> In striking contrast to the reception of Josephus' writings by Christians, Jews seem to have been altogether unaware of his works for almost a millennium after the author's death. Nothing in the voluminous Hebrew and Aramaic rabbinic literature from late antiquity betrays a knowledge of Josephus' narrative despite the deep theological significance attached to its central theme, the destruction of the Jerusalem Temple. Intriguing parallel stories, such as the legend that the rabbinic sage Yohanan ben Zakkai prophesied to the general Vespasian that he would become emperor, suggest the circulation of common traditions about the history of the first century, but there is no evidence that rabbinic Jews read any of Josephus' extant works before the Middle Ages.[10]

Goodman does not consider that the legend about Yohanan ben Zakkai may itself be an attempt (*the* attempt?) to supplant Josephus as the one who laid claim to have given the prophecy about Vespasian's rise to be *imperator*, a claim known to Josephus's younger Roman contemporaries including Suetonius, who makes reference to it. Everything about Josephus's reactions to the alleged calumnies of Justus of Tiberias indicate that the people of Tiberias knew about Josephus's works in the period before the end of the first century. So the traditions associated with the earliest rabbis from Tiberias could not have been ignorant of Josephus.

The presumption that the rabbis and the transmitters of the early Rabbinic tradition knew nothing of Josephus rests on yet another fallacy. Josephus and Herod Agrippa II were both present at the siege of Jerusalem. If the later Rabbinic tradition can transmit traditions about Rabbi Yohanan ben Zakkai's escape from Jerusalem during the siege, those same traditions could not plead complete ignorance about both Josephus and Herod Agrippa II. If they bear witness in any way to Agrippa II and the siege of Jerusalem, they surely must have known about Josephus and his role in the conquest of Jerusalem.

To the point: if no one is entitled to the claim that the people of Tiberias and Sepphoris did not know Josephus, then no one is entitled to the claim that the rabbis did not know of Josephus. This is to say that the earliest rabbis could not have been ignorant of Josephus even if they wanted to be; and the later rabbis of late antiquity could not have been either. The nonexistence of Josephus in the earliest traditions of the Talmud, whether Palestinian or Babylonian, cannot be construed as merely inadvertent. Yet, it rarely receives sustained comment,[11] as if it was and is to be expected, because presumably the rabbis either had no interest in Josephus or that Josephus's historical works were irrelevant to late antique Jewish traditions.

To speak of Josephus's silences concerning Paul and the earliest Christians is also to gesture in part to the Herodians, and in particular to three of the four children of Herod Agrippa I, king of Judaea from 41–44 CE. Marcus Julius Agrippa (27/28–92/93 CE?), Berenice (b. 28 CE), and Drusilla (38–79 CE) all encountered Paul, if we are to believe the Acts of the Apostles; and all three are featured in Josephus's narratives. Josephus does not speak of any personal interactions with Berenice, though her presence in Rome in the company of Titus gives reason to believe that Josephus could not have avoided coming into contact with her. Nor does he speak about any personal contact with Drusilla (who was only a year younger than Josephus and died in the eruption of Mt. Vesuvius in 79 CE).[12] He does, however, indicate a personal relationship with Marcus Julius Agrippa—that is, Herod Agrippa II—king of Chalcis in southern Lebanon (and adjoining territories), who bore the same name as his father Herod Agrippa (or Agrippa I). Agrippa II was well known to Josephus before the War with the Romans and the years afterward. Josephus counted on him for some of what he knew or learned about the Herodians.[13]

Josephus and Agrippa II appear to have been on agreeable terms in the context of the War with the Romans, and on friendly terms through the writing of Josephus's *Jewish War*. The relationship may well have soured subsequently, since Josephus presents a more negative and condemning portrait of Agrippa II in his *Antiquities*. All the same, Josephus provides enough details about Agrippa II in the *Jewish War*, the *Antiquities*, and the *Life* to underscore just how much or how little of Roman and Jewish life escaped Agrippa II during the first century. Agrippa II would not have been ignorant of much of what transpired in the social and political world of Jerusalem in Judaea and in the localities around Sepphoris and Tiberias in Galilee.

Agrippa II's oversight of the Temple and the office of the High Priest was particularly noteworthy from 56 to 66 CE, as he was responsible for the deposition of more than five of the High Priests appointed during this period. Agrippa II was undoubtedly responsible for the appointment of the High Priest Ananus son of Ananus, who instigated the judicial murder of James the brother of Jesus in 62 CE.[14] In appointing Ananus son of Ananus as High Priest, Agrippa II must surely have had some sense of how the rulership of the Herodians paralleled the rule of the line of the High Priest Ananus (Annas)[15] and those of his five sons (including Ananus) and son-in-law Caiaphas who variously served as High Priest in the first century.[16] Agrippa II also knew the apostle Paul, if we are to believe the account in Acts 25:13–26:32 that has Paul appearing before him as he waited to be sent to Rome for trial. This means that Agrippa II knew of both James the brother of Jesus and Paul the apostle in a way that makes it impossible to argue that he would have been ignorant of the Christian Jews.

Agrippa II's special oversight of the Temple during the period 56 to 66 CE overlaps also with Josephus's emergence into public life between 56 and 63 CE, according to his *Life*, which is to say that Paul's arrest in Jerusalem described in Acts occurred during Josephus's active years as a young man affiliated with the Pharisees in Jerusalem.[17] Curiously, Josephus deliberately leaves out of his *Life* any account of his activities in the period between 56 and 63 CE. One has to wonder why.

Agrippa II also knew the Emperor Claudius, and he knew Nero; and he knew Vespasian and his son Titus, although he seems to have had very little contact with Domitian and appears to have retreated into his provincial world during the reign of Domitian, when Josephus was still active in Rome. He knew as well one of Josephus's harshest critics, Justus of Tiberias, who at one time served as his secretary.[18] Agrippa II had the historical background and knowledge of Rome and the Romans as well as his fellow Jews or Judaeans to discern Josephus's many moods and complicities. As an almost exact contemporary of Josephus, and precisely because of his lineage, the various roles he played, and the families to which he was connected throughout the Roman Empire, Agrippa II was well placed as a reader and especially as a critic of Josephus's historical writings. That was certainly the case when Josephus completed the Greek version of his *Jewish War* a few years after the War with the Romans.[19] Had Agrippa II lived to see the completion of both the *Antiquities* and the *Life*, he most certainly could and would have exercised his prerogatives as reader and critic. He would have had his sister Berenice as testator to what he knew, if she was alive at the time.

Probably more than any one of Josephus's contemporaries who survived the Jewish War with the Romans, Agrippa II knew or could easily have discerned the extent of Josephus's silences across the broad swath of Jewish history in the first century; which is to say that he was just as important a witness to the first century as Josephus the son of Matthias; and perhaps more so because he was the last of the Herodians. Unfortunately, Agrippa II did not venture a history of Jewish life and institutions in the first century (and neither did Berenice). If he had, he very well would have offered the basis for an important comparison in the stories he would have told and those that Josephus did in fact tell and those Josephus deliberately left out or chose not to tell.

We shall have to keep this in mind in what follows. It is an important element of the story that cannot be written, since we do not have the sources for such an account, but it will have to be imagined, for Josephus's silences allude to so much that Agrippa II and Berenice knew that Josephus simply elided from his historical writings. In this regard it is worth recalling the words in Josephus's *Life* in one of the letters out of the sixty-two that Josephus claims Agrippa II wrote to him. Agrippa II wrote in relation to the *Jewish War* that "whenever you should next meet me, I myself will inform you of many things that are not widely known."[20] We can be sure that there were many other things about Jewish life and history in the first century that were not widely known, about which Josephus was ignorant or silent, but about which Agrippa II was well informed.

As an important source of information for some parts of both Josephus's *Jewish War* and his *Antiquities*; as one of the most prominent among Josephus's most well-placed and well-informed putative readers; and as someone who knew Paul, the apostle and missionary of the Christian movement, Herod Agrippa II could easily detect the resonances between the account of the conversion of King Izates of Adiabene narrated by Josephus and Paul's missionary activities among the Gentiles.

The story of the conversion of King Izates (or Izates II) had been known at least since 44 CE, the year of the death of Agrippa II's father, Herod Agrippa I. At that time Agrippa II was living in Rome as a member of the household of the Emperor Claudius. By the time Agrippa II was ruling over an extended territory including the previous domains of his uncle Philip the Tetrach (ruled 4 BCE–c. 34 CE) in 53 CE and superintending the Temple in Jerusalem, the Adiabene royals had established themselves in Jerusalem by building a palatial residence near the Temple Mount. Josephus begins his narrative of the conversion of Izates in *Antiquities* 20.17–96 within the general framework of the period when Cuspius Fadus was procurator or governor of Judaea (42–44 CE). The story was also well known to Judaeans because Queen Helena, the mother of Izates, had contributed to relief efforts to help the victims of famine in Judaea most likely in 44 CE. So long before Josephus presented his narrative of the conversion of King Izates in his *Antiquities* in the early 90s, the Judaeans knew about the conversion of the Adiabene royals.

Without question, the reception of Josephus's works was constrained by the cost of the production of his books and by the occasions during which Josephus had the books read to audiences in Rome.[21] He mentions some who purchased copies of his works, but he gives little indication of oral performances of the reading of his writings. Still, those Jews/Judaeans who survived the War with the Romans, such as they were, and who had the ability to read/hear Josephus's writings, would no doubt have appreciated the account of the Adiabene royals as a fitting tribute intended to preserve the memory of Queen Helena and her son King Izates for posterity. Almost no one who read it or heard it read was likely to forget the tale.

Of course, Agrippa II himself would have known the story before Josephus committed it to writing. It is, therefore, most likely that as Agrippa II listened (with his sister Berenice) to Paul give his apologia and describe his mission to the Gentiles (Acts 26:1–27) he would have thought about the parallels between what Paul was saying and what he knew of the conversion of the Adiabene royals and the two Jews/Judaeans (Ananias and Eleazar), who had contributed to that process. The parallels would not have escaped a hearer like Agrippa II, neither would they have escaped both of his sisters, Berenice and Drusilla (Acts 24:24), who would have had some sense of how Paul's activities reflected some of what obtained in the conversions of the Adiabene royals.

My discussion proceeds in five chapters. The first two chapters cover various aspects of Josephus and his silences as a methodological and historiographical problem for the history of early Christianity, while the remaining three chapters deal with Josephus and his contemporaries in Rome during and shortly after the reign of the Emperor Domitian (81–96 CE), including the likes of Tacitus, Pliny the Younger, and Martial; as well as the Christians of Rome who produced the work that has come down to us as First Clement.

Chapter 1, "Josephus, Paul, and the Early Christians: Before and after 62 CE," probes the question as to why Josephus is so reticent about the early Christians of Judaea and Rome and why he is completely silent about Paul the apostle, his older contemporary. I pay particular attention to the year 62 CE, which Josephus covers in different parts of his *Jewish War* and *Antiquities*, while maintaining complete silence about that year and his own activities in his *Life*, and suggest that his knowledge of events for that year make it impossible for him to claim ignorance about the early Christians, and possibly about Paul.

My point of departure for chapter 2, "Reading Josephus's Silences: Writing Paul Out of the Jewish Archives of the First Century," is Josephus himself. I use his own words about the silences of a previous historian who had lived in Syria, who nevertheless ignored Jews or Judaeans when he wrote a universal history. Josephus considers his silence unpardonable and provides reasons why he thinks the said historian ignored Jews and Judaeans. From this standpoint, I explore Josephus's own silences about Paul the apostle and the early Christian movement in Jerusalem, Galilee, and Rome. I point out that while some of Josephus's younger contemporaries among the Romans made sure to mention the Christians of Rome, Josephus seemed either indifferent or determined to be silent.

One important element of my discussion in this chapter involves the general state of the sources outside the canonical New Testament that attest to the Christian movement in the first century. Rather than focusing on the three passages in Josephus that are at the center of discussions about the Christian movement, I suggest a different point, namely, that great fire that destroyed most of the city of Rome in 64 CE. That is a matter of historical record. It is an event that is attested by Pliny the Elder, Tacitus, and Suetonius. Surprisingly, Josephus never mentions this event in any of his writings. I probe Josephus's silence about this catastrophic event and its impact on a nascent group associated with one Chrestus or Christus (as Tacitus reports it).

The Fire of 64 is an event about which Josephus could not possibly have been ignorant since he was almost certainly in Rome or nearby at the time. He gives an account of his mission to Rome in his *Life*, how he become friends with Nero's wife, and yet manages throughout his various narratives to avoid mentioning this most important event in the city's recent history and the light it sheds on Roman attitudes about the new "superstition" that had emerged from Judaea, according to Tacitus and Suetonius.

For a modern comparison, think of it this way: let us assume there was a prominent foreigner who was in New York City when the catastrophe of 9/11 took place in 2001. Now let us imagine that the same person returned to live in New York City a few years later. Having lived in New York City for about two decades, the same prominent person writes his autobiography, and in the autobiography he mentions that he visited New York City in 2001. However, he makes no mention of the event of 9/11, not does he allude to it in any of his writings which he produced while living in New York City all that time. What would we think? Naturally, we would suspect that the said individual had something to hide or that he wished to conceal the fact; and that perhaps there are aspects of the event he did not wish to acknowledge, make known, or discuss. One might even suspect that he intended to suppress the event entirely. Well, this is what Josephus does with the Fire of 64 CE that destroyed much of Rome. His younger contemporaries in Rome who wrote about the event connected it with the Christians of Rome.

Josephus's silence about the Fire of 64 CE may be his first most significant act about erasing the Christians of Rome from first-century history, the full effects of which will not be clear until we set his other silences in context: that he remained silent about so much while living in Rome in the last two decades of the first century.

I consider it an essential methodological premise that Josephus's *Life* (his autobiography) be compared with the autobiographical elements in the so-called seven authentic letters of Paul. The next section of the chapter, then, takes aim at the parallel lives of Josephus the Pharisee and Paul the former Pharisee. Here I compare Josephus's *Life* with Paul's Letter to the Galatians as two primary sources for first-century Jewish life. Against this backdrop I then discuss how Josephus's extensive treatment of Queen Helena and her son King Izates of the Royal House of Adiabene in Northern Mesopotamia broaches many themes that are found in Paul's biography: a Jewish mission to Gentiles, the conversion of Gentiles, the problem of circumcision and conversion; the role of proselytes in Judaism, the nature of Jewish Law, etc. Yet, Josephus has no interest in Paul who typifies in his mission to the Gentiles all these elements that Josephus describes in his various narratives about the Adiabene royals. In fact, the story about the Adiabene royals that Josephus tells sometimes reads as if it is meant as a counternarrative to Paul's mission to the Gentiles. My point here is to suggest that his preoccupation with the conversion of the Adiabene royals shows Josephus deeply interested in matters of Jewish missionary activity and the conversion of Gentiles. So at some level the missionary activities of Christian Jews, who were his contemporaries, would have attracted his attention. Yet, Josephus nowhere so much as hints at this reality.

The attention Josephus pays to the conversion of the Adiabene royals from Mesopotamia who emigrated to Jerusalem is fundamental to the story he tells. So it is not incidental to his understanding of what the kingdom of Adiabene meant to the Jews of the first century. The Royal palaces they built in Jerusalem near the Temple complex were a sight to marvel at. Queen Helena became a well-known personality in Jerusalem for her philanthropy, and in particular the role she played in buying grain from Egypt and distributing it to people in Judaea during a famine. Curiously, the historical time of the Adiabene narrative parallels the most active period of Paul's mission to the Gentiles. But Josephus, apparently, knew nothing, nor heard anything after the fact even from someone like Agrippa II who encountered Paul.

If it were left to Josephus, we should never know that a certain Paul, a former Pharisee and contemporary of Josephus's father in Jerusalem, was the central figure in the expansion of the nascent movement that began in Judaea with the preaching of Jesus and spread throughout Syria, Asia Minor, and ultimately found a home in Rome at the end of the first century, when Josephus was writing his *Antiquities*, *Life*, and *Against Apion*.

In the final part of the chapter, I add that the early writing called the *Didache* in many ways attests to communities of Christians whose self-understanding was inseparable from their sense of Jewishness. Their very existence, the sense of belonging to the God of David, attests to a self-consciousness of Christianity as patently Jewish: meaning that whatever they were, they did not think of themselves as situated outside of Jewish life, because they belonged to the God of David. The *Didache* attests to the earliest Christians in the way that Josephus's writings do not. I suggest in the end that Josephus attempted something akin to a historical *ostracism*, just as the ancient Athenians did when they voted to exclude members from their community by writing their names on *ostraka* (pieces of pottery) to vote them out. Josephus's silences were intended to effect the exclusion of Christian Jews from the archives of Jewish life in the first century.

Chapter 3, "Josephus and Martial in Flavian Rome: The Rhetoric of Silence and the Language of Derision," begins with a discussion of Josephus's *Life* as containing one of the most remarkable omissions and silences in the Josephus corpus. I point out that the promise Josephus made at the end of his *Antiquities* concerning three works that he intended to write is a promise that Josephus left unfulfilled. Not only did he renege on the promises, but the autobiography that he wrote subsequently left out more than half of his life even as he insisted that he had provided an account of his entire life. I call attention to this fact as an act of deliberate silence, the upshot of which was that Josephus refused to document Jewish life in Rome in the last three decades of the first century, an astonishing feat from the singular historian of Jewish life in the first century.

The rest of the chapter sets Josephus in relation to Martial, who claimed to be the most widely read poet in Rome in the later part of the first century. He was there for three decades. Martial's poetry is racy, bawdy, indecent, and sometimes obscene. Although Martial resorts to anti-Jewish derision, and should have attracted Josephus's attention, if Josephus was so concerned about it to write his *Against Apion*, Josephus never mentions Martial. This is curious because presumably everyone was reading Martial.

Socially, Martial could not have been ignorant of Josephus, if as seems abundantly clear, Martial was close to the court of the Emperor Domitian in all the ways that he describes his access to Domitian in his epigrams. As a corollary, if Josephus continued to receive favors from Domitian, it is well-nigh impossible to believe Josephus was also a stranger to those who were the familiars at Domitian's court, and certainly not a poet as famous and as current as Martial. As for Josephus, was there any Judaean more well known in Rome than the Judaean General who was captured by Vespasian and then lived in Vespasian's former apartment in Rome after the Jewish War?

Another way of thinking about Josephus is to think of him as a kind of representative figure, perhaps the most well-known Jew in Rome in the time of the Flavians. In this respect, whatever Martial said about Jews or "conquered" or "burned-out" Jerusalem was said partly and somewhat indirectly about Josephus. To respond to anti-Jewish calumny, Josephus did not write against Martial, ignoring the very person who was producing and disseminating his contemptuous epigrams and invective. Instead Josephus wrote against the Alexandrian grammarian Apion, who had been dead for nearly half a century. Why write against the dead when Martial was doing in the present what Apion had done in the first half of the century? Why attack Apion when Martial was a living representation of that same reality in front of Josephus? It is as if Josephus preferred a fictional altercation with a long dead and disgraced critic rather than engage his contemporaries living in Rome, all the while pretending, protesting, and pontificating that he was in fact addressing his contemporaries who poured scorn on Jews.

What is more, Philo Judaeus, his fellow Alexandrian, had disputed against Apion in the legation sent to the Emperor Gaius Caligula to plead the cause of the Jews of Alexandria after the riots of 38 CE. Philo had undertaken to respond to others who also calumniated Jews. So it was not entirely necessary for Josephus to write *Against Apion* when Philo had already covered much of the same terrain in works like *In Flaccum*, *Legatio ad Gaium*, etc.

I argue that Josephus's *Against Apion* is really an attempt by Josephus to rehabilitate himself after the assassination of Domitian in 96 CE. After praising the Flavians for so long, and after adverting in the concluding paragraphs of his *Life* how much he enjoyed the patronage of Domitian with barely a word about Domitian's tyranny and reign of terror that paralyzed the Roman Senate and many of Rome's elite, Josephus's situation became untenable once Domitian had been killed.

Josephus was not alone in this. Martial too found himself in a similar if more dire predicament. Martial tried to extricate himself from his own past and present by attempting a remake of his image among the citizens of Rome. When that refashioning did not work, Martial had to leave Rome to return to his native Bilbilis in Spain. It was an elected self-exile from Rome. He simply did not have a choice. His presence in post-Domitian Rome was no longer tenable.

Josephus, had he been an encomiast like Martial, would have been subject to the same fate. Pliny the Younger provides a captivating description in his *Panegyricus* of how a number of dastardly characters who had been part of Domitian's reign of terror were put on boats and sent into almost certain ruin by the Emperor Trajan. I do not suppose that Josephus was one of them. But he could have been if he had behaved as badly as they had.

Under the circumstances, Josephus needed to provide an account of himself. He had to defend himself now that the last of the Flavians had been eliminated and the Flavian dynasty, such as it was, had come to an end.

Josephus had to explain himself to the citizens and residents of Rome as to who and what he now was as "Flavius Josephus." He chose to defend himself as a Jew—not as a Roman who had taken the name of the Flavians, but as a Jew who could have the name Flavius but who still belonged as a Jew. It is this background that gives the *Against Apion* its surreal and fictive quality that is so often overlooked by historians. Josephus was defending his life, his Jewish past, and ostensibly a Jewish future that he himself had done very little to exemplify in the more than two decades he lived in Rome. For one who seemed to have given up on Jewish ways, Josephus now turned apologist and evangelist/missionary for the Jewish constitution (*politeuma*) and the superiority of the laws handed down by Moses. He writes about Jewish society as a *theokratia*, a theocracy, but does not use the more common word he employs in the *Antiquities*, where he speaks of Jewish rites and customs as *thrēskeia*,[22] which calls attention to both the cultic and ethical aspects of Jewish life. He did all this against the damning of Domitian's memory that was taking place in Rome at the time. *Against Apion* is as much an *apologia* as it is anything else. For that reason, I argue, it is also a self-parody. All the more so because Josephus never once even hints that living in the time of Domitian was as terrifying as some of his Roman contemporaries claimed. Once more, Josephus is engaged in dissimulation about all that is around him.

Chapter 4 considers the circle of Pliny the Younger, Tacitus, Suetonius, and other Romans who endured the times of Domitian and what they had to say about it after Domitian's assassination in September 96 CE. I detail the sense of fear that characterized Roman life in the fifteen years of Domitian's reign and how this background is critical for appreciating the Roman contexts of First Clement, Josephus's culpable silences about Domitian, and his deliberate silences about his living contemporaries in Rome.

It is a complement to the story that I recount in chapter 3 about Josephus and Martial. This time, I present the state of things from the perspective of non-Jews like Pliny the Younger, Tacitus, and their contemporaries in Rome who endured the years of Domitian. Their experience of fear and how they managed those times help us appreciate what it must have been like for the Christians who produced First Clement to live in Rome at this time. It is this reality that also contributes to the absence of any sources that attest to a significant Christian presence in Rome between 81 and 96 CE. Yet, without such a presence, the church in Rome would not have been sought out by the church of Corinth in helping resolve its internal difficulties, the request that led to the writing of First Clement.

Chapter 5, thus, contains an essay on the worlds of First Clement, which included Josephus, even if Josephus does not mention the Christians of Rome who produced First Clement. In his silence about the Christians of Rome during his nearly three-decade stay in the city, Josephus does something similar to what he did with the Fire of 64, which was linked to the Christians in the minds of the people of Rome. Josephus, as I note in chapter 2, never mentions that event in the books he wrote in the last decade of the first century. Here too, even as he lives among Christians in Rome, they are nowhere in any of his writings. He does not even try to say the most basic things that Tacitus and Suetonius would say about them in their respective historical works. In addition, the lack of any references in the extant writings of Tacitus and Pliny the Younger in particular, who lived in Rome at this time when Josephus was also a resident, points once again to the need to read the extant sources from Josephus and his contemporaries with care. For one might be tempted to use the absence of Josephus in Tacitus and Pliny the Younger, for example, as evidence that neither knew Josephus or knew about him. Yet, it is certain that they knew Josephus, since their contemporary and mutual friend Suetonius knew Josephus and mentioned him as if everyone else did as well (Suetonius, *Vespasian* 5.6).

Chapter 5, thus, contains an essay about the worlds of First Clement, various worlds to which Josephus was also not a stranger, even if Josephus never mentions or alludes to the group of Christians in Rome who produced First Clement. Of course, it is possible that Josephus might have been completely unaware of the community of Christians who produced First Clement. But again, we must wonder how credible this is. I suggest the possibility that Josephus's silence about Christians in Rome during his nearly three-decade stay in the city is similar to his equally palpable silence about his involvement in or knowledge about any synagogues in Rome during his long tenure in the city.

Chapter 5 also bears witness to three generations of Christians in Rome, beginning with Paul's generation, the generation that came after him, and the generation of the writer(s) of First Clement. Against so much of the presumed view that the letter was written in the time of Domitian, I argue that the letter was written in the immediate aftermath of the death of Domitian, when the church in Rome had some respite from its most recent troubles by pointing out a few clues that have been overlooked. By preserving the memory of Paul and of Peter (5; 47), First Clement also undercuts Josephus. For one would never guess from Josephus's writings of the 90s that a viable community of Christians, some of whom were Jews and were most likely located in the Jewish Quarter in Rome, existed in the city. This is a point I make in chapter 2, and it receives further elaboration here. I conclude the book with what it means to read the first century with and without Josephus's *ostrakon* against Paul and against the Christians of Rome, and of the implications of Josephus's silences for understanding the history of Christian origins, which is the history of "Christian Judaism" in the first century.

NOTES

1. Josephus, *Antiquities* 20.160–166; *Jewish War* 2.563; *Life* 193 and 216.
2. Louis H. Feldman, *Josephus's Interpretation of the Bible* (Berkeley: University of California Press, 1998), 80–82. See also Louis H. Feldman, "Josephus' Eulogy of Elisha" *Vigiliae Christianae* 36/1 (1994), 1–28.
3. Steve Mason, *Flavius Josephus: Life of Josephus* (Leiden: Brill, 2001), 99fn858.
4. Josephus, *Jewish War* 4.318–322 (LCL 210, 93–95 [with slight emendations]).
5. Josephus, *Jewish War* (LCL 210, 94–95).
6. The Acts of the Apostles is often compared with Josephus and his writings with variegated consequences and implications as to its historical value. See now the encyclopedic work by Craig S. Keener, *Acts: An Exegetical Commentary, 4 Vols.* (Grand Rapids, MI: Baker Academic, 2015). Keener covers the historiographical issues extensively in Volume 1.
7. Steve Mason, *Flavius Josephus: Life of Josephus* (Leiden: Brill, 2001), 20fn90, underscores this very point.
8. On the earliest traditions of the rabbis and Galilee see respectively, Catherine Hezser, *The Social Structure of the Rabbinic Movement in Roman Palestine* (Tübingen: Mohr Siebeck, 1997); Ben Zion Rosenfeld, *Torah Centers and Rabbinic Activities in Palestine, 70–400: History and Geographic Distribution*, translated from the Hebrew by Chava Cassel (Leiden: Brill, 2010); Naftali S. Cohn, *The Memory of the Temple and the Making of the Rabbis* (Philadelphia: University of Pennsylvania Press, 2013); Mark A. Chancey, *The Myth of a Gentile Galilee* (Cambridge: Cambridge University Press, 2002); Shaye J. D. Cohen, *Josephus in Galilee and Rome: His Vita and Development as a Historian* (Leiden: Brill, 1979). As well, Richard A. Horsley, *Galilee: History, Politics, People* (Harrisburg, PA: Trinity Press International, 1995); idem, *Archaeology, History, and Society in Galilee: The Social Context of Jesus and the Rabbis* (Harrisburg, PA: Trinity Press International, 1996); Charlotte Elisheva Fonrobert, Martin S. Jaffee (eds.), *Cambridge Companion to the Talmud and Rabbinic Literature* (Cambridge: Cambridge University Press, 2007); Joshua J. Schwartz and Peter J. Tomson (eds.), *Jews and Christians in the First and Second Centuries: The Interbellum 70–132 CE* (Leiden: Brill, 2018).
9. On Josephus's audience, see Steve Mason, "Audience and Meaning: Reading Josephus' Bellum Judaicum in the Context of a Flavian Audience," in Sievers and Lembi (eds.) *Josephus and Jewish History in Flavian Rome and Beyond* (Leiden: Brill, 2005), 71–100; and Steve Mason, "Should Anyone Wish to Inquire Further: The Aim and Audience of Josephus' *Judaean Antiquities/Life*," in *Understanding Josephus: Seven Perspectives*, edited by Steve Mason (Sheffield, UK: Sheffield Academic Press, 1998), 64–103.
10. *The Jewish War*, translated by Martin Hammond with introduction and notes by Martin Goodman (Oxford: Oxford University Press, 2017), xxxi.
11. Jack Pastor, Pnina Stern, and Menahem Mor (eds.), *Flavius Josephus: Interpretation and History* (Leiden: Brill, 2011).
12. Josephus, *Antiquities* 20.137–143.
13. On Agrippa II see, for example, Seth Schwartz, *Josephus and Judaean Politics* (Leiden: Brill, 1990), especially chapter 4, "Herodians After 70," 110–69; see also Martin Goodman, *The Ruling Class of Judaea: The Origins of the Jewish Revolt against Rome, A.D. 66–70* (Cambridge: Cambridge University Press, 1987), and more recently, Martin Goodman, *Rome and Jerusalem: The Clash of Ancient Civilizations* (New York: Knopf, 2007), 362–65; 402–5.
14. Josephus, *Antiquities* 20.160–166.
15. Luke 3:2; John 18:13.
16. On the parallel lives of the Herodians and the High Priests, see, for example, Martin Goodman, *The Ruling Class of Judaea*, 111–13.
17. Josephus, *Life*, 12; Acts 21:27–22:29.
18. Josephus, *Life*, 356.
19. Josephus, *Life*, 364–67.
20. Josephus, *Life*, 365 (Mason translation, Brill Josephus Project, 150).
21. The question of the intended audience of Josephus's writings is a complicated one. At a minimum he gives some indication of this by distinguishing between the Aramaic version of

the *Jewish War* and the Greek version of that same work. As for the rest of his Greek writings (the *Antiquities*, *Life*, and *Against Apion*), there is no reason to think that he did not intend them for audiences both in Rome and beyond, even if his primary readership may have been at Rome. See Steve Mason, "Of Audience and Meaning: Reading Josephus' *Bellum Judaicum* in the Context of a Flavian Audience" in *Josephus and Jewish History in Flavian Rome and Beyond* (Leiden: Brill, 2005) edited by Joseph Sievers and Gaia Lembi, 71–100. Mason argues for an audience in Rome. See, as well, the chapters by Steve Mason, John M. G. Barclay, and Hannah M. Cotton and Werner Eck in *Flavius Josephus and Flavian Rome* (Oxford: Oxford University Press, 2005), edited by Jonathan Edmondson, Steve Mason, and James Rives.

22. Josephus, *Against Apion* 2.145–147; cf. *Against Apion* 2.165.

Chapter One

Josephus, Paul, and the Early Christians

Before and after 62 CE

Among many questions about Josephus, Louis Feldman asks, "To what degree does he contradict himself in the earlier *Jewish War* and the later *Antiquities*, especially when they cover the same ground, as they do for the period from Antiochus Epiphanes to the outbreak against the Romans, and particularly in the attitude toward the Samaritans and the Pharisees? Is there a consistent pattern in the modifications he makes in his reworking of biblical narrative? Why is his history so uneven, including extraordinarily detailed discussions of certain personalities and events (notably the reign of Herod), as well as numerous, often extensive, digressions, for example, the suicide at Masada (which militarily was of little importance), the summary of Jewish law, and the conversion of the royal family of Adiabene?"[1]

Feldman continues: "How fair is he in his treatment of his opponents, whether individuals, such as Justus of Tiberias, or groups, such as the Samaritans? To what degree is he prejudiced because of the pension and many other gifts he had received from the Romans? To what degree did misogyny influence his judgments? To what extent do apologetic motifs influence his portrayal of events, particularly in his paraphrase of the Bible? How far has he been influenced by motifs from Homer, Herodotus, Greek tragedy, and novels, with which he was apparently so well acquainted, in his version of history?"[2] We might also ask: how far did Josephus go to exclude perceived opponents and other competitors from his account of Jewish life in the first century? How deliberately did he minimize their influence even when he mentioned them?

If Herod Agrippa II and his sisters Berenice and Drusilla knew the apostle Paul and controversy sparked by Paul's activities in Jerusalem and Judaea, then it is not an impertinent question to ask why the historian Flavius Josephus, our most important witness to Jewish life in Judaea, Galilee, and parts of the Diaspora in the first century, never mentions in any of his writings his older contemporary Paul, a former Pharisee, who claimed in one of his extant letters that in his earlier career he was advancing in Judaism beyond many of his contemporaries and presumably many Jews of his generation (Galatians 1:14). At the very least, we should like to know if Josephus knew anything about Paul, and if he did, why he makes no reference to him.

Certainly, a case can be made that Josephus's silence about Paul is to be expected. After all, Josephus was his much younger contemporary. Josephus was born after Paul had already abandoned the Pharisees and become an apostle for the gospel of Jesus the Messiah. In which case, Josephus's silence should be deemed the result of his general ignorance about Paul and his place in Jerusalemite society and the Christian world. But if he did know of Paul, then the question is no longer impertinent. Which is to say that Josephus's presumed ignorance cannot be taken for granted. There is yet another reason why it cannot be taken for granted, namely that Josephus's father Matthias was an exact contemporary of Paul's. If Matthias had any affiliation with the Pharisees or the circle of Gamaliel the Elder, he most certainly knew Paul the Pharisee who lived in Jerusalem or nearby in the years before Paul's conversion and call to the gospel of Jesus the Christ, if Paul was as well-known as a Pharisee as he claims. Matthias's knowledge has some bearing on how we assess Josephus's silence and his possible ignorance.

Furthermore, Josephus's silence about Paul is part of a much broader sentiment that Josephus displays toward the early Christian movement. The only Christian, Christian Jew, or Jew affiliated with Jesus of Nazareth that Josephus mentions in the last chapters of his *Antiquities* covering the last four decades of the first century before the War with the Romans (26–66 CE) is James the brother of Jesus. Given his reticence about the Christian Jews, we have reason to believe that if Josephus could have avoided mentioning James, the brother of the Lord (as Paul describes him in Galatians 1:19), he would have. But he could not because the judicial murder of James was part of social and political events of the year 62 CE that shocked many of the residents and citizens of Jerusalem. I shall discuss this momentarily.

At one point in his autobiography, Josephus, the native and resident of Jerusalem, and later resident of Rome, has this to say about one of his contemporaries, Simon son of Gamaliel. Simon knew Josephus well and Josephus's father Matthias too. They were all Jerusalemites. Josephus writes as follows:

> Now this Simon was from the city of Jerusalem, from an exceedingly brilliant ancestry, and from the school of the Pharisees, who have a reputation of excelling others in their precision with respect to traditional legal matters. This was a man full of insight and reason able to rectify matters that were sitting badly by virtue of his own practical wisdom.[3]

The brilliant ancestry of which he speaks is simply that Simon was the son of the great Gamaliel the Elder, with a hint that Gamaliel was also of astounding pedigree. Josephus also writes here about the Pharisees as if he does not belong to them or never did, even as he makes the specific point of Gamaliel as a most prominent member of the Pharisees, a group of people who have a reputation for their precision or accuracy or exactness (*akribeia*) about matters of the law. The word *akribeis* is also sometimes translated as "strict," and so the idea of "strictness" gets easily assimilated with the notion of being zealous or having a zeal (*zēlos*) for the law. Paul uses the self-description, being zealous (*zēlōtēs*) for his ancestral traditions, but more specifically for the traditions of the fathers (Galatians 1:14). Josephus also uses zeal for the law in describing others in his texts.

Josephus as an adult must have known more than a few of those Pharisees associated with the "school" of Gamaliel and as a lad some of his much older contemporaries associated with Gamaliel the Elder. If Josephus knew so much about Gamaliel and the Pharisees, and he knew Simon his son, it is almost certain that he knew many more of his associates than he discusses. In speaking of Simon and his ancestry, Josephus was relaying information about a fellow citizen of Jerusalem whose lineage and family he knew well; and he provides the basis for the conclusion that one cannot fully understand the role and standing of the Pharisees in the middle of the first century without accounting for and appreciating the role and influence of Gamaliel the Elder and his "school."[4] Josephus's silence about Gamaliel the Elder, then, is not a sign of his insignificance; it is quite the opposite, for he provides the advertisement of Gamaliel's profound influence but then resolutely gives no details about Gamaliel himself to fill out the advertisement. Invariably, Josephus denies to his readers the full story of the Pharisees and their impact on Judaean society in the middle of the first century.

Josephus's silence about Gamaliel the Elder undermines and frustrates virtually every effort made to write a history of the Pharisees in the first half of the first century, a reality that is often unacknowledged or understated in the scholarship.[5] We do not know the year Gamaliel the Elder was born; that may not be too unusual, we do not know this detail for so many ancients. We do not know when he died. Josephus does not provide it. This is unusual, since he died during Josephus's lifetime. Some historians accept the date of 52 CE, but there is no real basis for it. The best that can be said, given the time he flourished and the time during which his son Simon emerges as a leading figure in Jerusalem, is that Gamaliel the Elder died probably around the year 50 CE. The most recent edition of the *Encyclopaedia Judaica* makes no effort to suggest any dates for him, except to say that he "lived in the first half of the first century."[6] Even the tradition repeated in the *Encyclopaedia Judaica* that he was the grandson of Hillel, the great and legendary leader of the Pharisees, is more assumption than fact. As Jacob Neusner points out, neither the Hillel material nor the Gamaliel material found in the tractates of the Mishna claim a relationship between the two.[7] Still, there is no denying that Gamaliel the Elder was the most influential if not the most important leader of the Pharisees in the first half of the first century. This much Josephus substantiates. What other evidence emerges in the Acts of the Apostles also supports this.

Paul himself does not mention Gamaliel in any of his extant letters, but Acts 22:3, in a speech attributed to Paul, makes the connection that Gamaliel the Elder was Paul's teacher; or at the very least, that Paul came of age in Jerusalem in an environment shaped by Gamaliel. In fact, what Josephus says about Simon son of Gamaliel and the Pharisees around him applies to Paul; even without the testimony of Acts. When Paul writes that he was advancing in Judaism beyond many of his contemporaries, the world he is referencing is that same world shaped by Gamaliel the Elder that Josephus describes in his *Life*. So even if Josephus never laid eyes on Paul, the world that Paul belonged to as a Pharisee in Jerusalem was a world to which Josephus was not a stranger. Josephus surely knew better those Pharisees of his own generation like Simon the son of Gamaliel. No one in Jerusalem could escape Gamaliel's influence, and no one could plead ignorance about Gamaliel the Elder himself while he was alive, let alone underestimate his long-standing influence in Jerusalem. The later Rabbinic traditions about Rabban Gamaliel the Elder underscore this. Josephus's evocation of the world of Gamaliel the Elder draws him into the world of Paul, and in so doing indirectly substantiates Paul's claim to unbounded aspiration among the Pharisees.

Let me reiterate: Josephus had personal knowledge of Gamaliel the Elder and his son Simon and the influential world they created or inhabited in the middle of the first century in Jerusalem. That was the world to which Paul belonged before Josephus was born and with which Josephus became acquainted throughout his years as a citizen of Jerusalem. So it is highly unlikely, perhaps even impossible, that Paul would have made a visit to the city, as he promised to do in First Corinthians 16:1–4 (cf. Romans 15:30–33), during the lifetime of Josephus, without Josephus knowing that one of those who belonged to the circle of Gamaliel the Elder had been in the city. In reference to that visit, Paul expressed in Romans 15:31 his apprehensions about what awaited him in Jerusalem and the reaction of the "unbelievers in Judaea" and his fellow believers in Jesus Christ, "the saints" (*hagioi*). The expression that is translated "unbelievers in Judaea" is a very specific form that Paul uses. Paul uses a participle of the verb *apeitheō* (to disobey). So one may ask, exactly what is it that those who are disobedient disobey?

Paul prays that he may be delivered from literally, "those who do not obey" (*tōn apeithountōn*). These he set in juxtaposition with the believers, the saints (*tois hagiois*), in a clearly contrastive sense; and so suggests that "those who do not obey in Judaea" are the unbelievers of Judaea, those who do not believe the gospel of Jesus the Messiah, the Christ (*christos*). In so doing, Paul maintains that Jewish society can be divided into two basic groups: those who believe that Jesus is the Christ; and those who refuse to believe or to be persuaded. Paul assumed and anticipated that his presence would not go unnoticed by those very unbelievers who live in Judaea that he wished to be delivered from. His description is so total and comprehensive as if to say that the people of Judaea have heard the gospel of Jesus the Christ, but that many have chosen not to obey or believe or to be persuaded by it. At this moment in time, the "unbelievers of Judaea" included the likes of Josephus son of Matthias and Simon son of Gamaliel the Elder.

Years before, "the unbelievers in Judaea" would have included Gamaliel the Elder himself, unless one is to believe later tradition that claimed that Gamaliel became a Christian at some stage or that he was already a Christian in the way he is portrayed in Acts, a tradition which clearly owes to a fanciful imagination and a hopeful elaboration of the portrait of Gamaliel the Elder in Acts.[8] Before his conversion and call, Paul too would have been part of that large group of "the unbelievers of Judaea" who did not believe the gospel of Jesus the Christ. During those years he would have been well known to Simon son of Gamaliel. So, at this stage of Paul's life, given his storied past and his current vocation, Simon son of Gamaliel might well have known if Paul was in the city. Josephus too would almost certainly have known or learned that Paul was associated with James the brother of Jesus, the putative leader of the followers of the Christ (the Christians) in Jerusalem for nearly three decades, whom Josephus mentions in connection with the events of 62 CE.

More importantly still, the timing of Josephus's entry into public life at age nineteen (c. 56 CE) coincides with the probable dates of Paul's last visit to Jerusalem, according to the chronology of Acts 23–24 and the end of the governorship of M. Antonius Felix (52–59 CE/54–60 CE). The transition from M. Antonius Felix to Porcius Festus's governorship in Judaea (59–61 CE/60–62 CE) was a much anticipated event in Judaea, and by that time Josephus himself was well on his way to establishing his credentials as one of the promising young men in Jerusalem, if we are to believe his account in the *Life*. Even if he did not know the details of Paul's encounter with Porcius Festus as described in Acts 25:1–26:32, Josephus knew something then and a good deal more later about what the new governor did in his early days in

Judaea. Josephus writes extensively in *Antiquities* about both Felix (20.173–178) and Festus (20.182–197) and the way they governed Judaea; and about Felix also in his *Life* (13; 37). Much earlier, in the *Jewish War*, he wrote still more about Felix (12.8.247; 13.2.252–253; 14.1.271) than he did about Festus (2.182).

So why the total silence about Paul? Did Josephus the historian not wish to discuss Paul because it might bring him into conflict with his Roman patrons to whom he owed his life and his livelihood? Did he not wish to discuss Paul because it offended his own sensibilities as one previously affiliated with the Pharisees? Would it have exposed him to saying more about Gamaliel the Elder, the leading Pharisee of his day, about whose life Josephus also says next to nothing?

Did Josephus mean to exclude Paul from the archives of Jewish history because he personally objected to Paul's interpretation of the Jewish past and its future? Did he exclude Paul in order to eliminate his influence from Jewish life? Or is Josephus's silence about Paul merely the by-product of his general unease about Jewish messianism in the first century? Was it because writing about Paul would require Josephus to discuss Jewish messianic expectations in far more detail than he would have liked? Or, was it the fact that Paul and others like him, Christian Jews, believed in Jesus of Nazareth as the Messiah?

JOSEPHUS AND THE EVENTS OF 62 CE: THE UNLIKELY PROPHET JESUS SON OF ANANIAS

In a slightly different context, Louis H. Feldman touches on some of these questions when he explains why Josephus was reticent in writing about James the brother of Jesus and why on his reading it is unlikely that Josephus could have referred to Jesus as Messiah. Feldman insists, as well, that those who followed any number of self-styled messiahs in the first century were not written out of Jewish life.[9] Feldman's contention pre-empts and potentially precludes the questions I have raised about Josephus's exclusion, silence, or omission of Paul. In relation to the so-called *Testimonium Flavianum* in Book 20 of Josephus's *Antiquities*, he writes:

> To be sure, there were several claimants to the status of Messiah in this era, and those who followed them were not read out of the Jewish fold; but in view of the fact that Josephus nowhere else uses the word *Christos* (except in referring to James, the brother of Jesus, *Ant*. 20.200) and that he repeatedly suppresses the Messianic aspects of the revolt against Rome because of the association of the Messiah with political revolt and independence, it would seem hard to believe that he would openly call Jesus a Messiah and speak of him with such awe.[10]

Feldman's insistence about Josephus's repeated suppression of the messianic elements of Jewish life and thought puts a particular emphasis on the importance of this theme in Josephus's own thought. For Feldman, this clearly undermines the authenticity of the *Testimonium Flavianum*.[11] Josephus would not possibly have called Jesus the Messiah since this would put him back where he did not want to be: raising a red flag to any of his Roman audience, who would have found it a provocation, if nothing else.

All the same, if we insist with Feldman that Josephus's determination to understate or erase messianic sentiment is always partly political and partly apologetic, we are likely to overlook other ways in which Josephus's anti-messianic sentiment plays out. We are likely to understate the possibly personal side of that determination, and why, in spite of Feldman's view, Josephus may well have excluded some of his fellow Jews also because of their links to and evocations of messianic sentiment. If there was one Jew among Josephus's contemporaries about whom one could not write without discussing messianism, it is Paul the former Pharisee and apostle. Feldman does not consider the case of Paul as one of those followers of a messiah who might well have been written out of Jewish life in this period by Josephus.

On the matter of messianism and exclusion from Jewish life, Martin Goodman writes that "when the Christians claimed that Jesus was the expected Messiah, in the eyes of non-Christian Jews they were simply mistaken. They could be pitied or mocked for their folly, but there was no need to expel them from the Jewish fold."[12] Since Goodman writes about Christians in general, it is not clear that he has in mind the particular case of Paul the apostle. In his more recent work,[13] in the book, *Toleration within Judaism*, coauthored with Joseph E. David and Corinna R. Kaiser, Goodman points out how Pharisees and Sadducees in first-century Judaea found ways to cooperate and to disagree without their fundamental differences turning them into enemies, and without either party excluding the other from Jewish life. Goodman's view of toleration, however, seems to be in tension with his own earlier work on the ruling class of Judaea.[14] In that work, Goodman demonstrated quite convincingly that at times the differences that separated the ruling classes could be quite vicious and consequential. Josephus's own writings provide ample testimony of repudiation, faction, and violence, sometimes even murder. So the tolerance or toleration to which Goodman appeals may not always explain the nature, viability, and extremes of intra-Jewish differences in the first century.

Furthermore, Paul's own testimony in his Letter to the Galatians about how he pursued his fellow Jews who were part of the church of God, the followers of Jesus Christ, and wished to destroy them, means that in his own case Paul wished to exclude the Christian Jews from Jewish life. His form of exclusion was literal: he wanted them destroyed. If Josephus wished to do the same to Paul, he would be doing nothing that Paul himself had not tried to do to other Jews prior to his conversion and calling as an apostle of the gospel of Jesus Christ. The only difference is that we have no testimony from Josephus or about Josephus that he wished to do such a thing, and no evidence that he participated in any attempts to physically harm any Christians. Nor do we have any documentation that Josephus issued threats or maledictions against Christians or against the memory of Paul. At the same time, Josephus was no ideological or natural pacifist. He attests to his own participation in acts of violence in the context of the Jewish War of 66–70. But the fact that we have no such evidence about Josephus wanting to destroy Christian Jews is not proof that Josephus could not have been as incensed about the Christians as Paul the Pharisee was when Paul was hounding them and seeking to destroy them. If one Pharisee felt and acted this way, as Paul certainly did, he may not have been alone in this sentiment.

For my purposes, I am excluding the evidence of the Gospels, which describe the Pharisees as among some of Jesus's most active and disagreeable opponents. I turn, however, to the case of Jesus son of Ananias, which Josephus relates in his *Jewish War* 6.300–309.

According to Josephus, Jesus son of Ananias was arrested and scourged in 62 CE, but spared only because Albinus the procurator of Judaea believed he was deranged. Josephus writes that Jesus son of Ananias had been preaching woe against Jerusalem and predicting calamities against the people of Jerusalem for four years before the beginning of the war in 66 CE. He continued in total for a little more than seven years before he died in 69 CE while carrying on his activities. Josephus writes as an eyewitness to Jesus son of Ananias's pronouncements.

Josephus had emerged into public life and had been affiliated with the Pharisees for six years when Jesus son of Ananias started to proclaim woe on Jerusalem in 62 CE. The Acts of the Apostles also contains a description of Paul's arrest in Jerusalem at some time before 62 CE, though the exact date is disputed, whether nearer 55 CE or 59 CE. The dating depends on when Felix the procurator of Judaea was recalled and was succeeded by a new procurator Festus.[15] If Acts is an independent witness, then we have here a situation that Josephus would not have been ignorant of. Tessa Rajak hints at Josephus's silences about Paul when she writes at one point in relation to Paul's arrest in Jerusalem that "Festus was also the procurator who sent Saint Paul to be tried at Rome. This is not alluded to by Josephus, and it may have made little impression on non-Christian contemporaries at the time (Acts 24–6)."[16] This assumes that only Paul's fellow Christians (mostly Jews) would have cared about or been interested in his arrest by the authorities in Jerusalem.

Whatever the case, whether such public events in Jerusalem made little impression on other contemporaries who were not themselves related to the people at the center of the troubles, Josephus seems to have known quite well how Jesus son of Ananias fared in Jerusalem at this time. His account about how the leading men of the city thought about the pronouncements of Jesus son of Ananias and how they responded (*Jewish War* 6.300–309) makes this patent. Significantly, the story in the *Antiquities* about the murder of James the brother of Jesus also took place in the same year that Jesus son of Ananias began his preaching of doom, 62 CE. However, Josephus chose to tell the story of Jesus son of Ananias in connection with events closer to the end of the war with the Romans than in connection with the beginning of Jesus's proclamation of doom over Jerusalem. Unsuspecting readers would not necessarily make the link unless they have the chronology clearly in mind, namely: the appointment of Ananus son of Ananus as High Priest; the judicial murder of James the brother of Jesus before the arrival of Albinus as governor of Judaea; the deposition of Ananus as High Priest; the arrival of Albinus as governor; the beginning of the proclamation of Jesus son of Ananias. Here is Josephus's long paragraph.

> Four years before the war, when the city was enjoying profound peace and prosperity, there came to the feast at which it is the custom of all Jews to erect tabernacles to God, one Jesus, son of Ananias, a rude peasant, who, standing in the temple, suddenly began to cry out, "A voice from the east, a voice from the west, a voice from the four winds; a voice against Jerusalem and the sanctuary, a voice against the bridegroom and the bride, a voice against all the people." Day and night, he went about all the alleys with this cry on his lips. Some of the leading citizens, incensed at these ill-omened words, arrested the fellow and severely chastised him. But he, without a word on his own behalf or for the private ear of those who smote him, only continued his cries as before. Thereupon, the magistrates, supposing, as was indeed the case, that the man was under some supernatural impulse, brought him before the Roman governor; there, although flayed to the bone with scourges, he neither sued for mercy nor shed a tear, but, merely introducing the most mournful of variations into his ejaculation, responded to each stroke with "Woe to Jerusalem!" When Albinus, the governor, asked him who and whence he was and why he uttered these cries, he answered him never a word, but unceasingly reiterated his dirge over the city, until Albinus pronounced him a maniac and let him go. During the whole period up to the outbreak of war he neither approached nor was seen talking to any of the citizens, but daily, like a prayer that he had conned, repeated his lament, "Woe to Jerusalem!" He neither cursed any of those who beat him from day to day, nor blessed those who offered him food: to all men that melancholy presage was his one reply. His cries were loudest at the festivals. So for seven years and five months he continued his wail, his voice never flagging nor his strength exhausted, until in the siege, having seen his presage verified, he found his rest. For, while going his round and shouting in piercing tones from the wall, "Woe once more to the city and to the people and to the temple," as he added a last word, "and woe to me also," a stone hurled from the *ballista* struck and killed him on the spot. So with those ominous words still upon his lips he passed away.[17]

In its natural, chronological, and logical sequence this story should have been told in connection with the death of James the brother of Jesus through the machinations of the High Priest Ananus son of Ananus, Ananus's deposition, and the arrival of Albinus as the new governor of Judaea after Porcius Festus. One cannot resist the thought that the prophecy of Jesus son of Ananias may also have had something to do with the events that occurred during the time of the High Priest Ananus son of Ananus, whatever else one makes of his mental state, as his contemporaries eventually construed. Josephus, who was himself a witness to all of this, surely had a view of it, since he presents in the end an account of Jesus son of Ananias as if he accepts prima facie that Jesus was a true prophet, or at least, that he uttered a true prophecy. We may wonder, however, whether Josephus himself believed in 62 CE, after Albinus dismissed Jesus son of Ananias, declaring him deranged, that Jesus son of Ananias was to be taken seriously, and if not, at what point Josephus came to put any stock in Jesus son of Ananias's pronouncements.

I may add here that this raises some important questions about a tendency among scholars who might find even Josephus's claim of Jesus of Ananias's true prophecy as something of an embarrassment. After all, the ancients were supposed to have been so gullible and unintelligent that they always claimed things as prophecy after they had lived to see certain things realized—the technical term: *vaticinium ex eventu* (prophecy after the fact). Incidentally, Josephus also says that Jesus son of Ananias was proved right because his prophecy come true. In his case, all his contemporaries could bear him out that he had been preaching this for more than seven years nonstop. His contemporaries tested him repeatedly, but his message did not change, and in the end he proved to be right.

Many have noticed similarities between how the people of Jerusalem treated Jesus son of Ananias and the stories in the Gospels about how Jerusalemites reacted to Jesus of Nazareth's proclamation of doom over Jerusalem. What is often overlooked is that Josephus, who knew James the brother of Jesus of Nazareth, and wrote about James's death that same year some time before Jesus son of Ananias began his prophetic pronouncements, says nothing about the trial of Jesus of Nazareth and his crucifixion in his accounts of the previous generation; but finds no trouble telling this story about Jesus son of Ananias and the way he was accosted by his fellow Jerusalemites and severely beaten on the orders of the governor Albinus.

Josephus states without apology and in not so many words that Jesus son of Ananias predicted the destruction of Jerusalem in 70 CE. Or rather, Jesus son of Ananias was prophetic in spite of himself, in spite of being declared by Albinus as deranged. Even so, Jesus son of Ananias's activities as a prophetic voice are in some sense better than what Josephus himself describes in relation to his prophecy about Vespasian becoming emperor (*Jewish War* 3.400–407).

Now here is the interesting thing: If Jesus son of Ananias had been predicting doom since 62 CE, then Josephus knew of this prophecy before he went to Rome in 63/64 CE. He heard it repeatedly when he returned and discovered preparations or anticipations of revolt. It was probably ringing in his ears when he left Jerusalem to take up his command in Galilee in late 66 CE, whether he gave it any merit or not. In fact, in many ways it turns out that Jesus son of Ananias had been an inadvertent prophetic figure to Josephus long before Josephus surrendered to the Romans in Galilee in Spring 67 CE. Josephus does not describe his own reactions to the prophecy of Jesus son of Ananias in this way. But he provides all the evidence to suggest that few in Jerusalem could have lived between 62 and 66 CE, when the war began, without hearing Jesus son of Ananias. Given his positive portrayal of Jesus son of Ananias compared to other prophetic or messianic imposters, Josephus willingly or begrudgingly acknowledges Jesus son of Ananias as a true prophet.[18] At the same time, Josephus was in some difficulty because Jesus son of Ananias was considered deranged; and the behavior that Josephus ascribes to him suggests someone slightly undone and unhinged, though not threatening to those around him. He was not violent. He just seemed indifferent to much around him, and simply carried on his message, though others were violent toward him.

Josephus's various accounts of James the brother of Jesus and Jesus son of Ananias also make plain that the leading men of Jerusalem were always concerned about anyone who would disturb the peace of Jerusalem. If Paul the apostle had ventured into the city some years before 62 CE and had been the center of such unwanted attention, as he anticipated in his Letter to the Romans and as Acts recounts, it would have been well known to the inhabitants of the city. The fact that Paul himself anticipated in his Letter to the Romans that his presence in Jerusalem would be occasion for possible controversy, a disturbance, or upheaval in the city is testament to what must have been common knowledge among people in Jerusalem about his activities outside of Judaea. There are, then, a number of coincidences that raise a few questions, not to mention the fact that Josephus was also among the well-informed in Jerusalem during this time period and also claimed to have been even better informed later on when he came to write the *Jewish War* and the *Antiquities*.

JOSEPHUS AND PAUL IN HISTORY AND SCHOLARSHIP

So why do Josephus's interpreters almost never ask the question as to why Josephus is so generally reticent about the early Christians of Jerusalem and Judaea and why he is so completely silent about Paul, who was affiliated with the Pharisees? Why do Josephus's interpreters never inquire why he never mentions in any of his writings Paul the former Pharisee, who was almost certainly arrested by the authorities in Jerusalem during the period of Josephus's emergence into public life as one among the Pharisees? Why has Josephus's silence about Paul itself become a matter of silence by historians and students of Josephus and Jewish life in first-century Judaea?

The subject is not hinted at in a number of recent reference works. Neither *The Cambridge Companion to Paul* (2003) nor *The Blackwell Companion to the New Testament* (2010) broaches the subject. The most recent *Blackwell Companion to Josephus* (2016) has no discussion of Josephus and Paul, and no allusions to the theme or to its possible significance. There is a chapter on Josephus and the New Testament by Helen Bond (pp. 147–158). However, she does not raise the question of Josephus's omission of Paul in his writings. Why this is the case is unclear. Yet much of what she writes about the world inhabited by Josephus (pp. 147, 149, 153) and the world of the New Testament writings demands some kind of inquiry, interrogation, or inquest, and some answers.

It may simply be that those engaged in Josephus scholarship are not also equally immersed in Paul and Pauline studies. It could be as simple as that. But this is a question that goes beyond the issue of scholarly specialization. It is about a fundamental aspect of the first century and how we read and understand the first century with Josephus.

Scholarly specialization does not explain matters completely. For example, John M. G. Barclay, whose work bridges the divide between Josephus studies and Pauline studies, with substantial contributions to both Pauline studies and Jewish studies of the Mediterranean Diaspora and has translated Josephus's *Against Apion* for the Brill Josephus Project, barely touches on the theme of Paul's exclusion from Josephus's writings. In fact, his notion of Paul as "an anomalous Jew" in many ways provides a basis for considering just how someone like Josephus would have thought of Paul.[19] It is not an inquiry that Barclay pursues, however.

John Gager's latest work, *Who Made Early Christianity? The Jewish Lives of the Apostle Paul*, has a chapter titled, "The Apostle Paul in Jewish Eyes: Hero or Heretic?"[20] The chapter moves quickly from Paul's own representations of his Jewishness to later writers in the Middle Ages to the present. It is a chapter that seems to lack an adequate preamble. For even if one begins with Paul's own assertiveness about his Jewishness and with the claim that most of his contemporaries in the first century accepted this to be the case, we still have the basic fact that Josephus, one of those contemporaries, excludes him from the world of first-century Jewish life. One might be tempted to say that, according to Josephus, Paul did not have a "Jewish life." For, while Josephus provides many narratives of Jewish lives from among his contemporaries, Paul is not one of his subjects. For all intents and purposes, Paul's assertions about his Jewishness and his assertiveness to that end are irrelevant as far as Josephus is concerned.

Daniel Boyarin's writings on Paul have dealt with matters of inclusion and exclusion, universalism and particularism, and with the politics of identity. His most recent inquiries about Josephus and Paul as two Pharisees center on their views of law (*nomos*). In a lecture on June 25, 2014, at the Pontifical Gregorian University in Rome, Boyarin compares and contrasts Josephus and Paul without raising the question whether Josephus even deemed Paul worthy of consideration.[21] Without addressing the question, it is easy to assume that Josephus would have accepted Paul as a legitimate interlocutor among his fellow Jews; or that he would have thought his ideas and arguments about Abraham, Moses, and the prophets, to say nothing of the communities (churches) he founded, worthy of respect. Needless to say, the question of Josephus's silence hardly comes up in Boyarin's inquiries both here and elsewhere. Interestingly, in his lecture Boyarin mentioned in passing how little Josephus says about Jesus—and, almost as if following the standard script, continued without so much as an allusion to the fact that Josephus says even less about Paul: nothing. The two subjects are not unrelated, however.

In the broader world of Pauline scholarship the situation is not much better. Virtually all the major figures in Pauline studies ignore the question. It is not that Josephus never comes up in their respective inquiries. He sometimes does. There is usually an affirmation of his importance for early Christian studies. A good deal of the attention turns on Josephus and Luke-Acts or Josephus and Acts. But while some of the focus on Acts involves the portrayal of Paul in Acts and the nature of Paul's Christianity vis-à-vis his previous life in Judaism, scarcely does that lead to a question as to why Acts is so fully immersed in Paul's world, when for all intents and purposes, Josephus's accounts about life in Jerusalem and within Judaism before the War of 66–70 has nothing about Paul in it. The one exception has to do with the cycle involving Paul's arrest and his shipwreck during his sea voyage to Rome. Most interpreters note the parallels between Josephus's account of his travel to Rome in 63/64 CE in his *Life* (15–16), where he also describes in brief a shipwreck, and Paul's sea voyages and shipwreck, narrated in Acts 27–28.

N. T. Wright's massive *Paul and the Faithfulness of God* ranges masterfully over Jewish sources in the period before Paul and contemporary with Paul. Wright has much to say about Josephus.[22] However, he does not consider at any point why Josephus has no reference to Paul in his writings and why Josephus's silence about Paul matters or should matter. In this respect, the very evidence of the letters attributed to Paul in the canonical New Testament act strangely to preempt questions about Josephus's silence about Paul. This seems unobjectionable, for the simple reason that Paul's letters speak for themselves as attestation of Paul's relevance to Jewish life in the first century. It is peculiar, nevertheless, that the many who consider some of Paul's letters to be forgeries or pseudonymous have also not taken to Josephus's silence as a way of discounting most of the letters in the Pauline corpus in the canonical New Testament as inauthentic. But that is a subject for another inquiry.

The scope of N. T. Wright's *Paul and His Recent Interpreters* (2014) confirms this apparent indifference to Josephus's omission of Paul.[23] The fact that New Testament scholars can in the main go about Pauline studies, and even engage with Josephus, without ever asking the question about Josephus's silence about Paul makes plain that the silence did not in the end limit Paul's influence. But it does not help in any way to explain why Josephus might have intended it in the first place, or how this particular omission or historical silence affects our understanding of first-century Jewish life as sketched by Josephus. This is part of what makes Josephus's omission of Paul and his significance and influence in Jewish life in the first century so interesting and intriguing.

E. P. Sanders's studies on Paul hardly seem attuned to this question. It is not raised in *Paul and Palestinian Judaism* (1977), or in *Paul, the Law and the Jewish People* (1983). In his most recent, *Paul: The Apostle's Life, Letters, and Thought* (Fortress, 2016), which encapsulates a lifetime of work on Paul, Sanders discusses Josephus extensively and often makes comparisons between Josephus and other New Testament sources or with Paul.[24] However, never once, as far as I have been able to determine, does Sanders ask the question as to why Josephus himself never mentions Paul.

Mark Nanos, who advocates for what is described as "Paul within Judaism," is keenly aware of Josephus's narratives about Queen Helena and her son King Izates of Adiabene in Northern Mesopotamia and how the conversion of Izates to Judaism touch on issues that Paul discusses in his letters, in particular the Letter to the Galatians. Nanos discusses Josephus's narratives and how the circumcision of Gentiles is central the story of Izates. He calls attention to how Josephus too insists on the importance of circumcision as a mark of distinction for proselytes and for natural, ethnic Jewish males. Nanos, who prefers to describe Paul's Judaism now with the phrase, "apostolic Judaism," seems almost indifferent to the fact that Josephus, who writes so evocatively about the Adiabene royals, excludes Paul's so-called "apostolic Judaism" from his reporting about Jewish life in the first century. Nanos has written a great deal about Paul in his essays and books without ever raising the question why Josephus's Jewish world includes King Izates and Queen Helena but does not include Paul.[25]

It is worth noting, though Nanos often overlooks it, that while Josephus gives equal time to the two Jews who play a role in Izates's choice and decision as to whether he should be circumcised to be a true convert to Judaism (Jewish way of life), Josephus clearly indicates which position he approves. Eleazar the Galilean insists on circumcision, while the merchant Ananias thinks of it as optional if in fact Izates would encounter difficulties in his role as a monarch on account of the deed. Josephus presents Eleazar, whom he describes as a person very learned in Jewish traditions (like a Pharisee?), as the "good Jew" and Ananias as the "bad or indifferent Jew." Mark Nanos's arguments give the impression that Josephus's narrative establishes that both Ananias and Eleazar are Torah-observant Jews in good standing, as far as Josephus is concerned, without mentioning that Josephus's explicit statements about Izates and how he was protected by God are meant to substantiate the fact that his choice of circumcision was an act of great faith that God blessed, over and against the seemingly latitudinarian views of Ananias the merchant.

Interestingly, Eleazar's position, while consistent with what was thought to be a fundamental requirement for any proselyte, was the position Paul denied, and in so doing insisted that Christian Gentiles were not like proselytes. For Paul, circumcision was not required for Christian Gentiles. Paul's view in Galatians looks superficially very much like Ananias's view. The difference was: Paul was not seeking proselytes to Judaism as such in the way that Josephus, Ananias, Eleazar, and Paul as a Pharisee understood Judaism. Rather, Paul sought believers in Jesus as the Messiah. He sought converts, both Jews and non-Jews, to something that he understood and we might appropriately call "Christian Judaism." If Ananias, "the bad or indifferent Jew" when it came to the circumcision of Izates, can be included in Josephus's *Antiquities*, why not Paul? Similarly, the position of Ananias, "the bad or indifferent Jew," was the one also preferred and championed by Queen Helena, who is portrayed in Josephus's writings as a heroine and a great example of a Gentile convert to Judaism. Paul the former Pharisee could not be so objectionable, if he also advocated circumcision as nonessential for non-Jews, except of course in his case, he considered it as nonessential for conversion to believing in Jesus of Nazareth as the Christ, the Messiah.

Steve Mason's *Flavius Josephus and the Pharisees: A Composition-Critical Study*, considered a landmark of Josephus scholarship, explores in great detail Josephus's various descriptions of Pharisees throughout his writings and his self-presentation as someone affiliated with the Pharisees.[26] This is the case, even if, as Mason also notes, the Pharisees as a group "figures only incidentally" in his writings. The idea then that "one could write a fairly detailed account of Josephus and each of his four compositions without mentioning the Pharisees,"[27] is somewhat misleading. Mason's work shows that Josephus's sense of his public life was constructed in many ways in connection with his views of the Pharisees and their relationships with other groups within Jewish life. Josephus's sense of himself as a leading figure in the first century was framed by his thinking, connections, and criticisms of Pharisees.

On occasion Mason makes comparisons with Paul, but all too often they are cursory and brief. At the end of his "compositional-critical study" Mason offers the following assessment that indirectly contrasts with Paul. Mason cautions: "It should perhaps be stressed, in view of the history of scholarship on early Judaism, that Josephus's antipathy toward the Pharisees had only personal causes, as far as we know. He never attacks Pharisaic piety *per se*, as a system." He adds that Josephus shares their goal of *akribeia*, "strictness," in dealing with the Mosaic Law.[28]

> It should be quite illegitimate, therefore, to use the results of this study as supplementary evidence (along with, say, the Gospels and Paul) for the "defects" of Pharisaic religion. The crucial point here is that Josephus's perspective was that of a tiny minority in first-century Palestine: he was an avowed elitist. But we have seen ample evidence in his writings that the Pharisees enjoyed the steady and eager support of the ordinary people. Our author disdained both the Pharisees and the masses.[29]

One is tempted to ask whether Josephus's elitism applies to his view of others like Paul, or whether his disdain for the Pharisees, as Mason claims here, extends to "Paul the Pharisee" or "Paul the former Pharisee."

Mason's assessment that Josephus's perspective is that of a minority, while also insisting that Josephus is "our most valuable witness to the history of the Pharisees,"[30] creates something of a conundrum. If one of those who might offer an alternative to this minority view is not even part of the world that Josephus sketches, has the evidence not already been skewed in the direction of Josephus? Mason himself seems to preempt the comparison by precluding Paul as an independent witness for Pharisees in the first century.

Josephus discusses the Pharisees from a historical point of view as to their origins and their effects on Jewish society. He also discusses them as his contemporaries. So it boggles the mind that Josephus's fascination with Pharisees does not compel him at any point to discuss Paul, who was both a contemporary and also a Pharisee a generation before Josephus. Unfortunately, Steve Mason's approach to Paul as something of a hostile witness to the Pharisees indirectly sustains Josephus's silence about Paul. So the question remains as to why "Paul the Pharisee" or "Paul the former Pharisee" does not make any appearance in Josephus. Here is a simple fact: Paul was a Pharisee and a former-Pharisee before Josephus was born in 37 CE. No amount of imaginative or brilliant historiography on Josephus's part can change any of this. Paul's biography constitutes an alternative and antecedent tradition before Josephus himself ever thought of affiliating with the Pharisees.

As far as I know, Mason does not raise the question of Josephus's omission of Paul, nor does he allude to its possible significance for understanding Josephus in his highly influential studies that make up his *Josephus, Judea, and Christian Origins*.[31] It is not mentioned as well in the sections of his

Josephus and the New Testament that deal with characters in the early Christian movement;[32] nor does he consider it in the sections of Josephus's *Life* where Josephus could well have written about it. Mason's commentary on Josephus's autobiography also seems to overlook the parts of the *Life* where Josephus deliberately omits details of his life between years nineteen and twenty-six, a period of time that would have been most revelatory about how Josephus emerged to become a leading figure in Jerusalem entrusted with a delegation to Rome.

What this brief review indicates is that, for whatever reason, the question I am posing has not been thought by most scholars and historians to be worthy of consideration. Daniel R. Schwartz helps to elucidate the significance of the problem this way. While addressing the nature and scope of Christian presence in Josephus's writings, Schwartz suggests a resolution that touches on the idea of exclusion in Josephus. Schwartz analyzes Josephus's use of the word *phylon* (tribe) and concludes that Josephus had no need to write about Christians or "the tribe of Christians" because he did not consider them Jews. Schwartz's explanation is intriguing in the sense that it ends up somewhat ingenuously and unexpectedly undermining any attempt to absolve Josephus. Schwartz, for his part, wishes simply to state a fact. He writes as follows:

> If Josephus views the Jews as a *phylon*, himself as their historian, and the Christians as another *phylon*, then his failure to say much about them becomes much less surprising. That is, if Josephus viewed the Pharisees, Sadducees and Essenes as types of Jews, and accordingly devoted much space to them, he viewed Christians as non-Jews, a category parallel to Jews and not a subgroup within them.[33]

Schwartz's view seems plausible, but only up to a point. Exactly what does it mean to speak of "Christians as non-Jews, a category parallel to Jews and not a subgroup within them?" The idea of viewing Christians as non-Jews flies in the face of one simple fact: the earliest Christians were mostly Jews. So in what sense can Josephus think of Pharisees, Sadducees, and Essenes as types of Jews and not of the earliest Christians, Christian Jews, as another type of Jews? At best the Christian Jews are an anomaly, but they are no less Jews than Josephus himself, unless Josephus maintains categorically that to be a Christian is to be disinherited from being a Jew. In which case, the Christians are by their very nature to be excluded, they are to be treated as *minim* (heretics), who are cut off from Israel.

This is what Schwartz does not spell out, but this is the only basis upon which Josephus, according to Schwartz, can maintain that Christian Jews like Paul or James the brother of Jesus aren't Jews. It really has almost nothing to do with designating Christians as a tribe (*phylon*) of their own, so to speak. Schwartz finds support in Josephus's alleged view of Christians as non-Jews in contemporary Roman writers like Suetonius and Tacitus, and from Luke-Acts.[34] This seems questionable. But even if it were to be the case, it does not answer the most basic question of all: why would Josephus categorize Christian Jews as non-Jews in the first place?

This brings us back to exclusion. Schwartz's explanation means that Josephus intended to exclude Christians—and Christian Jews, to be exact—by defining them out of Jewish life (or Judaism). That is the upshot of Schwartz's description. On this basis, Josephus's silence about Paul would turn out to be a determined and deliberate silence. Schwartz himself does not consider the exclusion of Paul in this respect. His methodological essays in his *Reading the First Century*, which are designed to suggest how we may read the first century with Josephus do not raise the question of Josephus's exclusion of Paul and the earliest Christians in Judaea, whose imprint on first-century Jewish life is undeniable. In fact, Schwartz barely alludes to Paul as relevant to reading the first century.[35] Alan F. Segal, on the other hand, states without apology that Paul is "our best witness to the issues that affected first-century Jews." Segal adds that "in spite of his complex feelings about Judaism and his uniquely Christian perspective, Paul is, ironically, one of the most fruitful and reliable sources for first-century Jewish religious life."[36] We may conclude, following Segal, that to write about Jewish life in the first century without mentioning Paul, the former Pharisee, as Josephus does, is to provide only a partial story of the first century at best.

INTERPRETING JOSEPHUS AND HIS ROMAN CONTEMPORARIES

In the chapters that follow I shall attempt to address this omission of Paul and the early Christians in Josephus's writings dealing with the first century and other matters related to it. It is about the writing of history and the silences of history. Some of it will be concerned with how Josephus managed to live in Jerusalem in the middle decades of the first century, to be a witness to Jewish life and history, and yet say nothing about Paul, who presumably was resident in Jerusalem or somewhere in Judaea when he took on the task of persecuting members of the Christian movement that he said he sought to destroy (Galatians 1). Paul mentioned that he was known to all the churches of Judaea at this time. While he did not claim any special pedigree in the way that Josephus presented himself as a priest of Jerusalem from a family of priests and of royal Hasmonaean heritage (*Life*, 1–5), Paul did speak of himself as a Hebrew of Hebrews, of the tribe of Benjamin. He may not have been privileged, but he claimed to be advancing in Judaism or the Jewish way of life (*Ioudaismos*) beyond many of his contemporaries. Much of that advancement took place in Jerusalem a few years before the birth of Josephus. By the time Josephus was born, Paul was already a former-Pharisee-turned-apostle of the Christian movement. But apparently, Josephus knew nothing of Paul, whose mission to the Gentiles took place during the middle decades of the first century between 35 and 65 CE.

Other parts of my discussion will be about Josephus's residence in Rome and his participation in the social world of that city. Josephus settled in Rome in 71/72 CE for the rest of his life after the Jewish War of 66–70 CE, and yet also managed to say nothing about a Christian community in that city on the one hand, and about the literary and intellectual culture of the city on the other hand, including some of its noted luminaries like Martial, Statius, Tacitus, Suetonius, and Pliny the Younger. Ancient Rome was not spatially or geographically a large metropolis. Less than six square miles, roughly the equivalent of four times the size of Central Park in New York City, it was a manageable city, and most of its notable citizens knew each other. This is a basic fact that should not be overlooked.

It is this sense of personal physical proximity, of closeness, of shared space, of immanent social presence, if I may call it that, which gives to the historical reporting of some writers in Rome the gossipy feel of the sources and documentation they appeal to. One cannot read something like Suetonius's *Lives of the Caesars* without a sense that so much of the history is full of friendly and neighborly gossip. Everyone seemed to know a story or two about everyone else. Or take the Letters of Pliny the Younger, which in spite of their literary artistry or attempts to that end, still communicate a conviviality and personal knowledge of so many others who belonged to the city of Rome.

Just for comparison: when the poet Martial left Rome after his long stay in the city, he had been resident in the city for almost three decades, a few years more than Josephus. Martial's presence is attested both by his own writings and by his contemporaries. He was a literary presence. He is mentioned in the Letters of Pliny the Younger who knew him personally, and who even helped him financially when Martial was departing the city, as if leaving for exile, although he was returning to his native city in Spain.

In Rome Josephus first lived in apartments donated to him by the Emperor Vespasian. Vespasian had lived in those apartments before he became emperor, and for that reason alone, most Romans would have known who Josephus was. But, of course, they also would have known, if they knew anything about Vespasian and the Jewish War, that Josephus was the Judaean General who had surrendered and been captured by Vespasian's forces in Jotapata in Galilee, and who subsequently fought alongside the Romans in the siege and destruction of Jerusalem. In short, Josephus was probably one of the most well-known people in Rome during his residence in the city. Josephus would have been quite conscious of his surroundings: whom he socialized with, how he was received, etc. So it strains credulity to think that

Josephus could live in close quarters with others in Rome and yet be completely unaware of their presence. Without wishing to overstate a point I made previously: if Suetonius could refer to Josephus as if everyone knew him, and if Martial was the most well-read poet in Rome, it is almost certain that Martial knew Josephus and that Josephus knew Martial as well.

It is, therefore, not merely of academic interest to ponder Josephus's silences about others in the city of Rome, non-Jews and Romans like Pliny the Younger and the poet Martial, who were not exactly obscure, but about whom Josephus says nothing, even though Martial in particular made it a point to calumniate and ridicule Jews, and in one instance derided someone he referred to as the "circumcised poet."

The Christians and Jews of Rome in the years that Josephus lived among them in the city should also be a matter of considerable interest. So the trajectory of this work begins with Josephus and ends with First Clement, which was produced in the last decade of the first century in Rome about the same time that Josephus was writing what appears to be his final work, *Against Apion*. As an important corollary, I shall offer commentary about the silences of contemporaries and historians and how silence aids and abets the historian's craft and our perceptions of the past that historians like Josephus provide us. In this particular case we have a historian who towers over the first century because we have so few sources other than his own writings to tell us about Jewish life and thought in first-century Judaea and Galilee. Another way of saying all this is to say that this book is fundamentally about reading the first century with and without Josephus, who may not always be our most helpful resource when it comes to any number of his contemporaries and the early Christian movement at the end of the first century, in spite of the few passages in his writings that suggest some kind of attestation of the Christian movement.

A PRELIMINARY ANSWER TO OBJECTIONS

To anticipate: it may be objected that the Christians were in fact not such a prominent group and that Josephus's silences as I am describing them here amount to nothing more than an attestation of this fact. Or that Josephus had no reason to discuss them, so his silences are nothing out of the ordinary. In other words, if the Christians were so significant, Josephus would have mentioned them. Another objection is that, in fact, Josephus does mention Christians in a couple of places in his writings so to speak of silence is to misrepresent him. Furthermore, it could be argued that Josephus is silent about a lot of things that we would wish he wrote about, so not mentioning Christians or the fact that he does not write copiously about them does not amount to anything. To wish for more than he did is to demand from him what he did not set out to do. In any case, it is misplaced to suggest that every silence in Josephus is a matter of deliberate omission on his part.

The last objection gets to the heart of the matter. For it is one thing to acknowledge the silences in Josephus. It is quite another to say that his silence about a group, a particular person, an event, or an act is always deliberate. Doubtless, it is matter of fact that Josephus does not mention Paul. But should we then proceed with the inference that the silence is deliberate and ill-willed? It should be said that while no one would insist that all silences are deliberate omissions, and that not all the silences of historians are to be deemed malicious, in the case of Josephus we have reason to wonder. Those reasons demand that we learn how to read and to listen to his silences. Why?

Josephus himself calls attention to the silences of history by providing reasons in one case as to why a certain historian elided a particular subject from his history. Then there is Josephus's unique role as a historian (or *the* historian) of Jewish life in the first century. Josephus is self-conscious about this, and adverts to it on a few occasions. He also mentions the importance of archives in the writing of history, as for example, the Archives of Tyre (e.g., *Antiquities* 9.14.2; *Against Apion* 1.113, 125, 156, 158), which Josephus appeals to in order to dispute other narratives.

When Josephus, the priest from Jerusalem and former military general, became Flavius Josephus the historian, he knew by then that there were no archives of Jerusalem to speak of. As part of the Roman forces that lay siege to Jerusalem in 70 CE, he stood watch and witnessed the burning of the buildings that housed the archives. So virtually everything he wrote, his *Jewish War*, *Antiquities*, *Life,* and *Against Apion*, would be the beginning of a new archive or, at a minimum, a reference point from the Diaspora for a new archive of Jerusalem and Judaea. Recall that he explains the reason why he wrote the first version of his *Jewish War* in Aramaic: so that the Jews of Mesopotamia and beyond would have an accurate account of the events in Judaea and Galilee. In which case, what he includes and does not include, especially about his contemporaries, is critical and consequential.

For the earlier periods of Jewish history he could be challenged. There were other sources, including the Hebrew Scriptures and other historical writings and sources he himself had used. But for his times in Judaea the sources no longer existed, which is why it should not be a matter of indifference as to what Josephus includes or does not include. A historian always makes choices—and those choices often have a logic all their own whether acknowledged or not, whether implicit or explicit. Here, we may note again Louis Feldman's sense of the unevenness of Josephus's history as he enumerates the kinds of questions one has to consider in assessing Josephus's credibility as a historian. Feldman queries:

> Why is his history so uneven, including extraordinarily detailed discussions of certain personalities and events (notably the reign of Herod), as well as numerous, often extensive, digressions, for example, the suicide at Masada (which militarily was of little importance), the summary of Jewish law, and the conversion of the royal family of Adiabene?[37]

The unevenness cannot be separated from Josephus's choices. It is somewhat different when he is compelled by the outlines and details of a biblical narrative which in an important sense provide him a template but also constrain his ability to ignore some biblical characters. This is not to say that he is bound to depict each character equally in the way they are depicted in the Hebrew Scriptures. About the parts of his writing, say the renarration of Biblical history which can be checked and double-checked, Josephus turns out not to be such a trustworthy guide. As Feldman in particular and many others have noted, Josephus rewrites the Hebrew Bible sometimes so thoroughly and so dramatically as to have created his own version of the Hebrew Bible through his revisions and re-creations. Hence, Feldman titles his chapter on Josephus in this regard, "Josephus as Rewriter of the Bible."[38]

Josephus's will and determination to refashion what is supposedly sacred, raises all kinds of questions about the parts of Josephus's writings that cannot be tested against other sources or records, even if he is not unique within Second Temple Judaism for offering his own interpretations and revisions.[39] More significant still, it should raise questions about those personalities, events, and known facts about which he skirts furtively and those about which he is completely silent in his various historical accounts of matters in the first century.

As for the other three objections, it needs to be said that we find ourselves in a slight quandary. If the few passages in Josephus that mention Christians of some sort are authentic, then obviously Josephus thought them worthy of mention. They were not so obscure. If those passages are not authentic, then it means that Josephus excluded them. But the exclusion does not of itself prove that they were insignificant. Here we also need to distinguish between two types of exclusion. If Josephus excludes Christians as part of his ethnography of Jewish life in Judaea, it means one thing; if he excludes Christians as part of life in the city of Rome that is quite another.

In either of these instances, Josephus would be writing about Christians as a whole or in general. However, it is something else entirely when he does not mention someone like Paul, an older contemporary who was resident in Jerusalem and belonged to circles with which Josephus's father was familiar. Here too an objection could be made that Josephus did not know Paul or did not know anything about him, as I have already mentioned. Or that he probably had no idea that Paul would be so influential. But to say this would be to mischaracterize the facts. Josephus wrote his *Antiquities*, which included in its last two books the period covering the first century, in the 90s. By then he had behind him a long life that included his experiences as a native Jerusalemite and extensive contacts in Judaea, Galilee, and in Rome. He had a retrospective view of much of the first century. He had as a close personal acquaintance or friend a contemporary like Herod Agrippa II, who was also a witness to most of the first century and is attested to have encountered Paul. Moreover, if Paul's activities had anything to do with the Temple or with Temple officials, as it is reported in Acts and alluded to in some of his letters, it would not have gone unnoticed and unreported among the inhabitants of Jerusalem and among the priests whose preoccupation was the Temple and its sanctity.

From what we know of Paul's letters, he had already made an impact in founding communities in Asia Minor, Achaia, and Macedonia, and was well known in Rome, if we accept the testimony of First Clement, by the time Josephus made his visit to Rome at the head of a delegation from Jerusalem in 63/64 CE. Paul's influence was still felt in Rome in the last decade of the first century when Josephus was resident in the city, when the church of Corinth sent emissaries and a request to the church in Rome to intervene in helping it resolve its difficulties, a request that led to the writing of First Clement by the church in Rome.

It will be the object of this study to provide reasons as to why we should not read Josephus's silences as merely inadvertent lapses in historical documentation, and his silence about Paul in particular as a happenstance. I shall provide in the course of this study the documentation of the silences and will make a case for considering the silences as deliberate. It will be up to the reader to assess both the credibility of the documentation and the persuasiveness of my argument about Josephus's intentionality.

The reader may demure as regards the particulars of my argument about Josephus's intentions. He or she may choose not to accept my account. However, that is not tantamount to a valid objection. For it will be up to the reader to provide reasons or a reason why the documentation turns out as it does; and more importantly, how Josephus's silences are to be interpreted in light of his own views about the culpable silences of other historians.

This is the point: if Josephus considers it legitimate to judge other historians for their silences, then Josephus's silences cannot be excluded from the very judgments to which he subjects other historians. Josephus cannot and should not be immune from critical judgment, when the criteria for those assessments are based on his own judgment of other historians. I shall go a step further. By providing a logic for why another historian might be motivated to exclude certain fact, realities, and things from their history, Josephus shows both that he understands the implications of historical silences and also that he believes that those who engage in historical writing are prone to certain faults or failings, even vices, and are sometimes disingenuous in their writing of history on account of those vices. What is more, by the time Josephus rendered the judgment to which I am appealing he had had many years to think about his own work as a historian. So it was not judgment made in haste. It was well-considered. Over the previous decades he had formulated other programmatic statements about his craft as a historian in *Jewish War*, *Antiquities*, and *Life*.

As far as it goes, the Greek version of Josephus's writings that have come down to us contain testimonies relating to Christianity in only three places, and one of the three only by inference. They all appear in his *Antiquities*, and in this order, and they all involve the execution of a teacher or leader of a movement:

18.3.3:	Jesus, a great teacher and miracle-worker, was crucified by Pontius Pilate
18.5.2:	John the Baptizer, a popular preacher, was imprisoned and executed
20.9.1:	James, the brother of Jesus who was called Christ, was stoned to death

Of the three passages attested in the Greek version of Josephus, the one about John the Baptizer is the only one that is unambiguously unproblematic. (I am assuming that the Slavonic version of Josephus that has other parts not attested in the Greek is not to be trusted.) There is no attempt in that passage to identify any of John's followers, even though he is said to have had a phenomenal following; and there is no attempt to link John the Baptizer to the Christian movement (in the way the Slavonic version does). I simply take it for granted that a later Christian redactor who had read Josephus's *Antiquities* up to that point would have sought to make explicit the links between John the Baptizer and Jesus found in the Gospels and in Acts. The passage about James the brother of Jesus could have been subject to tampering by later redactors, but there is nothing in the passage to suggest that it has, since the phrase, "Jesus who was thought to be the Christ," is a statement Josephus could have made without difficulty as representing the views of others in Judaea and Galilee. It did not have to be Josephus's view. What is more, a later Christian redactor would probably have been inclined to remove the ambiguity or uncertainty by correcting it to read, "who was the Christ," not who was thought to be the Christ. In which case, I take the reference to James as authentic Josephus, as my previous comments imply. Again, any later Christian redactor who knew the *Antiquities* would also have likely made explicit that the High Priest Ananaus son of Ananus (Annas) who orchestrated the death of James was also a relative of Caiaphas the High Priest at the time of the crucifixion of Jesus. Josephus himself highlighted the unique honor due the High Priest Ananus (Annas) to have had so many sons and a son-in-law as High Priests.

As we can see, of the three central figures responsible for the emergence and spread of the Christian movement as attested to in the writings of the canonical New Testament—John the Baptist, Jesus of Nazareth, and the apostle Paul—only Paul is missing from the works of Josephus. Yet, he was the only one of the three who was a living contemporary of Josephus.

Naturally the first reference, the *Testimonium Flavianum*, the testimony or evidence of Flavius (TF henceforth), attracts the most attention. Not only is it an extended passage that mentions Jesus's teaching and his great influence. But it also mentions the crucifixion of Jesus on the authority of Pontius Pilate and speaks positively of Jesus as perhaps more than a wise man. The fuller passage insinuates that Jesus may be something more because he performed miracles, had a great following, and was believed to have been resurrected. If it is authentic, it does establish that Josephus thought of Jesus as more than an admirable human being who met a gruesome death.

The attention these passages have received in the history of reception of Josephus's writings is to be expected. At the same time, the attention they have received is in inverse proportion to the actual testimony they provide about the Christian movement. First, they are rather minimal, considering the nature of the Jesus movement as recounted in the writings of Paul, the Gospels, and the rest of the New Testament. Secondly, Josephus does not mention anyone else apart from James, the brother of Jesus. When he does, he does not mention him as a leader of the followers of Jesus, though the way he highlights him as the brother of Jesus who was called the Christ makes patent that James is to be understood and characterized in relation to Jesus the Messiah and the movement that was brought into being by Jesus. Thirdly—and this is significant—the historical moment in view, that is, the stoning of James sometime in 62 CE, means that Josephus was keenly aware of some matters concerning the Christians of Jerusalem and Judaea during his formative years. I have already addressed some of this.

But why only James, the brother of Jesus? Did Josephus maintain an interest in the brother of Jesus and in no one else associated with the Jesus movement? If James, then why not Paul, or even Peter, for that matter? Why does Josephus betray no interest in the one very important figure of the Christian movement who mentions in his own letters (Galatians 1) his involvement with the said James, among the leaders of the church in Jerusalem? What of the fact that the said individual (Paul) mentions in his letters that he intended to make a journey to Jerusalem, a visit that took place a few years before the events surrounding the death of James? Could Josephus have been really so ignorant of our person of interest, Paul the apostle, even as he provides these notices related to early Christianity?

Historians and Josephus's interpreters have also been indifferent to or uninterested in a related question. This time it is about Josephus and his presence among Christians (both Jew and Gentile) in Rome in the last two and a half decades of the first century. Again, I have already alluded to this. For some reason, interpreters of Josephus who even acknowledge his remarkable silences on other matters seem to underestimate the significance of this one; that Josephus lived in the same environment in Rome that produced First Clement, a document from the church of Rome to the church at Corinth that is deeply imbued with the Hebrew Scriptures.

A few recent compendia dealing specifically with Josephus as historian and as a Flavian seem not at all interested in the subject.[40] One cannot read First Clement without realizing how thoroughly Jewish the author(s) and the community behind First Clement understood themselves. First Clement quotes or refers to the Hebrew/Jewish Scriptures profusely. It takes for granted that Christianity or "being Christian" is Jewish and is completely naïve about anything approaching something like a conflict between something called "Judaism" and something else called "Christianity." It simply insists that Jesus is the Messiah. At the risk of overstating it, it may not be inappropriate to say that First Clement attests to something called "Christian Judaism" in the same way that Paul's Letter to the Galatians does, for example. First Clement does not make a point of identifying itself as wholly Gentile (comprised of non-Jews) or some mixture of Gentiles and Jews. It simply assumes that anyone can belong to this society, this new universal community. So presumably they are made up of Jews and non-Jews, with "Christian" as the adjective that qualifies this community of very Jewish origin and character. However, in Josephus's world of Jewish sects and groups, they do not exist. There are no Christian Jews even in Jerusalem. They do not exist in Rome, even if they existed in Judaea.

Here we seem to assume that the TF bears witness to some such grouping in Judaea and elsewhere because it mentions Jesus having a following among Jews and Hellenes. But the reference is inexact. Even if the TF is genuine, it does not distinguish in what sense the followers of Jesus constituted anything unique as such or common with other Jewish groups. Josephus does not mention them among the various groups he discusses.

Here is another critical feature: if the TF's reference to Jesus's followers is meant to signal Gentiles in the Mediterranean world, it is more than intriguing that the one person who is singularly responsible for that movement outside Judaea is never mentioned by Josephus. For this and the aforementioned reasons I shall not follow the fixation on the TF.

That fixation among some scholars and some nonspecialists alike is partly motivated by a longing to have Josephus say something affirmative about Jesus as Messiah. Others are equally determined to prove that it is a forgery so that it denies their opponents any attestation from Josephus about the supposed messiahship of Jesus. What often gets lost is that Josephus mentions any number of messianic pretenders in his writings. So the idea of someone claiming to be a messiah in and of itself does not prove that the TF is affirming, for example, what Paul means when he speaks of Jesus as Messiah, or what the Gospel writers mean when they do the same.

Besides even if we discussed everything that has been said about the TF, it would not add a single piece of discovery to what Josephus says about Paul, which is nothing. So the TF and the abundant scholarship surrounding it, or the current debate it generates within some circles, are almost irrelevant to our concerns here.

A few basic facts that should not be matters of dispute: First, Josephus was a contemporary of Paul. In this sense what Josephus knew or did not know about Paul is markedly different from what he knew and did not know about Jesus. One could understand if Josephus did not say anything about Jesus. After all Josephus was born in 37 CE a few years after Jesus's crucifixion, so if Josephus claimed he did not know anything about Jesus, he could be excused. He could claim that there was not much of a following for Jesus after his death, even if there are other sources that say otherwise. But not when it comes to Paul. Paul's later years parallel Josephus's early years. So simply saying that Josephus did not know Paul because Paul was a Diaspora Jew whereas Josephus was from Jerusalem is almost beside the point. It hardly settles the issue. After all, Philo of Alexandria was a Diaspora Jew and an older contemporary of Josephus. Yet Josephus mentions Philo on more than one occasion. He mentions other Jews from other parts of the Diaspora who were his contemporaries, including the Adiabene Royals from Mesopotamia who settled in Jerusalem.

Josephus mentions other contemporaries closer to home, many of them Pharisees. Paul was a Pharisee. Even if he had ceased to identify with the Pharisees when Josephus came of age, it strains credulity to think that Josephus, a resident of Jerusalem, would not have heard anything about this former Pharisee who was now spearheading a movement beyond Judaea and Palestine. In any case, Josephus's father Matthias was an almost exact contemporary of Paul, as I have already noted. He was well connected with the leading figures in Jerusalem. Josephus's father would have known something about Paul, if Paul was as reputable among the Pharisees and as troubling to the early Christians as he claims to have been.

Josephus's silence about Paul, then, should be treated with astonishment and a certain amount of incredulity. If he can mention Philo, if he knows James the brother of Jesus, then Paul, the founder of many of the Christian communities in the Jewish Diaspora, who also associates himself with the likes of James the brother of Jesus and with Peter the apostle and the Christians of Jerusalem, should have at least earned a minor biographical reference. That he is simply nonexistent in Jewish life in the first century, according to Josephus, is one of the most culpable silences of any historian of first-century Judaism.

To give some sense of Josephus's culpability, let us consider the following. Suppose Josephus had never mentioned Philo of Alexandria in any of his writings. What would the verdict be on Josephus's silence about Philo? We would have to come up with reasons why Josephus ignored one of the most important and most prominent Jews of the first century. We would not consider it a trivial matter. If for nothing else Philo was perhaps the leading intellectual of the Jews of Alexandra, one of the most illustrious communities in the Diaspora. Even if others did not follow his teachings, Philo's stature was fully acknowledged by his fellow Alexandrians. He was also part of an illustrious family whose influence reached to Judaea. One of his nephews, Tiberius Julius Alexander, who became prefect of Egypt in the 60s, was sent by the Emperor Claudius as governor of Judaea in 46 CE. Tiberius Alexander would be on the staff of Titus as he lay siege to Jerusalem in 70 CE. Josephus could simply not avoid Philo and his family even if he wanted to. Not so with Paul.

Paul was not from a family like Philo's, so perhaps he did not need to be taken that seriously. Still, Josephus wrote about others who were even less illustrious than Paul, including many rebels from Galilee who could not match Paul's education or influence. Whatever you think of Paul, he was responsible for one of the most important transformations in Jewish life and thought ever. All this happened in the middle of the first century (c. 32–c. 64). To write about Jewish life in the first century without so simple an acknowledgment of his existence and of his influence is stupendous on any scale.

Doubtless Philo's literary output dwarfs the remnants of Paul's letters found in the canonical New Testament. But there is a real question whether in spite of this difference in the volume of their respective writings Paul does not outshine Philo. This may be debatable. A good deal of Philo's output involves commentary on the Hebrew Scriptures (the Pentateuch in particular) often with the objective of reframing those scriptures to fit Philo's philosophical and cultural outlook. Josephus too routinely rewrote the Hebrew Bible. In a sense, Paul had no such need. He took for granted that the Hebrew Scriptures in the Greek translations available to him were good enough. Oddly, and while considered the innovator, Paul turns out not to have rewritten the Hebrew Scriptures or reframed them in the way that Philo and Josephus did in their different ways. As a contemporary of both Philo and Josephus, to excise him from Jewish life would be like Josephus excising Philo out of Jewish history of the first century.

Josephus, the priest from Jerusalem, a descendant of priests and a professional historian, took it upon himself to be the truth-teller in his writings of all matters Jewish. In addition to his professional self-understanding as a historian, Josephus was also writing as a participant and a witness to history in the first century. He cannot easily be separated from the substance and content of his writings. Like all historians and others who bear witness or claim to bear witness, what one chooses not to tell or represent matters as regards motives and the shape of the story that one tells. Josephus himself writes on these themes. If Josephus was aware of the Christian movement, of some of the followers of Jesus, of James the brother of Jesus, but chose not to give them any presence in his history, chose to exclude Christian Jews from his ethnography of first-century Jewish groups (sects, schools) in his *Antiquities* and *Life*, this cannot be deemed a mere accident. That exclusion requires comment. If he did not know, could not possibly have known, then that is another story. But as we shall see, Josephus did know or was close enough to people, places, and particular events not to have been ignorant of them.

ONCE MORE: THE EVENTS OF 62 CE

The events of 62 CE to which I have already referred amplify Josephus's silences in ways that cannot simply be overlooked, as if inconsequential to his silences about the early Christians of Judaea and Rome. As I have already discussed, sometime that year a common man in Jerusalem named Jesus began to proclaim, in the manner of a prophet, a message of doom to the hearing of the people of Jerusalem. This Jesus, the son of Ananias, may well have brought to mind of people of an older generation, among them Matthias the father of Josephus, events that had happened a generation earlier when one Jesus of Nazareth (the Galilean) had been crucified. The people of Jerusalem did not have to think that far back, however, to be reminded of that Jesus. Before Jesus son of Ananias began his proclamations, James the brother of that Jesus of Nazareth, the putative leader of the Christians in Jerusalem, had been murdered at the instigation of the High Priest also named Ananias.

The events of 62 CE are not that well known. But they provide an important clue to understanding certain aspects of the fate of early Christianity than is generally recognized. Josephus the son of Mathias related them in his *Antiquities* over thirty years after the events of 62 CE. What Josephus says about Jesus son of Ananias, what he relates about the High Priest Ananus son of Ananus, and about James the brother of Jesus who was thought to be the Christ, all indicate in various ways how his writings reveal and also pass over silently important elements of early Christian history that are essential for understanding the fate of Christianity in the first century.

Josephus's account of the murder of James the brother of Jesus is part of a narrative about the short-lived but momentous career of the High Priest Ananus son of Ananus which lasted all of about a few months (three months) and why the murder of James the brother of Jesus and the reaction of the leading men of Jerusalem that Josephus relates makes patent that the group of Christians (mostly Jews) among whom James was thought to be a leader were not an unknown and indistinguishable group of people in Jerusalem. They were an identifiable group with a recognized leader whose judicial murder was a source of concern for the leading men of Jerusalem.

Jerusalem was not a very big place. The leading men of Jerusalem were not an amorphous and unknown group of people. To belong to that circle was to know about a good deal that happened in the city. Josephus's father Matthias belonged to this group, by Josephus's own reckoning. Josephus describes his father Matthias as among the most respected men of the city for his wisdom and manner of life. Matthias was also well connected to the recognized leadership in Jerusalem and was close to members of the Sanhedrin, the ruling council. Josephus's father was, therefore, involved in some of the decisions made by the leading men of the city. If they did not include him in their deliberations, he certainly did know about those who did the deliberating and why the issues were matters of concern. So we must imagine that Josephus's father had some knowledge of who and what was involved in the decision to sanction the judicial murder of James the brother of Jesus. He almost certainly knew as well why Jesus son of Ananias was allowed to go on proclaiming his message of Jerusalem's doom for as long as he did.

What about Josephus himself? Josephus was twenty-five years old in 62 CE. He describes himself in his autobiography as one of the leading young men in the city, affiliated with the Pharisees between age nineteen and twenty-six (56 to 63 CE) and with the leading men of the city. Josephus would have learned much from his father and also from others associated and not associated with his father. These are social facts. How current was his knowledge at the time? If he is to be believed that he was as connected to the Pharisees as he claims, then we cannot overlook his personal knowledge of some of these facts. If we consider his links to the Pharisees together with his father's connection to the leading men of the city and the Sanhedrin, then it is almost certain that Josephus knew a lot of these facts as they happened—not later on in his life when he came to write his *Jewish War*, *Antiquities* or *Life*, while living in Rome. It should be understood as basic historical fact that neither Josephus's father Matthias nor Josephus himself would have been ignorant about the events surrounding the murder of James the brother of Jesus when it happened in 62 CE.

Two basic conclusions to be drawn: First, Josephus knew James the brother of Jesus. He knew Jesus son of Ananias as a preacher of doom over Jerusalem. He was well aware of the unease the Jerusalem leaders felt toward Jesus son of Ananias; he was also aware of how some segments of the leading men of Jerusalem in league with the High Priest Ananus son of Ananus felt about James the brother of Jesus. As he puts it, most of the fair-minded among the people and those who were zealous for the law objected to the manner in which James the brother of Jesus had been accused, condemned, and murdered/executed. It is not necessary to insist as some have that the conflict was a classic one between Sadducees and Pharisees because Josephus describes Ananus son of Ananus as a Sadducee and the subsequent objection to his deeds by a group "zealous for the law." They could be Pharisees but they need not be, as if only Pharisees are described by Josephus as being "zealous for the law." There are instances in his writings where he mentions others being zealous for the law without necessarily calling them Pharisees. He seems to place those who were fair-minded among the people in a category even much larger and broader than those "zealous for the law."

Second, and this follows from the first point, according to Josephus, the objection to the High Priest Ananus was widespread not just among those "zealous for the law," indicating some sympathy for James because he was respected by other Jews. The tendency to diminish this element of sympathy is often combined with any instinctive reflex that James's death had nothing to do with James as a Christian, presumably because there was no anti-Christian feeling among any Jerusalemites.

If there was conflict between the Christian Jews and the rest of the Jerusalemites, it is not given any expression in Josephus's account. In fact, the opposite appears to be the case. All indications are that there was no such general conflict. Perhaps the tolerance shown Jesus son of Ananias is some indication. So the Jerusalemites responded to James's death as they would to any other Jew who they believed had been unjustly prosecuted and sentenced to death. To say, however, that Josephus does not report general antipathy toward the Christians in his account is not quite the same thing as saying that the High Priest Ananus himself and those aligned with and associated with him may not have been motivated by anti-Christian sentiment.

Helen Bond goes so far as to insist, against any evidence whatsoever, that Ananus merely acted against James because James had become party to the factions aligned against Ananus.[41] There is nothing in Josephus's account to say that James had become a partisan. In any case, if James was a partisan, what would he have been a partisan of? What social capital or currency did he have to influence the sentiments and political aspirations of his fellow Jews as to who occupied the High Priesthood and who did not? Why would anyone care? In an odd twist, in determining to absolve Ananus of any antipathy toward James the Christian, Bond turns James into a far more important social and political actor, contrary to anything Josephus insinuates, and the historical record furnishes. Odd too that none of his supposed partisans were able to save him from his fate. Instead, James is mentioned as suffering a fate with others who are nameless as if insignificant characters in the internecine violence of Jerusalem politics.

Back to Josephus himself: Did Josephus count himself among the fair-minded in Jerusalem and Judaea who believed that James had been unjustly prosecuted and sentenced to death? Was he among those who were zealous for the law who believed that the High Priest had contravened the teachings of Torah? Or was he simply indifferent to what happened to James? Did he agree with the High Priest and the Sanhedrin? If not, why does he not say so? Should we simply assume that he was fair-minded and so objected to both the prosecution of James and his capital punishment?

Here, then, is an attempt to make sense of events in 62 CE surrounding the High Priest Ananus. For a period of about six months in 62 CE, between the departure of Festus the governor of Judaea and the arrival of his replacement Albinus, something changed in Jerusalem in part because of one man: Ananus the son of Ananus, the High Priest.

While the people of Jerusalem and Judaea waited for the new procurator Albinus to come from Alexandria, there was a political vacuum that many sought to exploit. Agrippa II sought to fill the vacuum by appointing Ananus the son of Ananus as High Priest. This was over and against the interests probably of the majority of the chief priests. As things turned out, Ananus proceeded quickly to demonstrate his power and authority. He had a group of people brought up on charges of contravening the law, tried, and executed. Among them was James the brother of Jesus.[42]

The leaders in Jerusalem saw this as an opportunity to get rid of Ananus. It was also to undermine Agrippa II and question his authority for appointing him in the first place. This too was to preempt anything that Albinus would do. Significantly, Ananus did not disappear. He continued to exercise some influence and to influence others. Josephus mentions later on that Ananus was bribed to oppose Josephus's command in Galilee (*Life* 194ff.). So we must understand that this was a person Josephus knew well.

The possibilities of violence during 62 CE gives us reason to believe that with the death of James, most of the Christians in the city of Jerusalem left the city. It was no longer safe for them to be there. The removal of Ananus as High Priest before the arrival of Albinus may have encouraged some to return, but it seems unlikely. After all, Ananus himself was not tried or ostracized. He remained among the chief priests and continued to influence others as late as the eve of the Jewish War when Josephus was in Galilee. We should therefore not assume that his removal would have been comforting for the Christians of the city, if any remained there. His continued involvement in matters in Jerusalem and Jewish national life suggests that perhaps the disapproval of the fair-minded people that Josephus mentions was somewhat qualified. If they found him so objectionable, their objections did not go beyond removing him from office. He continued to play a role in Jerusalem, but not as High Priest. Moreover, by the very nature or the rules of the Sanhedrin, he could not have gotten the conviction of James and the others without the participation of other chief priests. So while Josephus calls attention to those who objected to Ananus the High Priest, Josephus also provides the evidence to suggest there were some who sided with him, enough for him to be able to arrest James and the others who were thought to have contravened the law, and get them tried. There is next to nothing in the phrasing of Josephus's language here to suggest that it was a matter of strict observance to the Mosaic Law (*peri tous nomous akribeis*) that had brought James into opposition to Ananus. The phrase, "having acted illegally" (*paranomesanton*), from the verb "paranomeo," could mean simply doing anything considered unlawful or illegal.[43] Whatever it was, Josephus does not say exactly how James and the others accused had acted illegally, with a strong sense of having done something prohibited and deserving of the severest sanction, in this case death.

Perhaps, then, part of the objection to Ananus was mostly self-interested, that those others, the fair-minded and those who were zealous for the law, would not themselves become victims of his machinations. How real this was, Josephus does not quite say, but it could not have been far from the surface, if it is true that it was believed that Ananus had acted unjustly.

There are too many elements about the conflict between Ananus and the fair-minded and those who were zealous for the law that Josephus does not reveal. The fact that Josephus himself elides any description or discussion of his own activities during this period also raises questions about where he belonged and what role he played. What is striking, given this silence, is that a year later, Josephus was handed the responsibility of leading a delegation from Jerusalem to Rome to secure the release of a group of priests who had been arrested and sent to Rome.

Josephus's diplomatic mission makes clear that he was favored among those who were now in the ascendancy in Jerusalem. At a minimum most of these leaders played a role in the deposition of Ananus as High Priest, or were connected to those who did. Ananus does not seem to have overlooked any of this, which probably explains why he was willing to act against Josephus a few years later when Josephus was in command in Galilee (*Life* 192ff.).

In any event, when Josephus left Jerusalem for Rome, he had behind him the knowledge of the Christians of Jerusalem and the prosecution and execution of their putative leader, James the brother of Jesus (of Nazareth). While he was in Rome or nearby, the city suffered destruction by fire in July 64 CE. The historical account of Tacitus ties the event with Nero's persecution of Christians who were made scapegoats, even though most suspected Nero himself had a hand in the destruction planned to make room for his new palace he intended to build. Nowhere in Josephus's writings does he mention the Fire of 64, nor does he make any reference to the persecution of Christians in Rome by Nero during much of his reign, as indicated by Suetonius, and after the Fire, as reported by Tacitus.

If Josephus had mentioned this, he would have been forced perhaps to offer an explanation as to why the Christians were persecuted in Jerusalem by the High Priest (in 62 CE) and in Rome by Emperor Nero (in 64 CE). As it is, he provides very little in the way of a description of just what it was that made James the brother of Jesus so objectionable to Ananus that he found a way to convict him and have him executed. The comment that those who were fair-minded and zealous for the law thought James's execution unjust does not provide an explanation as to why James was the object of Ananus's prosecution in the first place and why Ananus wanted him dead. Nor does it furnish any reasons as to why those who tried James also found reasons to convict him of a capital offense. Moreover, Josephus does not mention the names of those who were also tried along with James, nor does he indicate whether they were Christians or not, and what kind of fate they also endured.

What may also be significant is that Ananus went about having James executed almost as soon as he became High Priest. Ananus did not last more than three months in the role on account of this and other dastardly acts. So it is doubtful that James had done something so recent as to be charged with a capital crime. In all likelihood Ananus had identified James as an objectionable character before Ananus was elected High Priest. So as soon as he was put in that role, he set out to get rid of him. Ananus's actions reflect a long-standing disapproval of what James represented in Jerusalem. That Ananus did not act alone also suggests that he had considerable support for his view. This brings us back to Josephus and his father Matthias. Curiously, Josephus says nothing about what his father thought about James and of his condemnation and death. Was Matthias among the fair-minded and those who were zealous for the law among the Jerusalemites? Did Matthias have a say in the prosecution of James, the brother of Jesus? Was Matthias opposed to Ananus as High Priest?

Between what happened in Jerusalem in 62 CE and Rome in 64 CE we have documentation about Christians in Judaea and in the imperial capital. In both places they were a well-recognized (and flourishing?) community that attracted the attention of the High Priest and the Emperor Nero respectively. In both instances an attempt is made to prosecute their leader(s) or to destroy them. The execution of James the brother of Jesus was no mere happenstance. Neither was Nero's persecution of the Christians of Rome. The justifications were different. Josephus does not furnish the proper basis for the first. For the second, Tacitus explains it was on a charge of arson. However, Tacitus provides no indication that there were any proper trials conducted to ascertain the truth of the charge.

By orchestrating the judicial murder of James the brother of Jesus, Ananus had set himself in opposition to those who used the occasion to seek his removal. Those events would have been known to the Romans, to whom the Jerusalemites had sent petitions complaining about the High Priest and demanding the speedy arrival of a new governor to curb Agrippa II and Ananus. After all, it was Nero who appointed Albinus to take over the governorship of Judaea after Porcius Festus. It is even possible that the murder of James the brother of Jesus may have emboldened Nero and his praetorian prefect Tigellinus to go after the Christians in Rome. I cannot prove this. But the general opprobrium in which the Christians were held and the knowledge that they derived from Judaea would have made any knowledge of the murder of James the brother of Jesus appear to non-Jews as a particularly condemnatory act that they too could emulate. Albinus's decision to remove Ananus son of Ananus was one of his more important official acts as governor of Judaea.

The news of James's death in 62 CE will also have filtered through the various Christian communities in Damascus, Antioch, Asia Minor, Greece (Corinth, Philippi, Thessolonika, etc.), most of the places where Paul and others had founded churches. Eventually, and perhaps sooner than later, it would have been known in Rome. If it was not known there, Josephus himself would have been carrying that knowledge with him when he arrived in Rome in 63/64 CE. By the time Josephus left Rome to return to Jerusalem, he had this event and the most recent Fire of 64 CE in the background. He does not connect them at any point, nor does he provide any commentary whatsoever about their relative significance. Tacitus's later account of the events surrounding the Fire and the role of Christians in the story shines a spotlight on Josephus's complete silence about the event.

JOSEPHUS'S SILENCES ABOUT THE HIGH PRIEST CAIAPHAS: SOME IMPLICATIONS

It may be worthwhile to mention that Josephus's silence about Paul and his brief reference to James the brother of Jesus are of a kind with his reticence about another figure of the first century, the High Priest Caiaphas, whose name he gives in full as Josephus/Joseph Caiaphas. Although Caiaphas is mentioned in the canonical Gospels and in Acts as one of the most prominent Jews in the first century and one who had various dealings with Jesus and his followers, Caiaphas appears in Josephus's *Antiquities* with no more than the dates of the beginning of his reign and the end of his tenure as High Priest.

The passage in which he records his deposition by Vitellius, the governor of Syria, also contains the end of Pontius Pilate's tenure.

> And so Pilate, after having spent ten years in Judaea, hurried to Rome in obedience to the orders of Vitellius, since he could not refuse. But before he reached Rome Tiberius had already passed away. Vitellius, on reaching Ju-

daea, went up to Jerusalem, where the Jews were celebrating their traditional feast called the Passover. Having been received in magnificent fashion, Vitellius remitted to the inhabitants of the city all taxes on the sale of agricultural produce and agreed that the vestments of the high priest and all his ornaments should be kept in the temple in custody of the priests, as had been their privilege before. At that time the vestments were stored in Antonia—there is a stronghold of that name—for the following reason. One of the priests, Hyrcanus, the first of many by that name, had constructed a large house near the temple and lived there most of the time. As custodian of the vestments, for to him alone was conceded the right to put them on, he kept them laid away there, whenever he put on his ordinary clothes in order to go down to the city. His sons and their children also followed the same practice. When Herod became king, he made lavish repairs to this building, which was conveniently situated, and, being a friend of Antony, he called it Antonia. He retained the vestments there just as he had found them, believing that for this reason the people would never rise in insurrection against him. Herod's successor as king, his son Archelaus, acted similarly. After him, when the Romans took over the government, they retained control of the high priest's vestments and kept them in a stone building, where they were under the seal both of the priests and of the custodians of the treasury and where the warden of the guard lighted the lamp day by day. Seven days before each festival the vestments were delivered to the priests by the warden. After they had been purified, the high priest wore them; then after the first day of the festival he put them back again in the building where they were laid away before. This was the procedure at the three festivals each year and on the fast day. Vitellius was guided by our law in dealing with the vestments and instructed the warden not to meddle with the question where they were to be stored or when they should be used. After he had bestowed these benefits upon the nation, he removed from his sacred office the high priest Joseph surnamed Caïaphas, and appointed in his stead Jonathan, son of Ananus the high priest. Then he set out on the journey back to Antioch.[44]

The juxtaposition of Pontius Pilate, who is mentioned in the first sentence, and Caiaphas, whose deposition occurs in the last, raises at least one question, if Josephus knew James the brother of Jesus and had known of his death for nearly three decades when he wrote these words in Rome in the 90s CE. Could Josephus have written about Pilate, Caiaphas, about the role of the High Priest at Passover, about the supervision of the Romans and the presence of the governor of Syria, and so on, without once thinking about what he had learned about the events surrounding the death of Jesus who was thought to be the Christ, that Jesus, the brother of James, under Pontius Pilate and Caiaphas?

If it were left to Josephus, we should never know that the High Priest who superintended events at Passover the year Jesus died had anything to do with the man from Galilee who was put to death by order of Pilate the prefect/

governor that particular Passover. We should say almost; because in fact, Josephus provides details to call attention to his silence about Caiaphas.

Even if we doubt the accounts in Acts that link Paul to Caiaphas, Caiaphas would most certainly have known about Paul if Paul was as active in pursuing the followers of the crucified Jesus of Nazareth as he described himself in Galatians. To later contemporaries, the murder of James the brother of Jesus through the instigation of the High Priest Ananus son Ananus, who was related to Caiaphas, would have called attention to Caiaphas's own role in the death of Jesus the brother of James a generation earlier. Josephus's father, Matthias, who was a contemporary of both Jesus and his brother James and was alive when James was put to death in 62 CE, would not have missed any of these connections. Although Josephus does not mention Caiaphas in his account of the High Priest Ananus son of Ananus, his earlier accounts of the house of Ananus (Annas) and of Caiaphas as one of the prominent members of that house compels the reader to supply the unstated details that Ananus son of Ananus, who orchestrated the murder of James the brother of Jesus, was a relative of Caiaphas who was High Priest at the time of the death of Jesus. Whether we wish to describe these realities as evidence of a conflict between the family of Jesus of Nazareth and the family of Ananus the elder (High Priest from 6–10 CE?) who was father-in-law to Caiaphas and father to Ananus the High Priest (who was appointed and deposed in 62 CE) is another question altogether. The basic facts are that two High Priests from the same family, some thirty years apart conspire to put to death two brothers.

If there was a Chronicle of the High Priesthood, as Josephus implies at *Antiquities* 20.261 and *Against Apion* 1.36, then there must have been material available to him about Caiaphas that he deliberately did not use or include in his *Antiquities*. Josephus himself provides a catalog of High Priests (*Antiquities* 20.226–227 // 224–251) that appears to derive from such a chronicle. So the fact that in the *Antiquities* he does not mention a single deed by Caiaphas, the longest serving High Priest of the first century, is no mere accident. Unless of course, all of that material dealing with Caiaphas was only available in Jerusalem and that material was destroyed with the Temple. But note: Josephus received certain things from the Temple on Titus's order. Some of this material may have been taken elsewhere before the final siege of Jerusalem. In any event, Ananias son of Nebedaeus, who served from 48–59 CE, an eleven-year term, similarly receives no portrait. Josephus simply mentioned that he was appointed by Herod king of Chalcis after he deposed the High Priest Joseph son of Camydus (*Antiquities* 20.100).

Incidentally, the later years of the tenure of Ananias son of Nebedaeus also involves the period of Paul's arrest in Jerusalem recorded in Acts 23:4–9 that precipitated his transport to Rome to face charges. As well, a number of former High Priests got involved in events in 66 CE: not only Ananias son of

Nebedaeus but also Ananus son Ananus, who had James the brother of Jesus murdered. Ananias son of Nebedaeus, for one, was killed by the Sicarii in 66 CE.[45] Josephus says little about him in the *Antiquities*, but he appeared to have little choice in having to say quite a lot about him in the *Jewish War*: much of it not very flattering (*Antiquities* 20.9.2–4; *Jewish War* 2.426–429 and 2.441).

Josephus's catalog of the High Priests in Israel's history in *Antiquities* 20.10 ends with a reference that the High Priests during the time from Herod to the destruction of the Temple had various functions; and he points out that the years that cover the high priests from the time of Herod the Great to 70 CE is 107 years. He does not name any of them here in part because he had mentioned them in the previous books, even though he does not discuss all of them. It is important to consider those he does not really discuss. *Antiquities* 20.9, however, contains the story of Ananus son of Ananus and the death of James the brother of Jesus. He ends that chapter with the appointment of Jesus son of Damnaeus after the deposition of Ananus son of Ananus by Agrippa II. It is impossible, then, to read the cycle from *Antiquities* 20.9 to 20.10 without wondering how the house of Annas, in the persons of Caiaphas and Ananus son of Ananus, dealt with the house of Jesus in the persons of Jesus of Nazareth and his brother James.

Then we have the fact that the High Priest's actions were official public acts. They were recorded, as we see in what happened with the vestments. In that passage Josephus points out that, on the three festivals and fasts, the vestments had to be procured and used as prescribed. One of those three festivals was Passover. The other two were Pentecost and Tabernacles (*Antiquities* 15.408). So every Passover, Caiaphas would have had to do his official duty for all of Jerusalem to see. It was an occasion of high drama that the Romans did not miss. In fact, they superintended it. Their control of the vestments ensured this. So somewhere in the official records there would be a description of exactly how Caiaphas conducted himself on Passover. So during that Passover when Jesus met his final end, no doubt, Caiaphas would have been involved. All of Jerusalem and Judaea would have heard what happened. Josephus, of course, records no deeds of Caiaphas on any Passover: not a single Passover. But his own account of the vestments and the three festivals (*Antiquities* 18.91–95) at which they were used compel us to imagine what might have happened and what did happen on that Passover. Surely on the Pentecost, following this particular Passover when Jesus died, Caiaphas would once again have had something to do. About this too Josephus has nothing to say.

So three times a year for almost two decades Caiaphas officiated at the pilgrimage festivals. That they were routine does not mean they were not eventful. That is why on many occasions the Roman governor made a special visit sometimes at Passover.

Ordinarily, we should have encountered Caiaphas again in *Antiquities* 20.9.1 in relation to the High Priest Ananus, who masterminded the judicial murder of James the brother of Jesus. But this time Josephus does not mention Caiaphas. He does not have to, it is implied. In doing so, Josephus calls attention to something like a historical conflict between the house of Ananus and the family of Jesus of Nazareth, that began with Caiaphas and came to an end with Ananus in 62 CE. In spite of what he says about Caiaphas in *Antiquities* 18, and all that he says about the High Priest and his role in Jewish life and in Judaean politics, Josephus manages to write about everything and everybody else without describing a single act or ruling of Caiaphas, even though Caiaphas was the longest serving High Priest of the first century. What can easily be lost sight of, given Josephus's silence, is that the last ten years of Caiaphas's reign coincided with the teaching and public ministry of John the Baptist and Jesus of Nazareth, and with the conversion and/or apostasy of Paul the Pharisee.[46] Josephus, nevertheless, does have a word to say about John the Baptist, and we are sure that Caiaphas too had an opinion about John, unless of course, Josephus would rather we take his own view as the one that most of the priests of Jerusalem held about John the Baptizer.

By any account and under any reckoning Josephus's silence about Caiaphas's acts and words is astonishing. If Caiaphas was the most important High Priest of the first century, he simply cannot be ignored. Too much of the story of first-century Jewish life in the period during which he was High Priest goes through Caiaphas; or cannot be understood without him. Sure Josephus mentions his name twice. But he provides no account of Caiaphas's deeds. Yet, as High Priest Caiaphas must have had an opinion about almost every matter of religious and political importance or consequence during his tenure in office. These views would not have been private, they would have been matters of public record. So then, whether we want to admit it or not, whether Josephus writes about them or not, Caiaphas must have had an opinion about the teaching and preaching of John the Baptist, of Jesus of Nazareth, and a few other perceived religious, social, and political miscreants between 18 and 37 CE, perhaps including Paul the Pharisee turned follower of Jesus the Galilean. Some such dossier must have existed in the private mind of almost every resident or citizen of Jerusalem about Caiaphas; and there was also an attendant public perception or understanding about the acts or deeds of Caiaphas. Josephus's silence about all this in the *Antiquities* renders Caiaphas mute, is if he was irrelevant to events in Judaea. That is simply not credible. It seems deliberate. To the point: one cannot render an account of Caiaphas without discussing John the Baptist, Jesus of Nazareth and his followers, the Nazarenes (or Galileans), Paul the Pharisee, etc.

It was better, then, not to give an account of Caiaphas as High Priest. It could be argued that silencing Caiaphas was one of the easiest ways of suppressing the social facts about the Christian Jews. For to write about Caiaphas and about how he conducted the affairs of the high-priestly office, negotiated the delicate and sometimes precipitous balance between his fellow Jews and the Romans, and managed the various factions in Judaean society, would have required Josephus to tell about Caiaphas and Pontius Pilate the Roman governor whose term also ended in 37 CE. These are the two officials whose tenures in office form the inclusio of the passage I quoted from Josephus a short while ago. Almost invariably, he would have had to write more specifically about the teacher or rabbi from Galilee named Jesus who was executed in c. 30 CE and about what precipitated his mission and what possibly became of his followers afterward. Josephus seemed determined not to give any legitimacy to the Christian Jews. But this leaves a gaping hole in Josephus's descriptions about the officials of the Temple and about Judaean politics and religious sensibilities in the years 18 to 37 CE. The omission of Caiaphas's acts seem pointedly deliberate.

What perhaps goes unmentioned is that in Rome the objections to Christians had something to do with the Christians originating as a movement that began in the Roman province of Judaea. In Judaea itself, according to Josephus's own account about the death of James, the leader of the Christian Jews was the subject of violence perpetrated by some of his fellow Jews, one of whom occupied the highest Jewish office, the office of the High Priest.

Josephus had known all this for nearly three decades when he came to write his *Antiquities* in Rome in the early 90s. So his relatively sparse treatment of the Christians of Jerusalem in his brief mention of James the brother of Jesus, his elimination of the Christian Jews as a viable Jewish sect among the various groups that he mentions in the *Jewish War* and the four schools that he describes in the *Antiquities*, his total silence about anything related to the messianism of Jesus of Nazareth and his followers, his complete silence about Nero, Tigellinus, and the Fire of 64 about which he was a living witness all point to a deliberate attempt on his part to write the Christian Jews out of his archives of Jewish life in the first century. He did this in Rome at a time when the Christians of Rome bore witness to their existence and viability in First Clement, a work which not only underscores the centrality of Paul to the churches of Rome and Corinth but also stands as a testament to those lauded in the Hebrew Scriptures as the ancestors of the early Christians.

In the preceding we have established that Josephus ignores a host of historical characters; and passes over in silence the lives of some of his most influential and important contemporaries: Gamaliel the Elder and Caiaphas among them. Whether this was intended to magnify his own importance is difficult to prove, though he adverts to his own importance in some many instances as to suggest that some element of this motivates his many omissions and silences about so many of his contemporaries that we should want to know about. So ignoring Paul may not have been an aberration. Nor does it suggest that Paul was insignificant. Still less does it prove the emptiness of Paul's claim that he was advancing in Judaism beyond many of his contemporaries when he abandoned the cause of the Pharisees and became an apostle for the gospel of Jesus the Messiah. In the chapter that follows I appropriate Josephus's own view that the silences of a historian are in some instances culpable silences. Josephus's words and his assessment of other historians will provide the basis for construing the reasons why Josephus himself might have ignored Paul and the early Christians of Judaea and Rome.

NOTES

1. Louis Feldman and Gohei Hata (eds.), *Josephus, Judaism, and Christianity* (Detroit: Wayne State University Press, 1987), 23–24.
2. Feldman and Hata, *Josephus, Judaism, and Christianity*, 24.
3. Steve Mason, *Life of Josephus: Translation and Commentary* (Leiden: Brill, 2001), 191–92, 98.
4. It is perhaps understandable if Josephus does not discuss Gamaliel the Elder in *Jewish War*, since it is his son Simon who is the focus of his attention; and by then Gamaliel the Elder was deceased. However, the absence of any note on Gamaliel in the *Antiquities* covering the period of his long prominence in Jerusalem is noteworthy; similarly, the lack of any references to him in relation to Josephus's discussion of the four schools within Judaism/Jewish life in both the *Antiquities* and the *Life*. In this respect, it is revealing too that Steve Mason's *Flavius Josephus on the Pharisees: A Composition-Critical Study* (Leiden: Brill, 1991), also has almost no discussion of Gamaliel the Elder.
5. See, for example, Jacob Neusner and Bruce D. Chilton (eds.), *In Quest of the Historical Pharisees* (Waco, Texas: Baylor University Press, 2007)
6. Fred Skolnik (ed.), *Encyclopaedia Judaica, Volume 7* (Farmington Hills, MI: Thomas Gale, 2007 [2nd Edition]), 364–65.
7. Jacob Neusner, *The Rabbinic Traditions about the Pharisees before 70: Part 1, The Masters* (Leiden: Brill, 1971), 341–76. See 15–21; 294; on the tradition linking Gamaliel and Simon son of Gamaliel to Hillel; *The Rabbinic Traditions about the Pharisees before 70, Part II: The Houses* (Leiden: Brill, 1971); & *Part III: Conclusion* (Leiden: Brill, 1971).
8. Pseudo-Clementine Recognitions, 1.65–71. See also Emil Schürer, *The History of the Jewish People in the Age of Jesus Christ, 175 B.C–A.D. 135, Volume 2*, revised and edited by Geza Verrnes, Fergus Millar, and Matthew Black (London: Bloomsbury, 2014 [first published 1983]), 368fn49.
9. See as well, William Horbury, *Messianism among Jews and Christians: Biblical and Historical Studies* (London: Bloomsbury T&T Clark, 2016 [2nd Edition]).
10. Louis H. Feldman, *Judaism and Hellenism Reconsidered* (Leiden: Brill, 2006), 329.
11. For some of the difficulties surrounding attempts to substantiate the authenticity of the TF see the important article by J. Carleton Paget, "Some Observations on Josephus and Christianity," *Journal of Theological Studies* N.S. 52:2 (2001), 539–624.
12. Martin Goodman, *Rome and Jerusalem: The Clash of Ancient Civilizations* (New York: Vintage Books, 2008), 555.
13. Joseph E. David, Martin Goodman, and Corinna R. Kaiser, *Toleration within Judaism* (Oxford: Littman Library of Jewish Civilization, 2013), chapter 3.
14. Martin Goodman, *The Ruling Class of Judaea: The Origins of the Jewish Revolt against Rome, A.D 66–70* (Cambridge: Cambridge University Press, 1987).
15. See now Craig Keener, *Acts: An Exegetical Commentary, Volume 4: 24:1–28:31* (Grand Rapids, MI: Baker Academic, 2015).
16. Tessa Rajak, *Josephus: The Historian and His Society* (London: Duckworth, 2002 [2nd Edition]), 72.

17. Josephus, *Jewish War* 6.300–309 (LCL 210, 265–69).

18. Cf. Tony Costa, "Is Saul of Tarsus Also among the Prophets? Paul's Calling as Prophetic Divine Commission," in *Christian Origins and Hellenistic Judaism: Social and Literary Contexts for the New Testament*, edited by Stanley E. Porter and Andrew W. Pitts (Leiden: Brill, 2013), 203–36; reference is to 229.

19. John M. G. Barclay, *Jews in the Mediterranean Diaspora: From Alexander to Trajan, 323 BCE –117 CE* (Berkeley: University of California Press, 1999), 381ff.

20. John Gager, *Who Made Early Christianity? The Jewish Lives of the Apostle Paul* (New York: Columbia University Press, 2015), 37–52.

21. Part of his argument from that lecture can now be found in Carlin A. Barton and Daniel Boyarin, *Imagine No Religion: How Modern Abstractions Hide Ancient Realities* (New York: Fordham University Press, 2016).

22. N. T. Wright, *Paul and the Faithfulness of God* (Minneapolis, MN: Fortress, 2013).

23. N. T. Wright, *Paul and His Recent Interpreters* (Minneapolis, MN: Fortress, 2014).

24. E. P. Sanders, *Paul: The Apostle's Life, Letters, and Thought* (Minneapolis, MN: Fortress, 2016).

25. Mark Nanos, *The Mystery of Romans: The Jewish Context of Paul's Letter* (Minneapolis, MN: Fortress Press, 1996); *The Irony of Galatians: Paul's Letter in First-Century Context* (Minneapolis, MN: Fortress Press, 2002); his essay in *Paul within Judaism: Restoring the First-Century Context to the Apostle*, edited by Mark Nanos and Magnus Zetterholm (Minneapolis, MN: Fortress Press, 2015).

26. Steve Mason, *Flavius Josephus and the Pharisees: A Composition-Critical Study* (Leiden: Brill, 2001).

27. Steve Mason, *Josephus, Judea, and Christian Origins: Methods and Categories* (Peabody, MA: Hendrickson, 2009), 186.

28. Mason, *Flavius Josephus and the Pharisees: A Compositional-Critical Study*, 375.

29. Ibid.

30. Ibid.

31. Steve Mason, *Josephus, Judea, and Christian Origins* (Boston: Hendrickson, 2009).

32. Mason, *Josephus and the New Testament* (Peabody, MA: Hendrickson, 2003 [2nd edition]), 147–250.

33. Daniel R. Schwartz, "Should Josephus Have Ignored the Christians?" in *Ethos und Identität: Einheit und Vielfalt des Judentums in Hellenistisch-Römischer Zeit*, edited by Matthias Konradt (Padeborn: Schöningh, 2002), 165–78. The reference is to 171.

34. Ibid., 174–75.

35. Daniel R. Schwartz, *Reading the First Century: On Reading Josephus and Studying Jewish History of the First Century* (Tübingen: Mohr Siebeck, 2013).

36. Alan F. Segal, *Paul the Convert: The Apostolate and Apostasy of Saul the Pharisee* (New Haven: Yale University Press, 1990), xvi.

37. Feldman and Hata, *Josephus, Judaism, and Christianity*, 23–24.

38. Louis H. Feldman, *Josephus's Interpretation of the Bible* (Berkeley: University of California Press, 1998), 14–73. Christopher Begg has an extensive list of articles exploring, like Feldman, Josephus's rewritten bible. See as well his *Josephus's Account of the Early Divided Monarchy: 8, 212–420* (Leuven University Press, 1993) and *Josephus's Story of the Later Monarchy: AJ 9.1–10.185* (Leuven: Peeters, 2000).

39. Feldman, *Josephus's Interpretation of the Bible*, 73.

40. For example, *Flavius Josephus and Flavian Rome*, edited by Jonathan Edmondson, Steve Mason, and James Rives (Oxford: Oxford University Press, 2005) and *Flavius Josephus: Interpretation and History*, edited by Jack Pastor, Pnina Stern, and Menahem Mor (Leiden: Brill, 2011), *Making History: Josephus and Historical Method*, edited by Zuleika Rodgers (Leiden: Brill, 2006). *Josephus and Jewish History in Flavian Rome and Beyond*, edited by Gaia Lembi and Joseph Sievers (Leiden: Brill, 2005).

41. Helen Bond, *Caiaphas: Friend of Rome and Judge of Jesus?* (Louisville, KY: Westminster John Knox, 2004), 82; also *A Companion to Josephus* (Oxford: Wiley, 2017), 82ff.

42. See Seth Schwartz, *Josephus and Judaean Politics* (Leiden: Brill, 1990), 166n37. Schwartz points out that Tessa Rajak, *Josephus: The Historian and His Society*, 151n17, is

about the only one who claims that this bit about the killing of James is an interpolation. What evidence does she have for it? None. It is just her conviction that Josephus would not have written it. Well, how would the Christian interpolator have known that in 62 CE James was murdered? Acts does not mention it. So she cannot claim that the person learned of it from Acts. The last mention of James is in Acts 21:18. He is very much alive and well.

43. James McLaren, "Ananus, James, and Earliest Christianity: Josephus' Account of the Death of James," *Journal of Theological Studies* 52 (2001), 15.

44. Josephus, *Antiquities* 18.89–97 (LCL 433, 65–69).

45. James VanderKam, *From Joshua to Caiaphas: High Priests after the Exile* (Minneapolis, MN: Fortress Press, 2004), 460.

46. Adele Reinhartz, *Caiaphas the High Priest* (Minneapolis, MN: Fortress Press, 2013): Chapter 1: Caiaphas in Context. See also James H. Charlesworth ed., *Jesus and Temple: Textual and Archaeological Explorations* (Minneapolis, MN: Fortress Press, 2014): He mentions in footnote 14 (p. 55) how Josephus manages to say nothing about Caiaphas even though he is dealing with matters that concern the High Priest; referencing *Antiquities* 18.

Chapter Two

Reading Josephus's Silences

*Writing Paul Out of the
Jewish Archives of the First Century*

According to Josephus, "[Titus] gave his troops permission to burn and sack the city. For that day they refrained; but on the next they set fire to the Archives, the Acra, the council-chamber, and the region called Ophlas, the flames spreading to as far as the palace of Queen Helena, which was in the centre of the Acra."[1] Josephus writes these words about an event to which he was an eyewitness: the destruction of his native Jerusalem and its famed Temple. Just as importantly, he bore witness to the destruction of the Archives. The loss of that repository of Jewish life, which receives very little comment from historians and scholars, determined Josephus's status and his singularity as the historian of Jewish life in the first century.

Steve Mason asserts in his preface for The Brill Josephus Project a consensus widely known and acknowledged by historians of the first century that no one can do without Flavius Josephus, not if one is interested in Jewish life in the first century. As he puts it:

> If Josephus boasts about the unique importance of his work (War 1.1–3; Ant. 1.1–4) in the fashion of ancient historians, few of his modern readers could disagree with him. By the accidents of history, his narratives have become the indispensable source for all scholarly study of Judea from about 200 BCE to 75 CE. Our analysis of other texts and of the physical remains unearthed by archaeology must occur in dialogue with Josephus' story, for it is the only comprehensive and connected account of the period.[2]

There is simply not another extant source to first century Jewish life in the Roman province of Judaea like Josephus. What he provides in terms of the range of his vision, the scope of his writings, and his personal involvement in matters religious, political, social, and military stand singularly against a landscape without much in the way of sources and documentation. Josephus's *Jewish War* (between 75 and 79 CE), *Antiquities of the Jews* (93/94 CE), his *Autobiography* or *Life* of Flavius Josephus (after 94 CE), a supplement to his *Antiquities*, and his *Against Apion* (c. 97) are unique sources for first-century Jewish history.

No one can do without him if one is interested in the relationship between Judaeans (or Jews), the people of Judaea, and Rome, as Martin Goodman has recently demonstrated in his captivating work, *Rome and Jerusalem*.[3] What, then, to do when Josephus is silent? What should it mean? Should it have to mean anything? If it should not mean anything, why not? The second quotation with which this chapter begins highlights an element of the "why not?" In 70 CE the buildings that held the archives of Jerusalem were destroyed, burned to the ground. Josephus was a witness to the event. Henceforth everyone, including Josephus, would have to consider the history of Judaea and Jerusalem without the archives of Jerusalem. The omissions and the silences of any new archive take on a significance all their own. As a unique source for reconstructing that archive, Josephus's writings and their attendant silences contribute to our very conceptualization and understanding of the new archive.

BEARING WITNESS: THE SILENCES OF HISTORY

To speak of the silences of history is to venture into a difficult arena. To speak of the silences of a historian is to wander into fields even more treacherous. For it presupposes that one can speak positively about that which remains hidden, unexpressed, or inarticulate. Given the singular importance of Flavius Josephus for the history of the first century, the implications of his silences may be incalculable.

However, an important advance can be made on the methodological significance of some of Josephus's silences as a historian and as a writer by referring to his own comments of historical criticism about other historians. The passage comes from his *Against Apion*. It reads as follows:

> That the omission of some historians to mention our nation was due, not to ignorance, but to envy or some other disingenuous reason, I think I am in a position to prove. Hieronymus, who wrote the history of Alexander's successors, was a contemporary of Hecataeus, and, owing to his friendship with King Antigonus, became governor of Syria. Yet, whereas Hecataeus devoted a whole book to us, Hieronymus, although he had lived almost within our bor-

ders, has nowhere mentioned us in his history. So widely different were the views of these two men. One thought us deserving of serious notice; the eyes of the other, through an ill-natured disposition, were totally blind to the truth. However, our antiquity is sufficiently established by the Egyptian, Chaldaean, and Phoenician records, not to mention the numerous Greek historians. In addition to those already cited, Theophilus, Theodotus, Mnaseas, Aristophanes, Hermogenes, Euhemerus, Conon, Zopyrion, and, may be, many more—for my reading has not been exhaustive—have made more than a passing allusion to us. The majority of these authors have misrepresented the facts of our primitive history, because they have not read our sacred books; but all concur in testifying to our antiquity, and that is the point with which I am at present concerned. Demetrius Phalereus, the elder Philo, and Eupolemus are exceptional in their approximation to the truth, and [their errors] may be excused on the ground of their inability to follow quite accurately the meaning of our records.[4]

One need not know in detail the specific identities of all the historical writers he mentions to appreciate Josephus's point.[5] Josephus is kind to those writers who err because they do not quite follow the records of other nations with the greatest competence. What I wish to draw attention to are the many ways in which Josephus's own words provide commentary about his own silences as both a contemporary living witness and as a historian of Jewish life in the first century. The distinctions he makes between Hieronymus and Hecataeus as historians of the Jews or Judaeans are relevant to his own silences about the early Christian movement within Judaean and Jewish society and in the larger Roman world.

It will be the objective of this chapter to show through a few episodes and historical moments that there were many occasions on which Josephus could have and should have written about Paul and the early Christian movement in Judaea, Galilee, and Rome. However, on almost every occasion Josephus chose not to. Josephus's almost total silence about Paul and other Christians in his writings is therefore not an accident of history or historiography. If it is not an accident, then, the evidence is not merely suggestive but almost incontrovertible that Josephus deliberately wrote Paul, in particular, out of Jewish history. By excluding him from his account of Jewish life in the first century, Josephus in effect delegitimated Paul and his unique contribution to the early Christian movement as an essentially Jewish tradition.

Josephus was a contemporary of Pliny the Younger, Suetonius, and Tacitus, all of them Romans who mentioned Christians in their respective writings. They also had some notion that the Christians had originated in Judaea. Josephus, a native of Jerusalem and of Judaea, who had intimate knowledge of Galilee, and later lived in Rome for more than two decades, barely mentions the early Christian movement in his works. If it is not too impertinent, we should have to ask in the end, borrowing his own language about the silences of other historians: what "ill-natured disposition" compelled him to be this silent about the Christian Jews? What motivated him to exclude from his account of Jewish life in the first century the most influential one among them in terms of the spread of the Christian movement beyond Judaea? What "blinded" Josephus to "the truth" about Paul?

EARLY CHRISTIANITY IN A ROMAN WORLD

First things first: All four canonical Gospels mention the High Priest Caiaphas and the Roman governor or prefect Pilate in their narratives about the trials and crucifixion of Jesus of Nazareth in Jerusalem in the province of Judaea (Matthew 27:11–26; Mark 15:2–15; Luke 23:2, 3; 18–25; John 18:29–19:16). At least one of them, Luke 3:1, also mentions that all of this took place during the time of the Emperor Tiberius. Outside of the New Testament writings, there is almost no documentation of this event around which the Christian tradition revolves. The paucity of evidence is compounded by the little information we possess about Pontius Pilate. The same four canonical Gospels also mention John the Baptist, an ascetic preacher, as a precursor to the mission and public preaching of Jesus of Nazareth; and describe how Jesus was baptized by John (Matthew 3:1–17; Mark 1:3–11; Luke 3:2–22; John 1:19–34). The beginning and end of Jesus's public mission, then, are framed by his encounter with John the Baptizer on the one hand, and with Caiaphas and Pontius Pilate, on the other.

In his *Antiquities*, Flavius Josephus mentions John the Baptizer (*Antiquities* 18.116–119), without any suggestion or even a hint that he had anything to do with the emergence of a new movement spearheaded by someone named Jesus from Nazareth in Galilee. *Antiquities* 18.55–64 contains Josephus's extended comments on Pontius Pilate, much of it not very complimentary. Within this section lies the so-called *Testimonium Flavianum* (18.63–64), which mentions the execution of Jesus, and is almost certain to have suffered at the hands of later redactors. For the time being, I only wish to establish the juxtaposition of the high priest Caiaphas and Pontius Pilate with some possible allusions to Jesus in Josephus's *Antiquities*. Josephus rounds off his portrait of Pontius Pilate by relating Pilate's departure from Judaea and his arrival in Rome shortly after the death of the Emperor Tiberius (37 CE).

Josephus's older contemporary, Philo Judaeus of Alexandria (c. 20 BCE to 50 CE), is just as uncomplimentary in his assessment of Pontius Pilate in his *Legatio ad Gaium* (299–305). At a minimum this links Pontius Pilate to the Emperor Gaius, who succeeded Tiberius, the one who had appointed Pilate as procurator of Judaea. Philo also had relatives who were conversant with matters in Judaea, and so he may well have known a whole lot more about Pilate than he writes. Josephus writes about Philo's brother Alexander the Alabarch (*Jewish War* 5.205), who made donations for the gold and silver plating for the Temple gates. Alexander is also mentioned by Josephus in relation to King Agrippa I in connection with certain financial dealings between the two (*Antiquities* 18.159). The connections between Philo's family and the Herodians were extensive. Philo's nephew Tiberius Julius Alexander, one of the sons of the Alabarch, at one time a regional governor in Upper Egypt (Tacitus, *Annals* 15.28.3), also served as the chief of staff for Titus during the Judaean War (*Jewish War* 5.45–6; 6.237). Philo could not have been ignorant of the major currents of Judaean life even if he wanted to. To say that he had intimate knowledge of what transpired there and should have said something about the early Christian movement would be to press the evidence.

As for the Romans themselves, for a very long time it has seemed that Tacitus (56–117 CE), that is, Publius (or Gaius) Cornelius Tacitus, Roman senator, governor, consul, and historian, presented one of the rare testimonies about Jesus and the origins of the Christian movement in his *Annals*, written toward the end of his life in 117 CE. It is a relatively late source for the origins of the early Christian movement. Yet it is unavoidable. If the passage in *Annals* 15.44 is genuine, then Tacitus was obviously dependent on some earlier sources that he does not name. Tacitus makes a passing reference elsewhere to using previous books. Given his long history in public life and within the Roman administrative system as senator, governor, and consul, he cannot be dismissed easily as an unreliable source without good and incontrovertible reasons.

After describing the great fire of July 64 CE, what Nero made of it by building a new palace, the suspicions that he may have caused the entire thing, how new precautions were taken to avert another fire, and if there was another one, how to fight it, how Nero tried to appease the populace, and so on, Tacitus proceeds to speak about what else was done beyond human effort to elicit some good fortune for the city of Rome. It reads as follows.

> The next thing was to seek means of propitiating the gods, and recourse was had to the Sibylline books, by the direction of which prayers were offered to Vulcanus, Ceres, and Proserpina. Juno, too, was entreated by the matrons, first, in the Capitol, then on the nearest part of the coast, whence water was procured to sprinkle the face and image of the goddess. And there were sacred banquets and nightly vigils celebrated by married women. But all human efforts, all the lavish gifts of the emperor, and the propitiations of the gods, did not banish the sinister belief that the conflagration was the result of an order. Consequently, to get rid of the report, Nero fastened the guilt and inflicted the most exquisite tortures on a class hated for their abominations, called Christians by the populace. Christus, from whom the name had its origin, suffered the extreme penalty during the reign of Tiberius at the hands of one of our procurators, Pontius Pilatus, and a most mischievous superstition, thus

checked for the moment, again broke out not only in Judaea, the first source of the evil, but even in Rome, where all things hideous and shameful from every part of the world find their centre and become popular. Accordingly, an arrest was first made of all who pleaded guilty; then, upon their information, an immense multitude was convicted, not so much of the crime of firing the city, as of hatred against mankind. Mockery of every sort was added to their deaths. Covered with the skins of beasts, they were torn by dogs and perished, or were nailed to crosses, or were doomed to the flames and burnt, to serve as a nightly illumination, when daylight had expired. Nero offered his gardens for the spectacle, and was exhibiting a show in the circus, while he mingled with the people in the dress of a charioteer or stood aloft on a car. Hence, even for criminals who deserved extreme and exemplary punishment, there arose a feeling of compassion; for it was not, as it seemed, for the public good, but to glut one man's cruelty, that they were being destroyed.[6]

As this passage stands, it brings together various elements of the traditions found in the canonical Gospels and other themes in early Christian history. Specifically, it mentions the execution of "Christus" by the procurator Pontius Pilate during the time of the Emperor Tiberius, and states unambiguously that Nero persecuted the Christians as scapegoats for the Fire of 64 CE. On these elements alone, this is a passage that should have appealed to early Christian apologists, many of whom wrote about the persecution of Christians. There are, however, a number of problems with the text that suggest possible and very likely later interpolations. The most significant of these problems is that it is not quoted in the extant works of any known early Christian writers before the fourth century. More than that, it is not even alluded to by any Christian writers. Even after the fourth century it is not well attested. So, as it stands, although it bears witness to a strong Christian presence in Rome in 64 CE, it does not commend itself without inherent difficulties about its attestation. So I shall set it aside and turn to another historian and contemporary of Tacitus, namely Gaius Suetonius Tranquillus, that is, Suetonius (69–122 CE).

Suetonius is known mostly for his *Lives of the Twelve Caesars*. At the time of writing this work he was also the secretary of the Emperor Hadrian. What he has to say about the Fire of 64 CE appears in his *Life of Nero*. Unlike the passage from Tacitus's *Annals* 15.44 just cited above, the sections in Suetonius dealing with the Fire of 64 CE do not make any claim that Christians were made scapegoats by Nero, and thus suffered persecution on account of it. About the fire itself this is what Suetonius says:

> When someone in a general conversation said: "When I am dead, be earth consumed by fire," he rejoined "Nay, rather while I live," and his action was wholly in accord. For under cover of displeasure at the ugliness of the old buildings and the narrow, crooked streets, he set fire to the city so openly that several ex-consuls did not venture to lay hands on his chamberlains although

they caught them on their estates with tow and fire-brands, while some granaries near the Golden House, whose room he particularly desired, were demolished by engines of war and then set on fire, because their walls were of stone. For six days and seven nights destruction raged, while the people were driven for shelter to monuments and tombs. At that time, besides an immense number of dwellings, the houses of leaders of old were burned, still adorned with trophies of victory, and the temples of the gods vowed and dedicated by the kings and later in the Punic and Gallic wars, and whatever else interesting and noteworthy had survived from antiquity. Viewing the conflagration from the tower of Maecenas and exulting, as he said, in "the beauty of the flames," he sang the whole of the "Sack of Ilium," in his regular stage costume. Furthermore, to gain from this calamity too all the spoil and booty possible, while promising the removal of the debris and dead bodies free of cost he allowed no one to approach the ruins of his own property; and from the contributions which he not only received, but even demanded, he nearly bankrupted the provinces and exhausted the resources of individuals.[7]

While Tacitus is expansive on the Fire of 64 CE, writing several long paragraphs, Suetonius is rather brief. Is it because he does not wish to repeat Tacitus? Suetonius mentions men of the highest rank and social standing, ex-consuls, who dared not put their hands on those who were tasked to create all the havoc, because they knew or believed Nero himself had ordered it. He says nothing about those who were reputed and accused to have caused it. Instead he attributes it all to Nero's plan, a point Tacitus also makes. Suetonius describes what it cost the city and its population, but again he makes no mention of Christians or any other group of people being made culpable for so much that had devastated the city. But was this because he had already discussed the punishments Nero meted out to those he found objectionable?

In an unexceptional reference to the Neronian Fire, Pliny the Elder, writing much closer to the event, mentions in Book 17.1.5 of his *Natural History* the destruction of certain ancient trees in Rome that were in existence until the Emperor Nero set fire to the city. Pliny writes without any intimation of whatever else the fire cost the city. It was as if the circumstances were so well known to his readers that it was not worth mentioning or alluding to any of it, so that he could cause no offense by lamenting the loss of ancient trees when so much else had also been lost. Unsurprisingly, there is no reference to the persecution of Christians anywhere in the *Natural History*. On the other hand, Pliny the Elder mentions Nero's culpability here without ambiguity.

Suetonius, for his part, states without embellishment in an earlier section of the *Life of Nero* that punishment was inflicted on the Christians, a race of men given to a new and mischievous superstition (*Life of Nero* 16.2). Suetonius mentions this in a context when discussing the sorts of prohibitions and new punishments that Nero devised. Here he makes no explicit mention of the Fire of 64 CE, which is not to say that some of these punishments that

Nero inflicted on the Christians could not have been linked to the fire. He writes very broadly about the scope of recriminations against the Christians in a way as to suggest that the Christians were targets of Nero's punishments during much of his reign, which suggests that they were likely subjected to these punishments both before and after the fire, and perhaps during the week of the fire as well. They may very well have been singled out when the fires raged in July 64 CE because they were deemed to be pernicious at a time when, according the Tacitus's account, all attempts were made to propitiate the gods of Rome.

Suetonius's broad description of recriminations against the Christians during the time of Nero is consistent with the sentiments recounted in Tacitus's *Annals* 15.44, whether the passage from the *Annals* is authentic or not. For if the Christians were already under suspicion and subject to abuse, it would have been easy for them to be made scapegoats during the Fire of 64 CE. If that was the case, then even if the line in Tacitus about Jesus Christ and Pontius Pilate is an interpolation, Suetonius's words in *Life of Nero* 16.2 suggests that the rest of Tacitus *Annals* 15.44 could in fact be about "Christus" and Christians and not one "Chrestus," another Jew, who is mentioned as an instigator of troubles in Rome during the time of the Emperor Claudius.

Could Tacitus and Suetonius have both or individually been confused about Christianity, "Christus," and the said "Chrestus" in the various reports about Chrestus and Christians in the *Annals* and the *Lives of the Twelve Caesars* respectively? Perhaps. Later writers attest to how easily "Chrestus" and "Christus" could be confused, interchanged, or conflated, at least as far as manuscript evidence goes. For if Tacitus meant "Chrestus" in *Annals* 15.44 and it was later changed to "Christus" by an interpolator, that would mean that Tacitus had no intention of linking the horrible Neronian persecution of 64 CE with the Christians but with a group of Jews and the memory of an earlier instigator named Chrestus, who had flourished during the time of the Emperor Claudius. That would not undermine Suetonius's claim that the Christians were subject to systematic recriminations and persecution under Emperor Nero. That claim, in all its generality, attests to the presence of Christians in Rome during the reign of Nero.

Tacitus and Suetonius aside, is it not too much to ask that a movement that began in Judaea should be attested in Rome for it to be believed to exist? Not entirely. Judaea belonged to Rome and its empire, so inquiring about the presence of Christians in Rome is not an irrelevant question. It allows us to gauge how quickly a movement of this kind would manifest itself in the imperial city, and if it had any presence there, what impression it made on the citizens of the city.

In a recent work, Bernard Green writes that "the silence of Tacitus about the Christians after Nero is significant" and "equally telling is the reticence shown by Josephus about Christianity."[8] Green leaves Tacitus's silence behind and tries to solve the puzzle about Josephus's silence about Christians. He suggests that "given Josephus's residence in Rome, it is more likely that Josephus's view of, or ignorance about, Christians was heavily coloured by the obscurity and isolation of the Roman Christian community." Green offers no evidence to suggest that this was in fact the case. Moreover, it does not quite explain the scope of Josephus's silences or ignorance (if we want to put it that way). For, as Green acknowledges, there is simply no reference to Christians "in his immensely detailed account of the religion and politics of Judaea."[9]

It is not complete silence, however. Green does not raise the oddity of what it would mean for Josephus to have known about the murder of James the brother of Jesus in 62 CE in Judaea and to be silent about Christians or Christianity in connection with his own presence in Rome in 63/64, and his later residence in the city for so many years after the destruction of Jerusalem in 70 CE. Or how Josephus's knowledge of James the brother of Jesus suggests a greater awareness of the early Christians than the scant testimony he provides in his writings suggest. Or the fact that, by mentioning the murder of James, Josephus himself bears witness to hostilities both latent and expressive toward the Christian Jews by non-Christian Jews, which invariably draws attention to the career of Paul who attests to this very hostility when he describes himself as someone who sought to destroy the Christians in his former life as a Pharisee. In other words, what little Josephus thought he was intimating by his mention of the murder of James the brother of Jesus reveals a great deal more than Josephus wished to reveal. If it mattered to the High Priest Ananus to have James murdered, then, somehow, the early Christians in Jerusalem were of some relevance or significance to the social politics of the city.

JOSEPHUS AND THE EARLY CHRISTIAN MOVEMENT: JERUSALEM, GALILEE, AND ROME

One point needs emphasizing. Given how much Josephus comments about Jewish factions, groups, and sects, it is curious that he has almost nothing to say about a group of Jews who were followers of a certain Jesus from Nazareth in Galilee and how they were understood in terms of the social politics of Judaea and Galilee. That historians and commentators are only able to draw on a couple of passages from his works that bear on the Christian movement is itself indication of a major absence or lacuna in Josephus's writings. However one assesses it, this looks very strange. For it gives the impression rightly or wrongly that Josephus had little or no knowledge of the movement, or that whatever he knew of it did not amount to much, and that for much of this early period they were insignificant.

Ordinarily, Josephus is seen as an important witness to Christianity because of two passages in the *Antiquities* where he mentions Jesus (or Joshua). *Antiquities* 18.63–63 contains the phrase "He was the Christ," and *Antiquities* 20:200 refers to a certain Jesus who was thought to be the Christ. The passage about Jesus being "the Christ" appears to contain a late Christian interpolation, for this basic reason: If Josephus believed that Jesus was the Messiah, then Josephus should have become a Christian. Since there is no evidence that he ever expressed such an idea, we must be more than skeptical about the statement. The second reference fares better but not by much. It occurs in connection with the execution of a certain James by the recently appointed high priest Ananus. The passage as it currently stands reads: "James was the brother of Jesus who was considered the Christ." To say he was considered the Christ means that Josephus is merely reporting an opinion. On the basis of these two passages one would have to say that Josephus has some knowledge of the early Christian movement, and so we could read these passages as evidence that he knew even if at a distance some traditions associated with Jesus and his brother James.

For my purposes Josephus's autobiography or *Life* is critical. Most of Josephus's *Life* covers a period of about six months sometime between 65 and 66 CE relating to the revolt in Galilee against the Romans and contested interpretations of that event. The bits of biographical information that Josephus provides of his life before 65 CE serve as a preface to the rest of the narrative. It is in the prefatory section that Josephus provides one of the most important clues that deserves much more attention that it often receives.

After discussing the origins of his distinguished family, Josephus states that he was born from his father Matthias in the first year of the reign of the Emperor Gaius. Gaius Iulius Caesar Germanicus was emperor from March 18, 37 CE to January 24, 41 CE.[10] Josephus confirms that he was born in 37 CE also in his *Antiquities* 20.268 that the thirteenth year of Domitian's rule (93/94 CE) was also his fifty-sixth.[11] Although I am discounting *Antiquities* 20:200 because of a likely later Christian interpolation, Josephus's own words establish that he was in Jerusalem in the decade of the 50s and the early 60s before he was asked to undertake an embassy to Rome in 63/64.

Josephus's election by authorities in Jerusalem to undertake an official legation establishes that he was in every sense a very public figure in Jerusalem. Which is to say that anything that happened in a public or in a semi-public way about anything in Jerusalem, especially anything concerning the Temple, would have been of interest to Josephus the priest. In his self-portrait Josephus describes a person who was friends of priests, well known to the priestly establishment, and also known among the Pharisees. If the early Christians had any public presence in Jerusalem, Josephus would most likely have known about it, if they had any dealings with the Temple or

Temple officials or had any significant interactions with Pharisees. Or at least there may have been rumors of such things.

On his way to recounting his visit to Rome, Josephus writes about his nineteenth year, when he returned from a three-year ascetic tenure with a teacher named Bannus. He leaves out a good seven years between 56 CE and 63 CE, the year of his return to public life, as he puts it, and then writes as follows:

> After my twenty-sixth year, indeed, it fell to me to go up to Rome for the reason that will be described. At the time when Felix was administering Judea, he had certain priests, close associates of mine and gentlemen, bound and sent to Rome, on a minor and incidental charge, to submit an account to Caesar. Wanting to find some means of rescue for these men, especially when I discovered that even in wretched circumstances they had not abandoned piety toward the deity but were subsisting on figs and nuts, I reached Rome after having faced many dangers at sea. For when our ship was flooded in the middle of the Adriatic, we—being about 600 in number—had to swim through the entire night. And when by the provision of God a Cyrenian ship appeared before us around daybreak, I and some others—about eighty altogether—overtook the rest and were taken on board. After we had come safely to Dicaearchaeia, which the Italians call Puteoli, through a friendship I met Aliturus: this man was a mime-actor, especially dear to Nero's thoughts and a Judean by ancestry. Through him I became known to Poppea, the wife of Caesar, and then very quickly arranged things, appealing to her to free the priests. Having succeeded, with enormous gifts from Poppea in addition to this benefit, I returned home.[12]

As he himself tells the story, Josephus arrived at Puteoli and then proceeded to Rome. Josephus would almost certainly have visited the *Transtiberim* on the bank of the Tiber, which housed the Jewish Quarter and which also contained the ports of call. He does not mention this, but he did not have to. It was common knowledge that most of the people from the East, especially Syria, and most of the Greek speakers settled there. Philo of Alexandria provides ample witness of what that "other side of the Tiber" meant to Jews or Judaens. On Caesar Augustus and his attitude toward Jews, Philo, quoting a letter from King Agrippa I to Emperor Gaius, writes as follows:

> He was aware that the great section of Rome on the other side of the Tiber is occupied and inhabited by Jews, most of whom were Roman citizens emancipated. For having been brought as captives to Italy they were liberated by their owners and were not forced to violate any of their native institutions. He knew therefore that they have houses of prayer and meet together in them, particularly on the sacred sabbaths when they receive as a body a training in their ancestral philosophy. He knew too that they collect money for sacred purposes from their firstfruits and send them to Jerusalem by persons who would offer the sacrifices. Yet nevertheless he neither ejected them from Rome nor de-

> prived them of their Roman citizenship because they were careful to preserve their Jewish citizenship also, nor took any violent measures against the houses of prayer, nor prevented them from meeting to receive instructions in the laws, nor opposed their offerings of the firstfruits. Indeed so religiously did he respect our interests that supported by well nigh his whole household he adorned our temple through the costliness of his dedications, and ordered that for all time continuous sacrifices of whole burnt offerings should be carried out every day at his own expense as a tribute to the most high God. And these sacrifices are maintained to the present day and will be maintained forever to tell the story of a character truly imperial. Yet more, in the monthly doles in his own city when all the people each in turn receive money or corn, he never put the Jews at a disadvantage in sharing the bounty, but even if the distributions happened to come during the sabbath when no one is permitted to receive or give anything or to transact any part of the business of ordinary life, particularly of a lucrative kind, he ordered the dispensers to reserve for the Jews till the morrow the charity which fell to all.[13]

Philo's references to prayer houses, Sabbath, religious philosophy, the dole, etc., makes abundantly clear that those in the district on the "other side of the Tiber" were part and parcel of the fabric of Roman life. You could no more live in Rome than be ignorant of the *Transtiberim*. Philo was speaking from personal experience, having been in the city on his legation to Gaius Caligula (c. 39 CE). Agrippa, from whom Philo presumably takes the account, knew the city very well. No one concerned about Jewish affairs could be indifferent to what transpired on the other side of the Tiber, Josephus included. Josephus's experience in 63/64 CE would probably have mirrored Philo's more than two decades before.

Josephus writes that he became well acquainted with Nero's wife, Poppaea Sabbina. Josephus makes clear that he came into Poppaea's graces through the patronage of a Jewish actor, Aliturus. The acquaintance and subsequent friendship of this otherwise unknown Jewish actor who could introduce Josephus to the wife of the emperor is essential to the story Josephus tells. In one sense, Josephus grants to Aliturus a role that is as important as Josephus's own as the leader of the diplomatic delegation from Jerusalem. Josephus implies that without Aliturus, acting almost as his ambassador to Poppaea Sabbina, Josephus's mission would have been frustrated. As Martin Goodman puts it, "Almost everyone in the Roman empire knew someone who knew someone who might be able to intervene, through however many links in the chain of patronage, at the center of power in the state."[14] When those links in the chain of patronage depended on people not in official positions but closely connected to those circles of influence through informal social links, they could be even more salubrious. Aliturus helped Josephus establish a personal bond with Poppaea that would eventually yield dividends for Josephus, as he added that he returned to Judaea with gifts from Nero's wife.

There is another important element to the story that Josephus does not emphasize, though it is assumed. It is not very likely that Josephus would have been tasked with this mission, nor would he have accepted it, if both Josephus and those who entrusted him with it did not expect a positive outcome from Rome. Josephus himself recounts in his writings any number of delegations sent to Rome from Jerusalem and Judaea to the emperors Claudius and Nero to address issues in the province of Judaea, often involving high priests or activities associated with the Temple.[15]

The recurrent problem about disputes that originated in the Temple precincts is part of the reason why we should expect that the controversy that brought Paul the apostle before the procurator Felix and his wife Drusilla and then Festus, Herod Agrippa II, and Berenice, would not have been unknown to most of the priests of Jerusalem. The kind of agitation that Paul had caused in Jerusalem belonged to a general class of disturbances that included the events that had led to the arrest of the priests whose case Josephus was supposed to plead before Nero.

That Josephus had been sent on a legation to rescue priests from Judaea who had been sent to Rome makes it certain that Josephus had dealings with leaders of the Jewish community in Rome and would most certainly have been acquainted with events in the Jewish Quarter during his extended stay in Rome. If there were Christians in Rome at this time who had any connections with the earliest Christians in Jerusalem, they would most likely have been resident in the Jewish Quarter. If there was any word going around about a new superstition (*superstitio*) that had arrived in Rome from Judaea, it was not likely that Josephus, himself a well-placed member of the priestly community in Jerusalem, would have heard nothing or would have been told nothing about it. He was, after all, acting in an official capacity about matters legal, political, and religious concerning the people of Jerusalem and Judaea. Yet, Josephus does not even hint of any such reality.

Keep in mind too that according to his later account of events in his *Antiquities*, a year before he took on the diplomatic mission to Rome, in 62 CE James the brother of Jesus was murdered. So Josephus arrived in Rome fully aware of who James was, what the brother of Jesus of Nazareth must have meant to people in Jerusalem and in Galilee, and why his murder mattered to the High Priest who instigated it. With this in the background, it strains credulity that Josephus would have cared nothing about what was said or done by and to Christians in Rome while he was in the city or somewhere nearby.

The overly curious might even ask where Josephus lived during his sojourn in Rome on this mission. To which priestly community did he present himself when he arrived in Rome? Which synagogues did he attend during his stay in the city? What social circles did he participate in during his extended stay as he waited for his pleas on behalf of the Judaean priests to be addressed? Could he have lived among his fellow Jews in the Jewish Quarter of Rome without hearing anything whatsoever about this new breed of Jews who believed that Jesus the Nazarene was the messiah? What about Aliturus who probably acted as his guide and confidant during this period? Someone in his line of work in Rome would have been privy to just about any kind of gossip worth hearing. How likely is it that Josephus would have been spared the wonderful details of Roman gossip in the company of someone like Aliturus?

Plutarch remarks in his *Roman Questions* that it was required that anyone who came to Rome on an official embassy had to register at the Temple of Saturn located at the foot of the Capitoline Hill in the northwest quadrant of the Roman Forum, almost at the center of Rome itself. That registry invariably brought to the attention of the leading citizens of Rome whoever was in Rome on official business. With a catalog of the kinds of persons within the embassy, the registry would also provide information about the connections between the various members of the embassy with other people in the city, and so on. In short, one could not be anonymous in Rome when on an official embassy from the provinces. Those who mattered and had the right to know would have known about your presence. Josephus and his Judaean embassy was no exception. Some of Josephus's earliest contacts in Rome would have been formed shortly after he and his embassy registered themselves at the Temple of Saturn.

Josephus is so economical about the details of his time in Rome that one might be tempted to think he had a relatively quiet and mostly anonymous presence in the city. However, in his *Jewish War*, when describing some of the attempts made to persuade him and his comrades to surrender, Josephus mentions that Titus sent the tribune Nicanor to urge Josephus and his fellow rebels to surrender. Josephus adds that he knew Nicanor from his previous first visit to Rome, which is why Titus had sent him to negotiate. As tribune, Nicanor belonged to the lower echelons of the military bureaucracy. He was probably one of many others within the military and imperial administration with whom Josephus become acquainted, and who subsequently had some role to play in matters concerning the provinces of Judaea and perhaps Syria, that had implications for those in Jerusalem and Judaea. If Josephus had supplied specific details of the priests he was in Rome to rescue, what specifically had led to their arrest and sequestration in the first place, and why there needed to be a special legation to appeal for their release, we would be better placed to know which parts of the imperial and military administration Josephus could not avoid, or even which members of the senatorial class he might have had reason to be acquainted with.

Under these circumstances, the pertinent question would not be whom else Josephus knew in Rome from his previous visit besides Nicanor and Aliturus that he does not mention in his writings, but rather how many people did he not know among the imperial household, for example. We might then ask about his silences in this regard and what it was that Josephus did not wish to reveal about his first visit to Rome.

Josephus sums up a tumultuous period in the life of the city of Rome (63–64 CE) and a most interesting period in his own life with two short sentences. I paraphrase: He arrived, made provision to have the priests released, and after he received gifts and benefactions from Poppaea Sabbina, he returned home. It is neat and tidy (*Life* 16). Josephus's silence betrays him, however. His circle in Rome during that first visit was probably a lot wider than he lets on in the *Life*, and he had substantially more knowledge of what transpired in the city than his two short sentences capture.

The fire that destroyed all but four sections of the city beginning on July 19, 64 CE was no ordinary event. Tacitus makes a point of this. Peter Lampe argues convincingly that the four sections of the city that were spared included the Jewish Quarter (Tacitus, *Annals* 15.40), the *Transtiberim*.[16] Naturally "those who had saved their own skins and had watched the fiery spectacle from the safety of the other shore became easy targets for suspicion of having set the fire. For demagogic purposes this situation must have appeared ideal. And Nero, himself under suspicion from the rumors of the populace, had every reason to think up a believable diverting maneuver to direct the people's wrath away from himself."[17]

Against this background Josephus's silence becomes even more deafening. This was not an event to be passed over by a historian of Jewish life who would write in his *Antiquities* about how God's providence guided and protected the Jewish nation both near and far. Could he not have used this event, still later, against the calumnies of Apion when he wrote *Against Apion*? What about the Emperor Nero? Hardly any Roman would have been uninterested in knowing what Josephus thought about him.

Josephus had his own way of dealing with Nero's reputation for cruelty and debauchery. He mentions at one point that he will pass over the unpleasant aspects of Nero's reign (*Jewish War* 2.250–251). He justifies this move both here and in his preface, because, as he put it, others have written about them and also because they are well known. This is terribly convenient. Josephus at once precludes objections and disarms his potential critics. He looks every part the loyalist and disingenuous for not addressing Nero's reputation. At the same time, he does not leave his readers to figure out this unartful silence. He alerts his readers to it, which is to say that Josephus gives us reason to believe that he was fully conscious of his silences; in some instances at least.

That he can also find it in himself to defend Nero is beguiling, since he writes in the *Jewish War* that Nero's success drove him to murder his family members, and in the *Antiquities* he chronicles other heinous crimes. In relation to the latter he goes out of his way to provide something of an apology for Nero. Josephus speaks of two kinds of contemporaries, some who play the role of critics and others who are sycophants. He complains about those who, because they received favors from Nero, are completely fawning and laudatory; and others, who condemn him completely and see nothing good in him because they despise him. The question is: Where does Josephus himself stand? Is he one of the fawning interpreters? No. But neither does he wish to condemn Nero completely. Could he have permitted himself to do so even if he tried? In any case, how does one speak kindly of someone who murders members of his own family? What motivated Josephus to approach Nero's character with such apparent charity? Why does he insist on defending Nero when he knows the details of Nero's crimes?

In many ways, Josephus was compelled to confront a basic fact: Nero's misdeeds were too well known and publicized to be ignored. Even making allowances for the gossip, rumors, and suspicions, Nero's deplorable acts were known to the Roman public. So neither Josephus nor any other sympathizer could ignore them or pretend they did not exist. The best one could do was to try to explain why Nero could be so cruel, whether he was acting in character, out of character, according some inherent instinct or nature, or whether he was somehow controlled by influences and other things over which he had no mastery. That seems to have been Josephus's approach. Josephus was not the only one who tried to find the reasons for Nero's cruelties.

Suetonius, who is often presented by some historians as a biased critic of Nero, still speaks commendably about other aspects of his reign. He does for Nero what he does in his portraits of all the twelve Caesars he writes about. He adopts a form that always requires him to speak of the accomplishments and good deeds of the emperor before commenting on the bad. About Nero, Suetonius is unabashed in stating that in some things Nero was actually to be commended for achievements that brought great benefits to his fellow Romans. It is only after presenting this "Good Nero" that he proceeds to detail the "Bad Nero." Significantly, he provides no excuses for the "Bad Nero." However, he does try to explain.

In Josephus's case, it appears that his association with Poppaea may well have influenced his estimation of Nero. Josephus seemed restrained in condemning in Nero the same types of cruelties he condemned in other historical characters he wrote about. Writing for a specifically Roman audience, Josephus also had to explain his own association with Poppaea and Nero or perhaps why he too received favors from him indirectly through Poppaea. Why was Josephus untroubled by receiving favors from a woman whose reputation was so sullied among the Romans that they believed her responsible in part for her husband's murder of two of his closest family members, his mother Agrippina in 59 CE and his first wife Octavia in 62 (Tacitus, *Annals* 14.1). Significantly, Nero married Poppaea in 62 CE not too long after these horrific events. Yet Josephus writes about Poppaea and her kindness to him without a hint of criticism.

Notice too that in all that Josephus says about Nero there is not a word about the Fire of 64 CE, an event about which he could not possibly have been ignorant. By his own testimony he was in Rome and its environs at this time and was especially favored by Poppaea. Poppaea died in 65 CE, not long after Josephus returned home, a fact Josephus also passes over in silence. There is no suggestion anywhere that Josephus remained in Rome through 65 CE and may have been there when Poppaea Sabbina was murdered.[18] This was also the same year in which Nero ordered his longtime advisor, the orator and philosopher Seneca, to commit suicide. To mention neither one of these events requires a studied disposition or choice. Josephus chose not to tell either story, though he was writing in the early 90s and to an audience that was still interested in Nero's regime and its horrors.

The Romans made comparisons between Domitian and Nero. Pliny the Younger, for one, regretted that one of his good friends Gaius Fannius had not brought to completion a historical work devoted to the time of Nero, for which he had long waited for its publication. Fanius published three books but died (c. 105) before he could complete the entire project about Nero's crimes and the many he had executed or exiled (Pliny, Letter 5.5.2–6). Josephus could plead ignorance that he was not in Rome in 65 CE. He could claim that in Seneca's case there was a charge brought against him that was supposedly substantiated in a judicial inquest, if one needed to make apologies for Nero. However, by the time he was writing both his *Antiquities* and his *Life*, the stories about both Poppaea's and Seneca's death, were common knowledge in Rome where Josephus lived in retirement supported by funds from the Flavians.

In Poppaea's case, no judicial story could be contrived. If Josephus had mentioned Poppaea's death, he would have had to comment on the stories making the rounds that Nero had kicked her when she was pregnant with their second child and that this was the cause of her death. Suetonius relates the story. These two instances of Josephus's deliberate silences about events occurring during and shortly after his stay in Rome between 63 and 65 CE provide the basis for the following conclusions:

1. Josephus deliberately suppressed whatever knowledge he had about the Fire of July 64, the role of Nero regarding the cause of the fire and the attendant recriminations that followed.
2. Josephus chose not to report much of his knowledge of Jewish life in Rome on this first visit. It stands in contrast to Philo's willingness and indeed his joy at showing what a vibrant community of Jews existed in Rome when he arrived in the city on his legation to Gaius Caligula. Had Josephus commented on Jewish life in the city, he would prob-

ably have been forced to say something about Christian Jews in Rome in 64 CE.
3. Likewise, Josephus left much of his social life and interactions in Rome in complete silence, making it nearly impossible even to discern what may have contributed to his own personal choices when it came to surrendering to the Romans in Galilee at the beginning of the Jewish War that ensued not too long after his return from Rome.

If he had not withheld these details, Josephus would have had to provide some account of just who the followers of "Christus" or "Chrestus" were (to use Tacitus's language) and how they managed to have emerged from Judaea and found a hearing in Rome. In short, he would have had to provide an early history of the Christian movement from its beginnings during the time of Pontius Pilate (whom he discusses, as we noted before) to the time of Nero. He chose not to. Now some historical markers:

62 CE	Josephus was in Jerusalem when James the brother of Jesus was murdered
63/64 CE	Josephus goes on a legation to Rome to secure release of Jewish priests
64 CE	Nero is suspected as the culprit in the fire in Rome that devastated huge swathes of the city
65 CE	Seneca takes his own life on orders from Nero
	Josephus returns to Galilee and Judaea, after a year or so in Rome with gifts from Poppaea Sabbina, the wife of Nero
66–70 CE	The Jewish War
68 CE	Nero commits suicide
70 CE	The destruction of the Temple in Jerusalem
73–76 CE	Josephus writes the *Jewish War*
93/94 CE	Josephus completes his *Antiquities*

Josephus lived in Rome in his retirement under imperial patronage, living off the largesse of the Flavian emperors: Vespasian, Titus, and Domitian. He was well known for two things: as being the Judaean general who had surrendered to Roman forces in Galilee and later joined in the siege of Jerusalem; and as the person who gave a prophecy about Vespasian's rise to the *imperium*. That prophecy was also tied to his repeated claims in the *Jewish War* that God, the God of Israel, had now chosen Rome and its emperors to do his bidding, and that the Romans were now favored in a way that the Jews were not. Part of the argument also required, interestingly enough, Josephus's elision of Jewish messianic expectation from almost all that he wrote in the *Jewish War*, *Antiquities*, the *Life* and in *Against Apion*.

Josephus's writings go so far as to divest Jewish messianic expectation of any realism. In fact, it is almost nonexistent. Reading Josephus, one would assume that the Jewish people in the Second Temple Period had never contemplated the idea of a Messiah.[19] The documents from Qumran, however, attest to Jewish messianic expectation as almost basic. Yet, Josephus excludes this most important theme from his works. Why? One answer is that it may have something to do with his reticence about the early Christian movement.

In his extensive work on Josephus's biblical interpretation and rewriting of the Bible, Louis Feldman confronts the different ways in which Josephus minimizes certain themes and virtually divests them of their significance or relevance. On Josephus's attitude toward Jewish messianic expectations, Feldman senses a deeply felt sensibility and conviction in Josephus which emerges in different ways in his treatment of certain characters like David and Hezekiah, or his approach to important themes or passages in Isaiah and Jeremiah. On Josephus's view of the triumvirate, David, Hezekiah, and Isaiah, Feldman hints at the possibility that Josephus is operating from a perspective that is decidedly set on counteracting Christianity. Josephus is far from indifference. His antipathy could be described as "silently anti-Christian." The phrase is not Feldman's, it is mine. But it seems inescapable given what Feldman proposes when he tries to find reasons for Josephus's practices. Feldman writes:

> Josephus may also have de-emphasized David, Hezekiah, and Isaiah, not only because of their close association with the messianic ideal but also because David and Isaiah had assumed special importance for Christianity. . . . Hence, to counteract the importance of David and Isaiah among the Christians, Josephus may have diminished their significance, just as, we may guess, he may be reacting against the claims of Christianity in the original version of the *Testimonium Flavianum*. (Ant 18.63–64)[20]

Feldman himself does not link this possibly anti-Christian vein in Josephus that he detects to the equally unmistakable silences about Christians in Josephus's writings. Again they seem inextricably linked, and provide a broader context for Josephus's silences as self-consciously and deliberately agonistic silences about Christians and Christianity.

If one can write about the *Antiquities* of the Jews without ever mentioning Jewish messianic expectation as part of those antiquities, then one has, in a brilliant stroke, undercut one of the foundations upon which Christianity rests, namely, that it is the fulfillment of Jewish messianic expectation. At this point, you don't have to debate Christian origins because it has no basis to stand on. Or Josephus has his eyes on his Roman benefactors and does not wish to introduce a theme that would put him on a collision course with Roman imperial religion. For, to speak of messianic expectations is to raise fundamental questions about Roman imperial claims of the divine variety.

The two are not mutually exclusive. They coincide at precisely the point at which Roman imperial claims of divinity compel action against the new religious movement out of Judaea associated with Christus. So Josephus's silence accomplishes two ends. First, he avoids having to deal with an important element of Jewish religion of the Second Temple Period that could resurrect some of the very sentiments that had led to Jewish opposition to Roman rule and the recent war in Judaea (66–70 CE), and second he avoids having to deal with Christianity, which is a problem for the Roman imperial cult as well. While his silence on Christians in Rome can be overlooked and even excused, since after all he did not have to write about the Christians if he did not want to, his silence about Jewish messianic expectation is inexcusable. Josephus erases from Jewish history of the Second Temple Period one of its most important aspects. The fact that he does it so nearly comprehensively shows the extent to which Josephus's personal and ideological commitments shape his *Antiquities*—and of course, much of the *Jewish War* and his *Life* are intended to show how deluded his fellow Jews were in attempting to fight against the Romans.

Arnaldo Momigliano touches on these themes in a slightly different context. While he does not speak of Josephus's silences in the way that I do, he suggests that Josephus's judgments seek to reshape Jewish thought and sensibilities; and a good deal of that has to do with reshaping Jewish messianic sensibilities:

> By blaming the disaster on the ruling class of his people (or example, Ant. Jud. 1.23), Flavius Josephus is far from secularizing his categories of judgment. He, of course, refuses to share those messianic hopes that had sustained the fighters. Going beyond a generic loyalty to the religion of the fathers (as expressed in Ant. Jud. 3.317–22 and elsewhere), Flavius is convinced that the prophets had already predicted Roman rule and the limits of its duration.[21]

So as Momigliano reads him, Josephus held to a refashioned messianic idea. He reconfigured messianic hope in such a way that one might be forgiven for not recognizing it in much of the history that he rehearses or narrates in the *Antiquities*. While Momigliano argues that Josephus is "far from secularizing his categories of judgment," in taking the particular stance that he does against both the messianism of the Hebrew prophets and what he considered the deluded messianism of some of his compatriots, Josephus did in fact secularize Jewish messianic expectation. Josephus the seer, who prophesied that Vespasian would be Roman emperor, plays the role of a "messianic prophet" to the Roman imperium. One had no need of Isaiah in these times. Josephus makes very little about Isaiah in the *Antiquities* as if Isaiah, one of the most central texts in Jewish messianism, had no significance for contemporary Jews. One would not know from Josephus's seeming indifference to Isaiah that Isaiah was so central to the liturgical lives of Jews, from the sectarians of Qumran to those of the first-century synagogues, and that the highest proportion of the readings from the prophets (*haftarah*) accompanying the readings from the Torah in the synagogues was from Isaiah. There were other sources, of course, for Jewish messianism.

Momigliano provides the following attestation of what Josephus in fact does and seems to come very close to saying that Josephus was partly disingenuous. Momigliano writes:

> On the one hand, he tells us clearly that Roman rule had been predicted by Jeremiah, Ezekiel, and Daniel (ant. Jud. 10.79, 10.276) as well as by the much older Azariah (Ant. Jud. 8.294–96, 2 Chron. 15.1), on the other hand, he eliminates certain aspects of the prophecy of Daniel. He omits the vision of the beasts, that is, of the empires in Daniel 7, whose reference to Rome is attributed to God himself in a very original passage from 2 Esdras 12.10ff. . . . and betraying some embarrassment, Flavius Josephus refuses to explain the prophecy of the divine stone, which breaks the statue of the empires in Daniel 2.34. He knew it had been reinterpreted as an oracle on the fall of Rome (ant. Jud. 10.210).[22]

In the end, as Momigliano notes, Josephus asks or demands to be trusted as a prophet in his own right, or at least a historian writing with prophetic insight: an authoritative interpreter of the Jewish past, its present, and its possible futures.

> Trusting in his prophetic talent, Flavius Josephus predicts the future and survives. As a survivor, he professes his loyalty to the God of the Fathers and to the laws of the Bible. But he is cut off from the two vital currents of the Judaism of his time: the apocalypse and the synagogues.[23]

So unless we learn to read Josephus's silences against the contemporaneous evidence, we will miss a great deal. That contemporary evidence includes, first, Josephus's own writings, which provide enough evidence to frame his silences and also to contextualize them; and second, the writings and documentary sources of his contemporaries, which often illuminate the contexts in which Josephus passes over silently what they draw attention to. Josephus's silences are, therefore, productive silences. We may call them "loud silences," precisely because he says so much else that make his silences almost impossible to ignore. One of his loudest silences, as I have been arguing, is the fact that Josephus does not mention Paul, the apostle and missionary of the early Christian movement, with whom he shared so many characteristics as a Pharisee in the middle of the first century.

AUTOBIOGRAPHIES OF TWO PHARISEES: JOSEPHUS'S *LIFE* AND PAUL'S LETTER TO THE GALATIANS

Josephus's *Life* and Paul's Letter to the Galatians are brief autobiographical accounts of two Pharisees who were contemporaries in the middle of the first century. What, then, does Paul do that Josephus does or does not do? Well, Josephus presents the autobiographical material as preface for a contested interpretation of the revolt in Galilee at the beginning of the Jewish War and his role in it. Paul, for his part, describes a contested situation in Galatia and the role of his fellow Christian Jews in their relations with Gentiles. Each has to defend himself: Paul the gospel he preaches; Josephus his supposed actions and possible negligence or collaboration with the enemy. From each we gain some sense of how they conceptualized and lived out their Jewish identities in a Roman world: what it is that mattered to them with respect to the deity, and what sort of life they believed was required of them. No reasonable person reviewing just this bit from Josephus and Paul would think the Paul was somehow a lesser Jew than Josephus.

Josephus chose the Pharisees. Paul had been a Pharisee before Josephus, and a self-described persecutor of the early Christians. Paul advertises his credentials as a Pharisee and his zeal in trying to destroy the early Christian movement. One does not have to know of the Acts of the Apostles to know this. What Paul says in the Letter to the Galatians he repeats in another form in his Letter to the Philippians. Paul the Pharisee became a follower of Jesus the Galilean; Josephus remained a Pharisee until, ironically, the Jewish campaign in Galilee in 65/66 CE. There is no historical evidence to suggest that Paul lived to see the beginnings of the Jewish War. Whether Josephus still conceived of himself as a Pharisee after his surrender to the Romans is an open question. His capitulation was the watershed event for Josephus. For Paul, his turnaround is the experience he describes in Galatians 1 and 2. It is not impossible to imagine that perhaps some aspects of the zeal that Paul attaches to his objections to the Christian Jews as characteristics of his allegiance to the Pharisees may have been present in Josephus the Pharisee as well. Josephus himself never describes himself in any way as to suggest that he was among the most zealous people in Jerusalem. If anything, he tries to cast himself as a person of moderation. At the same time, the ease with which he condemns and repudiates the acts of many of the contemporaries he writes about and the various motives he often ascribes to them do not incline to the view that Josephus was always at his most charitable. It should not be surprising if he repudiated the Christian Jews for all the arguments that he makes about the uniqueness, viability, and superiority of the Mosaic legislation and Jewish ways in the *Against Apion* in particular. We should not be surprised on account of this that he would go to such an extent to consign the early Christian movement to virtual nonexistence, making it irrelevant to

Jewish history as he sought to present it. A movement that thought of someone as "the Christ" had no place in Josephus's Judaism as described in *Against Apion*, and presumably had no place in the *Antiquities* either even if he wrote about James the brother of Jesus who was thought to be the Christ.

But not for Paul. In the first chapter of Galatians Paul provides the elements of a life that links him to Peter the Apostle and James, "the Lord's brother." The phrase, "the Lord's brother," is not incidental. At a minimum it establishes a simple fact. Although not one of the original disciples of Jesus, Paul came to know Peter in person and spent fifteen days with him. I should like to have known the conversations he had with Peter over those fifteen days. He also met James, but none of the other apostles (Galatians 1:18–19). If Peter presented to Paul some of the details of the life he had with Jesus, James would provide a family perspective. What did James tell Paul and what did Paul learn from James so that he would continue to believe what he already believed about Jesus and continue to proclaim what he declares from the opening of the letter to this very end? What did James affirm for Paul to continue to say that Jesus was the Son of God (Galatians 2:20) and that he lives his life to the crucified Christ who now lives in him?

In Galatians 2 Paul provides even more detail, this time about the visit "fourteen years later" (Galatians 2:1). On this occasion he meets not only Peter and James, whom he met the previous time, but also John, presumably the apostle. These three he labels "those reputed to be pillars." But he already knew that. He says this only because he is on his way to criticizing Peter and those who came from James. Here then Paul provides biographical details that establish once more that he is not an invented character or that the gospel he preaches is not at odds with those early disciples and those who knew Jesus of Nazareth. Once more, I should wish to know what he learned from John the apostle. He states emphatically that they affirmed his mission to the Gentiles as they acknowledged theirs to their fellow Jews. It was not a mutually exclusive affirmation as if Paul could not go to Jews or that the others could not go to Gentiles. It was merely a division of responsibility based on the nature of their respective callings, their histories, and their current or present geographical and cultural locations.

For our purposes the important thing is the link between Paul, James the brother of Jesus, and the apostles Peter and John. There is no better testament to Paul's link to the message of Jesus than for him to declare his relationship to these three. Josephus says nothing about Paul. Josephus has nothing in his works about Peter, nor about John, but he bears witness to James the brother of Jesus. So between Paul and Josephus they have in common a knowledge of James the brother of Jesus to which they attest in their writings; and Josephus has plenty to say about Jewish life and thought in the years during which Paul flourished as an apostle in the middle of the first century between 30 CE and 70 CE, between the death of Jesus the Galilean from Nazareth and the destruction of the Temple in Jerusalem at the end of the Jewish War. But even without Josephus, whose *Life* also offers an account of how he came to be a Pharisee or affiliated with the Pharisees, Paul provides something comparable and more primary still about the early Christian movement. He gives an account of his own life as a Pharisee who was converted to become a follower of Jesus the Galilean.

When set against the various autobiographical details that Josephus provides about himself in his writings, Paul's Letter to the Galatians, together with the other six so-called authentic letters, bear witness to a more salutary and commendable life of a Jew or Gentile in the first century than Josephus's. Paul fares much better than Josephus and another contemporary Seneca, the philosopher. Paul would not be accused as some of Seneca's contemporaries accused him of teaching one thing and living out something else, of writing moral treatises and living in such a way as to make null and void the ideas he promoted in those treatises. Rarely, if ever, does Seneca subject his own past actions to the philosophical analysis he pursues in his moral essays. It would have been most revealing for Seneca to have commented on his previous actions, subjecting them to philosophical criticism. As it is, he speaks of his present self, at the time of writing the philosophical letters and essays. But not his past. Paul, on the other hand, appears to have lived out his affirmation in Galatians 2:20–21. "I have been crucified with Christ, and I no longer live, but Christ lives in me. The life I live in the body, I live by faith in the Son of God, who loved me and gave himself for me. I do not set aside the grace of God, for if righteousness could be gained through the law, Christ died for nothing" (NIV). At the risk of misunderstanding, it needs to be acknowledged, against the prejudices of historians and literary critics, that Paul's life as attested in his writings was exemplary, even if we don't believe what he believed. Without prejudice to their religious or apocalyptic content, if one were to take Paul simply as a moral actor, his writings provide a more coherent morality than either Seneca or Josephus.

It will simply not do to say that the early Christian movement was a mass of conflicting and confused ideas if Paul is recognized as the center of the movement as it spread beyond Jerusalem and Judaea. Paul insisted on this much: it was *his* gospel and *he* was *the* apostle to the Gentiles, with a special task to proclaim the good news (*euangelion*) of Jesus the Son of God to the Gentiles, or the Nations. He laid all this out as clearly as could be in the Letter to the Galatians, and even dared anyone to contradict him: an angel from heaven or any mere mortal.

Some historians and New Testament scholars and critics suggest that his assertion is merely an emotional outburst or a self-aggrandizing exaggeration or wish fulfillment. But it is in fact at the heart of his argument about the nature of his authority and the content of the gospel he proclaims. Paul is so sure of himself, or of his gospel, that even if an angel from heaven should appear and proclaim something else other than what Paul preaches, Paul is emboldened to condemn that angel eternally. Now if you believe in angels, you might wonder what right Paul has in judging angels so categorically; and if you don't believe in angels, you may wonder still. However, Paul leaves it in no doubt that on this and this alone, he has it on better authority that he is in the right and everyone else is in the wrong, angels who dare to contradict him included.

Josephus does not mention to his Roman audience in his *Antiquities* the existence of an early Christian community inspired by a movement that began among the Jews of Judaea, even as he presents a good many Jewish factions and sects in his history to educate his Roman readership. The autobiographical elements in the opening chapter of Paul's Letter to the Romans, however, establish beyond dispute the existence of a community of Christians in Rome in the early 50s. To appropriate the language of Tacitus's *Annals* 14.55, Paul's letter attests that a "superstition" (from the Roman point of view) that began among the Jews in the Roman province of Judaea spread to Rome and found a hearing there. Suetonius, then, was not inventing or imagining a fictive group of Christians when he claimed that they had been subjected to recriminations during the reign of Nero (54–68 CE). The social background and the occasion of Paul's Letter to the Romans fall precisely within this period.

Paul's Letter to the Romans contains probably his most well-crafted and argued explanation of his understanding of Israel's past, Jewish messianic expectation, and the gospel of Jesus Christ. Unlike the other letters, Paul writes to a city he had not yet visited and to a community of Christians who as yet did not know him in person. Paul cannot even lay claim to have been the one who personally founded the church in Rome. However, he lists a whole host of characters connected to him who have been part of the church in Rome or are known by his recipients to be among his coworkers (Romans 16:1–23). So he writes to them with all the authority he claims as the apostle to the nations or the Gentiles. Here is the opening. It appears to be one sentence:

> Paul, a servant of Jesus Christ, called to be an apostle, set apart for the gospel of God, which he promised beforehand through his prophets in the holy scriptures, the gospel concerning his Son, who was descended from David according to the flesh and was declared to be Son of God with power according to the spirit of holiness by resurrection from the dead, Jesus Christ our Lord, through whom we have received grace and apostleship to bring about the obedience of faith among all the Gentiles for the sake of his name, including yourselves who are called to belong to Jesus Christ, To all of God's beloved in Rome, who are called as saints: Grace to you and peace from God our Father and the Lord Jesus Christ. (Romans 1:1–7 [NRSV])

He soon points out why he is eager to come to Rome (Romans 1:15). He even claims that the faith of the Christians in Rome is proclaimed throughout the world (1:8), and that he has always had them in mind: "for God whom I serve with my spirit by announcing the gospel of his Son, is my witness that without ceasing I remember you always in my prayers, asking that by God's will I may somehow at last succeed in coming to you." Paul indicates that he had always held the hope of visiting them, but has been prevented from coming, which is why he is so eager to visit them. The letter precedes the visit, almost as if preparing his way to be received by the Romans.

Josephus would write his *Antiquities* much later, about three decades later. Josephus too will be speaking to a primarily Roman audience (and just like Paul writing in Greek) to explain to them the ways of his ancestors and Jewish religious hopes and aspirations. In his introduction, Josephus makes clear that he is writing a history and maintains that he wants to set the record straight about the Jewish past, its form of government, and how God has guided the nation up to and including the present time that has recently witnessed a war with the Romans. Paul writes no such history. However, Paul presents in his Letter to the Romans a specific theological interpretation of Israel's history and of its religious hopes that sets him apart from the various interpretations that Josephus too writes about with unquestionable theological intent. Josephus pontificates here and there about those same hopes and of the Jewish future that Paul also writes about. The contrast between Paul's arguments and Josephus's equally theological interpretations in different sections of the *Antiquities* is all one needs to know about the different path that the gospel of Jesus Christ set for Paul the converted Pharisee as opposed to Josephus the conflicted Pharisee and sometime Roman apologist.

Both Josephus and Paul speak about how they stood comparison to their contemporaries. Josephus speaks of his distinguished background and how he was head and shoulders above his peers. He says some of this in the preface where he even points out how others might envy him on account of his lineage and his accomplishments. Paul, for his part, speaks of advancing in Judaism beyond many of his generation. He then speaks about what God did to reveal his Son to him. Josephus constantly speaks of how the deity providentially guides him and considers his choice of philosophical schools within Judaism as he finally settled on the Pharisees as almost providential. Paul, against opposition, speaks of his rights as an apostle in First Corinthians 9 and in Second Corinthians 11:16–12:10. Then in Philippians 3:1–11 he speaks about his confidence in the power of Jesus's resurrection and the fellowship of his suffering. In the middle of it he has this to say: "If anyone else has reason to be confident in the flesh, I have more: circumcised on the eighth day, a member of the people of Israel, of the tribe of Benjamin, a

Hebrew born of Hebrews; as to the law, a Pharisee; as to zeal, a persecutor of the church; as to righteousness under the law, blameless" (4b–6 [NRSV]).

Against this background, one can legitimately ask what Paul gained by becoming a Christian. Or more precisely, in the words of the historian Charles Freeman, "What Did Paul Achieve?" That is the title of a chapter in Freeman's recent book.[24] For Freeman, and in line with much received opinion, Paul was something of a corruptor of Jesus's teaching. He changed virtually everything, demanding a strong emotional commitment and disparaging much else:

> In the context of his belief that the Second Coming was at hand this was understandable. But the Second Coming did not come and Paul became something completely different. His letters, which had been received piecemeal by their recipients, were brought together as if they were to define Christian living for all time. The results were not always healthy.[25]

Freeman continues that "the rejection of the 'wisdom of the wise' easily led to an assault on reasoned thought" and that Paul's concerns over human sexuality "fed into paranoia about the lures of women and the 'evils' of homosexuality." Freeman adds that "the stress on sin might be developed into a denigration of human nature" and that "Paul's own ambivalence towards his Jewish background fueled anti-Semitism."[26]

This is a rather jaundiced reading of Paul. In what sense was Paul's so-called ambivalence about his Jewish background any different from Josephus's or Philo's? Weren't there already anti-Jewish riots in the ancient world before Paul and after? Freeman attempts a concession ostensibly because "Paul cannot be blamed . . . for the ways in which his letters were separated from their original context and used by Christians for other purposes." But Freeman's language is so prejudicial to the image of Paul that even the supposed correction turns into another diatribe. Freeman's faint praise is another occasion for denunciation. Freeman acknowledges Paul's capabilities as a rhetorician, and even speaks of his eloquence. Still, he laments: "Christianity would have been dramatically different if we had, for instance, fuller records of Jewish Christianity. There might never have been the antagonisms between Jew and Christian."[27]

"Fine literature," "impressive examples of ancient rhetoric," "most passionate," "impressive examples of ancient rhetoric"—these are not the characteristics of something one would wish away. Freeman professes not to wish that Paul had never happened. The oddity is that everything else he goes on to say is to have wished that Paul's Christianity had died some kind of premature death to save the world from its dastardly influences.

Freeman even writes as if there were no divisions, factions, and antagonisms among Jews in the first century before and after Paul; that a fuller record of so-called Jewish Christianity would show just how damaging Paul was for Christianity; and that there might never have been differences between Jews and Christians if Paul's mission and his teachings had not precipitated them. He presents a reality of first-century Jewish life and Judaism that is far removed from anything that is found in Josephus's *Antiquities, Jewish War*, or his *Life*. Freeman imagines a world that never existed. When he turns to what might have been for Christianity's future Freeman is all wistfulness founded on a fictional and imagined past that never was. According to Freeman:

> We would have benefited immensely from the survival of some of Apollos' speeches (although the Letter to the Hebrews may reflect some of his ideas.) Apollos may have preached only to an intellectual elite, in the tradition of Plato, but a more reasoned theology would have provided a useful contrast to the impassioned and highly emotional rhetoric of Paul.[28]

That we have a favorable view of Apollos at all is mostly due to Paul's commendation of Apollos in the Corinthian correspondence, and his insistence that both he and Apollos did not teach different things: that what Paul planted, Apollos watered (First Corinthians 1:1; 2:1; 3:6, 9; 16:12). The subsequent biographical sketch found in Acts 18:24–28 adds more detail.

So it is something of a fiction to suggest that Apollos and Paul were at odds on what they taught. It is not clear, in any case, what the so-called "more reasoned theology" in the mold of Plato would have looked like; and how badly Paul's so-called emotional theology would stand in its wake. The metaphorically impassioned language of someone like Plotinus, coupled with his asceticism, makes him just as rigorous in his denunciations of the body as anything Freeman decries in Paul's alleged "paranoia about the flesh." So does Freeman really believe that a theology based on Plato as is to be found in say Plotinus, Porphyry, or Iamblichus or other later Platonists is less impassioned than Paul's? Freeman seems to equivocate: "Paul will always remain controversial and enigmatic." Freeman's descriptions suggest a veritable neurosis on the supposition that Paul was a "Puritan."

> He was heroic in his endeavors but hardly attractive as a personality. Puritans seldom are. In a comparatively rare moment of insight (2 Corinthians 12:20), he recognised the bitterness and confusion he could bring to those he visited. Even the loyal Timothy seems to have been rejected for failing to live up to his mentor's expectations. The arrival of his letters must have been dreaded. No one could be quite sure what he would demand next or what idiosyncratic interpretations he might make of scripture or the message of Christ. They were, after all, personal to him and not part of an established tradition. For those who were attuned to the apostles who had actually known Jesus, his authority must have been suspect and the apparent vision of Christ hardly comparable to their eyewitness testimony. Yet, there have always been Chris-

tians—Augustine and Luther are good examples—who remain intrigued by Paul even to the extent of appearing to give his letters precedence over the gospels. They are the theologians who have given Paul the prominent place in Christian tradition which he occupies today.[29]

This is extremely tendentious and almost nonsensical. Paul was prominent in Christian tradition from the very beginning of the mission to the Gentiles. He was prominent long before Augustine, and certainly much longer before Luther.

So, "What Did Paul Achieve?" It has to be asked of the one who renders judgment whether there is any comparative dimension to that judgment. In other words, what did Paul achieve in comparison to others of his generation or others like him? If there is no comparative dimension, especially involving his contemporaries, then the standard against which he is judged is merely that which the person making the judgment chooses. Much of what Freeman presents is of this variety. So we should probably ask: what did Paul as a prominent Pharisee and Josephus an affiliate of the Pharisees in the first century achieve in their respective lives? If we wanted to broaden the scope, we might include Philo Judaeus or even Seneca. Could Freeman truly make the judgments he hands down on Paul if he were to compare Paul to Josephus, Seneca, and Philo Judaeus? Could Freeman say that Josephus was a better representation of Judaism than Paul or that Seneca was a more credible moral actor than Paul? Perhaps he might say Philo was a more intellectually capable and influential person than Paul. But even that would be debatable.

As to his notion that if Apollos had been the more prominent figure then we would have had a better Christianity, one wonders still. The supposition that the Letter to the Hebrews reflects his ideas does not in fact set him against Paul as Freeman seems to imply. There is nothing in the Epistle to the Hebrews that sets itself against Paul's teachings in Romans or in Galatians, for example. The notion that somehow Hebrews is more tolerant than either Romans or Galatians is an enlightened fabrication. Hebrews too understands Christianity and the death of Christ as the fulfillment of Jewish messianic expectation. If Freeman laments Paul's emphasis on the cross and resurrection, he should not pretend that the notion of the perfect sacrifice that does away with the ancient Hebrew/Jewish sacrificial system is any less radical. That is the viewpoint of Hebrews. Actually when he comes to write about the Letter to the Hebrews, Freeman seems to forget what he criticizes Paul for,[30] yet he still manages to present Hebrews as superior to Paul. Paul is somehow a retrograde for arguing for the end of the Old Covenant, and yet Hebrews is sophisticated and commendable even though it argues the same thing.

> The Letter to the Hebrews is important because it shows how worship of Jesus was developing, some thirty or forty years after his crucifixion, in communities that appear never to have read any of the gospels. . . . The letter has a

theological sophistication and coherence which is greater than anything to be found in the genuine letters of Paul. It is a vivid reminder of how mature the Christian communities had become in their worship even before the writing of any known gospel.[31]

It may be slightly intemperate to engage in a dispute about Paul's theological sophistication compared to that of the Letter to the Hebrews. There is very little in the Letter to the Hebrews that disagrees with Paul. Few would consider Paul's Letter to the Romans as any less theologically sophisticated than the Letter to the Hebrews. Freeman's comment about the maturity of Christian communities "even before the writing of any known gospel" is a theme that warrants more consideration than it is often given. In addition, if the writing of Hebrews can be located in a period earlier than Freeman and other scholars surmise, it would require a revision of our understanding of how early that sophistication took hold, and what relation they bear to the letters of Paul.

The tendency to separate Paul from other early Christian characters and sources and from the teaching of Jesus also demands at least a brief comment about Paul and his companions. However, this is not the place for it. It is tied to the nature of Paul's letters and arguments about their authenticity. That is the subject of another work.[32] Thus far I have been content to use only those parts found in the so-called authentic letters that bear on Paul's autobiography in my attempt to compare him to Josephus.

PARALLEL LIVES: PAUL AND THE ROYAL HOUSE OF ADIABENE

Paul's achievement and Josephus's silence about him or ignorance of him comes into still better focus when we set his story side by side with a story that Josephus tells about the royal house of Adiabene in northern Mesopotamia. Josephus tells the story in two versions: first, in the *Jewish War*, and then secondly in the *Antiquities*. The latter gives the full version of how Queen Helena and her son Izates changed their ways of life to adopt Jewish customs.

Josephus provides a tale beginning with the birth of Izates, one of two sons of Helena and King Monobazus, who had other children by other wives. The king apparently demonstrated a fondness for Izates in part because of a "word" that came to him when his wife Helena was pregnant with the child. Josephus mentions that Helena was Monobazus's sister and passes over the issue of the incestuous nature of the marriage without comment, although he is not sparring when he passes along rumors about the alleged incestuous relationship between Herod Agrippa II and his sister Berenice. Josephus emphasizes, however, the divine element of "a word" that came to Monobazus that the child would be great. The implication is that this is what made the king love Izates more than any of his children and also led him to decree that the child was to succeed him.

As Josephus tells the story, the other siblings were none too pleased. Knowing that he could be harmed by his siblings, King Monobazus sends Izates far away from Adiabene, as far as he could, it seems, to King Abennerig of Charax Spasinu at the confluence of the Tigris and Euphrates, a few miles inland from the Persian Gulf in what is today Kuwait. Charax Spasinu was an important point on the land route through the desert into the Parthian kingdom. It was one of the easternmost cities that the Roman Emperor Trajan visited on his Parthian campaign in 116 CE. Trajan is said to have lamented his age when he saw the ships arriving from India, saying that if he had been younger he might have ventured further east like Alexander the Great. The Chinese envoy Gan Ying is said to have visited it in 97 CE. Pliny the Elder discusses Charax Spasinu in his *Natural History* 6.31.

Izates lived the better part of his life before the death of Monobazus in this important city. He married the daughter of King Abennerig of Charax Spasinu. We pick up the story now from Josephus, and I shall quote him extensively as it deserves to be read in its entirety to appreciate its significance for the argument that I am proposing about Josephus's silences about Paul and the early Christian movement.

> Now during the time when Izates resided at Charax Spasinu, a certain Jewish merchant named Ananias visited the king's wives and taught them to worship God after the manner of the Jewish tradition. It was through their agency that he was brought to the notice of Izates, whom he similarly won over with the co-operation of the women. When Izates was summoned by his father to Adiabene, Ananias accompanied him in obedience to his urgent request. It so happened, moreover, that Helena had likewise been instructed by another Jew and had been brought over to their laws. When Izates came to Adiabene to take over the kingdom and saw his brothers and his other kinsmen in chains, he was distressed at what had been done. Regarding it as impious either to kill them or to keep them in chains, and yet thinking it hazardous to keep them with him if they were not imprisoned—cherishing resentment as they must—he sent some of them with their children to Claudius Caesar in Rome as hostages, and others to Artabanus the Parthian king with the same excuse.[33]

Now back in Adiabene Izates learns about just how much Jewish ways have infiltrated the royal household here too. This time it is his own mother:

> When Izates had learned that his mother was very much pleased with the Jewish religion, he was zealous to convert to it himself; and since he considered that he would not be genuinely a Jew unless he was circumcised, he was ready to act accordingly. When his mother learned of his intention, however, she tried to stop him by telling him that it was a dangerous move. For, she said,

he was a king; and if his subjects should discover that he was devoted to rites that were strange and foreign to themselves, it would produce much disaffection and they would not tolerate the rule of a Jew over them. Besides this advice she tried by every other means to hold him back. He, in turn, reported her arguments to Ananias. The latter expressed agreement with the king's mother and actually threatened that if he should be unable to persuade Izates, he would abandon him and leave the land. For he said that he was afraid that if the matter became universally known, he would be punished, in all likelihood, as personally responsible because he had instructed the king in unseemly practices. The king could, he said, worship God even without being circumcised if indeed he had fully decided to be a devoted adherent of Judaism, for it was this that counted more than circumcision. He told him, furthermore, that God Himself would pardon him if, constrained thus by necessity and by fear of his subjects, he failed to perform this rite. And so, for the time, the king was convinced by his arguments. Afterwards, however, since he had not completely given up his desire, another Jew, named Eleazar, who came from Galilee and who had a reputation for being extremely strict when it came to the ancestral laws, urged him to carry out the rite. For when he came to him to pay him his respects and found him reading the law of Moses, he said: "In your ignorance, O king, you are guilty of the greatest offence against the law and thereby against God. For you ought not merely to read the law but also, and even more, to do what is commanded in it. How long will you continue to be uncircumcised? If you have not yet read the law concerning this matter, read it now, so that you may know what an impiety it is that you commit." Upon hearing these words, the king postponed the deed no longer. Withdrawing into another room, he summoned his physician and had the prescribed act performed. Then he sent for both his mother and his teacher Ananias and notified them that he had performed the rite. They were immediately seized with consternation and fear beyond measure that, if it should be proved that he had performed the act, the king would risk losing his throne, since his subjects would not submit to government by a man who was a devotee of foreign practices, and that they themselves would be in jeopardy since the blame for his action would be attributed to them. It was God who was to prevent their fears from being realized. For although Izates himself and his children were often threatened with destruction, God preserved them, opening a path to safety from desperate straits. God thus demonstrated that those who fix their eyes on Him and trust in Him alone do not lose the reward of their piety. But I shall report these events at a later time.[34]

The story ends here with the promise of a further retelling. Josephus goes on to describe the consequences of conversion:

Helena, the mother of the king, saw that peace prevailed in the kingdom and that her son was prosperous and the object of admiration in all men's eyes, even those of foreigners, thanks to the prudence that God gave him. Now she had conceived a desire to go to the city of Jerusalem and to worship at the temple of God, which was famous throughout the world, and to make thank-offerings there. She consequently asked her son to give her leave. Izates was most enthusiastic in granting his mother's request, made great preparations for her journey, and gave her a large sum of money. He even escorted her for a considerable distance, and she completed her journey to the city of Jerusalem. Her arrival was very advantageous for the people of Jerusalem, for at that time the city was hard pressed by famine and many were perishing from want of money to purchase what they needed. Queen Helena sent some of her attendants to Alexandria to buy grain for large sums and others to Cyprus to bring back a cargo of dried figs. Her attendants speedily returned with these provisions, which she thereupon distributed among the needy. She has thus left a very great name that will be famous forever among our whole people for her benefaction. When her son Izates learned of the famine, he likewise sent a great sum of money to leaders of the Jerusalemites. The distribution of this fund to the needy delivered many from the extremely severe pressure of famine. But I shall leave to a later time the further tale of good deeds performed for our city by this royal pair.[35]

The story of Izates's conversion turns on the Jewish merchant named Ananias who became well known among the king's harem. Ananias managed to convert some of the women to Jewish ways. Izates also learned about Jewish religion and customs from Ananias. Izates remained interested but did not fully embrace it. However, when it was time to return to Adiabene after the death of his father, he brought Ananias along with him to Adiabene as his teacher, probably as his advisor and also to continue learning about Judaism.

When Izates arrived in Adiabene and found out that his mother too has been influenced by someone else and had already adopted Jewish ways, the die was cast. The person who so influenced his mother is yet another Jew, who is not named. Izates makes haste to follow suit. His mother Helena cautions him against being circumcised, however, because it might put him at odds with his people, who may object to his rule because he had become a Jew. He could lose his kingdom. Ananias agreed with Queen Helena, and counseled caution. Ananias suggested that Izates could be a practicing and observant proselyte to Judaism without the outward, physical sign of circumcision. So far so good: until Eleazar from Galilee arrives on the scene. Josephus does not say what brought Eleazer from Galilee to Adiabene. Josephus does not describe him as a merchant, but as someone very knowledgeable.

Interestingly, we have three regions now represented: a certain Jew already in Adiabene who influenced Queen Helena; Ananias with whom Izates returned from Charax Spasinu to Adiabene; and Eleazar the Galilean, who maintains that circumcision is essential for Izates's conversion to Judaism and insists upon it without regard to what might happen to him or his kingdom. They cover quite a bit of territory: from the Persian Gulf to Adiabene in northern Mesopotamia and from Galilee in Palestine to Adiabene. Between these three regions we must also imagine the movement of people, ideas, and sentiments that drew the Adiabene royals toward Judaism and Jerusalem. Similarly, we should keep in mind how Paul speaks of his missions to Arabia (the Nabataean Kingdom in the Transjordan), Damascus, Syria, Judaea, and finally Jerusalem in Galatians 1:11–24.

Eleazar the Galilean is sometimes described as a Pharisee by scholars, because Josephus writes about his zeal for the Law using much the same language that he uses to describe Pharisees elsewhere in his works. But why he makes no attempt to identify him as such, if in fact he was a Pharisee, seems odd. Josephus, after all, makes much of being affiliated with the Pharisees, so we should expect him to mention Eleazar's connections with Pharisees if in fact this were the case. It seems more than likely that Eleazar was not a Pharisee in any proper sense of the word. Either way, he was a contemporary of Josephus, a much older contemporary, since the conversion of the Adiabene royals occurred when Josephus was a lad. So also was Ananias the merchant who traveled from Charax Spasinu to Adiabene with Izates. While it may be overly optimistic to inquire whether Josephus knew more about Ananias than he provides in his tale, it may not be too much to ask whether he knew more about Eleazar of Galilee than he furnishes in his story.

In any case, if Eleazar was not a Pharisee, then we have here a representation of a Jew among Josephus's contemporaries who was zealous for the law in the way the Pharisees were, but probably did not belong to the party or sect of the Pharisees. Which is to say that there were some Jews in Judaea and Galilee who were strict about the law without being Pharisees. Beyond that, it would have been interesting to know what exactly brought Eleazar to Adiabene and why he had to pay his respects to King Izates. Was he paying his respects as an individual or as a representative of the Galileans? Josephus does not say. But the fact that he came to pay his respects and had the audacity to implore the king to do what was right may say something about his status, which again Josephus does not discuss. Furthermore, the narrative presents him as someone competent to challenge other people's interpretation of the Torah, and he did it authoritatively either because he had some kind of training in the Law, in an official sense, or that he was extremely knowledgeable about the Law in his own capacity as a deeply devout Jew, or both.

Incidentally the story also turns on a difference between a Diaspora Jewish perspective provided by Ananias, who was a merchant from Charax Spasinu, and Eleazar from Galilee in Palestine. Ananias is willing to rule that Izates can be a Jew without being circumcised, if circumcision will put both him and his kingdom at risk, and Ananias feared that his own life would be at risk because he would be blamed for having introduced Izates to a foreign cult (religion). He makes a concession and assures King Izates that God understood his predicament. Eleazar the Galilean, on the other hand, is categorical, and he offers his dictum without knowledge that the king had received different counsel from Ananias on the subject. At least that is how

Josephus's narrative reads. Josephus gives no indication that Eleazar was privy to the previous counsel of Queen Helena and Ananias. Eleazar simply expressed his conviction and said what he said because that was for him the proper interpretation of the Torah.

Eleazar's words, as presented by Josephus, are very specific. He not only accuses King Izates of ignorance but also of indifference bordering on unrighteousness.

> In your ignorance, O king, you are guilty of the greatest offence against the law and thereby against God. For you ought not merely to read the law but also, and even more, to do what is commanded in it. How long will you continue to be uncircumcised? If you have not yet read the law concerning this matter, read it now, so that you may know what an impiety it is that you commit.[36]

Josephus's language suggests that Eleazar was deeply knowledgeable about the law without implying that he had some kind of official role as a teacher of the Law. If Eleazar was a known teacher of the Law from Galilee, it would make Josephus's silence about this fact peculiar for what else he leaves out about Eleazar of Galilee.

Galilee had a vibrant Jewish social, cultural, and intellectual life in the period between the reign of Herod the Great (37 BCE–4 CE) and the outbreak of the Jewish War in 66 CE. The founding of cities like Sepphoris and Tiberias by Herod Antipas (before 20 BCE–after 39 CE) who reigned as tetrarch after 6 CE is testament to this fact. It would have been helpful if Josephus, who knew both Sepphoris and Tiberias well, had indicated which one of these two major cities in Galilee Eleazar the Galilean was connected to. If he was not in any way associated with any of the major cities of Galilee, where was Eleazar located before he arrived in Adiabene in Mesopotamia?

Josephus's unfulfilled promise to add more to the story about the Adiabene royals suggests that he had a good deal more material than what we have in his writings. Perhaps he had more on Ananias and Eleazar the Galilean that he would have provided in his subsequent additions, if he had gotten to them. It is intriguing to speculate if he had something to add about either Ananias or Eleazar traveling to Jerusalem to the Adiabene royal residences there; whether Josephus himself had ever been in those residences, what he knew of their contents, and what they contributed to the larger collection of Jewish archives in the first century. Might I suggest also, given Josephus's extensive knowledge about matters in Galilee, that he probably knew a lot more about Eleazar the Galilean than the brief description he provides here.

Eleazer convinced King Izates, who proceeded to get circumcised. Izates informed his mother and Ananias after the fact. As it turned out he did not lose his kingdom, and so all seems to have ended well. When Helena saw this, she became even more devoted to the God of the Jews. She made preparations to relocate to Jerusalem, which she did, and eventually built royal residences there. Josephus does not mention the building projects in Jerusalem, but he promised to add to the story at a later time; a promise he did not keep. In the meantime he tells the story of Helena's philanthropy to the people of Jerusalem.

Other elements of the story told by Josephus set up parallels between the royals of Adiabene and Paul. Josephus makes clear from the outset that this is a story of conversion to Jewish ways, specifically Jewish religious life and customs: he uses four different tags: first, "to worship God according to Jewish religion" (in reference to Ananias and the events in Charax); second, "to go over to them" (in reference to Helena's conversion); third, to follow Jewish customs (in reference to both the first and the second); and fourth, to undergo circumcision (in reference to Izates). Josephus, then, highlights that in spite of their fears, the Adiabene royals did not lose their kingdom and were protected by divine providence after Izates underwent circumcision. This in turn motivated Queen Helena to even greater deeds of piety and, when she settled in Jerusalem, more remarkable acts of charity.

These two elements resonate with Paul's biography but in the opposite direction. First, Paul's message to his potential converts, as he describes it in Galatians and elsewhere, expressly argues against circumcision as a sign of conversion, in his case, conversion to faith in Jesus as the Messiah of Jewish expectation. Circumcision does not avail much, according to Paul's gospel (Galatians). Secondly, Paul calls Gentiles to convert in much the same way that Ananias, the unnamed Jew who influenced Helena, and Eleazar the Galilean, implore the Adiabene royals toward conversion. Thirdly, Helena demonstrated her new kinship with Jews and Judaeans by her charitable acts toward the people of Jerusalem. Paul too demonstrates the kinship of his fellow Christians, Jews and Gentiles, by their acts of charity to the so-called "poor" in Jerusalem, the saints, the Church in Judaea.

Helena's presence in Jerusalem was itself a remarkable fact. There are other stories of other royalty coming to Jerusalem, betaking themselves to Judaism. Perhaps the most famous one is the Queen of Sheba narrative. In the New Testament we have the Ethiopian Eunuch. He traveled to Jerusalem as a Jewish pilgrim or rather, a proselyte and a pilgrim, only to discover something new in his Judaism and return a Christian. Helena and Izates learned about Judaism not in Jerusalem but from those who brought it to them where they were: Izates in the Persian Gulf; his mother in Adiabene in Mesopotamia. They both eventually embraced it, and then Helena moves to Jerusalem.

Helena adopts Jerusalem. She emigrates and becomes a Jew in every way. I use the word "adopt" deliberately. For it is the word that Paul will use to speak of foreigners who are made children of Abraham by the gospel he proclaims. Your adoption as sons: that is how Paul puts it in Romans 8:23;

9:4. This is implied in Galatians 3:26–4:7. The spirit of sonship leads the son to say, "Abba, Father."

There are some similarities also between the story of Helena and the Ruth and Naomi narrative in the Hebrew Scriptures. In the latter, Ruth returns with her mother-in-law and commits herself to the God of Israel. Naomi is destitute in a way, and it is Boaz, Ruth's relative, who saves her, and through him becomes part of the genealogy of Jesse, the father of David. Helena is royalty. She does not marry a Jew, nor does she need to marry. She brings some members of her family, all from Adiabene, and makes Jerusalem her home and the God of Abraham her God. At some later point, concerned about the state of things surrounding King Monobazus after the death of Izates in Adiabene, Helena returned to Adiabene. She died there, but her remains and those of King Izates were sent to Jerusalem to be interred in a splendid tomb she had built several stadia north of the city. Josephus provides the account in *Antiquities* 20.

The story Josephus tells has, as well, elements of the Joseph narrative in the Old Testament: the youngest son who is preferred by his father but is hated by his older brothers, who wish him harm. In this case the preferred son is sent away for his protection. In the Joseph story the other brothers sell him into slavery. Here in this narrative when the father is about to die, he recalls his favorite son; and when the father dies, the mother says this was his father's wish that he succeed him.

When Josephus retold the story of Queen Helena and her son Izates in the early 90s, he was preserving for history a memory that had been wiped out in the destruction of Jerusalem, as the Adiabene royal palaces constructed so sumptuously by Helena in Jerusalem had been destroyed in 70 CE. Helena's adopted city lay in ruins; and with it her own architectural and religious legacies in Jerusalem in both her palaces and her contributions to the Temple. Within a generation of Josephus's death, the kingdom of Adiabene would become Christian, if we are to believe the sixth-century *Chronicle of Arbela*. The chronicle assumes that Christianity reached Arbela at the turn of the century[37] and that Christianity was firmly established in Adiabene during the time of Trajan, who invaded Adiabene in 115 or 116 CE. This brought to an end the more than seventy-five-year rule of Adiabene by a Jewish dynasty, which includes the reign of Izates the son of Helena.

If we follow the *Chronicle of Arbela*, we would have to say that as Josephus was working on *Against Apion* Adiabene was receiving its first signs of Christian missionary activities, and at about roughly the same time that the church in Rome was engaged with the church in Corinth in the rapprochement that is captured by First Clement (98–100 CE). Josephus clearly showed no interest in mentioning the Christians of Rome. But it is doubtful that he would not have been interested in what obtained in Arbela, the capital of Adiabene of his beloved Helena, after her death. The first version of his *Jewish War*, written in Aramaic, was intended for an audience that included those of the kingdom of Adiabene. The *Chronicle of Arbela*, on a different note, makes the point that at the beginning of the second century Christianity had made its way to that part of Helena's Mesopotamia, from where she had migrated to Jerusalem in something like an Abrahamic summons from Mesopotamia to Canaan. The story comes full circle.

Suetonius (*Claudius* 18.2) writes that there were famines, severe food shortages (*assiduas sterilitates*) throughout the empire during the reign of Claudius (41–54 CE). This period covers Josephus's life from age four to seventeen. Josephus mentions one in Judaea and Jerusalem during which Queen Helena of Adiabene demonstrated her benevolence by purchasing grain in Egypt and distributing it to the inhabitants of Jerusalem and Judaea who were in need. The time of the famine in Jerusalem is put somewhere around 46–49 CE. Josephus lived through the famine, and so was an eyewitness to Helena's generosity and philanthropy. Whatever its precise dating, the famine presents another moment of Josephus's silence or indifference to matters Christian.

Paul too mentions the needs of the poor in Jerusalem in his Letter to the Galatians. He does not speak of a famine as such. But there are passages in Acts that speak also of a famine in Jerusalem during the time of Claudius (Acts 11:27–30); Claudius is mentioned in v. 28. In First Corinthians 16:1–4 Paul speaks of a collection for the church in Jerusalem. He does not say that it was about a famine in the time of Claudius. However, he does say that he has already discussed this with the Galatians (a reference to Galatians 2:10?). He provides further elaboration in Second Corinthians 8 and 9, indicating that the Macedonians are also involved in what he describes as "the service to the saints" (8.4; 9:1). Paul then writes movingly about generosity and those who have given even out of their poverty for others.

This is a testament to Christian generosity; of mostly Gentiles/Greeks to the church in Jerusalem at the time of need. If it coincides with the famine that Helena intervened with her purchase of grain, we have here Paul doing what Josephus commends Helena for; but without Josephus ever saying anything about Paul and the Christian Jews of Jerusalem. This was not a small undertaking. It may not have been on the same scale as Helena's generosity, but it was a clear indication of a church spread across Asia Minor, Achaea, Macedonia, and present in Rome, extending a helping hand to the church in Jerusalem. Is there a better representation of one *ekklēsia* made up of Jews and Gentiles than this?

Surprisingly, while Josephus writes effusively about Helena's charity, he knows nothing apparently and says nothing about the kindness and charity of the Christians in Rome, Corinth, and other parts of Asia Minor, Macedonia, and Antioch, who were involved in helping those in Jerusalem. Most critically, Paul mentions his collection to the people of Jerusalem in several of his letters (Romans 15:25–28; First Corinthians 16:1–4; Second Corinthians 8–9; Galatians 2:10) as to leave no doubt that this was indeed something uppermost in his mind and important to the expression of the new social reality of a church (*ekklēsia*) made up of Jews and Gentiles scattered the world over.

Of course, Josephus did not have to know what took place among the Christians in Rome, Corinth, Macedonia, Asia Minor, and Antioch as far as helping the Christians in Jerusalem and Judaea. Nor do I mean to suggest that Paul had a profile in any way comparable to Queen Helena of Adiabene. But I do want to underscore that what Paul does in rallying support of the Christians beyond Judaea to provide assistance to the Christians in Jerusalem and Judaea, who were mostly Jews, attests to a notion of a new *ethnos*, a new nation made up of Jews and non-Jews, that was far more radical than Helena's generosity suggested.

Was it only Helena's generosity that would have been known at this time in Jerusalem? Hardly, if Paul did what he says he did. In this case, it is not just one person or one royal family and their generosity but entire communities of people over a wide area, and at some distance from Jerusalem.

Without putting too fine a point on it, the story Josephus tells of Helena and her son King Izates is in many ways a counternarrative to Paul's mission to the Gentiles. Here is a story about members of a Gentile family from Mesopotamia who convert to Judaism and prove to be some of the most prominent of Jewish converts in the first century. Helena's philanthropy and benefactions to the people of Judaea are noted, her tomb in the "Tombs of the Kings" is a well-documented historical site. At a time when Paul is arguing for a particular kind of Judaism centered on Jesus of Nazareth as the Messiah, Helena and her son Izates convert to the very Judaism that Paul is reforming or renewing, as he understood it.

Josephus celebrates these Gentiles converted to the old ways at the same time that Paul is converting other Gentiles to "the gospel," "The Way," or "The Name," that is Christianity, and warning them in Galatians not to revert to the old ways or some version of it. It is almost as if Josephus and Paul are writing past each other. Josephus's interest in the story of Helena's and Izates's conversions, his recommendation for the rite of circumcision even if it would complicate Izates's relationship with his subjects, and his lengthy exposition of the story, suggests a deep interest in matters of religious proselytizing, conversion, and the role of foreigners within Judaism. Yet while doing all this, Josephus remains remarkably silent about Christians among his fellow Jews. They are simply nonexistent. But then there is James the brother of Jesus who was called the Christ.

Josephus's interest also highlights the currency of intra-Jewish debate about what a true convert to Judaism is, how they ought to live, and what ritual requirements are essential for conversion. The two advisors that Josephus mentions in his story of Helena and Izates present two different responses to Izates's dilemma about circumcision and its potential impact in his kingdom. Neither, it should be noted, denies that circumcision is important and essential for the male convert. The problem is whether this particular male convert, a king, whose subjects are not themselves Jews or converts to Judaism, or have not been required to convert to Judaism, should go through with the act that he has determined to be appropriate for himself. It may be significant that neither advisor suggests that his subjects too should be made to convert. Why? Because a forced conversion was never an accepted form within Judaism. Philo writes on this. Josephus too speaks in his own defense against forced circumcisions (*Life* 112–113; see also *Antiquities* 2.454; 13.319). Ironically, Paul accuses the Galatians of subjecting themselves to a kind of "forced conversion" by others who insist that they must be circumcised to be truly Christian. Paul ups the ante in Galatians: not that non-Jews have to be circumcised but that they do not need to become Jews in order to become children of Abraham.

It is interesting to consider what Paul might have said to Queen Helena if he had encountered her. Was Paul aware of her presence in Jerusalem when he delivered his collection to the "poor" in Jerusalem? Could Paul have been ignorant of her given the imposing structures of the Adiabene royal residence near the Temple Mount? Would Paul have affirmed her conversion to Judaism? Or would Paul have insisted that she convert again, or rather, believe in Jesus as the Messiah to be truly a child of Abraham, as he argued in Galatians and elsewhere?

We are back to the question as to why Josephus's references to the Christians in Judaea and beyond, both Jews and Gentiles. One can offer a defense of Josephus by saying that the case of the Adiabene royals was unavoidable. Their presence in Jerusalem was not to be missed. They had constructed magnificent palaces as part of the architectural wonders of the city. So even as a lad or a teenager in Jerusalem Josephus would have known about them and certainly would have known their generosity during the famine in the time of Claudius. The Christians among the people of Jerusalem were rather an obscure group and would be known only by those in the know, so to speak. Whatever it was they did was circumscribed. So he was simply ignorant of them. Such an explanation works well if all that matters is personal experience of a very narrow kind. Josephus's knowledge of James the brother of Jesus was also personal. For by 62 CE, Josephus was a young man in Jerusalem. He knew this event as a matter of personal experience, and so could not pretend to be entirely ignorant of the group of people to which James belonged and which made him so objectionable to the High Priest Ananus son of Ananus. His presence in Rome in 64 CE was also personal experience, and so he could not claim to be ignorant of the matters that

Tacitus later described about the Fire of 64 and the plight of the Christians in Rome at the time.

Josephus writes as a professional historian, and on this score, his presumed or supposed ignorance cannot be taken simply at face value. After all, much of what he wrote about the history of the Adiabene royals he did not gain from personal experience. He derived some of this material from his research into certain sources. Jacob Neusner and others have tried to point out what some of those sources might be. Josephus could just as easily have discovered what other things happened during the famine, a famine that he lived through himself. So not inquiring about anything else and then claiming ignorance does not help his own standing as a historian. If he considered it all irrelevant, that too was a choice. But on that score he leaves himself liable to the same charge that he levels against other historians for their silences. Besides, if he was so interested in stories of conversion to Jewish ways and customs, then the early Christian movement in Jerusalem, the rest of Judaea, Galilee, and elsewhere in the greater Diaspora presented the most interesting current case study. Even if he considered them an aberration, why did he stop there, when he found other groups within Jewish life, like the Essenes, worthy of note? In every way he seems to have decided that the Christian Jews did not belong in the archives of Jewish history.

The *Didache*, the God of David, and the Jewish Archives of the First Century

Unlike the *Chronicle of Arbela* which postdates Josephus by several centuries and provides a different ending to the story of Adiabene from the one Josephus celebrated, there is another source that attests to the early Christian movement that is closer to Josephus still, and offers commentary about Christian Jews. Because it is not found in the New Testament, it stands as an extracanonical witness to the early Christian movement. It is the work called the *Didache*. It represents unimpeachable testimony of what some of the earliest Christians actually looked like, over and against what they are often imagined to have been. In what follows I shall discuss the *Didache* on its own terms and also in relation to Paul's Letter to the Galatians before offering some comments about how it frames, contextualizes, and exposes Josephus's silences.

But before I do that, we need to recall Josephus's words about Hieronymus the historian who spent some time in Syria, according to Josephus, and yet managed to leave out the Jews or Judaeans from his history. Notice that in Josephus's words, being in Syria was practically like being in Judaea. It meant living just across the border, so to speak, from Judaea, or living practically within our borders, as Josephus put it. For the moment, and for the sake of the argument, this means that Josephus is just as guilty about the Christians behind the *Didache* as Hieronymus was about the Judaeans, if the *Didache* emerged out of a Syrian context, as some scholars have surmised. It would mean that Josephus as a Judaean must have known something about the communities behind the *Didache*. I shall not press the point any further, although a similar case could be made about the earliest Christians in Damascus and Antioch who are featured in Paul's writings.

Originally composed in Greek, the complete text of the *Didache* or The Lord's Teaching to the Gentiles/Nations by the Twelve Apostles was discovered in a manuscript in Constantinople (Istanbul) in 1873 by Philotheos Bryennios, Archbishop of Nicomedia. He published his findings in 1883. The manuscript, now called H54, is dated to 1056. Some version or form of it is mentioned by Eusebius of Caesarea (c. 260 to c. 339 CE) in his *Ecclesiastical History* at 3.25.4. Athanasius of Alexandria also mentions it in his famous *Festal Letter* (397 CE) where he gives his list of books for the New Testament canon. There he points out that the *Didache* and the *Shepherd of Hermas* are not canonical. Jerome mentions in his *De viris Illustribus* (c. 392 CE) that both the *Didache* and the *Shepherd of Hermas* are read and useful but are not canonical. So, it is possible that the *Didache* or some version of it was widely read up through the time of Eusebius of Caesarea, and even as late as Jerome. But by the fifth century, it clearly did not have the influence it might have had before. By then the leading theologians of the church had become more conscious of a clearly defined list of texts that they considered canonical; at the same time, they spoke in ways as to suggest that some texts, though excluded from the list, could be used in the church to good effect.

One of the great advantages of the *Didache* is that it attests to a group of churches within a wider collective or community, perhaps in a few towns and villages spread over an area large enough to envisage traveling preachers and teachers who moved from church to church. The *Didache* captures the community's sense of itself, its mores, its fundamental ritual of initiation—baptism—and presents a somewhat coherent view of its way of life. It is not strictly a manual of discipline, but it speaks about discipline. It is not strictly a liturgical text, but it speaks about the liturgy or things that are liturgical, or rather we should say that it speaks about rituals: of food, of baptism, of eating, of comportment, and so on.

It is written also not from the standpoint of an individual addressing another individual or someone's specific problem or controversy. There may be controversies behind some of the topics it discusses, especially when it speaks about the so-called hypocrites in relation to fasting. But the tone is one of outlining a plan for good conduct. So it is not incidental that it begins with the "Two Ways," much like the Book of Proverbs does in its early chapters. It sets forth a choice between good and evil and situates that choice in relation to "the gospel of the Lord," which is first mentioned in chapter 8 immediately after speaking of the hypocrites, and serves as an introduction to a version of the Lord's Prayer (8.2–3).

Much of chapters 1–4, which ends with the statement, "this is the path of life," could come out of the Old Testament or Hebrew Scriptures. The only distinctive difference is the mention in 4.1–2: "for where the Lord is discussed, there the Lord himself is. Everyday seek out the company of the saints, that you may find comfort in their words." Then in 4.3 it says: "Do not create a schism but bring peace to those who are at odds."

The piece about not creating a schism sounds like the situation described in First Corinthians. Basically, once the writer completes the Two Ways (1.1–5.2), he turns to elaborate on the community's ways: baptism, fasts, communal meal, thanksgiving (eucharist). There is a prayer at chapter 10 and then he deals with leadership, authority, and charismatic gifts in discussing the prophets and itinerants (11–13). He discusses the Lord's Day in chapter 14 and then the election of bishops and deacons in chapter 15. Chapter 16 sums up. Here he talks about human creation, sin, the world-deceiver, signs of the end, and a rupture or resurrection of the death at the sound of a trumpet. Chapter 16 is a kind of apocalypse.

However disparate the themes may appear, there is coherence in how the manual is composed. It provides an outline or framework of a community's understanding of itself and its basic sensibilities. Significantly, it presents a social reality, a shared understanding, and is also very clear about its boundaries. It speaks about what to avoid, that is, "what not to do," what to practice, and distinguishes between the haters of the truth (5.2), whom it mentions alongside persecutors of the good and those who love "the lie" in contradistinction to those who love the truth. There is little ambiguity when it speaks about the differences between the way of life and the way of death, the Two Ways. However, significantly, it demonstrates a good deal of forbearance toward differences in certain forms of practice when it discusses something like baptism. It is not particularly strict about one specific mode of baptism and does not insist that only one way of doing it is efficacious. Rather it maintains that if certain basic elements are present, then some variations are inconsequential (chapter 7).

One of its most distinguishing features relates to its similarities or differences from Matthew 6:9–13, which contains the canonical version of the Lord's Prayer. The *Didache* has its own version that is very similar to the version found in the Gospel of Matthew. In the way it appears in the *Didache*, the Lord's Prayer has to be reckoned one of its most important characteristics. It can be compared in this respect to the Shema: "Hear O Israel, the Lord your God is One; and you shall love the lord you God, with your heart, your soul and your mind." If the Shema is the lodestone of Hebrew religion, then the Lord's Prayer is the charter for Christians. So the fact that a version of it is present in the *Didache* is about all one needs to know about how clearly and self-consciously this community understood itself to be Christian, how they differentiated themselves from everyone else, and how the *Didache* stands in relation to the rest of the New Testament writings and to Jewish life in the first century.

It begins with a phrase about not being "like the hypocrites," namely those who fast on Monday and Thursday.

> But you should fast on Wednesday and Friday. Nor should you pray like the hypocrites, but as the Lord commanded in his gospel, you should pray as follows: "Our Father in heaven, may your name be kept holy; may your kingdom come, may your will be done on earth as in heaven. Give us today our daily bread. And forgive us our debt, as we forgive our debtors. And do not bring us into temptation but deliver us from the Evil One. For the power and the glory are yours forever." Pray like this three times a day.[38]

It is here too that the *Didache* makes its first mention of "the gospel," leaving little doubt that the particular prayer is one that the Lord had commanded. The *Didache* also anticipates and precludes an interesting theme, namely whether the Gnostic writings that emerged especially in the second century should be accorded the kind of valence that so many scholars and historians grant them. What do I mean? If the *Didache* is so clearheaded about what the gospel is, what the Two Ways are, what the basic rites of initiation and fellowship are, then it prompts the following question: From where do the Gnostic writers of the second century get the notion that they somehow have the "secret gospel" of Jesus? As far as the *Didache* is concerned there is nothing secret about this gospel. It is quite clear that the gospel is the way of life, and it demands the kind of righteousness that they are trying to live out.

The *Didache* can easily be outlined this way:

1:1	The Two Ways
1:2–4:14	The Way of Life
5:1–2	The Way of Death (briefly summarized)
6:1–3	Transition
7:1–4	On Baptism
8:1–2	On Fasts
9:1–5	On Eucharist
10:1–4	Prayers after meals. Your attitude toward Food
10:5–6	Prayer for the Church
10:7	Transition / On allowing "the prophets" to hold Eucharist whenever
10:8–11:3	How to Receive Itinerant Preachers, Prophets, etc.

11:4–6	The Dubious Itinerant Preacher
11:7–12	You Have to Test Them
12:	Do Not Be Gullible
13:	Receive Every True Prophet
14:	Lord's Day and Eucharist: What You Should Do
15:1–2	Appoint Bishops and Deacons
15: 3–4	Reprove and Correct One Another
16:	Watch Over Your Life

At 10:7 there is an important transition to the prophets, bishops, and itinerants called apostles. The first thing we should notice is that the apostles mentioned here are apostles in a general sense as compared to the Twelve Apostles mentioned in the title, which is in reference to the original twelve disciples of Jesus. The second thing to notice is that a prophet may also be an itinerant or could be in-house; and third, the bishop is definitely a resident bishop.

The *Didache* gives clear guidelines as to what constitutes acceptable teaching and behavior. First and foremost, the teacher, whether he is prophet, apostle, or bishop (I assume) should be received if and only if the teacher does what has just been described. If not, do not receive them. Verse 11:2 adds that the proper teaching will be for the increase in righteousness and the knowledge of God. The teacher seems to be set apart, sandwiched between what the *Didache* says about the prophet and Eucharist in 10:7 and what it says about the apostles and prophets in 11:3ff. If the traveling apostle is of dubious character, someone who is after money, he is a false prophet. Notice how the *Didache* joins the apostle to the prophet in this section. The point seems to be that the apostle is someone who is itinerant, has some claims to prophetic utterances, and may even evidence ecstatic experiences (11:4–6). The churches have to be on their guard. Again, the standard of what may be wrong with them is what motivates them; what they are demanding from you; what pretenses, etc., whatever you ask in the spirit, if you receive it, you better eat it (11:7–12).

However, there is no paranoia here. As it says in 12:1: "Let everyone who comes in the name of the Lord be received: but when you have tested them . . . ." In other words, do not be gullible, do not be naïve, there are charlatans out there. Beware (12:5). If he will not work, chances are he is a charlatan. This is very good advice, nothing out of the ordinary. The *Didache* admonishes, then encourages its churches to receive every true prophet. The logic is simple. If you apply the test as suggested, the only prophets or itinerant preachers you would end up receiving are the kind who are not likely to be charlatans. Then it recommends that the churches appoint bishops and deacons. Again, some basic requirements are set out: they should not be lovers of money; they should be truthful; and that those who play the roles of prophets and teachers should be approved in their respective churches (15:1–4).

From a doctrinal standpoint, the *Didache*'s approach is simple but not simplistic. It fastens itself to the traditions of the original apostles and of the Lord. The *Didache* not only claims to be the Lord's teaching, it also links the Lord's teaching to the twelve apostles. In the body of the work it makes a further link with a Gospel. For all this, the *Didache* curiously does not make any claim of authorship. It is an anonymous text. However, it is self-assured in its authority as "The Teaching of the Lord by the Twelve Apostles."

How would someone know "who the Lord is," if that person had not heard something about Jesus the Christ? Who would know who the twelve apostles are, if they have no knowledge of any of the written Gospels or some tradition which mentioned that Jesus had twelve disciples who are called apostles? If you do not already know this, the work gives you indications of these things. It makes reference several times to the Lord (5:1, 12; 14:1 and 3); to the child Jesus (10:2), to the Son of God (16.4), etc. It mentions "the Gospel" (8:2; 15:2; 15:3) as well as teachings of the Gospel, namely what the Lord said. It makes reference to the Lord in his Gospel (7.2) when introducing its version of the prayer Jesus taught to his disciples that we know from the canonical Gospels.

So whoever it is who wrote or compiled the *Didache* was clear about one basic fact: there is "a gospel," namely a teaching or proclamation (*euangelion*), to which he appeals. He does not use the phrase "the gospel" in a generic sense but seems to point to a particular work. It could be a written work, in which case its authority is enshrined by its very nature as a written work. Or it could be an oral tradition so specific in its outlines and details as to constitute a singular authoritative source. If so, it would probably have been entrusted to some individuals within the community or communities of the *Didache*. That individual or those individuals would be recognized as the trusted custodian(s) of the tradition. It is even likely that such an oral tradition would have been preserved in different parts, or that different parts of the tradition would be known and entrusted to well-appointed individuals who preserve the respective parts of that tradition; whether sayings, narratives, etc. So even as oral tradition there would be a clear sense of what the authoritative tradition is.

If you already know any of the four canonical Gospels or any others besides them, you can go and check which one it is closest to. As it turns out, the passages in the *Didache* that echo passages from the canonical Gospels are close to the Gospel of Matthew. If the writer has a particular Gospel among all the Gospels we know of, then it is Matthew or a version that lies behind Matthew. Interestingly, he refers to "the Gospel" as if his readers also know exactly what he is talking about.

In this important sense, the *Didache*'s authority is not *sui generis*. It depends on the Gospel (oral or written) known to both the writer (or writers) and the recipients of the teaching. Does it matter, then, if we don't know who wrote it or where it came from? Should anyone be worried about the fact that this could be deemed a forgery? Well, if it is a forgery what is it trying to forge? Nothing really. You could argue that it makes a claim to be speaking for the twelve apostles, so it is pretending to be something that it is not. But examination of the text itself tells us that it makes no such claim. There is nothing pseudonymous about it. It is merely saying something like this: this is the doctrine or teaching that we have received from the Lord through the twelve apostles. It does not insist on its own authority except that it directs the readers/recipients to the Gospel that they already have. The best way to construe the work, then, is as a manifesto or handbook or a summary of the teachings derived from the gospel of Jesus Christ and "the Gospel," which is precisely how it titles itself: The teaching of the Lord by the Twelve Apostles.

It can also be read as a commentary on "the Gospel." In some of its passages it paraphrases "the Gospel" to which it refers and sometimes comes close to quoting it, and along the way it makes some recommendations about certain liturgical practices and issues of church order. It is primarily a moral treatise: how the Christian is supposed to live. Which is why it begins with the basic premise of the "Two Ways." It is highly reminiscent of the language of Proverbs, or even some of the Psalms (and Wisdom Literature), as I have already indicated. There is a long tradition about the "two ways" in Judaism. The Epistle of Barnabas also has the Two Ways. The Two Ways elaborates on a theme that is common in Jewish moral instruction. It is found in some of the Qumran material (Dead Sea Scrolls) and clearly in the teaching of the Sermon on the Mount in the Gospel of Matthew: There is a way that leads to life and another that leads to death. Choose which one you prefer. This goes back even to Deuteronomy, Joshua, etc.

There are other things: In chapter 3 it has the refrain "my child," at different points in the chapter and also at the beginning of chapter 4. This is reminiscent of or similar to First John. It appears to mimic as well the structure of the moral exhortations found in Proverbs. The *Didache* seems very straightforward. It should be a surprise only to someone who does not want to believe that these ordinary Christians knew what they believed and how they interpreted their traditions. There is nothing technical here: no complicated theological argumentation. It is basically "Christianity Made Simple," if you like: there are two ways of life, choose the way that leads to life and avoid the one that leads to death. What could be clearer? It is all the theology they needed, at least as the writer or compiler has it.

The *Didache*'s title prompts an important question, however. If the *Didache* is the teaching of the twelve apostles, does that mean it is indifferent to the authority of Paul? After all, Paul was not one of the twelve disciples/apostles. Is this, then, a deliberate attempt to sidestep or challenge Paul's authority? If so, is it not ignoring Paul and his mission to the Gentiles in a way similar to Josephus's silence about Paul and the early Christian movement? Not exactly: for whereas Josephus has almost nothing to say about the existence of the Christian movement as such within Judaism or among the Gentiles, the *Didache* bears witness to a collection of churches with traveling teachers, appointed leaders, a social world, and institutionalized life with well-established rituals of initiation and fraternity.

What then of Paul and the "twelve apostles?" One possibility is that the work reflects a context that is unaware of Paul's mission to the Gentiles. At the same time, it is conscious or perhaps even anxious about itinerant preachers and prophets. It clearly distinguishes the apostles about whom it is anxious from the apostles of the Lord whose teaching it is proclaiming. So perhaps, it simply reflects a period in the history of the early Christian movement prior to Paul's established role in the movement, before he becomes the undisputed presence throughout Asia Minor, Macedonia, Achaea, and eventually Rome, to use just the testimony of his seven so-called authentic letters (at this point): First Thessalonians, Galatians, First and Second Corinthians, Romans, Philippians, and Philemon.

The particular historical moment from which it emerges may also explain other features of the *Didache*. There is mention of one written Gospel. There is not much said about the church among the Gentiles, even though the common translation of the title refers to the Lord's "teaching to the Gentiles" by the twelve apostles. The word used there should be translated more appropriately as "to the nations." The same word is used in 1:3. But there is much about distinguishing themselves from the so-called hypocrites who fast on Monday and Thursday (the standard days for fasting in the Jewish tradition). There is also an interesting reference to the God of David (10:6). Everything seems to speak of a milieu of Christian Jews who are keen to distinguish themselves from non-Christian Jews. By speaking of the God of David, the writer of the *Didache* makes a specific claim to Jewishness. That claim to Jewishness rests on an even more fundamental claim that the Christian Jews of the *Didache*, or followers of the Lord, are the followers of the Way of Life (in contradistinction to) the Way of Death that has been spoken about in Judaism for centuries. The work is a Christian Jewish text that also reflects on intra-Jewish debates without much reference to Gentiles as such.[39]

The question of the *Didache*'s relationship or connection with Paul will not go away, though. Must we take the reference to the twelve apostles in the title as literally as I have previously done? Significantly, the very notion of "apostle" that one finds in the body of the text is much broader that what the title suggests. In fact, other than in the title, the text itself makes no reference to the twelve apostles. It alludes to them, however, when it makes use of the phrase, "as the Lord commanded," and similar expressions. Fundamentally, it is the twelve apostles who were entrusted with what the Lord commanded. Within the body of the text itself it speaks about apostles in a way as to describe them as contemporaries. It seems to assume the notion of an *apostolos* as someone sent to deliver or carry or communicate a message. But it does not even say that they ought to have been sent by other churches or who exactly makes them apostles. It also does not distinguish them from teachers as such. But it seems to preserve a distinction between itinerants who may be prophets, apostles, or teachers and teachers and prophets who are not itinerant.

> And so welcome anyone who comes and teaches you everything above. But if the teacher should himself turn away and teach something different, undermining these things, do not listen to him. But if his teaching brings righteousness and the knowledge of the Lord, then welcome him in the Lord. But act towards the apostles and prophets as the gospel decrees. Let every apostle who comes to you be welcomed as the Lord. But he should not remain more than a day. If he must, he must stay one more. But if he stays three days, he is a false prophet. When an apostle leaves he should take nothing except bread, until he arrives at his night's lodging. If he asks for money, he is a false prophet.[40]

Incidentally, by the last line it has conflated prophet and apostle. It cannot be emphasized enough what the practice of this part of the *Didache* could do to save the church intolerable hardship and misery. That insouciant juxtaposition: money and/or prophecy has contemporary resonance. It is always contemporary.

The remainder of chapter 11, then, lays out what a false prophet might look like. Again the connection with money is ever present, but it is left to the last line. The overarching theme is the way the person conducts himself or herself. This picks up on the motifs in the Two Ways that opens the *Didache* and underlines how essential it is to discern the way of life in the life of a supposed prophet. Even more importantly, the pattern of the prophet's conduct is to be like the Lord's.

> [7] Do not test or condemn a prophet for speaking in the Spirit. For every sin will be forgiven, but not this sin. [8] Not everyone who speaks in the Spirit is a prophet, but only one who conducts himself like the Lord. Thus the false prophet and the [real/true] prophet will both be known by their conduct. [9] No prophet who orders a meal in the Spirit eats of it; if he does, he is a false prophet. [10] Every prophet who teaches the truth but does not do what he himself teaches is a false prophet. [11] You are not to condemn any prophet who has been approved as true, and who acts on behalf of the earthly mystery of the church, even if he does not teach others to do what he himself does,

since he has his judgment from God. For even the ancient prophets behaved in this way. [12] Do not listen to anyone who says in the Spirit, "Give me money" (or something else). But if he tells you to give to others who are in need, let no one judge him.[41]

The passage just quoted seems riddled with contradiction or at least confusion. Do not test (*peiradzein*) or judge (*diakrinein*) a prophet who speaks in the Spirit; do not condemn any prophet who is approved; but let no one judge if a prophet asks for money for those in need, which presumes that one may judge under different circumstances.

Verse 11 seems particularly at odds with everything else that precedes. It seems to suggest that a prophet might teach others to do differently than he does, ostensibly as a living contradiction of what he teaches. If so, he appears to be a false prophet, according to the previous passage. This seems a blatant contradiction or a reversal of the preceding.[42] The contradiction, however, looks less certain if we take seriously the qualifier: "a prophet who has been approved and is true." From this standpoint, "he who does not teach others to do what he himself does" is not to be equated with "he who teaches the truth but does not do it himself."

If we go back to the beginning of the section as to why one should not test or judge a prophet who speaks in the Spirit, a more fundamental consideration is in view, namely, that the prophet will reveal by his behavior whether he is true or false; and if he is already approved, then his judgment will come from God. Whatever the case, the truth about the prophet will be revealed by how the prophet behaves. At the end, *Didache* 11.12 concludes: "Do not listen to anyone who says in the Spirit, 'Give me money' (or something else). But if he tells you to give to others who are in need, let no one judge him." So, clearly, any prophet speaking in the Spirit and claiming that the Spirit demands money for himself can be judged a false prophet.

Some of this discourse is comparable to what obtains in Paul's discussion about prophets false and true in First and Second Corinthians. It could also be related to itinerants mentioned in the Letter to the Galatians. In other words, the social world attested to by these passages is not at all different from the social worlds described in Paul's so-called authentic letters. It does not establish any sort of dependence, of course. However, it does establish similar themes and concerns, and perhaps controversies. In both Paul's contexts and in the *Didache*, there is an emphasis on discernment: dealing with traveling teachers, prophets, and apostles, some of whom it turns out are opponents of Paul and of the teaching of the churches of the *Didache*.

Some of the opponents are referred to as hypocrites in both Paul's letters (in Galatians, for example) and in the *Didache*. In the case of the latter it seems somewhat puzzling. For if they are non-Christian Jews, why would they be hypocrites if they are doing what Jews have always done? In other words, a Jewish person who fasts on Monday and Thursday is not doing anything hypocritical. If, on the other hand, that Jewish person says that he or she is a Christian, but they will fast on Monday and Thursday, then the charge of hypocrisy is intelligible, but not by a whole lot, unless the insistence on fasting on those two days is a mark of differentiation intended to set them apart from other Christians, both Jew and Gentile.

Paul frames part of the argument in the Letter to the Galatians in these terms. Paul speaks of his opponents or those of the circumcision as hypocrites, and he applies the word to Cephas (Peter, the Apostle) for believing one thing and doing something else when he was in Antioch. So, while the *Didache* makes no reference to Paul and appears indifferent to the apostle to the Gentiles, it reflects at the very least the tensions underlying Paul's arguments in Galatians 2. This may also lend support to those scholars, and there are many, who guess that the *Didache* might have originated in Antioch in Syria, even if they do not appeal to the language about hypocrisy. The Antioch origin is not impossible, but we have almost no documentary evidence for it.

The social world of the *Didache* resembles the social world of Paul, even if Paul is not named or was not one of the original twelve disciples of Jesus. The particular references to "hypocrites" and "dogs" call attention to this. Our first inclination is to see the reference to hypocrites as relating to the Gospels where Jesus speaks of some of his fellow Jews as hypocrites, specifically referencing what the hypocrites do in the synagogue and when they fast (Matthew 6:2, 5, 16). *Didache* 9.5 then alludes to Matthew 7:6 when it insists that the Lord says: do not give holy things to dogs. Matthew 7:5 also refers to the one who judges without having first learned to judge clearly (or see clearly) as a hypocrite. So the allusion to Matthew 7:6 cannot be overstated. It is about those who are unbelieving within the house of Israel: do not give what is holy to dogs, do not cast pearls before swine.

To compare one's fellow Jews to dogs (*kysin*) is one thing, no matter how disparaging it may be, to compare them to swine (*choirōn*) is to raise the level of derisiveness and condemnation to another level. It is jarring and deeply offensive, since Jews are not to have any contact with swine. The *Didache* does not repeat the saying about swine. Whether this is intentional or not cannot be determined, though it might just be the case that it has been influenced by Matthew 15:26 where Jesus tells the Syro-Phoenician woman that it is not right to give the bread of the children to their little dogs (*kynariois*).

The clear relationship between the *Didache* and traditions about Jesus gives the impression that it may have nothing to do with Paul. It is easy, then, to miss the fact that the reference to the hypocrites and to the dogs could be a reference to Jewish malcontents or Judaizers, as I have already intimated. Paul uses one term in Galatians and the other in Philippians, while speaking of Judaizers. In Galatians, he refers to Peter's hypocrisy (*hypokrisei*) and the other fellow Jews who were caught up in it. Then in Philippians he refers to those of the "false" circumcision, as dogs (*kunas*). I say "false" circumcision because Paul implies it rather than states it. Paul's juxtaposition of *hē peritomē* (the circumcision) and *tēn katatomēn* (the mutilation) implies that the former is the true circumcision, to which Paul belongs, while the latter is the false circumcision. The rest of Philippians 3:3–11 spells it out. The "dogs" put confidence in the flesh (v. 4), just as Paul used to do as a Pharisee who was blameless with respect to a righteousness based on the law; whereas Paul, now, and his fellow believers, put confidence and glory in Christ Jesus.

In the *Didache* itself the terms "hypocrites" and "dogs" are deployed with respect to those who are baptized and those who are not baptized: that is, baptized followers of Jesus and everyone else. If the concern is with other Jews, then it is about intra-Jewish differences, since there is a concern also about fasting at the proper time. If, on the other hand, the concern is with non-Jews or other Gentiles, then it might refer to Gentiles. However, there is no indication that it has Gentiles in view. The work reads as primarily Jewish in context. So, "do not give it to dogs," alludes to Paul as well as the traditions behind the Gospels not because Gentiles are in view, but rather Jewish unbelievers; the ones who cannot be baptized because they do not believe in Jesus as Messiah; and other Jews who may be believers but who find the presence of Gentiles problematic or intolerable.

The *Didache* assumes some knowledge of the inclusion or exclusion of Gentiles, which cannot be far from the surface because it mentions the sacrifices of the Gentiles. It speaks of these sacrifices not as something distant or alien to its community or to its world, but as essentially part of its world. The baptized from the Nations participate in the Eucharist whereas the nonbaptized and nonbelievers among fellow Jews are excluded. This is Paul's world; or the world evoked by his letters.

Even the style of presentation of its moral injunctions and precepts, which seem contradictory to some interpreters—for example, about the true and false prophets—can be found in Paul's letters. I do not mean to suggest that the *Didache* is necessarily borrowing from Paul's letters, only that the way of arguing about *paraenesis*, moral instruction, shares certain characteristics with Paul. There is a pattern of elaboration that is consistent with certain forms of moral instruction that Paul also employs.

Do not eat meat sacrificed to idols, Paul says. That is the general rule. Then he adds, but if you are strong and it will not matter to your faith, you can eat meat sacrificed to idols. On the other hand, if it will be a cause for a weak or weaker brother stumbling (Romans 14:13), then please do not do it. In Alan Garrow's way of assessing the coherence of a text and the different hands at work in a text, Paul could not be the one saying all these three things one after the other (Romans 14:6 and 21). Then to end at Romans 14:22 with

"Blessed is the man who does not condemn himself [who is not condemned] by what he approves." Something similar is expressed in First Corinthians 10:23ff: Everything is permissible but not everything is beneficial. And then at 10:28 he instructs that one should act for the sake of the other man's conscience. Earlier in First Corinthians 7 Paul had done something like this regarding marriage:

7:1:	It is good for a man not to marry.
7:2:	But: since there is so much immorality, each man should have his own wife.
7:8:	Now: to the unmarried and widows: it is good to stay unmarried.
7:10:	To the married this command.
7:12:	To the rest I say this:
7:12ff:	About being unequally yoked:
7:25:	Now about virgins
7:23:	I would like you to be free from concern as I am
7:24–40:	Then rest on how to conduct one's self.

Interestingly chapter 8 is about food sacrificed to idols.

8:4:	We know that idols are nothing.
8:7:	But not everyone knows this, so we must be sensitive.
8:9–13:	Be careful your freedom is not occasion for someone else's fall: a stumbling block for the weak.

In Alan Garrow's way of reading things, the writer (Paul) is contradicting himself. Verse 7:1 contradicts 7:2; 7:8 contradicts what precedes it. Similarly, 8:4 is in tension with 8:7 and 8:9–13 defers to the weak as if in opposition to one's freedom. Or it cannot be the same person who is giving these different injunctions.[43]

To sum up: The *Didache* is self-conscious about what it is to be "a Christian" (*christianos*). In using the word *christianos*, it also evokes the social world described in the early chapters of Acts, where the author writes that the followers of Jesus were first called "Christians" (*Christianoi*) in Antioch (Acts 11:26). At one important point in the text the *Didache* speaks about determining how "a Christian" (*christianos*) who is passing through may live among you (12.4). It presumes that such "a Christian" is a person who fits the description of the kind of belief and practice that has been described in the preceding sections of the *Didache*. This self-consciousness about "being Christian" is a feature that can easily be overlooked. But it should not be underestimated. It is inextricably linked to the gospel of Jesus through the God of David (10.6). That link between the gospel of Jesus Christ and the God of David anticipates and precludes virtually every claim to possessing the true and secret gospel of Jesus made in the varieties of Gnosticisms found in texts of Jewish, Christian, or Babylonian provenance in the second century.

I end here with a section of the *Didache* that contains one of its references to the God of David, a section that is also probably the most redolent with themes found in Paul's letters to the Corinthians. It concerns table fellowship, Eucharistic meals, and Christian self-definition. To appreciate its significance, it is a section that begins with the version of the Lord's Prayer in 8.2–3 and ends with another prayer in 10.1–7. I quote it in full, minus the version of the Lord's Prayer that I have previously quoted:

> And with respect to the thanksgiving meal (eucharist), you shall give thanks as follows. First, with respect to the cup: "We give thanks, our Father, for the holy vine of David, your child, which you made known to us through Jesus your child. To you be the glory forever." And with respect to the fragment of bread: "We give thanks, our Father, for the life and knowledge that you made known to us through Jesus your child. To you be the glory forever." As this fragment of bread was gathered together from upon the mountains and was gathered to become one, so may your church be gathered together from the ends of the earth into your kingdom. For the glory and the power are yours through Jesus Christ forever. But let no one drink from your thanksgiving meal (Eucharistic meal) unless they have been baptized in the name of the Lord. For also the Lord has said about this, "Do not give what is holy to the dogs." And when you have had enough to eat, you should give thanks as follows: "We give you thanks, holy Father, for your holy name which you have made reside in our hearts, and for the knowledge, faith, and immortality that you made known to us through Jesus your child. To you be the glory forever. You, O Master Almighty, created all things for the sake of your name, and gave both food and drink to humans for their refreshment, that they might give you thanks. And you graciously provided us with spiritual food and drink, and eternal life through your child. Above all we thank you because you are powerful. To you be the glory forever. Remember your church, O Lord; save it from all evil, and perfect it in your love. And gather it from the four winds into your kingdom, which you prepared for it. For yours is the power and the glory forever. May grace come and this world pass away. Hosanna to the God of David. If anyone is holy, let him come; if anyone is not, let him repent. Maranatha! Amen."[44]

The reference to gathering the church from the four winds into the Lord's kingdom suggests that the communities behind the *Didache* do not conceive themselves parochially or provincially. The church whose purity they pray for, the church of the God of David, is universal. "If anyone is holy, let him come; if anyone is not, let him repent."

There is a sense here of a universal call to all and sundry. This ameliorates somewhat the polemical edge of its criticism of the "hypocrites," and stands in contrast to the Epistle of Barnabas with whom it shares the appropriation of the traditions linked to the Two Ways. Whereas the *Didache* has the Two Ways at the beginning, the Epistle of Barnabas has a portion of the Two Ways at the end. The Epistle of Barnabas is very direct in its criticism of non-Christian Jews and is far more caustic than the *Didache*. So the use of the Two Ways by both texts, the mention of the destruction of the Temple in Barnabas (16:1–4), but no reference to it in the *Didache*, and the general tone of Barnabas's criticism, give reasons to believe the *Didache* was written before the Jewish War.

The Epistle of Barnabas also expresses a wish that those who destroyed the Temple would rebuild it, which many scholars take to be a reference to Jewish hopes for rebuilding the temple until Emperor Hadrian built a shrine over the site (132–134 CE). Interestingly, some of the same scholars who accept the mention of the destruction of the Temple as clear indication that the Epistle of Barnabas was written after 70 CE somehow do not accept the absence of any reference to that event in the *Didache* as evidence that it was written before it, even though it is accepted by some of the same scholars that the *Didache* bears witness to traditions before 70 CE.

Barnabas mentions the destruction of the Temple, so it is not difficult to say that it was written after 70 CE. Similarly, a work like 4 Ezra also mentions the destruction of the Temple and indicates that it was written thirty years after that event. 2 Baruch, like 4 Ezra, also presumes the destruction of the Temple. Certainly, Josephus's *Jewish War* contains a description of the event. His autobiography or *Life* mentions the destruction of Jerusalem, as it must since Josephus's conduct in Galilee during the War takes up much of the *Life*. He does not, however, revisit the story in the *Antiquities*, which ends before the conflagration of the War against the Romans. He assumes that his readers know that event, and so he adds in the last paragraph in the *Antiquities* a note about possibly updating his material with another book on the subject. Curiously, his *Against Apion*, his last extant work, does not mention it, but speaks of the sacrifices in the Temple in the historical present as if the Temple still exists, even though every one of his readers would have known that not to be the case. The upshot of this is that what Josephus presumes as common knowledge among his audience determines whether Josephus mentions or does not mention the destruction of the Temple in the works he wrote after his *Jewish War*, which contained a description of the event.

When a work like the *Didache* makes no reference or allusion to the destruction of the Temple, one might be tempted to think that it is indifferent to the event, especially if it is also assumed that it was written after 70 CE. But that may not be the case. Its reference to the sacrifices of the Gentiles and to the Eucharist as sacrifice clearly implies that the Eucharistic sacrifice supersedes every other sacrifice. The fact that it makes the claim without invoking the destruction of the Temple may be the surest indication that it was written or compiled before the destruction of the Temple. Hence the extra importance of *Didache* 14, the section devoted to the Eucharist, where it combines material from Malachi 1:11 and 1:14b (*Didache* 14.3). The *Didache*, however, states that sacrifices be offered or are offered "in every place and at every time" by the Gentiles; whereas both the Septuagint, which it appears to be quoting, and the Hebrew of the Masoretic Text have it that sacrifices be offered or are offered "in every place" by the Gentiles (Nations). They do not have "every time." Why does this make any difference?

There is a possible allusion to a gospel tradition going back to John 4: Jesus's encounter with the Samaritan woman, where the woman says to Jesus that her people go to Mount Gerizim and not to Jerusalem; to which Jesus responds that a time is coming when people will worship God in spirit and in truth, and will not need to go to Jerusalem to worship. Admittedly, Jesus does not speak about offering sacrifice (4:19–24). However, offering sacrifice was the most characteristic element of worshipping in Jerusalem: the fact that one could offer sacrifices in the Temple. If the Nations can and should offer sacrifice to God wherever they are, as Malachi 1 states, then they do not need to go/come to Jerusalem. Not even at the times stipulated that one should go to Jerusalem to offer sacrifice. The *Didache* takes it a step further by saying that they can offer sacrifices at any time. If the Temple had been destroyed, this would have been the place to underscore the event. But the *Didache* makes no such attempt or allusion.

If the *Didache* was written after the Jewish War of 66–70, it probably would have reflected this too in its criticism of "the hypocrites," which is why it makes the most historical sense to believe that it was written no later than the year 66 CE. How much earlier than 66 CE is not that easy to determine. Whatever the case, everything we read about the *Didache*'s understanding of the role of apostles, teachers, and prophets suggests a very early conception of these functions or offices in the church; even the encouragement for the churches to appoint bishops indicates that it was not the norm, or that the idea had only recently begun to take hold. Most probably, however, the *Didache* reflects a historical moment not very far from the original apostles or followers of Jesus. If I had to guess, and it is a guess, I would suggest one of two possibilities: first, that the *Didache* emerges out of a community of Christian Jews in Judaea, perhaps not far from Jerusalem; and second, which I consider the more likely possibility, is that the *Didache* emerges out of a collectivity of churches in the towns and villages of Galilee, and may well have been composed long before the murder of James the brother of Jesus in Jerusalem in 62 CE. The idea of having itinerant preachers, prophets, or teachers, who should not be entertained for more than two days, and who circulate among a group of churches, makes Galilee, with its towns and villages, a conducive environment for such a group. Moreover, it is the region from where Jesus of Nazareth and his earliest followers ventured toward other parts of Judaea and Palestine.

It is well now to consider the scholarly consensus on the *Didache* and how this bears on Josephus's historiography and his silences. Robert Kraft, whose work on the Epistle of Barnabas has been central to discussions of the *Didache*, suggests a period between 50 and 66 CE for the earliest strata of material that make up the *Didache*.[45] Speaking of strata and compositional history also means that one has to provide different dates for the different strata. Kraft splits the difference. He believes the earliest sources for the text come from the mid-first century, but the current state of the text is from the mid-second century. Kraft also follows the German tradition of scholarship that the work came from Egypt. What he and others have going for them is that the text has a number of traditions juxtaposed, so that one can postulate that there are at least two or three layers in the way the text is put together. It is a compendium. But to say that it gives the impression of a layered text does not in and of itself provide the warrants or parameters for determining what may have been original and what was added later on; and still less in what sequence the supposed additions came. So the question as to what may have been added and at what stage is not trivial. Interesting, Alan Garrow's ingenious attempts at solving the problem of the redaction of the *Didache* eschews any questions about just when all those redactions took place. Garrow completely sidesteps the question of the dating of the work. Yet this is not irrelevant to his project and his claims, especially because there is virtually no manuscript evidence to support any of the stages that he claims in the redactional or compositional process.

What cannot be disputed is that the earliest layer is quite early indeed. The claim that the rest of it comes from the mid-second century is plausible. In which case, it would belong not to the original work but to its later redactors. That would make sense, but what constitutes the substance of the later redaction is nearly impossible to prove. Furthermore, it would not make sense to think that the second-century redactor was the original composer of the work, because by then there was much that would have made its teaching neither novel nor relevant, or even necessary. That is to say, after Ignatius of Antioch, Polycarp of Smyrna, Justin of Flavia Neapolis in Syria Palestine, and others, writing a work like the *Didache* in the middle of the second century would have sounded manifestly odd and out of place, and it would not matter if one were writing in Egypt or Syria.

Nancy Pardee has produced the most recent and up-to-date study of the structure and genre of the *Didache*. It builds on her 2002 doctoral dissertation at the University of Chicago.[46] In the main she follows Kraft's view of the many layers and comes out with four different stages of compositional history. Prudently she does not assign dates to the layers.

Her discussion of the two titles of the work in the manuscript tradition is helpful in pointing out that the use of "Didache" versus "Teaching of the Twelve Apostles" gives different indications as to which was probably the original. But it is not always clear from the few patristic references that they are all referring to the *Didache* as we know it now in the manuscript H54, especially because in some instances there is a clear reference to the Two Ways as a distinct body of work not at all related to the *Didache*. She accords pride of place to Pseudo Cyprian. More importantly, the patristic citations show that the text or some version of it was well known.

Pardee, in setting up her discussion, writes that for most scholars the consensus is that the *Didache* originates from the latter half of the first century or early second. As I have already indicated, the case can be made even more precisely than that, if we take seriously its relationship to the Epistle of Barnabas and its links to the Gospel of Matthew, both undisputed among scholars.

To repeat: The links with Barnabas rest on two factors primarily: First, the use of the Two Ways *logia* in Barnabas and the *Didache*, suggesting that they are mining the same resource; and second, the mention of the destruction of the Temple in Barnabas, which suggests that Barnabas was written after 70 CE. Another set of two factors can be added: first, the highly polemical edge of Barnabas compared to the *Didache*; and second, its constant citation of Old Testament passages in its critique of Judaism. So, while both the *Didache* and Barnabas share a context that is shaped by Jewish-Christian or Christian-Jewish concerns and perhaps controversy, the *Didache* is more sober in its expressions and certainly more self-conscious in simply setting forth instructions for behavior in a community of Christians, who were probably predominantly Jewish.

The links with the Gospel of Matthew put pressure on those determined to put Matthew late in the first century or perhaps even the second century. The *Didache*, if it is not quoting Matthew, is undoubtedly using the same traditions or sources behind Matthew. The uniqueness of its baptismal formula, which only Matthew has, makes it almost certain that it cannot be divorced from the Gospel according to Matthew. For my purposes, it is enough to establish that the earliest layer of the *Didache* belongs in the period between about 50 CE and 66 CE. I use 50 CE only because of Robert Kraft's view. In my own case, I should only like to insist that it belongs in the period before 66 CE, with a lot of emphasis on it being closer to 50 CE than later, given its possible allusion to the Council of Jerusalem mentioned in Acts and alluded to in Galatians. Another way of putting it is to say that it is close to the scenario described by Paul in Galatians as he claims occurred in Antioch, as I have already discussed.

Clayton Jefford of the Westar Institute and the Jesus Seminar offers in his article, "Locating the Didache," another alternative.[47] He mentions, for example, that the baptismal formula is too advanced because it is Trinitarian in its use of Father, Son, and Holy Spirit.[48] This seems quite mistaken. If baptism was the primary form of initiation for the followers of Jesus Christ, the question is what formula did they use? If Matthew 28:19 has the formula with Father, Son, and Holy Spirit, in what sense is that an advanced Trinitarian theological position? Mark 16:15–16 does not have the formula, but it speaks about baptizing those who believe. Luke does not have the formula either. Even Paul does not use that formula, as far as I know. So in every way the use of the formula is unique to Matthew among the canonical New Testament writings. For Paul and the others, it is usually about being baptized into the name of Jesus Christ. That is how Paul speaks in I Corinthians 1, for example. He speaks the same way in Galatians 3. There is nothing that is necessarily theologically advanced in the *Didache*. So to single out the baptismal formula as somehow the evidence of some advanced theological thinking when that formula can be found in Matthew with which it has other affinities is to look for uniqueness where it does not exist. Much of this presumes that so-called "advanced theological thinking" belongs to the second century.

If the relevance of the preceding discussion to Josephus's silences about Paul and Christian Jews still remains unclear, let me make it very explicit. The *Didache*'s discussion of fasting, first at 7.4 in relation to preparations for baptism, and later in connection with its version of the Lord's Prayer in *Didache* 8.1–3, document a Christian Jewish presence in a world to which Josephus was not likely a stranger: Judaea, Galilee, and perhaps Syria. The existence and viability of such a group of Christians shines a spotlight on Josephus's exclusion of Paul and other Christian Jews from the archives of Jewish life in the first century. It does this almost unwittingly and in the most unusual way.

When it mentions fasting, opting for Wednesday and Friday over and against Monday and Thursday, the *Didache* joins itself to a Jewish debate going as far back as the Book of Jubilees 6:23–28 (second century BCE), which elaborates with some seriousness how important it is to keep the proper feast days and festivals. The *Didache*, in its reference to fasting and the particular days on which to do it, joins itself to the contemporary debates represented in the Gospel of Matthew, and most significantly, the exuberance of that debate within rabbinic Judaism about the proper days for fasting. While the *Didache* does not provide an explanation for the position it adopts, it makes clear that its view opposes the Scribes and the Pharisees, when it follows this polemic almost immediately with its version of the Lord's Prayer.

The *Didache* makes patent, then, that it belongs to a group of Jews who fast on Wednesdays and Fridays, and who also have a unique creed, or rather, a special prayer that is both like and unlike other prayers previously said among the Jews of the first century. They learned this prayer from their Lord and master, Jesus Christ, the servant of David (*Didache* 9). They are not like most of their Jewish compatriots who do not pray like they do.

The *Didache* inscribes itself into Jewish history of the first century by picking a side in the intra-Jewish debate between Pharisees and non-Pharisees on the proper days for fasting. It interposes itself into contemporary Judaism by opting for the anti-Pharisaical position (and later Rabbinic position): the proper days to fast are Wednesday and Friday. In doing so, it makes a claim for the followers of Jesus as authentically Jewish and Christian and part of the fabric of first-century Judaism. Its use of the Two Ways and other language about Jesus as the servant of David confirm this. It thus makes Josephus's silences about the Christian Jews all the more curious. Without the testimony of Paul and the other writings of the canonical New Testament, the *Didache* puts paid to Josephus's deliberate acts of erasing Christian Jews out of Jewish life in the first century. The *Didache*, together with Paul's testimony in his letters, demands that we read the various sects or schools within first century Jewish life not as Josephus would have us read it, but with Paul and the communities behind the *Didache*, who also identified themselves as fully Jewish and fully Christian.[49] The *Didache* takes it for granted that anyone who believes the gospel that Jesus is the Messiah stands in good stead and will live truly as a *Christianos* (12.4).

The list of Josephus's silences that I have discussed in the pages preceding, each on its own, constitutes an important omission on Josephus's part.

1. No mention of what the early Christians in Rome endured under Nero; but Suetonius does.
2. No mention of the Fire of July 64 in Rome; but Pliny the Elder, Tacitus, and Suetonius do.
3. No mention of the *Transtiberim* (the district where the Jewish Quarter in Rome was located); but Philo of Alexandria and others do.
4. No mention of the Christian Jews in the first century; but Tacitus alludes to them; so too the *Didache* and the New Testament writings.
5. No mention of conversion of Gentiles and Diaspora Jews to Christianity; but he describes in detail the conversion of the royal house of Adiabene to Judaism.
6. No description of the early Christian movement and its links to Galilee; but he describes Judas of Galilee and his movement; and he mentions Eleazar of Galilee who was instrumental in the Adiabene conversions.
7. No description of the early Christian movement and their links to John the Baptizer; but he describes John the Baptizer, mentions that he had a great following but does not identify them.

8. Josephus does not provide a portrait of any Christian, Jew or Gentile, in all of his writings although he knows James the brother of Jesus; but he provides portraits of many individuals some major and some minor.
9. No mention of Paul; but his contemporaries among the last of the Herodians, Herod Agrippa II and his sisters Berenice and Drusilla, encountered Paul.

I shall add a tenth: As far as I have been able to ascertain, Josephus never mentions the village of Nazareth in Galilee anywhere in his writings. As commander of Jewish forces in Galilee, Josephus had intimate knowledge of most of the towns and villages of Galilee. He was especially knowledgeable about the larger cities like Gischala, Tiberias, and Sepphoris, the last of which was three and a half miles northwest of Nazareth. No doubt, Nazareth was an insignificant hamlet. Still, it is difficult to believe that in all of his time in Galilee and its environs, Josephus learned or heard nothing about Jesus of Nazareth or the Nazarenes, or traditions associated with Jesus and his band of followers a generation earlier. It is as if Josephus knows nothing of Nazareth in the way the canonical Gospels know nothing about Sepphoris.

Oddly enough, it is the insignificant Nazareth that becomes the basis for describing the followers of Jesus as such, so that in the Rabbinic tradition Christians are described as Nazarenes (*Nozerim*). The designation seems to have been current by the end of the first century. In Acts 24:5, Paul's opponents describe him as a leader of the sect of the Nazarenes (*ton Nazoriaon haireseos*). Josephus must have known this, if he knew of James the brother of Jesus. Josephus the native of Jerusalem and member of a priestly family that could trace Hasmonaeans on both sides of his family must have known that neither James nor Jesus were natives of Jerusalem.

To be sure, in the context of the Jewish War, for Josephus there was no particular need to be interested in an insignificant village like Nazareth. However, if Judas of Gamala and other self-styled messianic leaders were people of interest to Josephus, then one would think that he would have been interested in the followers of Jesus of Nazareth, who were, after all, a more recent phenomenon than Judas of Gamala who died in 6 CE. Certainly, Josephus had reason to discuss Judas of Gamala and his movement, the Zealots, in part because Josephus had to defend Gamala during the early stages of the Jewish War. He gives no hint that he had to defend a tiny village named Nazareth. Or was that too a detail that he suppressed?

Anyway, Josephus's literary and historical elision of Paul and other Christian Jews out of first-century Jewish history is almost clinical. It was also more effective than mockery, for it denied them both a historical witness and a historical past. Learning to read Josephus's silences leads to an even greater sense of Josephus's awareness of so many things Christian about which he chose not to write.

Josephus's own view that being in Syria was tantamount to being in Judaea is critical for assessing his own silences. That he also had extensive knowledge about the Jews of Judaea and Galilee means that he may not have been completely ignorant of what might have taken place in Syria in the years that Paul was involved in activities in Damascus and Antioch in Syria, in Arabia, and in Jerusalem, as Paul recounts in the Letter to the Galatians and elsewhere. Josephus's life in Jerusalem in Judaea and elsewhere in Galilee between his birth and the Jewish War of 66–70 CE provided him all the opportunities he needed to be acquainted with the nascent Christian movement among the Judaeans and Galileans of the first century.

If we insist on his ignorance, then it is a deliberate ignorance, which invariably leads one to think that he might well have wanted to suppress this reality. Josephus himself tells his readers that the belief in resurrection from the dead was one of the most distinctive views of the Pharisees (*Jewish War* 2.8.14 [163]; *Antiquities* 18.1.3 [14]). Consequently, it strains credulity to think that a self-proclaimed member or affiliate of the sect or school of the Pharisees would have taken no interest in a burgeoning movement that proclaimed the idea of resurrection as one of its most central beliefs. Josephus may simply have wanted to give it no representation because he did not think it worthy of its name. But that is precisely where he may have committed the greater fault: his ostracism of Paul and the Christian Jews.

Josephus claimed that Hieronymus the historian was motivated by malice and ill-will in excluding Jews from his universal history when he practically lived among them as a resident of Syria. Would it be too much to ask, following Josephus's own logic, whether he was determined to exclude Paul, for example, because he too was motivated by envy or some disingenuous reason, and not because he was ignorant? Those are his categories and his reasons for why a historian would do such a thing. They may not be ours, but they are surely the motives that Josephus recognized in his time and place. Once again: Did Josephus's "ill-natured disposition," to use his own words, "blind him to the truth" about Paul? Certainly, King Herod Agrippa II and his sisters Berenice and Drusilla were not ignorant of Paul, and so it is likely that Josephus was not ignorant either.

NOTES

1. Josephus, *Jewish War* 6.354 (LCL 210, 281).
2. Steve Mason, Series Preface, *The Brill Josephus Project*.
3. Martin Goodman, *Rome and Jerusalem: The Clash of Ancient Civilizations* (New York: Random House, 2007).
4. Josephus, *Against Apion* 1.213–218 (LCL 186, 1.23).
5. On details about the historical writers named, see John M. G. Barclay, *Flavius Josephus: Translation and Commentary, Volume 10. Against Apion* (Leiden: Brill, 2006), 121–25.
6. Tacitus, *Annals* 15.44 (LCL 322, 283).

7. Suetonius, *Life of Nero* 38.1–3 (LCL 38, 157).
8. Bernard Green, *Christianity in Ancient Rome: The First Three Centuries* (London: Bloomsbury T&T Clark, 2010), 53.
9. Ibid., 53.
10. Steve Mason, *Life of Josephus* (Leiden: Brill, 2001), 9; see also Tacitus, *Annals* 1.41.
11. Mason, *Life of Josephus*, 9n37.
12. Josephus, *Life* 3 (Steve Mason, *Flavius Josephus: Life of Josephus*, 21–27).
13. Philo, *Legatio ad Gaium* 155–158 (LCL, 77–79).
14. Goodman, *Rome and Jerusalem*, 76.
15. See Paul McKechnie, "Judean Embassies and Cases before Roman Emperors, AD 44–66," *Journal of Theological Studies* NS 56.2 (2005), 339–61.
16. Peter Lampe, *Christians at Rome in the First Two Centuries: From Paul to Valentinus* (Minneapolis, MN: Fortress Press, 2003), 47.
17. Ibid., 47.
18. William den Hollander, *Josephus, the Emperors, and the City of Rome: From Hostage to Historian* (Leiden: Brill, 2014), 35–37, reviews the dating of Josephus's first visit to Rome, but does not provide any evidence to support such an idea. Besides, if Poppaea died before Josephus left Rome to return to Judaea, then not mentioning her death and then writing as if she was still alive when he left for Judaea would involve Josephus in a piece of mendacity at the very least.
19. See now Matthew V. Novenson, *The Grammar of Messianism: An Ancient Jewish Political Idiom and Its Users* (Oxford: Oxford University Press, 2017).
20. Louis H. Feldman, *Judaism and Hellenism Reconsidered* (Leiden: Brill, 2006), 388.
21. Arnaldo Momigliano, *Essays on Ancient and Modern Judaism*, edited and with an introduction by Silvia Berti, translated by Maura Masella-Gayley (Chicago: University of Chicago Press, 1994), p. 75.
22. Ibid., 75.
23. Ibid., 77.
24. Charles Freeman, *A New History of Early Christianity* (New Haven: Yale University Press, 2009).
25. Ibid., 64.
26. Ibid., 65.
27. Ibid., 65.
28. Ibid., 65.
29. Ibid., 65.
30. Ibid., 66–71.
31. Ibid., 71.
32. F. B. A. Asiedu, *Paul and His Letters: Thinking with Josephus* (Lanham, MD: Lexington Book/Fortress Academic, 2019).
33. Josephus, *Antiquities* 20.2.3 (LCL 456, 19–21).
34. Josephus, *Antiquities* 20.2.4 (LCL 456, 21–25).
35. Josephus, *Antiquities* 20.2.5 (LCL 456, 27–31).
36. Josephus, *Antiquities* 20.44–46 (LCL 456, 411–13).
37. Jacob Neusner, "The Conversion of Adiabene to Christianity," *Numen* (13:2) 1966, 144–50; reference is to 144.
38. Didache 8.1b–3 (LCL 24, 429–31).
39. On the Jewishness of the Didache, see, for example, Huub van de Sandt and David Flusser (eds.), *The Didache: Its Jewish Sources and Its Place in early Judaism and Christianity* (Assen: Van Gorcum/Minneapolis, MN: Fortress, 2002).
40. Didache 11.1–6 (LCL 24, 435).
41. Didache 11.7–12 (LCL 24, 435–37).
42. Alan Garrow, *The Gospel of Matthew's Dependence on the Didache* (London: Bloomsbury, 2004), 1–155, has pointed to this as among the various contradictions in the text that suggest multiple hands and different stages in the composition or compilation of the *Didache*. He suggests five such stages, where others have only suspected one redactor.

43. This is not the place to engage the full scope of Alan Garrow's arguments about the Didache in his, *The Gospel of Matthew's Dependence on the Didache*. I merely indicate here the inherent problem of overlooking style in moral argumentation and insisting that what appears to be a style of argumentation is about contradictory assertions and must therefore be evidence of different hands at work in a text. The point is that style allows a person to argue with a structure that begins with a prohibition; then with a qualification, and then other exceptions to the prohibition. If this is not permissible in the way a single writer may argue, then there is a lot of moral argumentation in many writers that would be deemed the work of multiple hands.

44. Didache 9.1–10.7 (LCL 24, 431–33).

45. Robert Kraft, *Barnabas and the Didache* (New York: Thomas Nelson & Sons, 1965), 1–10; 46.

46. Nancy Pardee, *The Genre and Development of the Didache: A Text-Linguistic Analysis* (Tübingen: Mohr Siebeck, 2012). For earlier work on traditions of interpretation, see Clayton N. Jefford (ed.), *The Didache in Context: Essays on Its Text, History, and Transmission* (Leiden: Brill, 1995), and Jonathan A. Draper (ed), *The Didache in Modern Research* (Leiden: Brill, 1996). For the most recent discussion see, Jonathan A Draper and Clayton N. Jefford (eds.), *The Didache: A Missing Piece of the Puzzle in Early Christianity* (Atlanta: SBL, 2015).

47. Clayton Jefford, "Locating the Didache," *Forum*, Third Series 3.1 (Spring 2014), 39–68.

48. Ibid., 44.

49. In a slightly different context Daniel Boyarin concedes this point in connection with the dispute about fasting in the *Didache*. See Daniel Boyarin, *The Talmud: A Personal Take: Selected Essays* (Tübingen: Mohr Siebeck, 2017), 240–41fn46.

Chapter Three

Josephus and Martial in Flavian Rome

The Rhetoric of Silence and the Language of Derision

"It was the practice each year," Cicero recounted, "to send gold to Jerusalem on the Jews' account from Italy and all our provinces, but Flaccus issued an edict forbidding its export from Asia. Who is there, gentlemen, who cannot genuinely applaud this measure?" Cicero spoke as if the contributions made by Jews of the Diaspora to the peace of Jerusalem was tantamount to an act of thievery, robbing the Roman Empire of what was legitimately hers. He mentions measures to prevent such exports during his consulship and proceeds to describe the financial commitment of Diaspora Jews to Jerusalem as a superstition, a *superstitio*, even though it was no different in kind from Roman authorities levying taxes and sending the proceeds from the provinces back to Rome. "The Senate strictly forbade the export of gold on a considerable number of previous occasions, notably during my consulship," he asserted in self-congratulation.

> To oppose this outlandish superstition was an act of firmness, and to defy in the public interest the crowd of Jews that on occasion sets our public meetings ablaze was the height of responsibility. But the victorious Gnaeus Pompeius did not touch anything in the Temple after his capture of Jerusalem. In this he showed exceptional good sense—as he has on many other occasions—in that he did not give his detractors any opportunity for gossip in a city so prone to suspicion and slander. I do not believe that the illustrious commander was restrained by the religious susceptibilities of Jews and enemies, but out of respect for public opinion.[1]

Cicero did not disguise how much he cherished the conquest and subjugation of Judaea, though he praised the victorious general Pompey for his restraint in not despoiling the Temple in Jerusalem. That level of respect was particularly noteworthy, since as Cicero was about to underline, Pompey was under no obligation to treat Jewish *religio* with such deference.

"Every city," Cicero insists, "has its own *religio* and we have ours." With this premise, his audience naturally expects to hear him speak in such a way as to make obvious how Roman *religio* is better than every other kind. Cicero does not disappoint. He proceeds, inflecting his comments to press the point about how Jewish *religio* (or *superstitio*) stands in opposition to Rome's ambitions and its imperial might.

> Even when Jerusalem was still standing and the Jews at peace with us, the demands of *religio* of what they hold sacred [*istorum sacrorum*] were incompatible with the majesty of our Empire, the dignity of our name and the institutions of our ancestors; and now that the Jewish nation has shown by armed rebellion what are its feelings for our rule, they are even more so; how dear it was to the immortal gods has been shown by the fact that it has been conquered, farmed out to the tax-collectors and enslaved.[2]

The "immortal gods" have made null and void the Jewish sense of invulnerability and the attendant claims of divine protection. If Jerusalem was/is inviolable, it is only so because of the good-will of the Romans and their victorious general. "Conquered, farmed out to tax collectors and enslaved," Jews (or Judaeans) and Jerusalem can only be objects of scorn and derision. That was Cicero.

A little over a century later, Seneca the Younger, seemed to have his doubts whether indeed the conquered had not achieved an even greater feat than the conquerors: "Meanwhile the customs of this most accursed race [the Jews]," he lamented with great irony, "have achieved such strength that they are now received in all lands: the conquered have given laws to the conquerors." Seneca's scorn comes with equal amounts of admiration and resentment. Just as disturbing to Seneca, and again with noticeable jealousy: "The Jews, however, understand the origins of their rites, whereas the greater part of the Roman people do not know why they perform theirs."[3]

Seneca seemed to be replying to Cicero. But in the aftermath of the War in Judaea and the destruction of Jerusalem and the Temple in 70 CE Seneca's words had little or no resonance. Cicero's much earlier sentiments, written in connection with the actions of Pompey in 63 BCE, were much closer to what Romans felt about Jews, Jerusalem, and Judaea in the last three decades of the first century.

In the previous chapter I discussed Josephus's narrative about the conversion of the Adiabene royals and suggested that some of the themes in that story find parallels in the early Christian movement in the life of Paul and his mission to the Gentiles. I also argued that Josephus's presence in Rome during or after the Fire of July 64 CE meant that he could not have failed to mention this event, what it meant to the residents and citizens of Rome, and what it meant to the earliest Christians in any of his writings at various points when dealing with the Emperor Nero and his excesses without deliberate intent. In this chapter I wish to draw attention to other silences and omissions perhaps even more fundamental. I shall begin with one set linked to promises made by Josephus at the very end of his *Antiquities* about a number of works that he intended to write, promises that he did not keep. Once we have considered this, it will be clear that a number of the silences in Josephus are not simply inadvertent. They are deliberate. I shall then proceed to a discussion of Josephus and the poet Martial, who also lived in Rome for a substantial period of time in the last three decades of the first century. Although the references in Martial's Epigrams to Jews and Jerusalem are very few, they reflect widespread sentiments shared by most Romans at the time. To put it simply: most contemporary Romans felt nothing but contempt for Jews/Judaeans; and yet Joscphus did not address any of his Roman contemporaries directly about their contempt for Jews (or Judaeans). He preferred to address his concerns by engaging the work of the deceased Apion of Alexandria, even though Philo of Alexandria had already responded to Apion's calumnies and hostilities toward Jews. He did all this without acknowledging what Philo had done in responding to Apion or mentioning a single work in Philo's vast corpus; not even his *In Flaccum* or the *Legatio ad Gaium* that dealt with themes Josephus took in his *Against Apion*.

The one and only mention of Philo in Josephus's writings (*Antiquities* 18.25–60) is a reference made in the context of Josephus's description of Philo's role in the Jewish embassy from Alexandria to the Emperor Gaius Caligula that had to contend with Apion, who represented the delegation of Alexandria's Greek/Egyptian populace. The fact that Josephus described Philo as someone who was not "a novice in philosophy" is indication that Josephus knew some or the extent of Philo's writings. Yet Josephus wrote without ever once quoting, alluding to, or referring his readers to anything that Philo had written,[4] notwithstanding the fact that he sometimes seemed to be saying what Philo had already said.[5]

BROKEN PROMISES AND SEMI-AUTOBIOGRAPHY: THE SILENCES OF JOSEPHUS'S *LIFE* (C. 71–94 CE)

At the end of the *Antiquities*, Josephus signs off his great work of sixty thousand verses or lines by promising three additional works that he described as follows:

> Perhaps it will not seem to the public invidious or awkward for me to recount briefly my lineage and the events of my life while there are still persons living who can either disprove or corroborate my statements. With this I shall con-

clude my Antiquities, contained in twenty books with sixty thousand lines. God willing, I shall at some future time compose a running account of the war and of the later events of our history up to the present day, which belongs to the thirteenth year of the reign of Domitian Caesar and to the fifty-sixth of my life. It is also my intention to compose a work in four books on the opinions that we Jews hold concerning God and His essence, as well as concerning the laws, that is, why according to them we are permitted to do some things while we are forbidden to do others.[6]

The first project was to be a brief account of his lineage and the events of his life; the second a "running account of the war and of the later events of our history up to the present day," and the third a work in four books about what "we Jews hold concerning God and His essence," as well as those concerning the laws about what is forbidden and permitted. Some scholars have tended to assimilate the first and the second because we do not have an extant work from Josephus that looks to have fulfilled the promised second, though what has come down to us as his autobiography, the *Life*, has a rather long section devoted to the Jewish War. That construction is a mistake.[7] It should be admitted without much controversy that neither the *Life* nor the *Against Apion*—the two surviving works that Josephus composed after the *Antiquities*—completely fits the description of any one of the three proposed works that Josephus mentioned.

Furthermore, there is no record of a work that fulfills the promise of providing an account of "our history up to the present," nor is there any statement on Josephus's part that he planned to fulfill that promise in the future, beyond what he stated in the *Antiquities*. What is certain is that Josephus did not do what he promised. He passed over it in silence. A quick look at the *Life* also shows that it is disproportionately taken up with a section devoted to about six months of the Jewish War and so does not provide an account of the events of Josephus's life (*ton bion praxeon*) as promised at *Antiquities* 20.266 even though at the end of the *Life* he claims to have covered his entire life (*pantos tou biou*). Something does not add up. Here is an outline of the *Life*:

Life 1–6:	Ancestry
Life 7–12a:	Education
Life 12b:	From Age 18/19 to 26: Emergence into Public Life
	[Omission of any details about his seven years before public life]
Life 13–16:	Age 26: Diplomatic Mission to Rome
Life 17–413:	Six Months in Galilee during the Jewish War

Life 414–422: Late Stages of Jewish War: He Travels between Alexandria and Jerusalem

Life 423–429: Brief Comments about His Life in Rome / Final Testament

[Omission about his life in Rome from 71 to 94 CE, when he finished the *Antiquities*]

Life 430: Epilogue: Claims to Have Recounted His "Entire Life"

From this basic outline it is clear that Josephus excludes from his so-called autobiography the seven years leading up to his mission to Rome and the years of his life in Rome between the end of the Jewish War and the period during which he completed the *Antiquities*.

Let us take the standard view that Josephus finished the *Life* soon after the *Antiquities* in 93/94 CE. If he finished it in 94 CE, then it means the twenty-three years of his life in Rome (71–94 CE) are not covered. He simply does not tell us how he lived in Rome during those twenty-three years. The poet Martial does in some ways give us some clues as to how he lived during his times in Rome from the late 60s to the end of Domitian's reign (a subject to which we shall get to later in the chapter). If we add the seven years that Josephus also omits from his early years in public life in Jerusalem, from year nineteen to twenty-six when he was given the mission to Rome (c. 63 CE), then we have a full thirty years that Josephus simply does not account for.

Here is a fact remarkable in every way no matter how one construes it. In 94 CE, the fifty-seven–year-old Josephus set out to write an autobiography in which he deliberately left out thirty years of his life. That is more than half of his life. We cannot overlook this in our assessments of Josephus's *Life*. We have to take seriously that his silences are just as important as what he actually tells his readers. That is what should be interrogated, especially given the odd shape of what he chose to include. Compare Josephus's silences to some of the autobiographical details we find in the essays of Plutarch, the orations of Dio of Prusa, or even some of the letters of Pliny the Younger, and then you realize how unusual and intriguing are Josephus's silences, and how little he tells us about his life in Rome.

I should add at this point that there is yet another omission at the end of the *Life* that is as peculiar as any there is in Josephus. This has to do with a wife that he mentions in *Jewish War* 5.419, but who somehow is not part of his brief about his marriages and his domestic life at *Life* 414–415 and 426–429. I have discussed this in a different context, but it bears repeating here that such an act of erasure cannot have been unintentional.[8]

What sort of autobiography, then, is Josephus's *Life*? The *Life* makes the following claim about its contents: "These, then, are the things that occurred throughout my entire life, from them let others judge my character as they might wish."⁹ But he had stated earlier in the *Antiquities*: "Perhaps it will not seem to the public invidious or awkward for me to recount briefly my lineage and the events of my life while there are still persons living who can either disprove or corroborate my statements."¹⁰

A simple comparison would suggest that the two statements are not far apart. "The events of my life" from *Antiquities* parallels or is repeated in "the things that occurred throughout my entire life" in the *Life*. But appearances can mislead, as I have already insinuated. For one thing, the story told in the *Life* is not, in spite of the claim, all that occurred in Josephus's entire life. For another thing, the *Life* appears more as a supplement to the *Jewish War* than the *Antiquities*. It supports the idea that he was writing in part in response to Justus of Tiberias. Although the current consensus is that it could not have been written solely to refute Justus of Tiberias, the near exclusive focus of the work on the six months or so of his activities in Galilee are extremely odd for an autobiography. It still requires explanation. What is unmistakable is that the real details of his life outside of his activities during those six months of the Jewish War are very scant, extremely scant.

As well, one would expect naturally that an autobiography written in Rome in the last decades of the first century after more than twenty years of living in the city would include a minimal description of how Josephus lived during those years. But there is nothing in his *Life* that gives the slightest hint as to how he lived in Rome. This, in a work that claims to have given an account of his whole life. This speaks volumes.

Much of the scholarship on Josephus's autobiography is concentrated on three topics: First, the reason why he wrote the work; second, the role of Justus of Tiberias as instigator of the work; and third, the contradictions and inconsistencies between the *Life* and the *Jewish War*.¹¹ What is often overlooked is the much more glaring problem about the great omissions that I have highlighted in the outline of the *Life*.

In the introduction to his translation of Josephus's *Life*, Steve Mason makes a case for how Josephus's autobiography fits the way in which Plutarch describes the life of a successful statesman in his *Precepts of Statecraft*, a work almost certainly written after the life of Josephus. Mason provides an impressive catalog/list of correspondences between parts of the *Life* and various themes that appear in Plutarch's work. He then adds that the contemporary Roman context also valued a person's political life as a way of validating his character.

> In Rome, a man's character had traditionally been thought to be deducible from his ancestry and from his career in military and public service. These are just the points that concern Josephus. His five months in public/military office, after his paradigmatic mission to Rome, afford the only plausible evidence he can cite for his public achievements. Before the trip to Rome, he was very

young and perhaps relatively unknown; afterwards, he was first a prisoner and then a minor figure in the capital with no opportunity for public service. Brief though it was, the Galilean campaign was his period of glory as "general" and governor, and he must now make the most of it.[12]

So what Josephus does fits contemporary expectations from both a literary standpoint and a social standpoint. This confirms for Mason that the *Life* is a political biography.

It runs against a most basic fact about the *Life* and from Josephus himself. Nowhere does Josephus say that he was writing a political biography. Besides, he deliberately omits from this supposed political biography, if we are to believe Mason, the first seven years of his political life before he was entrusted with the diplomatic mission to Rome. That story should have been the opening or first act of his political biography. Then, of course, he is explicit that he was writing a work about his entire life. It is not just part of his life or his public/political career, but his entire life. It is that insistence that must draw us into considering the great omissions in the *Life* that Mason and others do not probe although they remain one of the most glaring aspects of the *Life*. However much the *Life* attests to parallels in Plutarch's description of what makes a successful statesman, Josephus himself claimed something that he did not actually deliver, as I indicated previously.

Plutarch, who gives the characteristics of the statesman that Mason calls attention to, nevertheless tells us a lot about what he does socially and personally in some of his essays. He too had a public/political life or career. The same with Dio of Prusa. The notion of a political biography as rationale can easily mislead, if it used to justify the exclusion of large portions of the autobiographer's life as irrelevant to that life. For under any circumstances the unapologetic and almost cursory exclusion of more than half of the life lived looks suspicious. This is what Josephus does. In the case of someone like Pliny, who was a younger contemporary of Josephus in Rome, his letters cover more than just his public career. Pliny wrote letters and preserved those letters as a literary monument to his very self. It was not merely about a political self or biography. Pliny's self-portrait in his letters was also part of the art of biography in the times in which Josephus lived. So we cannot simply appeal to the Plutarchian model of statecraft and contend that this is what sanctions or warrants Josephus's great omissions. It cannot explain away his silence about the entirety of his life in Rome, especially because Josephus made a promise that he dutifully did not fulfill. Mason appears to preclude this objection or sidestep the issue altogether when he writes about Josephus's life in Rome by describing it as a period when he was "a minor figure in the capital with no opportunity for public service." But that is not really the point. In other ways Josephus also claimed to be a prominent figure or at least someone not lacking in attention from the Flavian emperors.

Tessa Rajak's biography of Josephus ends with the aftermath of the conquest of Judaea and Josephus's writing of the *Jewish War* and moves to the remainder of his writings in the 90s. She has nine pages of an epilogue, without much in the way of any biographical details for the more than twenty years that Josephus lived in Rome. We have, then, a biography that does not include anything from more than the last twenty years of the subject's life. This is clearly not the fault of the biographer. Rajak gives a reason for this in the introduction, which in a way justifies the ending of her biography.

> I have been mainly concerned with Josephus' early life and writings, for, after that, information on his activities disappears almost entirely and, in any case, what he did must have become less significant and less dramatic. Also, the intimate connection between word and action was lost in his later years. None the less, the later works have been useful: not only the *Life*, a partial autobiography (though not of the interior modern kind) which deals in a new way with the events of A.D. 67, but also sections of the twenty-book *Antiquities*, and occasionally even the apologetic, pro-Jewish polemic, *Against Apion*, published in the mid-nineties. In the end, my interpretation of the first stages of his career has some consequences also for my reading of Josephus' development and of the kind of changes that he underwent—changes which, in my view, were rather limited.[13]

However, the reasons Rajak gives for the inconsequential nature of Josephus's later years misconstrue the import of those years and Josephus's silences about them. It is simply not credible that he excluded more than twenty years of his life because "what he did must have become less significant and less dramatic" or to suggest that "the intimate connection between word and action was lost in his later years." The fact that Rajak acknowledges that the *Life* is a "partial autobiography" is an admission of something not quite right. Exactly how partial is this partial autobiography? That is the question that needs answering, with some possibilities as to why Josephus chose to be so partial. It should be cause for asking whether indeed the supposed loss of "intimate connection between word and action" is not itself part of the effect that Josephus intended for the *Life*. The recent work of William den Hollander tries to fill out the details of what might have been Josephus's life in Rome in chapters 5 (Josephus and Domitian) and 6 (Josephus and the Inhabitants of Rome).[14] That effort also reveals just how scanty is the material available to work with from Josephus, if at all. Interestingly, Rajak does not raise the question about the omissions and the unfulfilled promises; and neither does den Hollander. The methodological significance of Josephus's omissions in the *Life* cannot be overstated.

If we must pay heed to Josephus as author, historian, and as a literary figure, we have to pay attention also to his deliberate art. The omissions are part of his rhetorical art. For a historian they loom large not only in terms of sources and evidence that are deliberately overlooked or elided, but in terms of the substance and rhetoric of the history written. In the case of a person's life it turns into questions of truth telling and self-representation. If Josephus claims to have told all, but in fact he has excluded more than half of his life, then we have a testament to the very character that he enjoins his readers to judge. Josephus is the man who insists that he has told everything, so to speak, but in reality has excluded more than half of his life. This is not exactly the most credible of witnesses.

We may speculate and probe as to why he does what he does. We nominally use the date 93/94 CE, the time of composition of the *Antiquities*, as the date for the *Life*. But it is just as likely that the *Life* was written after the death of Domitian. The main reason for this is that the way Josephus describes Domitia "continuing" what Domitian and before him Vespasian and Titus did in the benefactions he received implies just that. Domitia continued what Domitian had done. That is the natural sense of the syntax and the wording. As well, it has been pointed out that the work seems to have been written with haste and is full of all kinds of errors and misstatements of facts and changes in detail when compared to the *Jewish War*. The fact that the *Life* also does not do what Josephus signaled at the end of the *Antiquities* suggests the very strong likelihood that Josephus was compelled to complete the work when he did.

There are two possibilities: first is the obvious one to which he himself refers, that is, Justus of Tiberias's criticism of Josephus's *Jewish War* and his aspersions about Josephus's character. The second, I suspect, was that he had to finish in haste because Domitian had recently been assassinated. The event occurred on September 18, 96 CE, a little more than two years after the completion of the *Antiquities*. Josephus, at that moment in time, needed to defend himself in an environment in which he had lost his imperial patron. The Flavian dynasty had come to an end. The details he provides at the end about how he had been supported by the Flavians and how Domitia, the wife of Domitian, continued to render support, read as if it is meant to say that, like Domitia, Josephus had nothing to fear from anyone. Yet, he had to defend himself. The audience for the *Life* was not only those beyond Rome, especially in Roman Judaea, who had been exposed to Justus of Tiberias's criticism, but also potential readers in Rome who knew of how much he owed to the Flavians.

The idea that he could not have written so unambiguously about how much he valued the benefactions of the Flavians in the period after Domitian's death when most people outdid others to damn Domitian's memory overlooks a few things. It rests on a basic error, misunderstanding, or misrepresentation. The fact that Domitian's memory was damned or that people abhorred the way he had conducted himself did not mean that people also despised his brother Titus or his father Vespasian. They damned Domitian, not the memory of Vespasian nor of Titus. Josephus would not necessarily have been doing anything unusual by mentioning the advantages he had received from the Flavians—not even from Domitian. Josephus's statement that he had benefited from Domitian did not carry the risk that some of his interpreters assume. For, even the likes of Tacitus and Pliny the Younger, who expressed their disdain for the tyranny that prevailed under Domitian and repudiated Domitian, admitted that they had advanced in their careers under Domitian. To say that he had benefited from Domitian was no more a risk for Josephus than for Tacitus and Pliny to admit the preferments they enjoyed in the time of Domitian.

If, then, those who despised Domitian had to admit that they had prospered under Domitian, Josephus could make those very acknowledgments just as Tacitus does in his *Agricola*. The sequence of Vespasian, Titus, Domitian, and Domitia (with its specific language about "continuing"), therefore, lends support to the view that Josephus wrote the *Life* after the death of Domitian. That is the most natural way of reading his words. In any case, whether he wrote before or after the death of Domitian does not affect one important element of the *Life* that I have alluded to but now needs further elaboration: Josephus's decision to exclude any details of his more than twenty years of life in Rome from his autobiography. This deprived his contemporary readers and posterity of an account of Jewish life in Rome in the period from the conquest of Judaea to the end of the first century.

If you make a promise not under compulsion or duress that you will give an account of Jewish life (about "us") from the end of the War to the present (that is 93/94 CE) and then you end up writing a narrative in which you omit any details about your own life in the period in question, it cannot be because it was an inadvertent omission. Josephus simply refused to do what he had promised. This is one of the clearest signs of Josephus's most deliberate silences.

Josephus, it should be said, was eminently capable of giving a good account of Jewish life in Rome in the period after the War. We may take what he does in the *Jewish War* as example when he describes what obtained in the various communities that had encountered Titus before and after the destruction of Jerusalem. His description of the state of affairs in Syrian Antioch is particularly noteworthy with his portrait of a certain Antiochus, an apostate Jew, and how his various acts affected the Jewish community in Antioch and his father, who was head of that community. Now imagine if Josephus had attempted something like it for Rome between 71 and 94 CE. What would it have looked like?

It was one thing to blame the rebels in Judaea for what had happened to Jerusalem and the Temple and the destruction that had ensued on account of the revolt as he did in the *Jewish War*. It was quite another thing to venture to describe the current state of Jewish life in Rome and what Domitian had done to make life unbearable for Jews in the city and elsewhere. That was an entirely different proposition. That would have elicited a strong reaction from the imperial court and would probably have put Josephus's own life in jeopardy. If there is any doubt, one need only consider what Tacitus relates about his father-in-law Agricola and the interest of the imperial court in his demise. Josephus would not have been a stranger to that story as it unfolded until August 23, 93 CE, when Agricola died (Tacitus, *Agricola* 45.1). The execution of other senators shortly thereafter for literary activities would have made an impression on any writers at the time. Josephus promised the new works within a year of these deaths. He appears to have reconsidered. The recriminations that continued would have been reason enough for going silent on his promises. There could be other reasons more deeply personal as well (almost all related to his unwillingness to describe his own life and Jewish life in Rome).

It is almost as if because his readers knew about how he behaved during the War he could not conceal those details either in the *Jewish War* or in the *Life*. He acknowledged that much in the preface to the *Jewish War*. He repeats the performance in the *Life* as if trying to correct the record found in the *Jewish War*, with all the contradictions he serves up in the process between the two works. But, in this case, when his readers outside of Rome would never know how he lived in Rome among both non-Jews and his fellow Jews during the time of the Flavian dynasty, Josephus chose not to reveal anything. In which case, only those who knew him in Rome would have any idea about how he managed his life among them. Beyond Rome, no one else, and certainly not posterity, is given access to this part of his biography. As long as no one of his readers outside of Rome knew about any of this, he could not be judged properly. So the invitation he offers to his readers to judge his life and character based on what he produced in the *Life* is disingenuous at best. It is an invitation to judge on the basis of a patently incomplete account of his "whole life" deliberately constructed for that purpose.

For all these reasons, Josephus's omissions in the *Life* and his silences about his own life as a Flavian Jew in Rome are not just matters of biographical interest. They are important for assessing his role as a historian of the first century. As such they cover a much broader field than what I suggested previously in relation to the Christians in Judaea or Paul. This has to be the backdrop against which we have to inquire about the world around him that Josephus deliberately does not tell us about. It also provides the necessary context for an assessment as to whether Josephus was even aware of Christians in Rome. What we cannot say for sure is that he was not aware of Jews in Rome. That was simply not possible. They were there, and in great numbers, in the Jewish Quarter in the *Transtiberim*. His silence, then, is not proof of anything, except his determination not to speak about them and about his own life among them. Whether he was alienated, marginalized, or accepted without rancor, bitterness, or contempt, we shall never know. As for the Christians it is another story, never mind that his younger contemporaries Suetonius, Pliny, and Tacitus had some knowledge of Christians in Rome.

It is also not insignificant that Josephus does not describe the lives or the life of any individual Jews in Rome in his long residence in the city except to say that he had to deal with people of his own kind (fellow Jews) who brought charges against him. But he does not describe the life of a single Jew in Rome. Whether the silence about Jewish life in Rome extends to include the Christians in Rome is not something we can answer with any clarity until we have considered whatever else was going on among Josephus's contemporaries and what First Clement attests to. For this we shall have to wait for the next two chapters after which point we should be able to offer a possible answer to that question.

To reiterate: The fact that Josephus mentions Domitian's benefactions and those of his wife Domitia in the *Life*, together with all that he received previously from Vespasian and Titus, but says nothing about the tyranny and fear that reigned in the days of Domitian, is yet another one of the loud silences in Josephus. Again, this is not an accident. It cannot be explained away by claiming that he was writing about Jewish matters and not Roman ones. It cannot be considered irrelevant that Josephus passes over matters of grave importance concerning Jews in Rome and the rest of the Jewish Diaspora during the time of Domitian that affected his fellow Jews and were consequential for many people both Jews and non-Jews whom he knew in Rome.

Basically, his earlier *Jewish War* gives an account of his life through the War. It is not enough to say that his subject matter was the *Jewish War* and *Jewish Antiquities*, when he deliberately does not carry out a project he promised when he wrote his autobiography. It is in this autobiography that his more-than-two-decades life in Rome is reduced to a few editorial lines in something like a testament or will at the end. The final lines helped Josephus to avoid giving an account of his real circumstances, the worlds in which he lived, the choices that he made when he lived in Rome, what he avoided, and the kinds of scrutiny he endured, which are intimated in those final lines when he mentions some of the accusations brought against him. Those final lines belong to his strategy and his project as a historian of the first century.

What Josephus's Roman contemporaries describe in their various writings is testament to the scope of Josephus's diffidence and methodological silence about the period. Whatever we think about the Senate or the senatorial class in their struggles with the Emperor Domitian, the fact that Josephus's contemporaries among that class speak unanimously about an extensive reality about which Josephus says nothing should point us to what Josephus was capable of: what he suppresses or chooses to ignore. I mentioned something similar in the previous chapter about how Josephus described Nero and his excesses. That Josephus says nothing about the extensive attestation of Domitian's abuse of power is important for understanding the nature and implications of Josephus's silences. They should not be overlooked merely because Josephus says nothing about the period. To do so is to be complicit in his silences. Understanding the meaning of his silences requires interrogating not just what he wrote, but what he chose not to write about even when he had previously promised to do so.

THINKING ABOUT JEWS IN ROME

If the citizens of Rome had forgotten the sentiments captured in Cicero's *Pro Flacco* about Jerusalem, its Temple, the Jewish nation, its institutions, its conquests and defeats, Seneca made sure to remind his readers that they were to be pitied if they took on Jewish ways. The conquered were not supposed to give their laws to the conqueror. Even worse the Romans participate in rituals about which they knew little or nothing as to their origins and the reasons for doing them, whereas at least Jews know the reasons why they do what they do. If Cicero was clear in his calumny of Jews and Jewish ways of life in the words cited above in his defense of Flaccus the proconsul of Asia c. 59 BCE, Seneca seemed more ambivalent and perhaps even envious in the excerpt about the Jews at least knowing why they do the things they do. In the other excerpt Seneca sounds very much as if sharing the opinion of his contemporaries when he writes in rather harsh and vicious language that the Jews are a most accursed race (*sceleratissime gentis*), if Augustine is to be believed that he is quoting from Seneca's lost *De superstitione* in City of God 6.11.

If Seneca's *De Superstitione* had been lost to them when Josephus become permanently resident in Rome and was producing his *Antiquities*, *Life*, and *Against Apion* in the last decades of the first century, they would still have other living contemporaries to remind them of what they were supposed to think about Jews, Moses the lawgiver, and Jewish ways of life (Judaism).

If people had forgotten Cicero, if Seneca in Augustine is not to be trusted, we still cannot get away from Marcus Fabius Quintilianus (35–c. 96), the well-known teacher of rhetoric in Rome. Quintilian was an almost exact contemporary of Josephus (37–c. 100). He was also well connected. He was Pliny the Younger's teacher (Pliny, Letters 2.14.9; 6.6.2); he may have also had the poet Juvenal as a student. The poet Marcus Valerius Martialis (c. 40–c. 102) mentions him in one epigram, which also sounds like a dig at Quintilian when Martial writes that he has risen above his paternity and advanced beyond his station in life. Martial's apparent kindness comes with some gall (Epigram 2.90).

Quintilian did much to challenge the authority of Seneca among his generation. He complains that all the young people were reading Seneca. He did his very best to point out the deficiencies in Seneca and implored his students and everyone else to imitate his much better style. He criticized Seneca's style, if not his life. Quintilian described Jews as a pernicious people or race who were destructive to others (*Inst. Oratorio* 3.7.21). He may well have shared Seneca's views. So even without Augustine's testimony about Seneca's *De superstitione*, we have Quintilian saying something almost exactly as Augustine claims Seneca had said. Pliny was by education linked to Quintilian and by social life linked somewhat strangely to Martial, as we shall see in the next chapter.

If Quintilian was not enough, Pliny and his generation almost certainly shared in the sentiments of Tacitus.[15] It was simply a reminder of what it was they were supposed to think and believe about Jews, Judaeans, and their ways of life. However, against these settled convictions about Jews and Judaism in the cultured circles of his friends, Suetonius recalls with some possible sympathy an event from his youth about the effects of the Emperor Domitian's policies on the *fiscus Judaicus*, the Jewish contribution to the public chest or treasury.

> Besides other taxes, that on the Jews was levied with the utmost vigor, and those were prosecuted who without publicly acknowledging that faith (*qui velut inprofessi*) yet lived as Jews (*Iudaicam viverent vitam*) as well as those who concealed their origin and did not pay the tribute levied upon their people. I recall being present in my youth when the person of a man of ninety years old was examined before the procurator and a very crowded court, to see whether he was circumcised.[16]

Suetonius does not mention exactly where this took place, though the reference to a procurator suggests it probably took place in one of the provinces and not in Rome itself. There were procurators of the public treasury in Rome. However, he would probably have said so if the event had taken place in Rome. One does not have to have been present to know what a humiliating experience this must have been for the ninety-year-old man who had to submit to this public inspection of his mark for being a Jew. It seems to have made an indelible impression on the young Suetonius, who states that during Domitian's reign the collection of the *fiscus Judaicus* tax took on new forms hitherto unimagined.

Whereas Suetonius mentions this personal experience in being a witness to this public degradation and the shame that came with it, Josephus mentions instead the origins of the tax during the time of Vespasian (*Jewish War* 7.6.6) in the aftermath of the destruction of the Temple and Jerusalem in 70 CE, as if he knew nothing of the humiliating experiences his fellow Jews had to endure. In Josephus's defense it needs to be acknowledged that when he completed the *Jewish War* in 75 or 76 CE, he could not have foreseen that in the near future Domitian would make the lives of his fellow Jews more onerous in the way that the tax, the *fiscus Judaicus*, was collected. However, he seems to have shown a certain indifference to the humiliations wrought by Domitian when he wrote his *Life*, shortly after completing his *Antiquities*, in 93/94 CE, at the height of Domitian's reign of terror. Rather than mention how much his fellow Jews suffered under Domitian's terror, he called attention to the personal privileges he received from Domitian.

Living in relative comfort, Josephus defended the continued support he received from Domitian at about the same time period when Suetonius witnessed that scene involving the ninety-year-old man that Suetonius came to describe later in his adulthood in his book, *The Twelve Caesars*. How could Josephus be silent about the harassment and humiliation of so many of his compatriots? For the time being, what I wish to suggest in this juxtaposition of Suetonius and Josephus on the *fiscus Judaicus* is that it brings us face to face with Josephus's many silences once more; and this time in connection with the reign of Domitian in a dramatic way.

In the previous chapter, I discussed the many ways in which Josephus appeared to skirt certain themes and topics related to Nero's reign. I made the point that Josephus deliberately did not include anything relating to the Fire of 64 CE probably because he did not wish to say anything untoward about Nero, and also most likely because he did not want to discuss the Christians or the Christian movement. In objection to that suggestion, it could be argued that not mentioning the persecution of Christians during the time of Nero, as Suetonius did, was nothing unusual since Josephus did not live in Rome during most of Nero's reign. He merely visited for a short though memorable period. One could still excuse him for not mentioning the Fire of 64 simply as an oversight, though it strains credulity. When it comes to what took place in Rome under Domitian, however, it is nearly impossible to excuse Josephus for one simple reason. Josephus was a resident of the city for most of the Flavian period, from the moment he returned with Titus to Rome after the Jewish War to his death near the turn of the century. We have no evidence to suggest he lived anywhere else. So Josephus could not have missed anything of significance during the reign of Domitian that ended ingloriously with his assassination in September 96 CE. Josephus's silence about Jewish humiliation in connection with the enforcement of the law about the *fiscus Judaicus* during the reign of Domitian serves as an introduction and a point of departure for his complete silence about the presence of Christians in Rome at this time as well.

To appreciate the nature of Josephus's silences, it will be important to relate him to Martial,[17] who arrived in Rome in 64 CE. It is not known whether he arrived before or after the fire that began on July 19 that destroyed most of the city. Though the latter seems more likely. Anyway,

Martial never mentions the fire itself in any of his epigrams. But he does make reference in his epigrams to the palace that Nero built after the Fire, the so-called Golden Palace. Curiously, Martial's arrival coincides with Josephus's first visit to the city on the legation to rescue some Jewish priests from Jerusalem who had been imprisoned there. At that time, Josephus became well acquainted with Nero's wife Poppaea Sabina. Josephus must have heard or learned something about Seneca and the Pisonian plot against Nero at this time. Josephus returned to Galilee and Judaea and soon became involved in the events leading up to the Jewish War of 66–70. Having surrendered to the Roman forces, and then entered into their service, Josephus would return to Rome after that war in the spring of 71 CE. From that point Josephus would be permanently resident in Rome.

Martial would be likewise, except for a year spent in Forum Cornelii in Northern Italy in 87 CE where he composed his Book 3 (Epigram 3.4), and until he finally departed in 98 CE to return to his native Spain (Epigrams Book 10).

As Martial was preparing to go back to Spain, Josephus was writing his last major work, *Against Apion*. Neither writer mentions the other in his writings, which gives the strange impression that they were not even aware of each other's presence in Rome for all those years. The impression is false, however. Neither Josephus nor Martial could have been ignorant of each other. Here again is one of those silences: this time on the parts of both Martial and Josephus. Both were connected to Emperor Domitian. Josephus mentioned his connections with the Flavian dynasty in his *Life*, beginning with Domitian's father Vespasian, through to his brother Titus, and finally to Domitian himself. Martial mentioned his connections in various ways by appealing to Domitian in his epigrams, praising Domitian's rule and benefactions to both city and empire. He mentions one of the important members of Domitian's court, Parthenius the imperial chamberlain, as a close friend through whom he passed on his poetry to Domitian. How Martial and Josephus could have avoided each other and be completely ignorant of each other for almost thirty years seems well-nigh impossible, if we add to this the fact that Martial was also one of the most celebrated writers in Rome during the time of Domitian.

FLAVIUS JOSEPHUS OF ROME

Josephus settled in Rome under suspect conditions. If his description of his capture by Roman forces is credible, Josephus was probably one of the few Judaeans or Jews who could ever live in Rome incognito.

> Having thus survived both the war with the Romans and that with his own friends, Josephus was brought by Nicanor into Vespasian's presence. The

Romans all flocked to see him, and from the multitude crowding around the general arose a hubbub of discordant voices: some exulting at his capture, some threatening, some pushing forward to obtain a nearer view. The more distant spectators clamoured for the punishment of their enemy, but those close beside him recalled his exploits and marvelled at such a reversal of fortune. Of the officers there was not one who, whatever his past resentment, did not then relent at the sight of him. Titus in particular was specially touched by the fortitude of Josephus under misfortunes and by pity for his youth. As he recalled the combatant of yesterday and saw him now a prisoner in his enemy's hands, he was led to reflect on the power of fortune, the quick vicissitudes of war, and the general instability of human affairs. So he brought over many Romans at the time to share his compassion for Josephus, and his pleading with his father was the main influence in saving the prisoner's life. Vespasian, however, ordered him to be guarded with every precaution, intending shortly to send him to Nero.[18]

Josephus had one important final act to play upon his capture that no one saw coming, though when he enacted it, it was not received as readily and as heartily as he had hoped. The thought of him being kept a prisoner to be sent to Nero sprung him into action. It would indeed have been bizarre for Josephus to end up in Rome a bound prisoner, when he had not too long before been in the presence and confidence of Nero's wife Poppaea. He seemed determined to prevent total humiliation. So he acted.

On hearing this, Josephus expressed a desire for a private interview with him. Vespasian having ordered all to withdraw except his son Titus and two of his friends, the prisoner thus addressed him: "You imagine, Vespasian, that in the person of Josephus you have taken a mere captive; but I come to you as a messenger of greater destinies. Had I not been sent on this errand by God, I know the law of the Jews and how it becomes a general to die. To Nero do you send me? Why then? Think you that [Nero and] those who before your accession succeed him will continue? You will be Caesar, Vespasian, you will be emperor, you and your son here. Bind me then yet more securely in chains and keep me for yourself; for you, Caesar, are master not of me only, but of land and sea and the whole human race. For myself, I ask to be punished by stricter custody, if I have dared to trifle with the words of God.[19]

It is important to note that, according to Josephus's own words, Vespasian did not believe him at first, and thought the whole thing was a "cunning trick" to procure his safety.

To this speech Vespasian, at the moment, seemed to attach little credit, supposing it to be a trick of Josephus to save his life. Gradually, however, he was led to believe it, for God was already rousing in him thoughts of empire and by other tokens foreshadowing the throne. He found, moreover, that Josephus had proved a veracious prophet in other matters. For one of the two friends in attendance at the private interview remarked: "If these words are not a nonsensical invention of the prisoner to avert the storm which he has raised, I am surprised that Josephus neither predicted the fall of Jotapata to its inhabitants nor his own captivity." To this Josephus replied that he had foretold to the people of Jotapata that their city would be captured after forty-seven days and that he himself would be taken alive by the Romans. Vespasian, having privately questioned the prisoners on these statements and found them true, then began to credit those concerning himself. While he did not release Josephus from his custody or chains, he presented him with raiment and other precious gifts, and continued to treat him with kindness and solicitude, being warmly supported by Titus in these courtesies.[20]

In the paragraphs preceding the ones just cited, Josephus describes his difficulties with his fellow rebels in the town of Jotapata. At one point he mentions that when he was captured, his mind turned to certain prophecies and oracles that he was aware of, and he began to consider some of his most recent dreams and what they might imply in relation to those oracles. He appears to have made up his mind about what he might say to Titus or Vespasian after these reveries. In so presenting himself, he also goes out of his way to say that he had the ability to interpret God's ambiguous oracles.

This is what he says about his thoughts when Titus sent the tribune Nicanor to persuade Josephus and his colleagues to surrender. Nicanor, Josephus tells his reader, was someone of his acquaintance from his previous stay in Rome (*Jewish War* 3.346).

> While Josephus was still hesitating, even after Nicanor's assurances, the soldiers in their rage attempted to set fire to the cave, but were restrained by their commander, who was anxious to take the Jewish general alive. But as Nicanor was urgently pressing his proposals and Josephus overheard the threats of the hostile crowd, suddenly there came back into his mind those nightly dreams, in which God had foretold to him the impending fate of the Jews and the destinies of the Roman sovereigns. He was an interpreter of dreams and skilled in divining the meaning of ambiguous utterances of the Deity; a priest himself and of priestly descent, he was not ignorant of the prophecies in the sacred books. At that hour he was inspired to read their meaning, and, recalling the dreadful images of his recent dreams, he offered up a silent prayer to God. "Since it pleases thee," so it ran, "who didst create the Jewish nation, to break thy work, since fortune has wholly passed to the Romans, and since thou hast made choice of my spirit to announce the things that are to come, I willingly surrender to the Romans His intention to surrender and consent to live; but I take thee to witness that I go, not as a traitor, but as thy minister."[21]

If we are to adopt Josephus's own language, we will have to say that his prophecy to Vespasian was a shrewd conjecture about what was in the air about the supposed man from the east who was to rule the whole world. While Josephus does not say that others were also apprised of the said oracle in the way he describes it elsewhere, his comments here suggest that the common notion of the said oracle lay behind his "shrewd conjectures" and his own dreams about surrender and what his fate would be.

From Josephus's *Life*, he provides the following account of his capture and the treatment he received on Vespasian's orders:

> After the siege of Jotapata I was in the hands of the Romans and was kept under guard, while receiving every attention. Vespasian showed in many ways the honour in which he held me, and it was by his command that I married one of the women taken captive at Caesarea, a virgin and a native of that place. She did not, however, remain long with me, for she left me on my obtaining my release and accompanying Vespasian to Alexandria. There I married again. From Alexandria I was sent with Titus to the siege of Jerusalem, where my life was frequently in danger, both from the Jews, who were eager to get me into their hands, to gratify their revenge, and from the Romans, who attributed every reverse to some treachery on my part, and were constantly and clamorously demanding of the Emperor that he should punish me as their betrayer. Titus Caesar, however, knowing well the varying fortunes of war, repressed by his silence the soldiers' outbursts against me.[22]

If Josephus is to believed, he lived mostly under suspicion. That in itself is not surprising. However, earlier, he had written in the *Jewish War* that he had been given assurances by his friend Nicanor when he approached Josephus to persuade him to surrender, after the two officials who had previously been sent to him failed to convince him. Josephus let it be known that the Romans admired him for his courage and did not wish to harm him, and that Vespasian would not have sent a friend of his to persuade him if he wished to harm him (*Jewish War* 3.346–349).

What is surprising is how well Josephus carried on or appeared to carry on untrammeled by so much of what he had witnessed and experienced. The equally pedestrian manner in which he reports Titus encouraging him repeatedly to take whatever he thought would be of value to him after the destruction of the Temple and the city of Jerusalem seems so out of place, given the scale of the calamity Josephus had witnessed and endured among his fellow Jews and the Roman army.

> Again, when at last Jerusalem was on the point of being carried by assault, Titus Caesar repeatedly urged me to take whatever I would from the wreck of my country, stating that I had his permission. And I, now that my native place had fallen, having nothing more precious to take and preserve as a solace for my personal misfortunes, made request to Titus for the freedom of some of my countrymen; I also received by his gracious favour a gift of sacred books. Not long after I made petition for my brother and fifty friends, and my request was granted. Again, by permission of Titus, I entered the Temple, where a great multitude of captive women and children had been imprisoned, and liberated all the friends and acquaintances whom I recognized, in number about a hundred and ninety; I took no ransom for their release and restored them to their

> former fortune. Once more, when I was sent by Titus Caesar with Cerealius and a thousand horse [calvary] to a village called Tekoa, to prospect whether it was a suitable place for an entrenched camp, and on my return saw many prisoners who had been crucified, and recognized three of my acquaintances among them, I was cut to the heart and came and told Titus with tears what I had seen. He gave orders immediately that they should be taken down and receive the most careful treatment. Two of them died in the physicians' hands; the third survived.[23]

We have here the difficulties Josephus encounters for being known as a traitor on both sides of the war between the Romans and the people of Judaea. Much of what he presents is to show that in spite of the suspicions Titus kept faith in him. When Titus departed Alexandria for Rome, he took Josephus along. Josephus continues his narrative to underscore that what benefactions he received from Titus were honored by his father Vespasian who went so far as to accommodate him in the house he himself had occupied before he became emperor. He was now as familiar (*familiaris*) as any friend (*amicus*) or family (*familia*) of the emperor.

> On our arrival in Rome I met with great consideration from Vespasian. He gave me a lodging in the house which he had occupied before he became Emperor; he honoured me with the privilege of Roman citizenship; and he assigned me a pension. He continued to honour me up to the time of his departure from this life, without any abatement in his kindness towards me. My privileged position excited envy and thereby exposed me to danger. A certain Jew named Jonathan, who had promoted an insurrection in Cyrene, occasioning the destruction of two thousand of the natives, whom he had induced to join him, on being sent in chains by the governor of the district to the Emperor, asserted that I had provided him with arms and money. Undeceived by this mendacious statement, Vespasian condemned him to death, and he was delivered over to execution. Subsequently, numerous accusations against me were fabricated by persons who envied me my good fortune; but, by the providence of God, I came safe through all. Vespasian also presented me with a considerable tract of land in Judaea.[24]

There is an important story to be told about Josephus's landed property in Judaea, which has attracted the interest and stimulated the imagination of novelists, but about which Josephus in fact sheds little light on how he managed those holdings from Rome, who it was who oversaw his lands, and how he benefited financially from them. Perhaps much of the envy he claims to have attracted from his fellow Jews comes from this one fact: that this general who had turned on his own people was now profiting in no small measure from land in the very place that he had helped the Romans conquer. He concludes the *Life* with a brief dossier of his domestic affairs:

> At this period I divorced my wife, being displeased at her behaviour. She had borne me three children, of whom two died; one, whom I named Hyrcanus, is still alive. Afterwards I married a woman of Jewish extraction who had settled in Crete. She came of very distinguished parents, indeed the most notable people in that country. In character she surpassed many of her sex, as her subsequent life showed. By her I had two sons, Justus the elder, and then Simonides, surnamed Agrippa. Such is my domestic history.[25]

He now addressed any who would doubt him with a résumé of how he had continued to be favored by the Flavian emperors throughout his life in Rome, and with one more notice (to his enemies?) about the financial boon he enjoyed because he was exempted from taxes on his lands in Judaea.

> The treatment which I received from the Emperors continued unaltered. On Vespasian's decease Titus, who succeeded to the empire, showed the same esteem for me as did his father, and never credited the accusations to which I was constantly subjected. Domitian succeeded Titus and added to my honour. He punished my Jewish accusers, and for a similar offence gave orders for the chastisement of a slave, a eunuch and my son's tutor. He also exempted my property in Judaea from taxation—a mark of the highest honour to the privileged individual. Moreover, Domitia, Caesar's wife, never ceased conferring favours upon me. Such are the events of my whole life; from them let others judge as they will of my character.[26]

If nothing else, Josephus continued to live off whatever subventions and privileges he received from the Flavians. He seemed to be assured that the benefactions of Vespasian, Titus, Domitian, and Domitia, proved his right standing among his fellow citizens of Rome, both Jews and non-Jews.

At this point he turns to Epaphroditus, his patron: "Having now, most excellent Epaphroditus, rendered you a complete account of our antiquities, I shall here for the present conclude my narrative."[27] This ending works well to suggest that Josephus's time in Rome (up to whenever he completed the *Life*) had been an unqualified success, and that his life story actually concludes the antiquities of the Jews (or Jewish nation). It is not only that his *Life* is a literary supplement to the *Antiquities*, but that the life that Josephus's lived is a fitting end to the antiquities (the memorials and history) of the Jewish people. If so, then the invitation for others to judge his character is an invitation to judge him in relation to all the characters that he describes in the *Antiquities*.

The issue of Josephus's character is a troublesome one. For he himself calls attention to his changes of mind, pretenses, betrayals, cunning, opportunism, and a host of other strategies that he uses to maneuver through the difficult circumstances that he often found himself in. To try to provide a character sketch would require a substantial volume in its own right, and even then I am not sure that one can provide a portrait that makes sense or gives coherence to the many moods, choices, sentiments, and acts of Josephus, to say nothing of his own often contradictory and self-consciously self-serving interpretations of those actions. His autobiography does not provide a detailed account of the actions of his whole life, as he claims at the end. As I mentioned previously, it concerns his actions during the Jewish War, and it is written in part to counter allegations by his detractors, among them Justus of Tiberias, that Josephus's account in his *Jewish War* is full of errors and mendacity (*Life*, 336–340).[28]

JOSEPHUS'S *JEWISH WAR*, THE TRIUMPHAL PARADE, AND VESPASIAN'S TEMPLE OF PEACE

To those Jews living in the immediate aftermath of the destruction of Jerusalem in 70 CE, it was an abomination. Josephus does his best to override or conceal this sentiment, but it could not have been lost on him even as he watched the triumphal procession as a guest of Vespasian and Titus in Rome in 71 CE.

Josephus gives a detailed account of the events both from the standpoint of an eyewitness and also as an interpreter and historian of the Jewish people. His account is harrowing and makes for wrenching reading even so many centuries after the events. Throughout Josephus is almost apologetic, repeatedly underscoring the folly of the rebellion, Titus Caesar's various attempts to have the citizens of Jerusalem surrender, and the recalcitrance of the leaders of the rebellion. In so many different ways, and in spite of the brutality and violence meted out against the resistance, Josephus still casts Titus as a reluctant conqueror who was forced to his deed by the Jewish resistance. He even goes further to say that Titus never intended to burn the Temple and that it was the act of a careless soldier that set the Temple ablaze. Others offered a different view. There is, for example, an allusion to the event in Valerius Flaccus's *Argonautica* which is sometimes mentioned as an alternative to Josephus's claims about Titus's reluctant destruction of the Temple. The allusion is more impressionistic than fact, and it lacks historical merit.

But even so, the plunder that followed the destruction of the Temple and the fact that the implements (or their replicas) from the Temple were displayed in the triumphal procession, and then subsequently memorialized on the Arch of Titus gives some indication that Titus may not have been as innocent as Josephus presents him. There is a curious detail about Josephus's eyewitness account of the procession in Rome, when he says that the Menorah that was on display looked different from the one that he knew from the Temple. He adds that he as a priest knew exactly what it looked like, as if to say that what was on display was not exactly what was in the Temple. So in all likelihood a replica of some sort had been made. (There is some debate about this, as in fact, the one displayed on the Arch of Titus does not match the description found in the Torah.)

The entire pageant put on during the triumphal celebration was designed to leave a lasting impression on the minds of everyone about the momentous nature of the victory over the Jews of Judaea and Galilee and the astonishing achievement of dispossessing the Jews of their most sacred objects and the destruction of their most important city and its Temple. Josephus was duly impressed with the pageantry. Josephus gives a fulsome account in *Jewish War* 7.132ff.

> It is impossible adequately to describe the multitude of those spectacles and their magnificence under every conceivable aspect, whether in works of art or diversity of riches or natural rarities; for almost all the objects which men who have ever been blessed by fortune have acquired one by one—the wonderful and precious productions of various nations—by their collective exhibition on that day displayed the majesty of the Roman empire. Silver and gold and ivory in masses, wrought into all manner of forms, might be seen, not as if carried in procession, but flowing, so to speak, like a river; here were tapestries borne along, some of the rarest purple, others embroidered by Babylonian art with perfect portraiture; transparent gems, some set in golden crowns, some in other fashions, swept by in such profusion as to correct our erroneous supposition that any of them was rare. Then, too, there were carried images of their gods, of marvellous size and no mean craftsmanship, and of these not one but was of some rich material. Beasts of many species were led along all caparisoned with appropriate trappings. The numerous attendants conducting each group of animals were decked in garments of true purple dye, interwoven with gold; while those selected to take part in the pageant itself had about them choice ornaments of amazing richness. Moreover, even among the mob of captives, none was to be seen unadorned, the variety and beauty of their dresses concealing from view any unsightliness arising from bodily disfigurement. But nothing in the procession excited so much astonishment as the structure of the moving stages; indeed, their massiveness afforded ground for alarm, and misgiving as to their stability, many of them being three or four stories high, while the magnificence of the fabric was a source at once of delight and amazement. For many were enveloped in tapestries interwoven with gold, and all had a framework of gold and wrought ivory.[29]

Josephus goes on to describe how various episodes and scenes from the war were depicted: all this to bring to life to the Romans what had been done in their name on the battlefields and how their unending felicity has been vouchsafed.

> The war was shown by numerous representations, in separate sections, affording a very vivid picture of its episodes. Here was to be seen a prosperous country devastated, there whole battalions of the enemy slaughtered; here a party in flight, there others led into captivity; walls of surpassing compass demolished by engines, strong fortresses overpowered, cities with well-

manned defences completely mastered and an army pouring within the ramparts, an area all deluged with blood, the hands of those incapable of resistance raised in supplication, temples set on fire, houses pulled down over their owners' heads, and, after general desolation and woe, rivers flowing, not over a cultivated land, nor supplying drink to man and beast, but across a country still on every side in flames.[30]

There was a particular emphasis put on displaying the sacred objects of the Jews that had been pillaged from the Temple to demonstrate Rome's triumph over the god/God of the Judaeans. At this point, Josephus also cursorily presents an apology for the Romans as justified conquerors, who reluctantly defeated a deluded and obstinate people.

> For to such sufferings were the Jews destined when they plunged into the war; and the art and magnificent workmanship of these structures now portrayed the incidents to those who had not witnessed them, as though they were happening before their eyes. On each of the stages was stationed the general of one of the captured cities in the attitude in which he was taken. A number of ships also followed. The spoils in general were borne in promiscuous heaps; but conspicuous above all stood out those captured in the temple at Jerusalem. These consisted of a golden table, many talents in weight, and a lampstand, likewise made of gold, but constructed on a different pattern from those which we use in ordinary life. Affixed to a pedestal was a central shaft, from which there extended slender branches, arranged trident-fashion, a lamp being attached to the extremity of each branch; of these there were seven, indicating the honour paid to that number among the Jews. After these, and last of all the spoils, was carried a copy of the Jewish Law, then followed a large party carrying images of victory, all made of ivory and gold. Behind them drove Vespasian, followed by Titus; while Domitian rode beside them, in magnificent apparel and mounted on a steed that was itself a sight.[31]

If there were any doubts:

> The triumphal procession ended at the temple of Jupiter Capitolinus, on reaching which they halted; for it was a time-honoured custom to wait there until the execution of the enemy's general was announced. This was Simon, son of Gioras, who had just figured in the pageant among the prisoners, and then, with a halter thrown over him and scourged meanwhile by his conductors, had been hauled to the spot abutting on the Forum, where Roman law requires that malefactors condemned to death should be executed. After the announcement that Simon was no more and the shouts of universal applause which greeted it, the princes began the sacrifices, which having been duly offered with the customary prayers, they withdrew to the palace. Some they entertained at a feast at their own table: for all the rest provision had already been made for banquets in their several homes. For the city of Rome kept festival that day for her victory in the campaign against her enemies, for the termination of her civil dissensions, and for her ordinary hopes of felicity.[32]

In the final analysis, Vespasian's euphemistically named Temple of Peace would serve as the living memorial of the triumph in Judaea. Together with the Arch of Titus it would enshrine in Roman memory the historic destruction of Jerusalem and its famed Temple. When Josephus wrote the *Jewish War*, the Temple of Peace had only recently been completed in 75 CE. One is tempted to think that Josephus in fact wrote the Greek version of his *Jewish War* to coincide with this fact.

> The triumphal ceremonies being concluded and the empire of the Romans established on the firmest foundation, Vespasian decided to erect a temple of Peace. This was very speedily completed and in a style surpassing all human conception. For, besides having prodigious resources of wealth on which to draw he also embellished it with ancient masterpieces of painting and sculpture; indeed, into that shrine were accumulated and stored all objects for the sight of which men had once wandered over the whole world, eager to see them severally while they lay in various countries. Here, too, he laid up the vessels of gold from the temple of the Jews, on which he prided himself: but their Law and the purple hangings of the sanctuary he ordered to be deposited and kept in the palace.[33]

Henceforth, no one needed to say a word about what it meant to be a Jew or a Judaean or a citizen of the city of Jerusalem. Vespasian made sure of all this by erecting his Temple of Peace, where he put on display some of the artifacts taken from Jerusalem. And what peace? And for whom? And at what cost in human lives—and Jewish lives in particular?

The Adiabene royals who made Jerusalem their home were caught up in these events. Josephus does not mention them in the context of recounting the scenes at the triumphal celebration in Rome in 71 CE. But earlier in the *Jewish War* (6.352–357) he describes how they were taken as captives by Titus. Like other inhabitants of the city, they were caught up in the siege of Jerusalem. Queen Helena's Adiabene also had joined the Jewish side in the fight against Rome, even when other Jewish communities had kept apart from it. Titus did not forget this when some of those royals from Adiabene in Jerusalem came pleading for their lives. He spared their lives, but only so he could send them as captives to Rome. They suffered a fate worse than Josephus, who had already gained his freedom as he helped Titus and the Romans in their campaign against the Jews in Judaea and Jerusalem.

> On the same day the sons and brothers of king Izates, who were joined by many of the eminent townsfolk, entreated Caesar to grant them a pledge of protection. Though infuriated at all the survivors, Titus, with the unalterable humanity of his character, received them. For the present he kept them all in custody; the king's sons and kinsmen he subsequently brought up in chains to Rome as hostages for the allegiance of their country.[34]

It is instructive that in his later retelling of the story of Queen Helena and her son Izates and the royal house of Adiabene Josephus stopped short of rehearsing the tragic end of that dynasty even though he had promised to give an extended account after his description of their conversion to Judaism in *Antiquities* (20.2.1–4; 20.4.1–3). That fuller narrative never came, though in many ways, it was unnecessary unless he intended to include information that he had not provided in the account in the *Jewish War*. Josephus preserved the memory of Helena and the royal house of Adiabene in the *Antiquities* under the banner of how God had been faithful in preserving their kingdom though they had feared the consequences of converting to Judaism. That theme sits awkwardly with the end of the dynasty in the destruction of Jerusalem, which is probably why Josephus did not continue the story in the *Antiquities*. He probably stopped short of telling the rest of the story because he knew too well about how the Adiabene royals had fared after they ended up in Rome. Josephus was close to Vespasian and Titus at that time. He may even have seen those captive royals on display during the Triumphal procession in Rome staged for Vespasian and Titus that he described in the *Jewish War*. He comments about foreign rulers that were bound as war captives in the procession. However, he quietly skips over the fact that he had all but given indication of the Adiabene royals in such terms already.

Queen Helena could never have imagined this when she set out to leave such monuments to her family in the royal palaces they built in Jerusalem and the tomb they constructed to inter their remains. That it all transpired within a generation would have been an intolerable reality for any family. They had uprooted themselves from Northern Mesopotamia and then become extinct after settling in Jerusalem. It seemed a cruel fate. Tactfully, Josephus chose not to comment on these issues, though in other contexts he was quite prepared to decide who had been protected by God and who had not. Josephus's logic of divine presence or providence could be very elastic. If we follow Josephus's point that the Adiabene royals were taken as captives on account of the role played by Kingdom of Adiabene in the revolt in Judaea and in Jerusalem, then it is most likely that they were executed in Rome. Josephus himself most certainly knew what had befallen them. The Romans always seemed to know which foreign adversaries had provided aid and support to their enemies, and how many of their adversaries they had put to death.

Tacitus mentions in his *Histories* 5.12.3 that he had heard that the total number of the besieged in Jerusalem in 70 CE numbered around 600,000. Josephus says 1,100,000 perished most of them Jews (*Jewish War* 6.420–426). Josephus then says (6.420) there were 97,000 captives (so approximately 100,000). The number of captives is almost certainly a figure Josephus derived from official Roman sources; besides the fact that he was also an eyewitness and a member of Titus's staff. As for the nominal population of the city before the pilgrims arrived for Passover in 70 CE Josephus does not say. However, in two different places he suggests that at the time of Passover the pilgrims (or the population of the city) were 2.5 million (*Antiquities* 2.280) and 3 million (*Jewish War* 6.423). If those figures are anywhere near accurate, then Josephus's 1,100,000 dead is not unthinkable, since the siege took place during the week of Passover and so most of the pilgrims were trapped.

Although Josephus writes in his own defense at the end of his *Jewish War* that he had consulted official accounts of the siege, had used Vespasian's diaries, and had received official approval for his narrative from Titus and even had his works read in public, none of this prevents a skeptical audience from wondering about his numbers. After all, in a macabre way and in a manner consistent with the Roman thirst for blood, as the gladiatorial games attest, the high figures may be said to magnify Vespasian and Titus for having destroyed so many.

Yet, Josephus could also be accused of inflating the figures of the casualties, ostensibly to raise the figure of the Jewish dead either to support his own view of the infinite folly of the rebellion or the unimaginable suffering and desolation of the destruction of Jerusalem or both. So for the sake of the argument, I shall use Tacitus's number. Tacitus, at least, cannot be accused of such sentiment. He seems to speak for a kind of official Roman senatorial position. If we then subtract the approximately 100,000 who were taken captive, then the death toll for the Jewish population is approximately 500,000. That is the death toll from a few weeks or months and in an area not more than 250 acres. That is a catastrophe by any estimation ancient or modern.

In the Rome of the first century, after 85 CE, one could not miss the Arch of Titus. From the *Transtiberim*, on the west bank of the Tiber, it was less than seven hundred yards or meters. So anyone in the Jewish Quarter could see it. It loomed large over the landscape. It was a constant reminder to both the old and most recent residents of the Jewish Quarter (some of whom were prisoners of war brought from Judaea, some of whom had been on display in the triumphant procession in 71 CE) of what had taken place in Jerusalem, and how the Temple had been destroyed. If they happened to be near the Arch of Titus, they could also see on the bas-relief in the inside of the south-facing pillar a depiction of the triumphant processing with some of the implements that had been taken from the Temple, most notably the seven-stick candelabra (the Menorah). No one writing to a Roman audience could pretend these events had not happened; that the Temple was still standing, or that its treasures had not been looted by the Romans, and that the Romans had not put on a pageant to celebrate their destruction of Jerusalem. Josephus could not pretend otherwise as a writer, nor could he pretend his fellow residents of Rome did not know all of this.

How, then, did Josephus fare among the Romans beyond the circle of the said Epaphroditus to whom he dedicated his *Life*? Jonathan Price argues that Josephus kept to himself so as not to be an embarrassment, in part because his Greek accent would have sounded awkward if he had tried to engage the literati in Rome.[35] It was not the fact that he wrote in Greek. After all, many of those literary types were bilingual; nor was it the subject matter of his works but rather that he was not an unabashed supporter of the Roman cause: so Price surmises. This second argument seems very strained. Anyone who read the *Jewish War* would not have doubted that Josephus was unabashed in his defense of the Roman cause. It is that book that would have made Josephus's literary reputation until the early 90s when he set to writing the *Antiquities*. By then the mood in Rome was decidedly different with the Emperor Domitian superintending even literary works as *censor*. We should not assume, then, that the reception Josephus might have received in the 70s and 80s was the same that would have obtained in the 90s.

It is quite obvious that Josephus could not have dedicated the three works he wrote after the *Jewish War*, namely, *Antiquities*, *Life*, and *Against Apion* to the Emperor Titus or any other Flavian patron. Perhaps he could have dedicated the *Life* to an imperial patron since in it he partly praises Nero. But most of the *Life* is a justification of himself, which he had done in part in the *Jewish War* but not with the singular focus with which he does so in the *Life*. So even dedicating the *Life* to a Flavian would have been a stretch. Of course, *Against Apion* is a justification of Judaism and Jewish life, with a long-deceased anti-Jewish protagonist and propagandist as foil. Why would any Roman of senatorial rank and imperial pretensions want to have anything to do with it?

More pressing is the question as to why Josephus's contemporaries in Rome do not pay him more attention. Or perhaps did not wish to do so, given his past? Suetonius, who mentions Josephus in relation to the accession of Vespasian, provides nothing in the way of a biographical note, almost as if to say, "Everyone knows who Josephus is." It seems peculiar too that none of Josephus's contemporaries of literary note who lived in Rome at some point during Josephus's lifetime mention him: from Martial (40–120), Statius (c. 45x55–c.96), Tacitus (c. 56–117), Dio of Prusa (40–115), Epictetus (c. 50x60–c. 135), Plutarch (before 50 to after 120), there is not a word. Still Suetonius is a credible witness, even if a much younger contemporary of Josephus. He was after all born probably in 69 or 70 CE, the year of the destruction of the Temple in Jerusalem. Suetonius also calls Josephus an "honorable man." Is that meant ironically? Or was this somehow Suetonius's version of how the Romans viewed Josephus even at the time of his capture, as represented in Nicanor's solicitations encouraging Josephus to surrender? Almost everyone who knew of Josephus in Rome would almost certainly have known that he was a betrayer to the Jewish cause. Was it so honorable on his part to betray his *patria*, when to the Romans betraying one's *patria* was an offense deserving of something worse than death? Could he be an "honorable man" if he could not be trusted by his own? Or was he honorable because of what he had done for the Romans?

Was this Jewish general who had betrayed his own people that obscure as Price claims? Price is convinced that Josephus "refrained from public performance entirely." He notes that Josephus does not mention any public reading of his writings.[36] Josephus's absence from contemporary literary culture and performance, while significant, if in fact that was the case, is not tantamount to his obscurity. There is reason to object then to some aspects of Price's conclusion:

> Josephus' self-professed identity, his manner and style of writing, and his own interests, kept him isolated in Rome for the last thirty years of his life. This was partly the result of Roman prejudice, as can be gauged from Tacitus and Juvenal. Josephus, in his lifetime project, not only did not shed his Jewish identity but emphasized it. Josephus' exclusion was also partly self-imposed. His interests and literary purposes, as well as his artistic technique, remained profoundly provincial, despite his location in the capital. His enduring concerns are what ultimately gave his writings their main content and character. Yet we know *more* about Judaism because Josephus did not reach for *Romanitas*, as did other Roman historians writing in Greek, like Dionysius [of Halicarnassus] and Appian [of Alexandria].[37]

Price seems unwilling to acknowledge that there is as much *Romanitas* in the *Jewish War* as there is Jewishness. There is equally as much *Romanitas* in Josephus's self-designation as Flavius Josephus receiving benefactions from the Flavians as there is Jewishness in detailing his pedigree in the opening paragraphs of his *Life*. Price reads the *Jewish War* and everything else Josephus wrote as exemplifying the same sensibilities, which is simply not the case. In any event, even if Josephus wanted to, he could not have lived an obscure life in Rome.

According to Josephus himself, on the day of the triumphal procession in Rome celebrating the victory in Judaea and Jerusalem, the Romans shouted their approval when the Jewish general Simon son of Gioras was executed. That could have been Josephus's fate. No doubt a few Romans knew that as well. In short, Josephus would have been well known as the Jewish general who escaped the fate of Simon son of Gioras because he had the good sense to surrender to the Romans and was now living in his retirement among them through the patronage of the Flavians.

Steve Mason suggests that Josephus's connections with the Flavians were nothing special, even though at the end of his autobiography Josephus mentions the benefactions he received from the Flavians as something worth shouting about. Mason discounts them.[38] He notes that even the tax reprieve

Josephus mentions receiving from the Flavians was nothing remarkable. Others had received such benefits. Mason insists that even being granted Roman citizenship was nothing exceptional since Jews in Rome had citizenship and that Josephus was simply a captive slave who had been given his freedom. Stated in these terms, Josephus is a freedman; and so the Flavian's freedman. It just so happens that a lot of freedmen also had quite a bit of power. Martial, for example, goes out of his way to attack them for putting on airs and arrogating to themselves too much power; forgetting who they once were. Mason's devaluation of Josephus's benefactions is a bit odd. But he could be right.

Still, if they were nothing special, why would Josephus mention them? Sure, as Mason points out, the most well-connected Jews shortly before and during Josephus's lifetime were the Herodians who were on the friendliest of terms with the Julio-Claudian emperors. Josephus could not have counted himself in the same class as these kings and princes. Mason compares Josephus to them, and surely enough Josephus emerges the poorer. But then Mason seems to overlook his own sources.

First of all, Josephus makes particular mention of the fact that he was among maybe three people in all of Judaea who had the ability to write a literary work of the sort that he did in Greek. Never mind that he first wrote the *Jewish War* in Aramaic and then produced a second version in Greek. Second, Josephus mentions his friendship with Agrippa II, notes that he received sixty-two letters from him, quotes two of them, and mentions Agrippa as part patron and one of his most important readers, who also supplied information about the War. In so doing, he places himself among the elite in Jewish society in both Rome and Palestine. Thirdly, why would Agrippa pay him any heed if Josephus was merely an imposter? Fourth, Josephus presents himself as having acted in a way that accords with Agrippa's own attitude toward Roman power and the foolishness of the Jewish opposition to Rome, including his own compatriots in Galilee where he was commander. That is why the speech of Agrippa II that he provides pretty much follows the same arguments that Josephus himself uses in his self-presentation when he tries to dissuade his compatriots from opposing the Romans. Fifth, and this goes back to the question of Josephus's status: let us assume that he was a captive of Vespasian's. In the event, he also became a military attaché of some sort. In other words, here was a prisoner of war who had surrendered to his enemies and then taken on the role of collaborator. This is not an insignificant fact. Josephus plays a role that was noted by both the Romans and his fellow Jews. Otherwise the criticism of someone like Justus of Tiberias would have had little substance. So he was not simply a slave, as Mason wants to put it.

The exact value of the benefactions is another matter. However, I shall maintain that if they were nothing to shout about, Josephus would probably not have mentioned them. Given his circumstances, and what the alternative could have been, they amounted to something substantial, though to someone else they would have been ordinary perhaps. All the same, he was a Jew who lived in the former apartment of Vespasian the emperor. Not many could have said that they dwelled in the previous residence of the man who had become emperor. That must have counted for something, even to the so unimpressed among the Romans who sometimes sneered at Jews.

Both Martial and Statius speak about Jews in their respective works, so it is highly probable that they knew or knew of Josephus, perhaps the most prominent Jewish literary figure in Rome in the last decades of the first century. Then there are Josephus's silences about his literary peers (or perhaps he did not consider them his peers). Josephus himself never mentions Seneca (d. 65), Martial, Statius, or Epictetus in his writings. But no one would be inclined to take this as a sign of the obscurity of these figures in Rome. In the same way, we should not assume that the silence about Josephus is a testament to his obscurity. There may be other reasons of which we are not aware. I have also shown already that Josephus's silences about Christians in Rome belong to this larger reality of what is said about whom. Josephus himself leaves a good many things out of his historical writing. Those silences need to be seen in their proper contexts.

The silence of his contemporaries about Josephus is probably a testament to his marginalization, which is not quite the same thing as being obscure. Josephus's identity remained a problematic one. His difficulties did not merely surface when he became resident in Rome. His very status as someone who had changed sides during the war with the Jews made him a problematic character to both Jews and non-Jews. As we saw previously, he attests to this himself when he writes that during the siege of Jerusalem when things went badly for the Romans some of the soldiers tended to accuse him of disloyalty or worse, and when things seemed to go badly for the Jews they too felt Josephus had revealed their plans to the Romans. As someone playing the role of an intermediary or mediator, moving back and forth between his past as a general of Jewish forces (in Galilee) and his present as an advisor or collaborator with the Romans, he could not necessarily have anticipated his future. What he would become in Rome when he arrived there in the spring of 71 CE was not obvious. The literary life he took up was probably the least unobtrusive, problematic, and controversial. Whether he would remain uncontroversial in his writings was another question altogether. At the same time, to the extent that Josephus could not fully participate in all things Roman, he marked himself as a problematic character to those who encountered him in Rome.

Nevertheless, he put his Jewishness fully on display in his *Antiquities* and his *Life*; he then provided a spirited defense of the Jewish past and present in *Against Apion* which did not make it any easier for him to even pretend that he was fully Roman in his sensibilities and sympathies. If anything, he went out of his way to censure some important aspects of Roman life. This was not a sure way to endear oneself to the senatorial class and the literati in Rome. Judging from the likes of Tacitus and Martial, the cultured prejudice of the patricians and Roman elite toward Jews and Judaism was commonplace in Roman society.

Martial's epigrams and Tacitus's ethnography make sobering and disturbing reading. Yet these are the people Josephus would have had to have associated with. Even if he did, it is highly unlikely he would have thought himself beloved in such company. Worse still was the environment that existed in Rome in his later years during the reign of Domitian. It was not the first time Romans had feared for their lives because of the ways of a tyrant or a murderous regime. They had known some such reality under Gaius Caligula and then Nero. Josephus himself had chosen not to write about Nero's crimes when he came to write his *Life*. He also knew about Gaius Caligula by reputation and wrote extensively about him in Book 19 of the *Antiquities*.

It may be worth considering how Josephus reflected about his own experiences among the Flavians when he considered the sordid details of Caligula's reign, since he seemed relatively unconcerned about the patronage of the Flavians on the one hand, and on the other hand, determined not to put so much of Nero's reign under scrutiny, having received favors from his wife Poppaea. Yet, one wonders how Josephus could have lived under a tyrant without qualms.

One is put in the mind of Seneca's *De ira* 2.33.3ff., where Seneca describes a man who was invited by the Emperor Caligula to attend a banquet on the very day that Caligula had ordered the execution of one of his two sons. Seneca implored patience, so that he would not lose the other son. It is rather macabre but full of realism: Here is the text.

> Gaius Caesar had placed the son of Pastor, an illustrious Roman knight, under arrest, annoyed by his elegance and his foppish haircut. His father begged that he grant him his son's life. As though that were a reminder to punish him, Caesar promptly ordered the execution. But so as not to be totally impolite towards the father, he invited him to dinner that day. Pastor arrived without a look of reproach on his face. Caesar gave him a huge toast to drink, setting a guard over him. The poor man went through with it, as though he were drinking his son's blood. Ointment and garlands were sent for, and orders given to see if he would put them on. He put them on. On the very day that he had carried his son off to burial—or, rather, had failed to carry him to safety—he reclined with ninety-nine other guests, downing the sort of drinks that would hardly have been decent even at a birthday party for his children, an old man with the gout. Not a tear did he shed the while, not a sign of grief did he allow to escape him. He dined as though his plea had succeeded. Why? you may ask. He had another [son]. (*De Ira* 2.33.3–5)[39]

Although Josephus lived in much better circumstances and was never in the position in which Pastor found himself, a question remains: just how freely did Josephus live with the patronage of the Flavians? To what extent did he have to calibrate whatever he wrote in relation to this? What forms of censorship did he succumb to, and what forms of self-censorship did he employ? It is not easy to answer any of these questions. For the writings of contemporary writers like Martial, Tacitus, and Statius do not necessarily offer ready clues to figure out how they managed these issues, let alone how someone like Josephus could have carried on alongside them.

The works of poets and other dramatists who produce their writings under a tyrannical regime is not so easy to interpret, especially when they are dealing with how to criticize a tyrant. If you can get into trouble for doing so, in drama, in poetry, etc., how do you do it? Tacitus knows all about this, and so did Pliny and many of his peers, a reality to which I shall attend in the chapter that follows.

Imagine Josephus in an environment like this. It would not have been easy for Josephus to style himself as a poet or writer, when it was a well-known fact that he was a turncoat. Josephus could never under any circumstances have been critical of the Flavians. Josephus was not at liberty to write whatever he wanted, however he wanted it. The real problem for Josephus was rather how far he could praise the Flavians, and especially in his later years whether he could openly praise Domitian. Martial and Statius did, and perhaps as poets who depended partly on imperial patronage and approbation for their survival, they could not avoid playing the role of encomiasts. Does this excuse their praise of a tyrant or are they complicit? What about claims that they offered criticism in spite of it all?

Even for an established writer like Statius it may not always be clear when his supposed criticism of the tyrant is to be taken at face value, especially if the work was received at the time it was written as unproblematic and only later took on the attributes of defiance.[40] There is a most profound and interesting question: when is praise not praise but ironic criticism? When is praise satirical? How do you know? You may never know. But the fact that it is juxtaposed with other elements means one better think twice about it. It compels a double-take. Could it be read as "suspended criticism," living in a kind of suspended animation until the right circumstances come along to create the conditions for it to be read as such? But if it is so cryptic, then what is the use?

Take Tacitus's *Agricola*. It was written in homage to his father-in-law. But could anyone read it without thinking of the world around them, and how to deal with tyrants and sycophants? Not likely. So whatever we make of its intentions, it resonates and compels the reader to think twice about prevailing circumstances. Tacitus surely took this into account. He did not write the work until after Domitian's death. There was reason for that, which I shall discuss later. Even in a work by a dramatist, if the character first praises the emperor and then seems to change his mind later on, the mere fact that the change occurs is important. Whether that is enough to say that the later posture is the true posture and so the original position was a fake is not necessary. People do change their minds, so it is in character. The literary culture of the second half of the first century adds a lot to our understanding of the cultural context within which Josephus experienced his marginalization. His very presence in the literary circles of Rome would have been problematic and disorienting for all concerned, Josephus included.

One might consider Josephus among the Roman Stoics of the first century. Still, his Stoicism might have been deemed feigned, perhaps to curry favor. In an environment where Domitian started eliminating some of the most prominent Roman Stoics, what exactly was Josephus thinking when he presented himself as having been affiliated with the Pharisees in Jewish society, and describing the Pharisees as like the Stoics among his fellow Jews? Something here seems to be lost in translation, or to be missing in Josephus's understanding of his audience.

Take Tacitus and the virtues that he praises in his father-in-law in *Agricola*. Then let us picture a scene where Tacitus encounters Josephus either when Domitian's terror was in full force or after Domitian's assassination. What would Tacitus have thought of Josephus? Would we be surprised if Tacitus sneered at or ignored Josephus? Tacitus praises his father-in-law for retiring from politics so as not be a sycophant to a tyrant. Josephus, on the other hand, is dependent on a tyrant whom he dares not criticize, and worse, he presents the murderous tyrant as somehow of commendable character for not denying him his privileges, when he knows full well how many of the senatorial rank have lost their lives on account of the tyrant's cruelty. Worse still, Josephus would have his readers believe not only that Vespasian and his Flavian dynasty were good for Rome, but that he as a Jew had been endowed with prophetic insight to make bold a prediction that Vespasian would be raised to the *imperium* when he surrendered to Roman forces at the beginning of the Jewish War. Could none of this have mattered? They most certainly did.

In both Tacitus and Suetonius's story involving Vespasian we have something of a common understanding that Vespasian was ordained for the *imperium*. Josephus will tell a similar story, but in Josephus's version he himself is the protagonist in the story, whereas in both Suetonius and Tacitus's version Josephus is absent. The story deals with the interpretation of the oracle that Josephus claims misled his fellow Jews into revolt, whereas he himself saw it as a sign that Vespasian would rule the world as the man from the east that the oracle mentions. Josephus claims that he made this representation to Vespasian at the time of surrendering to the Roman army in Galilee, which secured his freedom and also brought him into the service of the emperor.

Actually, Josephus tells two stories in different places in the *Jewish War* that he does not repeat in the *Life*. At *Jewish War* 6.312–313 he describes the said oracle that was applied to Vespasian in terms very similar to how both Tacitus and Suetonius describe it.

> [One] will find that God has a care for men, and by all kinds of premonitory signs shows His people the way of salvation, while they owe their destruction to folly and calamities of their own choosing. Thus, the Jews, after the demolition of Antonia, reduced the temple to a square, although they had it recorded in their oracles that the city and the sanctuary would be taken when the temple should become four-square. But what more than all else incited them to the war was an ambiguous oracle, likewise found in their sacred scriptures, to the effect that at that time one from their country would become ruler of the world. This they understood to mean someone of their own race, and many of their wise men went astray in their interpretation of it. The oracle, however, in reality signified the sovereignty of Vespasian, who was proclaimed Emperor on Jewish soil. For all that, it is impossible for men to escape their fate, even though they foresee it. Some of these portents, then, the Jews interpreted to please themselves, others they treated with contempt, until the ruin of their country and their own destruction convicted them of their folly.[41]

However, in the earlier part of his narrative where he details the campaign in Galilee and his own command as general of the Jewish forces opposing the Romans in *Jewish War* 3.8.9, as I quoted previously, he makes himself the voice/interpreter of the oracle. Josephus is the protagonist in the story who claims to have offered his interpretation as a prediction to Vespasian, which in turn endeared him to the future emperor.

The second version is fundamental to Josephus's self-portrait as a Jew who changed sides, but who did so because he believed their mission was suicidal and founded on dubious premises. Of course, it raises the question as to why he joined the revolt in the first place. He answers and tries to preclude this objection by saying that he tried to persuade his fellow Jews from the course of action they eventually took but could not, and so he accepted command as general of the forces in Galilee.

On the specifics of his behavior leading up to his surrender to the Roman forces, he offers an extended description of what obtained in the Jewish camp among his fellow fighters and rebels, how he tried to influence them, and what finally became their lot, given that they were encircled and besieged by the Roman forces with almost no way of escape from the town of Jotapata.

Whatever the accuracy of his account of the behavior of those around him, one wonders about how much Josephus is to be believed about his own motives and actions. One wonders too about whether the absence of Josephus from Tacitus's version of the story is deliberate. After all, Tacitus also complains of some historians (plural, though he could mean just one) who write favorably about the Flavians.[42] Did he have Josephus in mind? Some scholars suspect that he did. If that is the case, then he had reason to elide Josephus from his account. In any event, the story about Vespasian's conquest and his rise to the *imperium* would have made the rounds in Rome. Whether or not everyone knew or believed the version told by Josephus in his *Jewish War* and in his *Life* is difficult to say. All the same, it is highly unlikely and perhaps doubtful that Tacitus had no idea of Josephus's version of the event, given how interested Tacitus was in Jewish matters. Tacitus would have his own moments in his *Histories* where he disparages Jews and their customs.

MARTIAL AND THE "CIRCUMCISED POET": THE POETICS OF CONTEMPT

Among Josephus's contemporaries, though, it is Martial whose silence about Josephus raises the most interesting questions as to how both he and Josephus could have avoided each other for more than two decades. Martial, the great stylist of the epigram, will take the contempt and mockery of Jews and Judaism to a level of literary respectability making it all the more curious why Josephus does not mention him and vice versa.

It might be said that the kind of verses that Martial writes to disparage Jews are few and far between and therefore not representative; or that we do not find many of them in our sources. But this would be to misunderstand what obtains here. They need not be profuse to prove the fact that the Jews of Judaea were humiliated or that Jews in Rome were treated with contempt. These were social, political, and spatial facts. They were enshrined in architectural monuments, coins, and in laws: the Arch of Titus; coins mentioning *Judaea capta*; the renewed law of the *fiscus Judaicus*; etc. They did not have to be repeated by anyone for them to be real, not even by poets. If the poet repeats or alludes to them, as Martial does, when he mentions "burned out Jerusalem" and the paying of tribute, he is merely calling attention to what is visible around him, known, and understood. He was not inventing them. To appropriate them was simply to remind his readers and his audience of what was already the case. So when he does mention them, they take on added significance. Statistics in this case are almost useless. Nor is the fact that Martial's epigrams about Jews and Jerusalem belong to his obscene epigrams and that these obscene epigrams make up only 10 percent of his entire output.

J. P. Sullivan provides the statistics. Martial published 1,172 poems between 85 and 101 CE in twelve books of epigrams.[43] Commenting on Martial's output, Sullivan writes:

> Of these there are only eighty six which a Victorian amateur of Latin literature would blush to offer in a literal English translation, which is considerably less than eight percent of the work. This is a surprising statistic in the light of

Martial's reputation as a pornographic classic like Catullus, Petronius, Juvenal, and Strato of Sardis.[44]

The Victorian amateur in this quotation is Walter C. A. Ker, whose Loeb translation of 1919 has the objectionable material in Italian. Sullivan gives the distribution of the said material across the books:

> The distribution of the grosser epigrams throughout the twelve books is interesting: five in Book 1; twelve in Book 2; eight in Book 3; none at all in Books 4 and 5; four in Book 6; nine in Book 7; none in Book 8, which specifically excludes them (8.1), being addressed to the Emperor Domitian; seven in Book 9; two in Book 10; but twenty-nine in Book 11 and ten in Book 12 (which may suggest a backlog from earlier eras but, more likely, derives from Martial's disillusionment with his prospects of patronage and his retirement to Spain).[45]

What does this distribution say? Many things, but none can be argued with any certainty, except for the fact that Martial excluded any of the objectionable material in the epigrams in Book 8 sent specifically to the Emperor Domitian and did not include any in Books 4 and 5, both of which also had a good deal of material dealing with Domitian. That may seem to support his later claim in Book 11 that Domitian put a curb on the freedom of expression, which supposedly then justifies the proliferation of such verses in Book 11. But this may be a ruse, and it appears most of his contemporaries did not buy it. Most of his epigrams were written during Domitian's reign: all of the first nine books, plus the original version of Book 10, which was later revised after the death of Domitian, and after Martial had already published Book 11 in which he tried to present himself as anything but a sycophant of Domitian.

Martial could defend himself to some extent that he had been restrained in his earlier books. Before the pivotal Book 8 he had already presented twenty-five (25) in his first three books alone; and in the two immediately preceding Book 8, he had presented thirteen (13). His output in Book 11, twenty-nine (29) epigrams, was only slightly higher than what he had done in the first three books, so obviously if one is counting in terms of how much he presented per book, then Book 11 is highly unusual. One possible explanation, and I cannot prove it, is that he wished to be forgiven for his excessive adulation of Domitian by being more obscene, knowing full well that he had an audience that enjoyed his bawdy and crude humor.

In any case, it does not do much to support J. P. Sullivan's earlier speculation that Martial "though an adept flatterer by necessity, was not necessarily, in my critical opinion, a natural writer of amusing or interesting obscene verse, hence the frequent grossness and reliance on sexual explicitness."[46] If he produced more of them at a time when he sensed a great danger to his life, livelihood, and reputation, then "natural writer" or not, he had made it part of his repertoire as a writer. So whether he wrote his earlier pieces "almost as fillers for the *libelli*, the personally circulated and highly complimentary slim volumes which Martial presented to potential or existing patrons before gathering them together annually at the request of his booksellers"[47] is irrelevant.

Defending Martial seems an unenviable task, but it has not prevented many scholars from doing so. Some go so far as to take at face value all of Martial's protestations of his innocence. Take, for example, Peter Howell's 1972 preface for the Modern Library edition of a selection of Martial's epigrams. Howell excuses Martial of all malice, even though Martial himself on occasion suggests otherwise. Howell writes:

> As Martial himself says, he does not write about gorgons or harpies: mankind is his concern. It is his acute perception of human nature, and boundless interest in the life around him, that makes him so permanently interesting. But his concern with mankind is not malicious. He is careful to make this absolutely clear in the Preface to Book I, where he states categorically that he has not satirised [sic] any real people, not even under fictitious names. Admittedly, under the early Empire, he would have been ill-advised to attack people of any importance, for emperors tended to discourage personal attacks. But Martial's warm-hearted character would in any case have avoided spitefulness. As a result, his verse may have lost some spice for his contemporaries, but it has gained timelessness and universality.[48]

Howell's account of Martial's supposedly "warm-hearted character" that eschews spite and is allergic to malice may seem almost unrecognizable to an average reader of the biting and scathing wit that infuse Martial's epigrams. There are other elements too. Why does this matter? J. P. Sullivan acknowledges in his *Martial: An Unexpected Classic* what everyone recognizes about Martial. "The strong sexual element in Martial's work has been a serious obstacle to several generations of readers. . . . It cannot be buried, as it is an important factor in our understanding and judgement of not only Martial, but also his audience and Roman literature in general."[49] The relationship between the sexually explicit material and other themes in the epigrams demand serious attention. They are not unrelated. Sullivan revises slightly upward his statistic for the obscene material. Thus Sullivan adds: "Although only ten percent of his epigrams would be regarded as obscene nowadays, over twenty percent (310 poems), most pejorative, relate to women, real or fictitious." He continues: "As might be expected, much of his misogynous satire is directed at the violation of the proper boundaries between the sexes and between social classes. But this is only part of the story: deeper forces are at work."[50]

Those deeper forces need to be taken seriously; Sullivan provides an extended discussion. At the same time, when it comes to sentiment, statistics are revealing but they can also conceal or mislead, and so may not always be as pertinent as they appear. Yes, it does matter that almost 10 percent of the time Martial writes obscene epigrams; and yes, it does matter that more than 20 percent of the time his epigrams address women, and most often pejoratively. These two instances make clear that he has a penchant for obscenity and is an unabashed misogynist. More importantly, in some instances the two overlap with vile and almost sadistic effect. But what do we say when Martial has less than ten epigrams dealing with Jews or the destruction of Jerusalem? Are these epigrams inconsequential in the scheme of things? After all, if it is a matter of statistics, then given the large corpus of his epigrams, they are miniscule: a fraction of 1 percent. Here is where the statistics can fail us, and most miserably.

In one important sense, Martial did not have to write a single epigram about Jews or the destruction of Jerusalem. As I already indicated, all around him there were reminders that mocked and ridiculed the Jews of Judaea.

A sentiment does not even have to be articulated for it to be real or potent. Most sentiments are unexpressed, but they have living force in the way people think, view the world around them, and act. How often a particular sentiment is articulated or expressed is simply a matter of repetition, it is not about the origin of the sentiment or its currency. It has more to do with how it is cultivated or nurtured, whether inwardly or out of public view, or outwardly and in full view of the world. So when dealing with sentiment, statistical frequency is not the ultimate sign of its viability or potency. That it is expressed at all is a sign of the acceptance of the sentiment by those by whom and to whom it is expressed. When it comes to sentiment, a single epigram, phrase, or gesture is enough. In some instances, what is most deeply held is often unexpressed. The occasional outburst is sufficient proof.

> Your overflowing malice, and your detraction everywhere of my books, I pardon: circumcised poet (*verpe poeta*), you are wise! This, too, I disregard, that when you carp at my poems you plunder them: too circumcised poet (*verpe poeta*), you are wise! What tortures me is this, that you, circumcised poet (*verpe poeta*), although born in the very midst of Solyma [Jerusalem], corrupt my boy. There! you deny it and swear to me by the Thunderer's Temple. I don't believe you: swear, circumcised one (*verpe*), by Anchialus.[51]

Martial mocks the "circumcised poet," who wishes to swear by the Thunderer's Temple. In mentioning the Thunderer's Temple Martial may be doing one of two things. First, he had the circumcised poet, the Jew, swear by the Temple of Jupiter in Rome. This has the effect of suggesting that this Jew is an inauthentic Jew; and second, that this Jew, whom he later describes as born in the very heart of Jerusalem (Solyma), has no temple in Jerusalem to swear by or that he chooses not to swear by it. Martial then presses the point of his inauthenticity by refusing to accept his swearing by Jupiter. For his part, he would consider this inauthentic Jew credible if only he would swear by Anchialus.

The name "Anchialus" has been something of a puzzle. In Ker's translation he provides a note that it is a reference to the boy who is supposed to have been defiled, abused, or used by the circumcised poet. Others have suggested that it is a corruption of a Jewish phrase, "as the Lord wills," which the Romans heard as "Anchialus;" or that it might refer to a character in Homer. The name "Anchialus" was also well attested among slaves and freedmen.[52] Whatever the referent, it is meant to be scornful or contemptible.

In the immediate context of Book 11 of Martial's epigrams in which he presents these verses about the circumcised poet, the preceding epigrams express a variety of sentiments; some touchingly endearing and others wicked and vile. Epigram 11.91 is an epitaph for Canace, a young girl who died aged seven. Martial writes endearingly and with great sympathy. Yet immediately following he is at his unpleasant best.

> To Zoilus:
> "He speaks erroneously, Zoilus, who calls you vicious. You are not vicious, Zoilus, but vice itself."[53]

In the one immediately following that addressed to the circumcised poet, he writes to yet another poet, Theodorus. One wonders if Theodorus the poet is also "the circumcised poet." Be that as it may, Martial wishes him dead.

> The flames have destroyed the Pierian dwelling of the bard Theodorus. Is this agreeable to you, you muses, and you, Phoebus? Oh shame, oh great wrong and scandal of the gods, that house and householder were not burned together![54]

Whether the burning of the house and the supposed scandal of the gods for not burning Theodorus together with his house has any bearing on Martial's reference elsewhere to "burnt out Jerusalem" is difficult if not impossible to determine (7.55). More significant perhaps is that Martial turns immediately in the next epigram to the circumcised poet from Jerusalem. Is it a coincidence? Who might this circumcised poet be who criticizes Martial and is accused of plagiarizing his works? It could not possibly be Josephus who is being mocked here? Josephus never indicated that he wrote verses. The representation does not necessarily have to be true for Josephus to be the target, however.

Elsewhere Martial is more perverse in his derision. Epigram 7.55 begins harmlessly enough on the theme of gift-giving and the mutual exchange and reciprocity that binds the gift-giver and the recipient. It soon turns phallic and homoerotic. It ends with a Jew who offers a gift in exchange, it seems, for burnt-out Jerusalem. His is a gift in return paid with his *mentula*.

Chrestus, if you return no man's presents, then don't give any to me or send any in return for mine; I shall think you sufficiently generous. But if you make return to Apicius and Lupus and Gallus and Titius and Caesius, you will perform fellatio, but not on me; mine is well-behaved and diminutive, but only one *mentulam* that comes from burned-out Jerusalem, one condemned to pay taxes.[55]

The ease with which Martial combines his bawdy humor with the destruction of "burned-out Jerusalem" in order to mock Chrestus (Greek for serviceable, useful, good for its kind), whoever he may be, or the Jew who is here represented by his *mentula*, is shocking. The Jew, like Chrestus, is serviceable in so many different ways for Martial's purposes—and not one of these purposes is good.

Menophilus covers his person with a sheath so enormous that it alone would be sufficient for the whole tribe of comic actors. This fellow I had imagined— for we often bathe together—was solicitous to spare his voice, Flaccus; but while he was exercising himself in the view of the people in the middle of the exercise ground, the sheath unluckily fell off; behold, he was circumcised (*verpus erat*).[56]

Martial seems somewhat neutral, here, in that he describes his real or imagined friend Menophilus with whom he went to the baths as having conned him: for while he had all along assumed the contrary, he found that he was in fact circumcised, when Menophilus lost an unusually large sheath that he used to cover himself only to reveal that he was circumcised. Even if one is willing to read 7.82 as somewhat harmless, it is nearly impossible to think that 7.55 should also be read as merely "benign." To do so would be to misconstrue its intent and the effect it has on those who enjoyed it and repeated it, to say nothing of the mind-set that entertains these thoughts and commits them to writing and wider publication.[57]

At a minimum Martial has nothing of Suetonius's apparent horror about what it meant for a ninety-year-old man to submit to inspection to find out whether he was circumcised or not; and less so of the hundreds of thousands who were destroyed in the burning of Jerusalem in 70 CE. Martial's epigram 7.55 is as caustic about the Jew paying the *fiscus Judaicus* as Suetonius's recollection of Jewish humiliation and degradation is tinged with sympathy. If Martial was the most read poet in Flavian Rome, one would have to assume that most Jews in the city would have endured a measure of humiliation and contempt in the city from Martial's effects alone. It is highly unlikely that any Jews would have found the literary salons of Martial's peers and contemporaries welcome places of social interaction. The moods created by Martial's epigrams would have been decidedly hostile and demeaning to them.

In two epigrams in Book 1, Martial makes reference to the district across the Tiber (*Transtiberinus*). In the first, he makes reference to a Jewish hawker (1.41), in the second (1.108) he mentions a friend Gallus, who lives across the Tiber. Gallus owns a beautiful house there, Martial writes, "I admit, but it is on the other side of the Tiber (*Transtiberinus*)." Martial probably intends this to be a reminder that this was not the best of neighborhoods. Martial was therefore not a stranger to the Jewish Quarter, as he assures Gallus that he must pay him a visit, a morning call, a visit that he deserves even if Gallus's house was much farther afield. He, after all, could gaze upon where Gallus lived from across the "other side" of the Tiber, as it were, in the Campus Martius, which was in the northwestern quadrant of the city.

Interestingly, Vespasian's apartment that became Josephus's home when he first settled in Rome after the Jewish War was located on the Quirinal Hill. Martial's apartment above the baths of Agrippa in the Campus Martius was within 1,500 yards (or let's say a mile) from Josephus's residence. We do not know if Josephus remained in this location for all of his life in Rome. But irrespective of where he lived later, it was not likely that he would have been a stranger to the Jewish Quarter. Nor could he have lived in Rome for all those years and not have heard, read, or known about Martial and his epigrams.

Martial directed his readers to look for his first book of epigrams from "Secundus, the freedman of the learned Lucensis" (Epigram 1.3). They had their bookselling operation behind Vespasian's famed Temple of Peace near the Roman Forum. It is acknowledged that the Temple of Peace was one of the most magnificent structures in Rome when it was completed by Vespasian. No one in Rome could miss its grandeur. It was an imposing edifice. Pliny the Elder described it thus:

> But this is indeed the moment for us to pass on to the wonders of our own city, to review the resources derived from the experiences of 800 years, and to show that here too in our buildings we have vanquished the world; and the frequency of this occurrence will be proved to match within a little the number of marvels that we shall describe. If we imagine the whole agglomeration of our buildings massed together and placed on one great heap, we shall see such grandeur towering above us as to make us think that some other world were being described, all concentrated in one single place. Even if we are not to include among our great achievements the Circus Maximus built by Julius Caesar, three furlongs in length and one in breadth, but with nearly three acres of buildings and seats for 250,000, should we not mention among our truly noble buildings the Basilica of Paulus, so remarkable for its columns from Phrygia, or the Forum of Augustus of Revered Memory or the Temple of Peace built by his Imperial Majesty the Emperor Vespasian, buildings the most beautiful the world has ever seen?[58]

For Pliny the Elder, the Temple of Peace was one of the architectural wonders of the world. Josephus lived even closer to the Temple of Peace than to Martial's residence.

Any mention of the Temple of Peace brought with it memories or remembrances of the conquest of the Jews of Judaea, the destruction of the Temple in Jerusalem, and the subsequent burning of the city. The phrase, "burned-out Jerusalem," that Martial used in Epigram 7.55 should be understood as a byword that easily came to most Romans living in the shadow of Vespasian's Temple of Peace. Josephus and the other Jews of the city of Rome could not escape its contemptible resonances even if they tried. The small number of epigrams that Martial devoted to the derision of Jews and Jerusalem, then, should not dispose us into thinking that Martial meant no harm. I cannot follow John Gager's rather sanguine review of Martial of all the main texts, Epigrams 7.30; 7.35; 7.82; 11.94.[59] Nor am I persuaded in relation to the literary circles to which Martial, Juvenal, and their kind belonged that, with respect to Jews and Judaism, "Roman attitudes undergo an unmistakable change at the end of the first century, from benign satire to real aversion."[60] Martial's attitude is far from benign.

Martial intends to be cruel. At the same time the level of ridicule in his epigrams about Jews and Jerusalem, while crude and obscene, has its parallel in some of what Josephus endured in the midst of the Jewish War in Judaea. At the moment when Jerusalem was set on fire Josephus speaks about the ridicule he endured from his fellow Jews in all the attempts he had made to dissuade them from war (speaking at times like Agrippa II). It is a scene in his *Jewish War* that reads almost as if Martial had this in mind when he used the phrase "burned-out Jerusalem" to demean the so-called "circumcised poet." Here is what Josephus says about the reaction of some of the Jewish brigands in seeing Jerusalem and nearby towns set on fire by the Romans:

> [The] Romans, having routed the brigands from the lower town, set the whole on fire as far as Siloam; the consuming of the town rejoiced their hearts, but they were disappointed of plunder, the rebels having cleared out everything before they retired to the upper city. For the latter showed no remorse for their evils, but rather bragged of them as blessings. Indeed, when they beheld the city [Jerusalem] burning, they declared with beaming faces that they cheerfully awaited the end, seeing that, with the people slaughtered, the temple in ashes and the town in flames, they were leaving nothing to their foes. Josephus, however, even at the last, never flagged in his entreaties to them on behalf of the relics of the town; yet for all his denunciation of their cruelty and impiety, for all the counsel offered to secure their salvation, the only return which he obtained was ridicule.[61]

Devoid of its phallic language, Martial's epigram about burned-out Jerusalem would not have read any differently to Josephus from what Josephus had endured from his fellow Jews prior to the destruction of Jerusalem, even as they stood at the sight of the burned-out Temple. Martial deepens the wound, but tragically it was one that had first been inflicted on Josephus by his fellow Jews. Martial made doubly sure by his lurid symbolism that the wound worsened.

The interesting question is how and why Martial escaped Josephus's censure. Why did Josephus not respond to Martial's calumnies? In abstraction, the question can be evaded. But to evade it is to assume that Josephus knew nothing of Martial's verbal denunciations, humiliations, and cruelties toward Jews. It becomes harder still to believe Josephus's ignorance or indifference, when we see what Josephus was prepared to write about Apion, the deceased Alexandrian Greek and contemporary of Philo, in his late work, *Against Apion*.

According to Josephus, one of the main reasons he took up the task of writing *Against Apion* was to respond to people in Rome who were repeating scurrilous attacks on Jews and Judaism made by the Alexandrian Greek writer Apion of the first half the first century. Josephus provides no names, no circles of influential or known individuals who were supposedly engaged in these calumnies that required a written response from him. Nor does he mention any written work among his contemporaries living in Rome at the time in this respect. What we do know are two basic facts. First, during his lifetime Apion already stood among his contemporaries in Rome in the first half of the century as a discredited figure. Second, the most widely read poet living in Rome in the second half of the first century was Martial. So, if anyone needed to be responded to it was Martial, who was an exact contemporary of Josephus, not Apion, who was long-since deceased. Or did Josephus write *Against Apion* after Martial had returned to his native Spain c. 98 CE? Even if that were the case, it would still not explain why he needed to respond to Apion's calumnies that were supposedly being repeated in Rome, when Martial and his living contemporaries were manufacturing new ones and rehearsing some old slurs as well.

AGAINST APION: HISTORICAL CRITICISM, *PROTREPTIKOS*, AND *APOLOGIA*

Steve Mason argues for *Against Apion* as a *protreptikos*, so that it has to be read as Josephus's call to philosophical conversion, because he presents Judaism as a philosophy. The better part of Mason's proposal has to do with another argument about what Josephus says about Jewish law and constitution. In other words, Josephus presents an account of what Judaism looks like as a *politeia*, political and social order. Then he makes the case that it has more ancient laws, better laws because they are practical, not like those of

Plato's Laws; and that the form of government is also divine and universally applicable. There are certainly elements in *Against Apion* that dilate on common themes found in other treatises designed to be read as a call to philosophy, as Mason shows in the most recent article on the subject.[62] Others are not so sure.[63]

The essays that make up a recent volume on *Against Apion* provide the layout of the terrain.[64] In their introduction John R. Levison and J. Ross Wagner point out the different approaches adopted in the respective papers. For my purposes, the most interesting part is the differences between Steve Mason and the other scholars who write about the rhetoric and objective of *Against Apion*.[65] Levison and Wagner comment as follows:

> Mason's conclusions are indeed not shared by all contributors. Van Henten and Abusch . . . understand the whole of Contra Apionem as forensic rhetoric. Moreover, Kasher, whose article on Josephus' rhetorical style we have already introduced, describes the purpose of Contra Apionem in altogether different terms from Mason when he writes, "Josephus cannot be suspected of having desired to encourage proselytism among the Gentiles. At most, I feel he sought to arouse sympathy for Judaism and to refute prejudices and deliberate calumnies by way of persuasion. It is certainly beyond doubt that he was well aware of the Emperor's policy on conversion in his day."[66]

Van Henten and Abusch contend it is a piece of forensic rhetoric; Mason says it is a *protreptikos*, so not forensic but somewhere between epideictic and deliberative rhetoric; between shared ideals and an exhortation to action.[67] Mason overstates the case, if only because Josephus does not say that he is writing to compel any such action, though it would be presumed if those who requested it were in fact thought to be desirous of such action or sympathetic toward it. The only remaining complication is the timing of the treatise, and here others have an important objection.

If Josephus is writing at a time under Domitian where the charge of *maiestas* can be directed against someone for following Jewish ways, then the entire notion of a *protreptikos* is vacuous. Who would be so mad as to do what would lead to their prosecution under the crime of *maiestas*, of minimizing the grandeur or greatness of Rome? Mason's own view that this is a measure of Josephus's courage is question begging. Would Josephus not be exposing himself to more personal accusation and calumny? What kind of courage would this be when he mentions that a slave in his employment made accusations against him to Domitian? If anything, it would be completely foolhardy and maddening for Josephus to do so by putting out a treatise urging conversion to Judaism under Domitian's tyranny. It is more probable that he wrote it after the death of Domitian, in which case, Mason's invocation of Josephus's courage would be irrelevant.

Even then why he took on the posture he did needs explaining. First and foremost, it needs to be acknowledged that the element of newness that Mason and others see in *Against Apion* is not always as it seems, nor what they claim. For example, Josephus's emphasis on theocracy (*theokratia*), a word he coined in 2.165, is not fundamentally different from what Josephus says about aristocracy in the *Antiquities*, as Salisbury points out in his article. Some of the calumnies mentioned in *Against Apion* are also present in the *Antiquities*: libel of the ancestors of Jews as lepers; Jews have not contributed to civilization; the nature of Jewish worship; atheism; misanthropy; practices such as Sabbath, circumcision, food laws, etc.[68]

Per Bilde's argument, Josephus's determination to "defend his own writings by placing them on a par with the Jewish Bible" seems closest to the truth.[69] Comparing *Jewish War* (1.3, 18; 3.340–408), *Antiquities* (20.264–266), *Life* 1–6, and *Against Apion* 1.1–56, Bilde demonstrates that Josephus always asserts his qualifications for truthfulness by appealing to his "priestly status, prophetic gift, and first-hand knowledge" of events to "describe the authors of the Jewish canon and his own qualifications as a Jewish writer of history."[70] In fact, Josephus conflates a number of things that on review prove to be mistaken, since his own works contain errors that the writers of the scriptures are not supposed to have made.

Bilde's argument, as summarized by Wagner and Levison, sees *Against Apion* 1.1–105, then, as Josephus's justification of himself in "response to Greek criticism of his own Jewish War and Antiquities."[71] Bilde does not separate the issues surrounding criticism of the *Jewish War* from the criticism of the *Antiquities*. He does not consider the relevance of someone like Justus of Tiberias, Josephus's own silences, his rewriting of biblical narratives, and the proposed book that he never wrote and how all of these relate to what became the *Against Apion*.

Against Mason, it should be clear that the entire treatise cannot be solely a *protreptikos*, because it picks up from where the *Antiquities* left off, with Josephus trying to convince an apparently non-Jewish but presumably sympathetic audience of the superiority of the Jewish way of life (in the singular). Josephus seems to have expected his audience to be sympathetic even when he disparages their traditions: Greeks, Romans, everyone. This is odd in so many different ways. Next to this is the connection between *Against Apion* and Josephus's *Jewish War*, *Antiquities*, and *Life*. Josephus clearly mentions the links between *Against Apion* and the *Antiquities* to indicate that he is continuing what he did there. But the reason why he must take on this new task is not as transparent as he claims. Why this kind of work? Why now? Why write against Apion, who has been dead for a few decades? Why Apion when others more recent and alive had written more directly against Jewish ways? Others like Martial?

There are significant differences in tone between *Against Apion* and the *Jewish War* as well. In the *Jewish War* Josephus presents himself basically as a Jew and a Roman whose sympathies and commitments are with the Roman cause. He is prepared to give up much in order to live out a Roman life. He still maintains that he remains a Jew, but much of his Jewishness, if we call it that, has been surrendered literally and figuratively to a Roman cause and a Roman life among the Flavians. He presents the Romans as divinely ordained to rule the world, and he invests the Flavians with authority vouchsafed by God. He also writes in a prophetic mode (Mason acknowledges this) and speaks like a prophet. He interprets dreams and so on. He is an oracle. He continues in a similar vein in his *Life*.

Against Apion takes a different tack that is partly acknowledged in various responses to the work. John Meyer addresses *Against Apion* in the context of a discussion about commonalities and differences among Jews of the first century under two headings: "A Culture of Sectarianism," and "Common Judaism."[72] Meyer quotes Josephus's description of the unanimity of Judaism in *Against Apion* and wonders how this fits with the different sects or groups that Josephus mentions in the *Jewish War* and the *Antiquities*. Either Josephus is "obfuscating for the purposes of apologetics," Meyer writes, or the differences in the various schools did not affect their essential unity, "certainly no more than did the divisions among the Greeks between Cynics, Epicureans, and Pythagoreans." Meyer adds:

> Indeed, for Josephus, the differences between the Greek sects or philosophies was much more fundamental than that between Pharisees, Sadducees, and Essenes, who for all their divisions, were still committed to observance of God's Torah around questions of Sabbath, kashrut, circumcision, and confession of Shema. In short, the "sectarianism" of the Second Temple period did not preclude inclusiveness or a sense of a "pluralistic" Israel.[73]

It is not clear if this is really how Josephus sees things. Josephus presents the various groups as distinct philosophical schools among the Greeks with different views that do not belong together. If it is his point to argue what all Jewish groups hold in common, that is not a problem. But if that is the intention, he does not do a very good job of it. However, if his point is to say that all Jews have the same views about the most fundamental questions that he addresses elsewhere, then he is contradicting himself. For in the *Antiquities* and in his *Life* he presents the various groups he profiles within Jewish life like the various philosophical schools among the Greeks. Here in *Against Apion*, however, Josephus insists that there are no contradictory statements about God among various Jewish traditions and that there are no differences among them as to how they conduct their lives. He insists on a basic unanimity that is as comprehensive as it is singular. That cannot be supported by his own writings, or the sources, as Meyer's comments show.

More importantly, Josephus's claims about unanimity are linked directly to biblical texts. It is to the biblical tradition that he grants the notion of unanimity that he first puts forth.

> For we have not an innumerable multitude of books among us, disagreeing from and contradicting one another, [as the Greeks have,] but only twenty-two books, which contain the records of all the past times; which are justly believed to be divine; and of them five belong to Moses, which contain his laws and the traditions of the origin of humankind till his death. This interval of time was little short of three thousand years; but as to the time from the death of Moses till the reign of Artaxerxes king of Persia, who reigned after Xerxes, the prophets, who were after Moses, wrote down what was done in their times in thirteen books. The remaining four books contain hymns to God, and precepts for the conduct of human life. It is true, our history has been written since Artaxerxes very particularly, but has not been esteemed of the like authority with the former by our forefathers, because there has not been an exact succession of prophets since that time; and how firmly we have given credit to these books of our own nation is evident by what we do; for during so many ages as have already passed, no one has been so bold as either to add anything to them, to take anything from them, or to make any change in them; but it is become natural to all Jews immediately, and from their very birth, to esteem these books to contain Divine doctrines, and to persist in them, and, if occasion be willingly to die for them.[74]

Josephus goes on to add that it is not unthinkable that Jews would hold on to their divine doctrines, preferring death to surrendering those doctrines. He had himself provided attestation of this in his *Jewish War* 1.1ff. He reiterates in *Against Apion*.

> For it is no new thing for our captives, many of them in number, and frequently in time, to be seen to endure racks and deaths of all kinds upon the theatres, that they may not be obliged to say one word against our laws and the records that contain them; whereas there are none at all among the Greeks who would undergo the least harm on that account, no, nor in case all the writings that are among them were to be destroyed; for they take them to be such discourses as are framed agreeably to the inclinations of those that write them; and they have justly the same opinion of the ancient writers, since they see some of the present generation bold enough to write about such affairs, wherein they were not present, nor had concern enough to inform themselves about them from those that knew them; examples of which may be had in this late war of ours, where some persons have written histories, and published them, without having been in the places concerned, or having been near them when the actions were done; but these men put a few things together by hearsay, and insolently abuse the world, and call these writings by the name of Histories.[75]

The distinction he draws initially is between divine doctrines that are found in scripture, and considered inviolate, and the variegated opinions or the inclinations of respective writers that are found among the Greeks and other nations. This is not necessarily a description of the various schools of thought among Jews as Josephus described them in the *Antiquities* and in his *Life*. It is a conception of scripture, which he presents as a fundamental difference separating Jews from Greeks and everyone else. He then slips into a different mode of argumentation by comparing his historical writing to those of others who supposedly have written what they neither witnessed nor learned from trusted sources what they did not know. That changes the terms of the debate considerably. It conflates two quite different realities. However, for Josephus they are not so different. For he assumes that the antiquity of the Jewish past is founded on the historical data of trusted sources. This is a characteristic he is prepared to grant to his own work as a historian but will contest in the case of other historians both ancient and contemporary.

As a piece of historical criticism, Josephus's *Against Apion* achieves what it sets out to do. The oddity is that we do not hear of Apion until the second book. But even this turns out to serve Josephus's purposes well. For he concentrates the first book on the historical works of three writers: Manetho, Chaeremon, and Lysimachus, whose works on Egyptian history provide the occasion for Josephus's historical criticism. This serves as prelude to his assessment of Apion's writings. Ironically, it is the very success of his historical critical work that also leaves him open to questions as to why he took on the task of responding to Apion's writings and not one of his living contemporaries.

Josephus seemed sensitive to this possible criticism. At the beginning of Book 2 he openly expresses his own misgivings as to why the refutation of Apion is necessary.

> In the first volume of this work, my most esteemed Epaphroditus, I demonstrated the antiquity of our Semite race, corroborating my statements by the writings calumnies of Phoenicians, Chaldaeans, and Egyptians, besides citing as witnesses numerous Greek historians; I also challenged the statements of Manetho, Chaeremon, and some others. I shall now proceed to refute the rest of the authors who have attacked us. I am doubtful, indeed, whether the remarks of Apion the grammarian deserve serious refutation. Some of these resemble the allegations made by others, some are very indifferent additions of his own; most of them are pure buffoonery, and, to tell the truth, display the gross ignorance of their author, a man of low character and a charlatan to the end of his days. Yet, since most people are so foolish as to find greater attraction in such compositions than in works of a serious nature, to be charmed by abuse and impatient of praise, I think it incumbent upon me not to pass over without examination even this author, who has written an indictment of us formal enough for a court of law. For I observe, on the other hand, that people in general also have a habit of being intensely delighted when one who has been the first to malign another has his own vices brought home to him. His argument is difficult to summarize and his meaning to grasp. But, so far as

the extreme disorder and confusion of his lying statements admit of analysis, one may say that some fall into the same category as those already investigated, relating to the departure of our ancestors from Egypt; others form an indictment of the Jewish residents in Alexandria; while a third class, mixed up with the rest, consists of accusations against our temple rites and our Jewish ordinances in general.[76]

Josephus still manages in other ways to create that unanimity. I discussed earlier how he excludes messianic expectation from Jewish history and theology in the *Antiquities*. Yet much of what comes out of the prophets, especially Isaiah, and their use by first-century Jewish sources, is unintelligible without it. Among the library of texts found in the caves of Qumran, texts from Isaiah are the third in number, after Deuteronomy and Psalms. In *Against Apion*, Josephus does not celebrate being a Roman, nor the fact that he is among the most competent of writers in Greek among his compatriots. He is not fulsome in his praise of things Roman and Greek and what have you. On the contrary, he is in the oppositional camp. In the guise of doing a history of the origins of his people, he can now castigate the other nations for being second-rate to Jewish political life, religious life, and yes, philosophy. Notice the emphasis on his people as opposed to being a Roman and a Jew. Of course, the fact that it is presented as to a Gentile audience does not quite overcome that it is also a polemic against Gentiles or rather the non-Jewish nations for having the wrong religious beliefs, rites, and laws. How is this supposed to appeal to them, if they entertain the kinds of scurrilous accusations made against Jews?

Martin Goodman, in an article on "Josephus's Treatise Against Apion," seems to overstate the case for the continuities between the *Antiquities* and *Against Apion*.[77] It is fine to say that Josephus continues his apologetic objective in *Against Apion* as he had in *Antiquities*. However, it does not explain the distinctive elements of *Against Apion* or even why Josephus saw the need for it, if as Goodman also believes, it was a timely piece and not really about a mid-century debate concerning the historical Apion. Goodman accepts that it was probably written just at the time of Domitian's demise, and sees it as a courageous work that insists on Jewish uniqueness; so that Josephus both heralds his being a Roman and a Jew in equal measures.[78] Goodman also suggests that Josephus's *Antiquities* presents a Judaism at variance with Roman ways, and therefore goes against the Flavian propaganda that was fostered by the Triumphal procession and the monuments in Rome that celebrated the defeat of the Jews, and that Josephus was also undermining the anti-Jewish slanders of his contemporaries in the era of Domitian's harsh policies on the *fiscus Judaicus*.

Goodman understates that Josephus too contributes to the Flavian propaganda; he had already done that in the *Jewish War*. There Josephus mentions matter-of-factly that Vespasian imposed a poll tax of two drachmas on every Jew no matter where they lived, and for the collection to be transferred to the Capitol in Rome, a sum which was previously paid to the Temple in Jerusalem (*Jewish War* 7.218). All of this belongs to his sentiments in 75/76 CE. When he came to the *Antiquities* and his *Life*, although he wrote both works in the thick of Domitian's repressive and recriminating tactics about the *fiscus Judaicus*, Josephus never mentioned the *fiscus Judaicus*. It is only if one does not pay attention to his *Jewish War* that Josephus can be presented as anti-Flavian in the *Antiquities*. In the *Jewish War* he signals his pro-Flavian views unabashedly, and often in juxtaposition with his strident criticism of his fellow Jews in Galilee and Judaea. In the *Antiquities* and especially in his *Life*, his sympathies toward the Flavians are captured both in his praise of the Flavian emperors and in his silences: namely, the atrocities that he refuses to mention or to criticize.

What is more, the *Antiquities* purports to be a historical project. So its polemical intent is not nearly as present as its historiography. Whatever seems anti-Roman, if indeed that is the intent, is presented in the form of an interpretation of "our ancient ways." *Against Apion*, on the other hand, is categorical and emphatic: this is what Josephus wishes to defend about the Jewish way of life. Goodman overlooks or understates the tensions between the *Jewish War* and the *Antiquities*, as well as the differences between *Against Apion* and both the *Jewish War* and *Antiquities*. When we consider them all together, it looks more like Josephus is writing in his own defense: not for Judaism, as such, but for himself, as someone who had maintained a pro-Flavian posture for much of his time in Rome but now needs to revise his position or remake himself.

How could Josephus not have been pro-Flavian? He was supported by them! There is not a single word against any of Domitian's policies. So Josephus looks more like Martial and others who found it extremely problematic to give a new account of themselves now that Domitian was dead and his memory damned. At the risk of overstatement, Josephus's defense of Judaism or the Jewish way of life in *Against Apion* is a pretext for Josephus's refashioning of himself after the death of Domitian.

Still, Goodman is right that a line passes from the *Antiquities* to *Against Apion*, with Josephus providing a classic *apologia*. This means that he has a specific case to make to his audience about Judaism and its viability in the late first century. In this respect, there are a number of issues to disambiguate. First, and this Goodman himself notes, why does Josephus smooth over almost all the differences he presents about Jewish groups in the *Antiquities*, and then say that what he is doing here is merely a continuation of what he did there? Anyone could check to see that that was not in fact the case. Second, why if he has contemporary detractors or claims that there are people still spewing the calumnies perpetrated by Apion does he not name any of them? Finally, why does he avoid his contemporaries in Rome who had produced calumnies of their own much worse perhaps than Apion, if we are allowed to put it that way?

The very staging of the dispute with Apion in Book 2 of *Against Apion* has much artificiality about it as to constitute a kind of shadow boxing. The real object of Josephus is not Apion. Apion happens to be a safe and convenient target, a foil for what Josephus needs to do. I suggest that part of that need was Josephus's own complicated relationship with the Flavians and the most recent historical past now that Domitian was dead, the same Domitian that Josephus praised or at least did not dare to criticize in his *Life*.

To appreciate this, we need to consider the history of Josephus's literary output and what he announced as his next projects after the *Antiquities* and the *Life*. At the end of the *Antiquities* Josephus signaled that he intended to write more works. This made plain Josephus's intention to append an autobiography to the *Antiquities* and his intention to write another work of a deeply theological nature. That he mentions that the theological work would be in three books indicates that he already had a plan for the work and perhaps even an outline. As things turned out, he did in fact write the *Life* or autobiography. But there is no indication that he ever wrote the three books "concerning our Jewish opinions about God and his essence, and about our laws" what it is permitted to do and what is proscribed. The projected work had a specifically apologetic intent: God and his essence, our laws, what is permitted to us and what is proscribed. As apologetics go, it would most likely have served the functions that Arnaldo Momigliano mentions in the following excerpt.

> A religious apology is not only a defense; it is, above all, a confrontation. This is its interest. An apology compels the believer to justify himself in the eyes of the world and to find, outside of idle custom, reasons of faith that have a universal value. A belief is opposed to a different belief in order to test its value and to see how it meets those demands that opponents raise through their objections. Thus, an apology invariably implies an examination of conscience, even when the din of war and love for oneself are not conducive to a calm consideration and tend to corrupt the debate by resorting to lawyerlike arguments. But a conscious reader understands, from what the apologist says and from what he does not say, that which appears to be the highest, unquestionable and original content of his religion, so that it can be offered without fear to the criticism of adversaries. Thus an apology invariably points to those elements that in a given time and for a given current of thought appear to be basic to a religion, those elements that have been affirmed as its reason to thrive and to be appreciated if not followed by other men. The choice of such elements is then used to weigh how the action of adversaries or, better, of current of thought in the surrounding world, have affected apologists by imposing their presuppositions to a greater or lesser extent, thus compelling the apologists themselves to deal with those very presuppositions.[79]

In its stead Josephus produces the *Against Apion*. Why the change? What exactly does the *Against Apion* do that made it an acceptable replacement for the previously intended project? Or should the question rather be: what compelled Josephus to write *Against Apion* and why the urgency, when he already had a project in mind, probably well outlined? As I mentioned earlier, something must have happened to compel Josephus to drop his intended project to write *Against Apion*.

Even if he finished the *Life* within a year of the *Antiquities* (I have already suggested the possibility of a different chronology), making the date of the completion of the *Life* 94/95 CE, we would have to place the combined *Antiquities-Life* at 95 CE, and this is on the most expedited writing schedule. We would still have to allow for some time for Josephus to respond to what he claims were criticisms of the *Antiquities* (93/94 CE) that he was responding to in *Against Apion*.

So allowing at least a year for the responses to come in, this puts the possible year of composition of *Against Apion* at 96 or 97 CE. This is awfully close, perhaps too close, for it not to have anything to do with the demise of Domitian and the end of the Flavian dynasty, in whose benevolence Josephus lived in retirement in Rome. Although I cannot prove it, I have already hinted at the view that, in all likelihood, Josephus wrote *Against Apion* after the assassination of Domitian in September 96. He abandoned the earlier apologetic project without necessarily abandoning some of the themes that he had planned for that project. For we soon discover that *Against Apion* deals with Judaism and its laws and constitution. The theological elements about God and his essence that he mentioned for the previous project barely show up in *Against Apion*. It shows up in a different guise: other motifs supplant it that still allow Josephus to speak about how the God that Jews worship is markedly superior to what anyone else worships. In one sense, then, for Josephus, *Against Apion* becomes a timely replacement for his previously planned theological-political treatise. The timeliness was almost certainly not of his own choosing. The social, political, and rhetorical occasion of the work may also explain why Josephus does not in fact address any of his living contemporaries who were writing calumnies against Jews, as we have already seen in the works of Martial.

JOSEPHUS'S SELF-PARODY: REREADING *AGAINST APION*

Before concluding this chapter, I wish to add here by elucidating why Josephus's *Against Apion* ought to be read as part of the literature on the post-Domitian context. Those who were afraid to write during Domitian's reign started to write and publish almost immediately after his death. Those who had been able to publish their works during his reign, and did not write in praise of Domitian, continued as usual. But for those who wrote in praise of Domitian, some effort was required to explain their past sycophancy and their present relevance and legitimacy. Although not a praise poet, Josephus still had some explaining to do, even if he had not been the most outlandish of Domitian's encomiasts. He still presented the Flavians, whose name he bore, as honorable and worthy emperors, Domitian included. Josephus's *Against Apion* served partly as a medium for remaking Josephus to his fellow Romans by what it did not say about Rome and Romans and what it did say about Greeks and Egyptians and everyone else who derided Jewish ways.

Josephus would most likely not have published *Against Apion* even as early as 95 CE when Domitian put to death his own cousin Flavius Clemens on the charge of adopting Jewish ways. Suetonius is clear on this. More to the point, after Domitian, the charge of adopting "Jewish ways" that had been prosecuted under the notion of "*maiestas*" (causing injury to the empire) would no longer be so feared. Only then could Josephus write so openly and critically of all things Greek and most things non-Jewish.

The putative Gentile audience for Josephus is both real and fictional. The fiction is that it is that audience that imposes itself on Josephus to write a work like *Against Apion*. Actually, he could have said as little as he could, since some of the arguments or the themes at least had been addressed in the *Antiquities*. In fact, the very opening lines of *Against Apion* suggest that Josephus is engaged in forensics. He uses the language of the courtroom. He presents himself as an advocate for the defense, and frames his discourse as a piece of forensic rhetoric.

Against Apion is Josephus's attempt to correct the representation he made of himself in the *Jewish War* as a Roman and a Jew. In *Against Apion*, there is hardly a mention of Josephus's *Romanitas* (Romanness). None. He sets about to speak boldly of the superiority of Judaism and the Jewish way of life as to make him practically anti-Roman. The elements of *protreptikos* help to disguise the aim; but it is there, and it is unmistakable in his trenchant criticism of Greek and Roman ways.

I suggest, then, that we read the *Against Apion* as an *apologia pro vita sua*. It is in defense of Josephus's own way of life. Not what he was before, but what he wished to be at the time of the writing. Thus, it is also Josephus's *Apology* for Judaism against all detractors. However, it is not a Judaism that actually exists as such but an ideal that Josephus would like to portray. (It could even serve as an anti-Christian polemic.) As such it is an apologia for an idealized Judaism that Josephus himself may not have practiced and had certainly not defended previously in the way that he does in *Against Apion*. It also has the function of a *protreptikos* for a revived or reconfigured Judaism of Josephus's making. On these terms it is doubtful how many Romans or Jewish sympathizers would have been persuaded by it. This pattern is not unusual. Josephus is rehabilitating himself at a time when he seems to have realized that his attempt to make himself into a full-fledged Roman has not succeeded. He turns back the clock. Or rather he repents of his past to present himself as an unapologetic Jew: in religion, ethos, ethnicity, philosophy, and commonwealth. It can also be read as Josephus's *final testament*.

He was not the only one among the residents of Rome who attempted a makeover in the aftermath of Domitian's death, as I have mentioned previously. Martial had done something similar in trying to ingratiate himself with the new regime by denouncing his own past as a praise poet of Domitian. Josephus had not written any praise poems of the likes of Martial's epigrams to and about Domitian. However, Josephus had praised Domitian, and showed no signs of repudiating in the slightest Domitian's atrocities during that reign of terror described by some of his contemporaries in Rome. He owed his living to the Flavians, and with the end of Domitian, Josephus too had come to an end. At this point, he remakes himself into a very different image of the one who had written the *Jewish War*. At this point in his life, he seems to have determined that he had nothing to lose. He exits the Roman stage on his own terms as a Jew, a native of Jerusalem, and of Judaea. One question remains, and it is worth asking it again: How truly free had Josephus been as a citizen of Rome and as a guest of the Flavians?

In review here are some of the details. Josephus wrote the *Life* in response to reaction to his *Jewish War*. Then he writes *Against Apion* partly in response to his *Antiquities*. He does not say that anyone objected to his *Life*. So we may set that aside as not germane at least initially to his *Against Apion*.

In the process of writing *Against Apion* he gives an account of himself and a justification of all the writings: *Jewish War*, *Antiquities*, and the *Life*. It lends to *Against Apion* an unmistakable sense of a defense of his very life, an *apologia pro vita sua*. But because Josephus does not acknowledge or admit this *apologia* in defense of his own life that he wishes to disguise, he is forced into theoretical and methodological considerations about history and historiography; how history is done and what he, as a historian, makes of the craft of history. All this is rather belated. He had all this in mind long before he wrote the *Against Apion*. He had some conception of this before he set out to write the *Jewish War*, and in fact, the influence of Polybius may already be present in that work.[80] It is here, however, in *Against Apion* that he presumably has the opportunity to set out specifically what he thinks of the art or craft of history. He mentions Polybius of Megalopolis by name in *Against Apion* 2.84.

Josephus establishes a seamlessness between himself or what he does as a historian (he had written an accurate account), the keepers of official records (those priests appointed to keep genealogical lists and so on), and the prophets of old who recorded the events recorded in scripture. He compares the last to the traditions of writing and record-keeping among the Chaldeans and Egyptians; and invests the Hebrew prophets with a kind of infallibility that he contrasts with the Greek writers of history who lacked proper records, and himself as clearly not like the Greek writers he criticizes on so many fronts. He says they are full of mendacity and error, why, because they write for all the wrong reasons, not about being historical, seeking the truth of what happened, but to impress as writers, or to object to others with whom they stand comparison, or to win favor for their display of wit. In short, they excel at their literary qualities, but not at the truth that should be rendered. He charges the entire Greek tradition of historical writing and historiography with these faults.

Trouble is, almost all the infractions he mentions the Greek historians committing are to be found in Josephus himself. If we take out the notion that he has some historical documents behind his work, he too, in spite of those sources, contradicts himself, makes mistakes, is rhetorical and self-serving at times, and does not always seem to be as concerned about the truth of history when he offers not just different interpretations but even different facts of the same events. In doing so, he distorts the authority of the Hebrew past and misrepresents his own qualities as a historian.

So while he is nearly correct in his historical criticism of the shortcomings of the Greek historical tradition, he does not seem to have overcome them in his own work as a historian, in spite of the fact that he has better resources or at least claims to have them, and has the benefit of also knowing the deficiencies of the past writers. To repeat their mistakes or shortcomings is to be in a much worse situation than they were. How does Josephus overcome this charge? That he does not even acknowledge that he may have been at fault in committing the same errors as those he criticizes is quite damning. For it leaves him open to any critic who can just point out his contradictions in the way that he claimed to do about the Greek historians and writers. It remains a mystery why the critical sensibility he displays when assessing other historians did not lead to self-criticism and reconsiderations of his own historical descriptions and arguments from the *Jewish War* to the *Antiquities* and the *Life*.

His spirited defense of his truthfulness with regard to what he does in the *Jewish War* is difficult to challenge; it can withstand criticism. As an eyewitness to some of the events, and for keeping records, and then offering his final product to those who were in a position to question his account, he has a lot going for him. They serve him well. The only problem is when he comes to write the *Antiquities* and then presents certain things in the *Antiquities* that contradict what he has done in the *War*. That he does not acknowledge any such reality when he is writing *Against Apion* in his last years is troubling. He may have been right when he did the *Jewish War*; but if he offers a different account and interpretation in the *Antiquities*, then he is no longer without contradiction; he is close to the mendacity he accuses the Greeks of.

A second element to *Against Apion* that stands out is Josephus's relentless mockery and abuse of Apion, who was deceased even before Josephus became a Pharisee (55/56 CE). Josephus calls him a liar, a deluded incompetent bore, a miscreant, and worse.

Josephus's invective against Apion pays the latter in his own coinage, using highly piquant and derisive language. At one point he calls Apion an ass and a person without a brain. All this, while Josephus never says a word about someone like Martial, a living contemporary poet, who was heaping abuse upon invective at a nameless or unidentified "circumcised poet." Nor does Josephus allude to Seneca who called the Jews an accursed race (*sceleratissime gentis*) as Augustine recounts in *City of God* 6.11 (cf. Tacitus, *Annals* 13.2). Or to Quintilian, who said something similar. He would not have known what Tacitus would write later in his *Histories*, but he surely knew those who were maligning Jews and Jewish ways of life among the educated elites in Rome, since he invokes a world in which criticism of his views were entertained. Those criticisms were invariably linked to the place of Jews in the world in general and their status in Roman society.

If Josephus could write so trenchantly against Apion, why did he not do so against Seneca or Martial, both of whom had expressed their disdain for Jews? Or was it rather that by speaking of those who were susceptible to Apion's calumnies he intended his *Against Apion* to serve as a rebuttal to them as well? Apion, as I noted, made an easy target. With a memorable sobriquet, "the world's gong" (*cymbalum mundi*), foisted on him by the Emperor Tiberius, Pliny the Elder wrote that Apion was more a gong of his own renown, more self-promotion than anything else.

I am following here Cynthia Damon's brief biographical sketch[81] with additions from Josephus's portrait at the beginning of *Against Apion* 2.

> Apion, an Egyptian by birth, trained as a grammaticus, succeeded the distinguished Theon as the head of the famed Library in Alexandria, the Museum (c. 20 CE). He had established a reputation as a great contributor to Homeric scholarship and had published a handbook of Homeric expressions (Glossary of Homeric Expressions). He was known in Alexandria, and traveled extensively, lecturing in Rome and Greece. According to Seneca (Ep. 88.40) he was called (*ho homerikos*), as if the very embodiment of Homer. He also had a reputation for demagoguery; when he represented the Greek citizens of Alexandria against their Jewish neighbors in the events and legations surrounding riots in Alexandria in 38 CE. In this event, he stood on opposite sides with the philosopher Philo Judaeus, who gives an account of the encounter in his *Legatio ad Gaium*. Josephus covers the event in *Antiquities* 18.257–259.

The choice of Apion as the focus of Josephus's refutation was not merely serendipitous. Apion was the public face of anti-Jewish sentiment expressed by a Greek who demanded Roman sympathy and judgment. So Josephus's choice made perfect sense except for the fact that it seemed cowardly when there were living contemporaries who were spewing vitriol and making virulent attacks against Jews. The choice, then, cannot be considered without some consideration that in Apion Josephus had made a preference as to whom among the potential anti-Jewish writers he would take on. Apion was his preferred choice. His claim that he picked Apion because there were many among his contemporaries who accepted and repeated his calumnies makes it impossible to dissociate Josephus's preference from what his contemporaries said and thought about Jews and whatever calumnies were being manufactured or produced in Rome in the 90s when Josephus wrote *Against Apion*. The only documented sources are the few epigrams of Martial and the writings of Seneca (Ep. 95.47; QN 4.1) from the previous generation. As for sources dealing with aspects of Jewish life deemed strange by Romans we have the poems of Persius, the satires of Juvenal, and the still earlier works by Horace and Ovid, some speaking about Sabbath and dietary laws and the like.

In point of fact, Romans did not need Apion's old and inveterate Egyptian calumnies to indulge their contempt for Judaeans or Jews. The monuments and artifacts in Rome associated with the destruction of Jerusalem and the burning of the Temple told their own tales, expressing a rhetoric of contempt, derision, and humiliation. Josephus himself lived within sight of these monuments, memorials to a living reality. Josephus could just as easily have written an ode to Jerusalem and to the Jewish past; he, after all, was reminded of these facts daily. The monuments in Rome did more than anything Apion could have done for contemporary Roman attitudes about Jews, Jerusalem, Judaism, and Judaeans.

Josephus needed a foil, not for his apologia for Judaism, or Judaism in Roman dress, as Barclay suggests, or a *protreptikos* as Mason's construes it, but rather for his own refashioning of himself in a post-Domitian era. He was not the only one who had to remake himself. Even apologists for Martial cannot quite overlook his own verbal acrobatics in trying to dissociate himself from the maligned Domitian, now that Domitian was dead. As Peter Howell writes somewhat reluctantly, "Martial's flattery of Domitian may seem gross to us (for example, the frequent comparisons, if not identifications, with Jupiter), and his abuse of him after his assassination is indefensible, though it is hard to blame him for knowing on which side his bread was buttered.[82] Yet the same Howell claimed there was no malice in Martial.[83]

All the loose threads in *Against Apion* that do not quite fit into a pattern are easy to tie together once we see this logic: First, Josephus writes to remake his past and to recast his own personhood as a Jew, who remains always a Jew, whether he is Roman or not. Second, Josephus presents Judaism as the most ancient society compared to both Greek and Roman societies. Third, all the arguments Josephus makes against the Greeks are applicable for the most part to Rome and to Romans whether it is about the vanity of its histories, the preference of rhetoric over truth, the errors of the gods, and so on. Fourth, whatever Josephus says about the constitutions of the Jews (previously the aristocracy of the Jews in the *Antiquities*) indirectly opposes tyranny as a form of government and can thus be read as a critique of what had transpired under Domitian, even if he continued to receive benefactions from him. If pressed, Josephus could always say that he was a "son" of Vespasian and a brother of Titus and Domitian, and a better friend to Titus than to Domitian.

I should add a fifth: all the vehemence that Josephus directs against Apion, all the ridicule and scorn he pours on him, contain the kind of riposte he would have liked to have sent Martial's way, if he had ever encountered his epigrams about Jews. I have argued that he did, or that he could not have missed them. The choice of Apion as the target allowed Josephus not to have to make the difficult choice of writing against his living contemporaries. (Martial will claim such a posture himself at the opening of his first book of epigrams that he shall not name any living opponents.) Since those among them who remained sympathetic to Apion's kind of vitriol against Jews were part of the audience against which Josephus wrote, we will have to assume that what was good for Apion was good for them too.

Shaye J. D. Cohen's piece on Josephus and historiography in *Against Apion* seems to misrepresent what Josephus is doing.[84] Yes, Josephus criticizes Greek historians, but he does so because they have the greatest reputation for being masters of the craft. That criticism has to do with the question of antiquity; why, if they are the masters of the craft, are they full of contradictions and why have they ignored Jews in their universal histories? The next plank of Josephus's argument is to say that the Egyptian historians (some of whom are also Greek) also got their history of the Jews wrong. The fact that they are Egyptian does not mean they are not Greek. But Josephus emphasizes being Egyptian since that is the locus of the Jews who are under attack. This sets him up to take on Apion, who is both Greek and Egyptian. There is no contradiction here. In any case, Cohen's ways of resolving the alleged contradictions are peculiar: (1) Josephus is a sloppy thinker; (2) he failed to homogenize his sources; (3) he revised *Against Apion* several times and did not notice the roughness; and (4) he knowingly used "less-than-perfect arguments in his defense of what he took to be the truth."[85]

Even assuming Cohen to be correct, this has little bearing on Josephus's characterization of Apion. At 2.12 Josephus writes: "Such is the amazing statement of the scholar (*grammatikos*). Its falsity does not need to be argued, but it is quite evident from the facts."[86] The sarcastic reference to "the scholar" and his "amazing statement" piles irony upon sarcasm.[87] At 2:25 he refers to the "amazing Apion." At 2.15 Josephus describes Apion as the most "accurate" or "precise" (*akribas*) scholar (*grammatikos*) who cannot get his facts straight and is full of mendacity.[88] Josephus calls Apion a liar on many occasions. It is probably his favorite tag. At 2.29, he is the "original Egyptian" or "first among the Egyptians," who nevertheless disparages his homeland. At 2.42 Josephus refers to him as "the noble Apion," who slanders with such ignominy the Jews of Alexandria in order to repay his fellow Alexandrians for the Roman citizenship bestowed on him. Apion spews nonsense (2.116), is full of ignorance (2.3ff., 2.26, 2.37, 2.38, 2.130), and lies with arrogance (2.26, 2.28, 2.80, 2.85, 2.89). At 2.88 he is the greatest imbecile.[89]

Josephus had previously dealt with Apion in *Antiquities* 18.257–260 in relation to his role in the Alexandrian riots that led to the various legations to Gaius Caligula in 39 CE. In the account in *Antiquities*, Josephus made it clear that Apion had a long-standing reputation of despising the Jews of Alexandria. The account Josephus presents in *Against Apion* 2.33–78 bears on that earlier history. However, Josephus does not bring into his current discussion any of that material. It is as if it did not matter. Yet everything he said about Apion among his fellow Eygptians the first time alludes to it. It raises the question once more of why he needed Apion for this new project. He claims that Apion still had influence: But this justification of his choice of Apion as the object of his criticism still does not fully explain why he had to respond to Apion at this particular moment in time:

> I shall now begin to refute the remaining authors who have written something against us, and in venturing a counter-statement against Apion the "scholar," it occurred to me to wonder whether it is necessary to make the effort. For some of what he writes is similar to what has been said by others; some things he has added in an extremely artificial manner; but most is of the nature of burlesque and contains, if the truth be told, gross ignorance, as if concocted by a man who is both despicable in character and a lifelong rabble-rouser. However, since most people, because of their folly, are captivated by such language rather than by literature of a serious nature, and enjoy insults, while finding expressions of praise irksome I have deemed it necessary not to leave even this man unscrutinized, since he has composed a charge against us as though in a lawsuit. Besides, I notice that it is also the case that most people are particularly delighted whenever someone who has begun to slander another is himself convicted of vices pertaining to himself. Now it is not easy to follow Apion's discourse or to know for sure what he intends to say. Roughly—as his material is in great disorder, with lies all jumbled up—some of what he says falls into the category as the material we have already scrutinized concerning migration of our ancestors from Egypt; some is a charge against the Judeans who reside in Alexandria; thirdly, there is mixed up with these a charge concerning the ritual practiced in our temple and the rest of our rules.[90]

The Loeb translation captures the mood better than this less literal translation by John Barclay of the first line of this paragraph. Simply put, Josephus is in doubt whether Apion is worthy of criticism. Because if his calumnies fit the description that Josephus gives them—confused, pure buffoonery, based on ignorance, full of error and lies, etc.—then truly there is some doubt whether they are worth a rebuttal, especially if what he is saying also mimics what others have said; and if Josephus has provided objections to those others. So why do it? Josephus justifies his effort by saying that Apion's calumny remains current, since his views are being repeated among Josephus's contemporaries. But why did they need to repeat them? For what purpose? After all, if it had to do with the Temple, well the Temple had been destroyed and the Romans had made sure to commemorate that in monuments in Rome. If it had to do with the "rest of our rules," that too seemed unnecessary. After all, a defeated and vanquished people could not claim that what they believed or the God they worshipped was all that creditable. So why even keep those rules? Besides, both Greek and some non-Greek writers had been objecting to this for some time now. So what was so novel about repeating Apion's calumnies after 94 CE?

Through *Against Apion* 2.1–7 Josephus does not mention that others are repeating Apion. That comes much later. The two reasons he gives here are 1) that Apion is caught in his own lies and slanders, and it is delightful to expose him on that account; and 2) that most people are charmed by what is abusive rather than literary works that are intent on truthfulness, so he would not want those characterized by folly to think they knew what was truly the case. Oddly, though, in exposing Apion's slanders and lies, Josephus also tends to be abusive rather than simply stating his case about Apion. He cannot help mocking and ridiculing Apion for his rank dishonesty and contemptuousness.

In *Against Apion* 1.1–5 he speaks of certain individuals who questioned his *Antiquities* and who depend on the previous calumnies of other writers. Ostensibly these are the writers he deals with in Book 1. He does not mention Apion among them. The impression one forms is that the criticism of his *Antiquities* was not motivated by what people had read in Apion. Josephus's contemporaries were reading or using some of the sources he takes up in Book 1. This explains in part his hesitancy about dealing with Apion in Book 2. It is almost as if it was not planned. But he had to find a place for Apion. It allows him to castigate a first-century writer, though not quite a contemporary, rather than the older historical sources, some going back more than four centuries, that he deals with in Book 1: Manetho, Lysimachus, etc. It served a useful purpose to pick on the discredited Apion. It was easier to mock him than to try to mock Martial, for example, even though Martial was the more present threat. More than that, the argument against Apion in Book 2 of *Against Apion* allowed Josephus to remake his identity and self-representation as a Jew and a Roman citizen from Judaea in contradistinction to Apion, the Alexandrian Greek and Roman citizen from Egypt.

No longer an apologist for Rome and its empire, Josephus re-presents himself as a Jew first and a Roman second, devoted to the laws and constitutions of Judaean religion and polity, even if the center of that religion no longer exists (the Temple) and even if the polity in any real and meaningful sense can only be found in communities in exile. As one of the Flavians, or a beneficiary of the Flavians, he exits the Roman stage with Domitian, the last of the Flavian emperors. He signs off *Against Apion*, congratulating his friend, a Gentile, a lover of truth; not like Apion and those like him: "To you, Epaphroditus, who are a devoted lover of truth, and for your sake to any who, like you, may wish to know the facts about our race (*genos*), I beg to dedicate this and the preceding book."[91]

In the end, Josephus seems to have recovered himself and returned to an original position that he held as a Jew in Judaea and Galilee, or wished to be seen as such, or both. *Against Apion* makes no accommodation toward Roman ways or being a Roman as the distinction for this particular Jew. To the contrary: at a time when a Hellene like Plutarch was crafting an elaborate intellectual and cultural rapprochement between being Greek and being Roman (in his *Parallel Lives*, in particular), Josephus seems to have given up completely at this late stage in his life on any such reconciliation (if ever it were possible) between being a Jew and being a Roman who had betrayed the Jewish cause.

One may recall here the experiences of both King Herod Agrippa I and King Herod Agrippa II. The later was Josephus's friend and contemporary. In many ways Josephus claimed to be not very different from Agrippa II. He advertised this much in his *Jewish War* and *Antiquities*. In fact, the speech he reports of Agrippa II in the *Jewish War* 2.346–401 warning the people of Jerusalem not to revolt at the beginning of the War is quite similar to the assertions Josephus himself makes in his objections to his compatriots about the folly of rebelling against the Romans. However, in the end Josephus seems to have turned in a direction closer to the sentiments of Herod Agrippa I, if the letter to Gaius Caligula as reported by Philo in his *Ad Gaium* truly reflects what Agrippa I actually said or wrote.

In a long letter in which he made a plea to the Emperor Caligula to refrain from desecrating the Temple in Jerusalem, Agrippa I concluded as follows.

> If I should recount the benefits conferred on myself by you, the day will be too short, and besides it is not suitable to treat a primary task as an appendage to another subject. And indeed even if I hold my peace the facts themselves break into speech and cry aloud. You released me bound fast in iron fetters, who does not know it? But do not clamp me, my emperor, with still more grievous fetters, for those which were then unbound encompassed but a part of my body, those which I see before me are of the soul and must press hard on every part of its whole being. You thrust away the ever imminent terror of death, you kindled fresh life in me when dead with fear, you awakened me as though I

were born anew. Maintain your bounty, my emperor, that your Agrippa may not bid farewell to life, for it will seem as though my release was not given to save me but that a victim to heavier misfortunes I should come to a more notorious end. The greatest gift of fortune that man can possess you granted to me, a kingdom, in the past of one country, later of another and a greater when you added Trachonitis as it is called and Galilee. Do not after granting me favours in super-abundance take from me bare necessities, and after restoring me to light of fullest radiance cast me anew into deepest darkness.

I renounce all that brilliance, I do not beg to keep my shortlived good fortune. I exchange all for one thing only, that the ancestral institutions be not disturbed. For what would be my reputation among either my compatriots or all other men? Either I must seem a traitor to my people or no longer be counted your friend as I have been; there is no other alternative, and what greater ill could befall me than these? For if I still keep my place in the list of your companions I shall lie under an imputation of treachery, unless my homeland is guarded unscathed from every kind of mischief and the temple is untouched. For you great potentates safeguard the interests of your companions and those who take refuge with you by manifestations of your absolute power. But if your mind harbour any hostility to me, do not imprison me as Tiberius did, rather do away with any idea of future imprisonment and at the same time bid me take myself out of the way forthwith. For of what value would life be to me whose one hope of salvation lay in your goodwill?[92]

The self-representation of Herod Agrippa I captured here by Philo anticipates Josephus at every turn. Agrippa I, who had once been bound under orders from the Emperor Tiberius, became a free man and a ruler of his people, who now pleads that he not be turned into a traitor. Josephus had been a traitor to the Jewish cause, was made a prisoner bound in chains, and was subsequently released from his bonds. He would be a witness not merely to the desecration of the Temple, but to its destruction. He would have to live with the pillaging of its contents, and with the commemoration of the event in Rome in pageant and architectural monuments. He would have to endure the calumny of Romans for much of his later years as a citizen and resident of Rome. *Against Apion* captures almost unwittingly the inherent contradictions of a good deal of Josephus's Roman self; a Roman self that he had finally come to reject or wished to reject.

While Josephus may not have written explicitly and directly against Roman ways in *Against Apion*, everything he said about Greeks, their historians, their pretenses, their religions, their polity, everything he said in comparison, criticism, and refutation (and at times denunciation) served a double purpose: Josephus was opposing Roman ways, as well. There is then a trajectory from the *Jewish War* to *Against Apion*. It can be missed if we overlook the particular occasion which prompted Josephus to abandon his projected work on the nature of God and his essence and the rules that govern Jewish lives, and in its stead, to write *Against Apion*. In responding to Apion in

Book 2 of *Against Apion* he mentioned something about "our rules" much like what he anticipated with the rules that govern Jewish lives in the abandoned work; but he did not address that part about God and his essence. Perhaps, he no longer had to. If *Against Apion* proves anything, it makes patent that ultimately Josephus could not disavow his Jewishness, even if he had longed ceased to be affiliated with the Pharisees. Whether he was prepared to change his name from Flavius Josephus back to Josephus son of Matthias, now that the Flavians were no more, we will never know. That he does not explicitly criticize Roman ways but finds himself free to criticize all things Greek is a literary conceit of some ingenuity, even as he claims contemporary relevance while remaining manifestly silent about all of his living contemporaries.

NOTES

1. Cicero, *Pro Flacco* 67–68 (LCL 324, 515–17).
2. Cicero, *Pro Flacco* 69 (LCL 324, 517–19 [slightly altered]).
3. Seneca, *De Superstitione*, quoted by Augustine, City of God, 6.11: *Augustine: The City of God Against the Pagans* (Cambridge, Cambridge University Press, 1998), 264.
4. For a brief assessment of the various positions taken by respective scholars on Josephus's knowledge of Philo, see Louis H. Feldman, *Josephus and Modern Scholarship: (1937–1980)* (New York: De Gruyter, 1984), 410–18.
5. See in this regard, Gregory E. Sterling, "'A Man of the Highest Repute': Did Josephus Know the Writings of Philo?" *Studia Philonica* 25 (2013), 101–14; Maren Niehoff, "Josephus and Philo in Rome," in *A Companion to Josephus* (Sommerset, UK: Wiley, 2015), 135–46; and her, *Philo of Alexandria: An Intellectual Biography* (New Haven: Yale University Press, 2018), 89–90; 105–6.
6. Josephus, *Antiquities* 2.267–268 (LCL 456, 141–45).
7. Feldman, *Josephus and Modern Scholarship*, 387–88.
8. Menahem Stein, *Josephus:* Against Apion *[and]* Life (Tel Aviv, 1968 [in Hebrew], originally published in 1932/33), 177 n. 5, quoted by Daniel R. Schwartz, "Josephus in Recent Hebrew Scholarship," in *A Companion to Josephus* (Oxford: Wiley, 2016), 420, attempts to make sense of this.
9. Josephus, *Life* 430a. Steve Mason, *Flavius Josephus: Life of Josephus* (Leiden: Brill, 2001), 172.
10. Josephus, *Antiquities* 20.266 (LCL 456, 141).
11. The fundamental work here is Shaye J. D. Cohen, *Josephus in Galilee and Rome: His Vita and Development as a Historian* (Leiden: Brill, 1979).
12. Mason, *Flavius Josephus: Life of Josephus*, xlvii.
13. Tessa Rajak, *Josephus: The Historian and His Society* (London: Duckworth, 2002), 6.
14. William den Hollander, *Josephus, the Emperors, and the City of Rome: From Hostage to Historian* (Leiden: Brill, 2014).
15. The nature of Cornelius Tacitus's views and sentiments is a complicated one. While most historians take a straightforward view and read his comments about Jews and Jewish ways in his *Histories*, for example, as caustic and demeaning, and have referred to him as anti-Jewish and anti-Semitic, Erich S. Gruen recommends a less straightforward view of Tacitus's words and his language. He proposes that he be taken seriously for the irony in his writing and the humor in some of his descriptions. Whether this resolves all the problems entailed in writing history or ethnography in an ironic mode is an open question. See, in particular, Gruen's *Rethinking the Other in Antiquity* (Princeton: Princeton University Press, 2010). For another

view of Tacitus as ethnographer, see Benjamin Isaac, *The Invention of Racism in Classical Antiquity* (Princeton: Princeton University Press, 2004).

16. Suetonius, *Domitian* 12.2 (LCL 38, 349–51).
17. On Martial and his Roman context, see J. P. Sullivan, *Martial: The Unexpected Classic* (Cambridge: Cambridge University Press, 1991); Ruurd R. Nauta, *Poetry for Patrons: Literary Communication in the Age of Domitian* (Leiden: Brill, 2002); William Fitzgerald, *Martial: The World of the Epigram* (Chicago: University of Chicago Press, 2007); and Victoria E. Rimell, *Martial's Rome: Empire and the Ideology of Epigram* (Cambridge: Cambridge University Press, 2009).
18. Josephus, *Jewish War* 3.392–398 (LCL 487, 115–17).
19. Josephus, *Jewish War* 3.399–402 (LCL 487, 117).
20. Josephus, *Jewish War* 3.403–408 (LCL 487, 117–19).
21. Josephus, *Jewish War* 3.350–354 (LCL 487, 103–5).
22. Josephus, *Life* 414–417 (LCL 186, 151–53).
23. Josephus, *Life* 418 (LCL 186, 153–55).
24. Josephus, *Life* 423–425 (LCL 186, 155–57).
25. Josephus, *Life* 426–428 (LCL 186, 157).
26. Josephus, *Life* 428–430 (LCL 186, 157–59).
27. Josephus, *Life* 430 (LCL 186, 159).
28. On Josephus's views and criticism of Justus of Tiberias see Seth Schwartz, *Josephus and Judean Politics* (Leiden: Brill, 1990), 141ff. See also Tessa Rajak, *Josephus: The Historian and His Society*, 146ff.
29. Josephus, *Jewish War* 7.132–141 (LCL 210, 545–47).
30. Josephus, *Jewish War* 7.142–145 (LCL 210, 547–48).
31. Josephus, *Jewish War* 7.145–152 (LCL 210, 548–49).
32. Josephus, *Jewish War* 7.153–157 (LCL 210, 551).
33. Josephus, *Jewish War* 7.158–162 (LCL 210, 551–53).
34. Josephus, *Jewish War* 6.352–357 (LCL 210, 479).
35. Jonathan Price, "The Provincial Historian in Rome," in *Josephus and Jewish History in Flavian Rome and Beyond*, edited by Joseph Sievers and Gaia Lembi (Leiden: Brill, 2005), 101–18. The reference is to 104–5.
36. Ibid., 105.
37. Ibid., 118.
38. Mason, *Flavius Josephus: The Life of Josephus*, 168n1742.
39. Seneca, *Moral and Political Essays* (Cambridge: Cambridge University Press, 1995), 71.
40. See Stephen Harrison (ed.), *Blackwell: A Companion to Latin Literature* (Oxford: Blackwell, 2005), 73–74.
41. Josephus, *Jewish War* 6.312–313 (LCL 210, 269–71).
42. On Josephus in Rome and among the Flavians, see now the account by den Hollander, *Josephus, the Emperors and the City of Rome*.
43. J. P. Sullivan, "Martial's Sexual Attitudes," *Philologus-Zeitschrift fur antike literature und ihre Rezeption*, Volume 123.1–2 (1979), 288–302: Reference is to 288.
44. Ibid., 288–89.
45. Ibid., 289.
46. Ibid., 289.
47. Ibid., 289.
48. *Martial: Epigrams*. Selected and translated by James Michie. Introduction by Shadi Bartsch (New York: Modern Library, 2002), xxxi.
49. Sullivan, *Martial: Unexpected Classic*, 185.
50. Ibid., 185.
51. Martial, *Epigrams* 11.94 (Ker translation, LCL vol 2, 303: adapted).
52. Cf. Louis Feldman, *Jew and Gentile in the Ancient World: Attitudes and Interactions from Alexander to Justinian* (Princeton: Princeton University Press, 1993), 156.
53. Martial, *Epigrams* 11.92 (Bohn Classical Library, 1897 [henceforth, Bohn translation]), 538.

54. Martial, *Epigrams* 11.93 (Bohn translation]), 538.
55. Martial, *Epigrams* 7.55 (LCL 95, 119; adapted).
56. Martial, *Epigrams* 7.82 (LCL, Vol. 1 [1919–1920], 479; adapted).
57. Cf. Shaye J. D. Cohen, *The Beginnings of Jewishness: Boundaries, Varieties, Uncertainties* (Berkeley: University of California Press, 1999), 351–59.
58. Pliny the Elder, *Natural History* 36.24[101–102] (LCL 419, 79–81).
59. John G. Gager, *The Origins of Anti-Semitism: Attitudes toward Judaism in Pagan and Christian Antiquity* (New York: Oxford University Press, 1985), 56–57.
60. Ibid., 59.
61. Josephus, *Jewish War* 6.363–365 (LCL 210, 481–83).
62. Steve Mason, "Contra Apionem in Social and Historical Context: An Invitation to Philosophy," in Louis H. Feldman and J. R Levison, *Josephus's Contra Apionem: Studies in Its Character and Context* (Leiden: Brill, 1996), 187–228; reference is to 217ff., where Mason argues for *Against Apion* as a *protreptikos*.
63. Steve Mason (ed.), *Understanding Josephus: Seven Perspectives* (Sheffield: Sheffield Academic Press, 1998), 194–246.
64. *Josephus' Contra Apionem: Studies in Its Character and Context with a Latin Concordance to the Portion Missing in Greek*, edited by Louis H. Feldman and John R. Levison (Leiden: Brill, 1996).
65. Ibid., 18–20.
66. Ibid., 19.
67. Ibid., 216.
68. Ibid., 20–21.
69. Ibid., 20.
70. Ibid., 20.
71. Ibid.
72. John Meyer, "Jewish Culture in Greco-Roman Palestine," in *Cultures of the Jews: Volume 1. Mediterranean Origins,* edited by David Biale (New York: Shocken Books, 2002), 149–57.
73. Ibid., 153.
74. Josephus, *Against Apion* 1.38–42 (William Whiston translation [slightly amended]).
75. Josephus, *Against Apion* 1.42–47 (William Whiston translation).
76. Josephus, *Against Apion* 2.1–7 (LCL 186, 293–95).
77. Martin Goodman, in an article on "Josephus's Treatise Against Apion," in *Apologetics in the Roman Empire*, edited by Mark Edwards, David Goodman, Simon Price in association with Christopher Rowland (Oxford: Oxford University Press, 1999).
78. Ibid., 55ff.
79. Arnaldo Momigliano, *Essays on Ancient and Modern Judaism*, edited with an introduction by Sylvia Berth and translated by Maura Masella Gayley (Chicago: University of Chicago Press, 1994), 58.
80. Louis H. Feldman, *Judaism and Hellenism Reconsidered* (Leiden: Brill, 2006), 358–60; Shaye J. D. Cohen, *The Significance of Javneh and Other Essays in Jewish Hellenism* (Tübingen: Mohr Siebeck, 2010), 119; cf. idem, "Josephus, Jeremiah, and Polybius," *History and Theory* 21 (1982): 366–81. See also A. Eckstein, "Josephus and Polybius: A Reconsideration," *Classical Antiquity* 9 (1990): 175–208; Frank W. Walbank, "'Treason' and Roman Domination: Two Case-Studies, Polybius and Josephus," 258–76 in idem. *Polybius, Rome, and the Hellenistic World: Essays and Reflections* (Cambridge: Cambridge University Press, 2002); and Gregory Sterling, "Explaining Defeat: Polybius and Josephus on the Wars with Rome," in *Internationales Josephus-Kolloquium, Aarhus* 1999, edited by J. U. Kalms (Munster: Lit, 2000), 135–51.
81. Cynthia Damon, "Pliny on Apion," in *Pliny the Elder: Themes and Contexts*, edited by Roy Gibson and Ruth Morello (Leiden: Brill, 2011), 131–45.
82. Peter Howell, Preface, *Martial* (Modern Library), xxxii.
83. Ibid., xxxi.
84. Shaye J. D. Cohen, "History and Historiography in the Against Apion of Josephus," *History and Theory* 27.4 (1988), 1–11.

85. Ibid., 3.
86. John M. G. Barclay, *Flavius Josephus: Translation and Commentary, Volume 10: Against Apion* (Leiden: Brill, 2007), 175.
87. Ibid., 174n42.
88. Ibid., 177n53.
89. Ibid., 171fn12.
90. Josephus, *Against Apion* 2.1; Ibid., 170–73.
91. Josephus, *Against Apion* 2.296 (LCL 186, 411).
92. Philo, *Legatio ad Gaium* 323–329 (LCL 379, 161–63).

Chapter Four

Martial, Tacitus, Pliny, and Friends

On Fear, Suspicion, Exile, and Death in Domitian's Rome

In his essay, *On Being a Busybody*, Plutarch provides the following testimony about an experience he had in Rome and an insight into what it must have been like to live during the later years of Domitian's reign. "When I was once lecturing in Rome," he writes, "that famous Rusticus, whom Domitian later killed through envy at his repute, was among my hearers, and a soldier came through the audience and delivered to him a letter from the emperor. There was a silence and I, too, made a pause, that he might read his letter; but he refused and did not break the seal until I had finished my lecture and the audience had dispersed. Because of this incident everyone admired the dignity of the man."[1] Dio of Prusa adds further confirmation to the state of affairs in the following two excerpts.

> It fell to my lot to be exiled on account of my reputed friendship with a man of good character and very closely connected with those who at that time were Fortune's favourites and indeed high officials, a man who lost his life on account of the very things which made him seem fortunate to many men, and indeed to practically everyone, I mean his connection by marriage and blood with these officials; the charge brought against me being that I was that man's friend and adviser—for just as among the Scythians it is the practice to bury cupbearers and cooks and concubines with their kings, so it is the custom of despots to throw in several others for no reason whatever with those who are being executed by them.[2]
>
> I want to render you an account of this sojourn of mine, since I believe that the time remaining to me is going to be very brief. Well, how I bore my exile . . . and, besides all this, bearing up under the hatred, not of this or that one among

my equals, or peers as they are sometimes called, but rather of the most powerful, stern man [Domitian], who was called by all Greeks and barbarians both master and god, but who was in reality an evil demon; and this too without fawning upon him or trying to avert his hatred by entreaty but challenging him openly, and not putting off until now, God knows, to speak or write about the evils which afflicted us, but having done both already, and that too in speeches and writings broadcast to the world, not being goaded by madness or desperation to do these things, but trusting in a greater power and source of aid, that which proceeds from the gods, though most men scorn it and deem it useless.[3]

The focus of this chapter is the culture of fear and suspicion that prevailed in Rome during the reign of the Emperor Domitian, a world that Josephus did not document. Given how troubling it was for anyone to write about contemporary events in these times for fear of reprisal—even death—Josephus's silence about the Jews of Rome may have been an act of self-censorship. At the same time, as I demonstrated in the previous chapter, his silence about the Jews of Rome is not attestation that there were no Jews in Rome. We should, therefore, consider the possibility that his silence about Christians in Rome is also not attestation that there were no Christians in Rome in the time of Domitian. This inference is supported by the testimony of his Roman contemporaries who mentioned or alluded to Christians in Rome not only in the days of Nero but in the period subsequently, even if they did so in writings that appeared in the early second century. I have in mind here Tacitus, Pliny the Younger, Suetonius, and Juvenal.

Josephus's self-censorship about Jewish life in Rome may also have been imposed on him simply because he was a Flavian and as such chose not to describe contemporary Jewish life in Rome or anywhere else. This meant that he did not have to expose exactly how difficult it must have been for an ordinary Jew to be in Rome in the last three decades of the first century. He did not have to write anything in an environment so full of the fear, suspicion, and debilitating anxiety that had disabled so many of his Roman contemporaries. A corollary of Josephus's silence or reticence in this climate is that he did not have to reveal a specific reason as to why he chose to ignore anyone or any other groups in Rome. His totalizing silence covered everyone and everything. This may be urged as an objection to the claim that he ignored the Christians of Rome deliberately.

For the objection to be sustained, however, it must countermand the historical and interpretative implications of Josephus's description of the murder of James the brother of Jesus (who was called the Christ) in Jerusalem during the brief tenure of the High Priest Ananus son of Ananus in 62 CE. That account made Josephus a witness to Christian presence in Jerusalem if not in all of Judaea between the time of his birth and the judicial murder of James. It carries similar historical weight as his description of John the

Baptizer in his *Antiquities* 18.116–119, though the account about James does not give any details about his life and activities as Josephus provides about John the Baptizer. Nevertheless, in the aftermath of James's death, Josephus could not pretend that he knew nothing of the Christian Jews of Jerusalem and Judaea. Consequently, any studied indifference on his part about Christians anywhere outside Jerusalem and Judaea, including Rome, which became his home after the Jewish War, involved a deliberate choice. I shall have more to say about this in the next chapter.

What follows in this chapter attests once again to the range and scope of Josephus's silences, for if we were dependent on him as witness to the age, we would know nothing about what his contemporaries bore witness to. This also provides the necessary backdrop for my discussion of First Clement in the next and final chapter.

Dio Chrysostom, that is, Dio of Prusa in Bythinia, was like Plutarch of Chaeronea in Boeotia, an outsider to the world of intrigue, preferment, and prestige that characterized political and cultural life in Rome in the second half of the first century. Each in his own way experienced and witnessed matters in Domitian's Rome both near and far. As philosophical writers and social and political commentators they offer insights that can orient our approach to the Emperor Domitian and his times and how in particular those who lived during Domitian's reign understood their experiences. Their contemporaries like Pliny the Younger and Tacitus are sometimes dismissed easily as partisans of the senatorial class, some of whom stood in opposition to Domitian. That cannot be said of Dio Chrysostom and Plutarch even if they too had friends among that class. Hence, my beginning with these passages from their writings about the reign of Domitian to orient us for this chapter.

The first quotation sets the scene: in this offhand comment about what he experienced during one of his lectures in Rome, Plutarch brings his readers into the uneasy and disquieting world of the senatorial class during Domitian's reign. Here we have a soldier delivering a letter from the Emperor Domitian to L. Junius Arulenus Rusticus as if being served a summons.

Arulenus Rusticus must have known instinctively that the way the letter was delivered to him and the occasion upon which it was delivered were not purely by accident. Plutarch must have suspected this as well in mentioning the silence that fell on the audience listening to his lecture when a soldier came in and moved through the audience to hand-deliver the letter to Rusticus. It must have been an awkward and eerie silence, as the audience waited to see what Rusticus would do with the letter just delivered to him. The very act of seeking him out in the audience to deliver the letter was meant to dramatize something close to the presence of Domitian's *imperium* and its reach into wherever and whatever public activity a senator was engaged in. Or was it an intrusion into a private gathering?

It was a lecture, there was an audience. So whether it was held in a private villa, in someone's residence, or in a more public venue, there was both a sense of privacy and a feeling of public gathering that allowed the soldier to enter that audience, make his way through them, and hand-deliver the letter in the full gaze of those gathered. The letter was to one man and one man alone. Yet, though private on this score, it was turned into a public event. That was intentional.

Rusticus had the effrontery to delay opening the emperor's letter, and so advertised that his own dignity mattered more to him than the emperor's. Rusticus's gesture suggested too that it was preferable to listen to Plutarch's lecture than to read the emperor's letter right then and there even though both the lecturer and the audience had given him permission to do so. If Rusticus gained in reputation on account of this, he also put the emperor in his place, so to speak; and that was not to be admired. If "everyone" admired Rusticus's dignity, then by admiring his dignity those very admirers made him odious to Domitian. Whatever Domitian's reputation may have been at the time, Rusticus clearly risked his own in behaving as he did. Plutarch does not say what became of Rusticus's reputation from the point of view of the court or whether his behavior was reported to the emperor, or how long after the incident Rusticus was put to death.

We may ask again: how private was this audience or how public was it? Plutarch does not say, but it all depends on how one construes the nature of the occasion and its social meaning. We should like to know who else was in the audience other than Arulenus Rusticus among the writers, philosophers, and senators of the day. Was Helvidius Priscus the Younger present? What about Herennius Senecio? Both were also executed by Domitian in 93 CE? Was Plutarch privileged to have Pliny the Younger present, a noted friend of Helvidius, Senecio, and Rusticus? Or for that matter Marcus Aquilius Regulus who, according to Pliny, wrote a work after their deaths denouncing both Rusticus and Helvidius? Was anyone associated with the Stoic philosopher Musonius Rufus anywhere in that crowd? What about Quintilian, the noted teacher of rhetoric and teacher of Pliny the Younger?

What about Martial? Would he have been welcome here among the likes of Plutarch and Arulenus Rusticus, who is not mentioned anywhere in Martial's epigrams, although there is a stock-character "Rusticus" ("bumpkin") who appears in Martial's epigrams? Did Martial mingle with this crowd when he was known to have been so fond of Aquilius Regulus, and had written several epigrams in praise of his talents and about his friendship (2.93, 5.63, 6.38, 7.31, 7.16)? What about Josephus? Was he to be found among Plutarch's listeners? If he was not, did he hear any of the gossip that emanated from this event about Rusticus's dignity?

Martial mentions invitations to dinner (*cena*) frequently in his epigrams, and sometimes boasted about his presence at them. This gathering was no *cena* or a convivial occasion linked to one. As Plutarch himself indicates in his *Quaestiones Convivales* 1.1, half of the time, the occasion lent itself to mocking and being mocked. His *Quaestiones Convivales* capture some of the mood. On this particular occasion, Plutarch appeared to be giving a lecture as if at a literary or a philosophical club. It is in this seemingly philosophical or literary setting that Rusticus received the letter from the emperor delivered by a soldier. What was the urgency? Was that not precisely the point? It could not wait, and yet, in reacting as he did, Rusticus let it be known that it could wait. In all likelihood, his indifference to the presumed urgency of the emperor's letter could easily be interpreted by the friends of the emperor or his informers as an affront.

Dio Chrysostom provides a slightly different kind of commentary in two parts. In the first notice from him, we learn of the reasons for his exile. It is all very plain. He happened to be a friend of the person who had run afoul of Domitian. His association with the condemned man was his passport to exile. In the second comment, he attests to his defiance, the help of the gods, and his own philosophical disposition (he says more about this in *Oration* 13) in not being silent in the face of a despot who demanded to be called "master and god" but who, to him, was in truth an evil demon (*daimona poneron*). These are strong words. It is not language that one finds in Pliny the Younger, Tacitus, or Suetonius, all of whom express strong disapproval of Domitian's reign. It is a measure of what Dio Chrysostom took to be one of the most deplorable expressions of political power he had witnessed. It is in this world superintended by "a demoniac," if you will (to borrow Dio Chrysostom's language), that Martial and some of his friends flourished.

The conditions of Dio's exile appear to have been milder compared to some others that Domitian banished from Rome. In Dio Chrysostom's case he was banished from Rome and Italy, it seems, as well as his native Prusa and the province of Bithynia. He would write after his exile in the first passage quoted above about how he survived his exile without losing his friends. In *Oration* 13 he mentions how he turned the conditions of his exile into an exercise of living out the philosophical life. Few, it seemed, were so fortunate to have offended Domitian and escaped with their lives to become philosophers, so to speak.

> I began to consider whether this matter of banishment was really a grievous thing and a misfortune, as it is in the view of the majority, or whether such experiences merely furnish another instance of what we are told happens in connection with the divinations of the women in the sacred places. For they pick up a chance clod of earth or a stone and try to see in it the answer to their enquiry. And, so the story goes, some find their clod light, while others find theirs so heavy that they are not able even to move it easily. "May not exile after all," I thought, "and poverty, yes, and old age too and sickness, and all

such things, appear heavy to some and grievous, but to others light and easy?"[4]

After considering the heroes of the past like Homer's Odysseus he decided to consult the Delphic Oracle as to what cause of action he should take. "And then when I consulted him," he writes, "he gave me a strange sort of reply and one not easy to interpret. For he bade me to keep on doing with all zeal the very thing wherein I am engaged, as being a most honourable and useful activity, 'until thou comest,' said he, 'to the uttermost parts of the earth.'"[5] So Dio took to life "on the road" in a manner akin to a peripatetic but almost surely in the mold of a Cynic philosopher: "And the men whom I met, on catching sight of me, would sometimes call me a tramp and sometimes a beggar, though some did call me a philosopher. From this it came about gradually and without any planning or any self-conceit on my part that I acquired this name."[6]

Either by design or by circumstance, Domitian seems to have dared Dio Chrysostom to live out the philosophical life for which he was reputed. Domitian may even have taken a cue from Nero, when he banished a number of philosophers including Musonius Rufus, who was Dio Chrysostom's teacher in Rome. Ironically, Dio ended up following in the footsteps of his teacher. Musonius Rufus was banished by Nero and the later recalled by Vespasian. Dio would be banished by Domitian and would in turn be recalled by Nerva.

Nerva's accession and his decision to recall all those who had been exiled by Domitian restored Dio Chrysostom to his native Prusa and renewed a long-standing friendship he had with the new emperor. The end of Dio's exile came with a request from Nerva for him to visit the new emperor in Rome. Unable to fulfill the request because of illness, Dio made sure to remind his fellow citizens of Prusa that his regret was not so much the personal attention and benefits he would have received from such a visit but what would have accrued to the benefit of Prusa. In a number of his *Orations*, Dio stressed his love of Prusa, and his choice of Prusa over all other places where he was welcome to live and make his own. While Dio had a standing invitation to return to Rome, someone like Martial appears to have received a not so formal request to leave Rome soon after Nerva's accession. And Josephus? Perhaps an equally informal importunity that he did not quite belong now that the last of the Flavians was gone.

MARTIAL'S EPIGRAMS: SOCIAL CONTEXT AND HISTORICAL FRAMEWORK

Books 10, 11, and 12 of Martial's epigrams present a set of interlocking realities that elicit many questions about the way Martial writes and presents himself. The first matter of significance is that Book 10 was issued twice: once before he wrote Book 11, which followed it normally, and a second time after Book 11 had already appeared. Book 11 was issued shortly after Domitian's assassination, while Martial's friend Parthenius was still alive, the same Parthenius who had often acted as a go-between for his epigrams to reach Domitian. The second version of Book 10 revises the book in a way that takes into account Domitian's assassination and the immediate aftermath of his death.

Book 11 has the special characteristic that it praises Emperor Nerva for ushering in a time of greater liberty (*libertas*) that is contrasted with the recent times under Domitian. Martial appears to signal this new liberty by presenting more obscene poems in this book than in any of the other book of epigrams he published. This proliferation of obscene poems in Book 11 is designed to lend credence to the view of Martial as someone who suffered as a poet who was not able to express himself freely during Domitian's reign. That is the pose, and not a very convincing one. For all intents and purposes, it is fraudulent. There was nothing that prevented Martial from writing the kind of obscene poetry that proliferates in Book 11. What is worse, he had in previous books engaged in this very same kind of posturing in relation to Domitian. So the idea that in his previous books he had been so constrained in his liberties as a poet is farfetched. He had on so many occasions justified his art of the obscene by appealing to the spirit of the Saturnalia. Far from being sincere in his later condemnation or repudiation of Domitian, as Ker and others have intimated, Martial was rather at his disingenuous best. He seemed to be joining in the repudiation of Domitian, the *damnatio memoriae* instantiated by the Roman Senate about Domitian; and secondly, engaged in a project of self-fashioning to present himself to his Roman audience and readership.

The reason for Martial's pretense to his lost liberties now regained has a lot to do with what he had elided in his representations of Roman society in much of his adulatory and sycophantic praise of Domitian in his epigrams. Martial had done much to gloss over the simple fact that Domitian's Rome was dominated by fear, suspicion, and insecurity to a degree that his fellow Romans had not experienced since the time of Nero. They lived in a world of informers; no one knew who would be the subject of a *libellus* or a summons to which they had to respond. On occasion, Martial's epigrams mentioned the informers, delators (*delatores*). He seemed naturally intrigued and terrified by the individual who only reads *libelli*, the kind of person one ought to fear at a dinner party. He sometimes toyed with the idea of how one would have to answer an indictment for what was said at a dinner party. They are scattered throughout the various books of the epigrams that one can easily miss their import. It is in these scattered references that one senses what lies underneath. But they do not present themselves to the reader unambiguously.

For even in these moments Martial seems to undercut the seriousness of what is in view for the sake of a laugh. There is one such occasion when he mentions an informer in Epigram 11.66:

> To Vacerra, "You are an informer, a calumniator, a forger, a secret agent, a slave to the unclean, and a trainer of gladiators. I wonder, Vacerra, why you have no money."[7]

Vacerra (that is: "blockhead") is involved in professions that generally earn the ire of most of his fellow Romans. Yet in spite of his multifaceted activities he is poor. Vacerra seems a fictional character: quite the opposite of what was expected of him for being so multitalented. Couched in these terms, Martial lessens the exceptionally deadly consequences of Vacerra's deeds as an informer. Martial can have it both ways. He does not have to say anything about what he thought about any real informers he knew or knew of, informers who had special claim to notoriety during the reign of Domitian, some of whom may in fact have been his friends or at least people he was closely associated with, including one Regulus whom we shall encounter shortly.

To appreciate Martial's possible complicities, we will have to assess the nature of Martial's sexual humor and the social background of that humor in the Roman baths. Once we see this connection, we will be able to say without reservation that Martial's liberties and those of his contemporaries, as far as the social world of the baths were concerned, continued unabated during the Flavian period. There were no such restrictions on his sexual humor. If anything, there may have been more liberties toward it, since it appears that most of the *literati* engaged in it, including Pliny the Younger and Nerva, who succeeded Domitian as emperor.

If then there were no constraints on Martial's liberties as a poet of Sotadics (to use the specific and precise language that Pliny employs to describe them), what liberties did he ever lament in his epigrams other than his own personal misfortunes here and there of being a client in need of patrons? Not many, and in fact, he seems to have been immune from the real dangers faced by most of his contemporaries who lived among informers. His occasional allusions and references to these dangers are the only signs that we have from him that he was somewhat indifferent to them because he was not entirely too disadvantaged by them.

> BOOK I.
> TO THE READER
> "I trust that, in these little books of mine, I have observed such self-control, that whoever forms a fair judgment from his own mind can make no complaint of them, since they indulge their sportive fancies without violating the respect due even to persons of the humblest station; a respect which was so far disre-

garded by the authors of antiquity, that they made free use, not only of real, but of great names. For me; let fame be held in less estimation, and let such talent be the last thing commended in me. Let the ill-natured interpreter, too, keep himself from meddling with the simple meaning of my jests, and not write my epigrams for me. He acted honourably who exercises perverse ingenuity on another man's book: For the free plainness of expression, that is, for the language of epigram, I would apologize, if I were introducing the practice; but it is thus that Catullus writes, and Marsus, and Pedo, and Getulicus, and every one whose writings are read through. If any assumes to be so scrupulously nice, however, that it is not allowable to address him, in a single page, in plain language, he may confine himself to this address, or rather to the title of the book. Epigrams are written for those who are accustomed to be spectators at the games of Flora. Let not Cato enter my theatre; or, if he does enter, let him look on. It appears to me that I shall do only what I have a right to do, if I close my address with the following verses: Let him not make them his own, by the false interpretation which he puts upon them."[8]

Now that he has dismissed Cato, Martial turns to usher him out even more programmatically and to ask why he makes an entrance only to be let out. Can the reader even pretend to play the role of the moralizing Cato? Not quite. Who, then, is the right interpreter of Martial's verses? What constitutes a false interpretation and what constitutes the true? If the reader is warned not to play the role of Martial's censor and to write his epigrams for him, does it mean that Martial's plainness of expression admit of no conceits and are as transparent as daylight? He speaks directly once more to the Reader in the first epigram of Book 1:

> The man whom you are reading is the very man that you want—Martial, known over the whole world for his humorous books of epigrams; to whom, studious reader, you have afforded such honours, while he is alive and has a sense of them, as few poets receive after their death.[9]

Has Martial not taken to pretenses when he declares to the reader that he, Martial, has already achieved immortality or worldwide fame in his lifetime what many poets hope for when they are dead? Is it really true that he is known "over the whole world?"

After a set of epigrams on the censoriousness of his fellow Romans and their inconstant and variegated tastes in literature, he turns to the emperor. Epigrams 1.4 and 1.5 are in dialogue with each other. Martial speaks in the former, the emperor responds in the latter.

> 1.4: TO CAESAR.
> "If you should chance, Caesar, to light upon my books, lay aside that look which awes the world. Even your triumphs have been accustomed to endure jests, nor is it any shame to a general to be a subject for witticisms. Read my verses, I pray you, with that brow with which you behold Thymele [a dancer]

and Latinus [a jester] the buffoon. The censorship may tolerate innocent jokes: my page indulges in freedoms, but my life is pure."

1.5: THE EMPEROR'S REPLY.
"I give you a sea-fight, and you give me epigrams: you wish, I suppose, Marcus, to be set afloat with your book."[10]

In this pose, the emperor acknowledges what Marcus Julius Martialis expects or at least hopes for, that his book of epigrams will receive approval. The emperor, in his role as censor, and especially in arrogating to himself the title of perpetual censor (*censor perpetuus*) supervenes whatever poetry Martial writes. Martial makes a plea for the censor to ease up on his censoriousness. The emperor should not object to innocent jokes; or rather he should tolerate innocent jokes because, after all, Martial's pages indulge in freedoms, but Martial himself is better than his jokes, for in life, he is pure. Martial here takes what he proposed earlier to his readers and reframes it for the *censor perpetuus*, the Emperor Domitian. But who determines what freedoms are appropriate? Is it the poet or the one who holds the censorship? Martial may mock the censoriousness of his fellow Romans, he may even dismiss the opprobrium of some of his readers; but he does not have it within his "freedoms" to instruct the censor how to do his work. Yet this is precisely what he does, while claiming purity for his life, even if his verses are not so pure. Still, he claims innocence for his epigrams.

But why should anyone believe him when he says in the preface that all he is doing is engaging in sport? That he has been self-controlled, that he has been fair in his judgments? Or that he has not named names and mocked them as he alleges the poets of old did? The proof of his epigrams is that he does not do all these things as he claims in the preface. He does name names, or at least give names to his victims; and yes, he does offer bad judgment as well, and in many instances he is not self-controlled. The simplest reading of that opening paragraph is that it is a ruse, or at the very least a pretense: Martial does not actually do a lot of what he claims to do, and he does much more that he claims not to do. Herein lies the conundrum or one of the conundra of a satirist or comic poet who writes in the first person.

Before proceeding, a word or two about the satirist who writes in the first person: The satirist is almost never out of character. The satirist who writes in the first person always risks self-parody. It is almost unavoidable. For once you take up that role, you cannot ask to be thought of as being a satirist only part of the time and on occasion and not all the time. You can never give it up unless you do so completely and resign from that occupation. Otherwise what obtains is that the satirist manipulates his readers by turns claiming to be speaking out of character and in character, and in the process creates any number of personas mostly to conceal what it is the satirist, as both character and historical person, believes or does not believe. The world inhabited by the satirist becomes a disorienting hall of reflecting mirrors with multiple images reflecting off and onto each other. Either the satirist owns up to his satirical self as his true self or he is part of the game of reflecting mirrors, and he owns up to all those many faces with their unique and sometimes conflicting and disorienting selves. One way to think this is to imagine the satirist as a hologram with multiple images representing the thing itself.

At the risk of overstating it, satire is essentially an art inherently deceitful and disingenuous in its moral claims. If satire does not pretend to moralism, then it can lay claim to something less harmful with respect to both its targets and to itself. Yet, because it is fundamentally an art of mockery, and insists on exposing what it considers essentially ridiculous, it cannot escape its putative claims to some kinds of moral standards. Without those putative claims it would also not achieve its desired effect. To add to this conflicted moralism, mockery by its very nature exposes not just the thing or the one who is mocked but unmasks the one doing the mocking. He who mocks, who scoffs at what he sees around him, is by turns supercilious, upright, and moral or pretentious, affected, and dishonest. Martial cannot pretend not to take on any of these guises.

Most of the time satire ends up being self-serving. In the bewildering and confused moral landscape created by the Roman satirist, the only thing that seems to endure is a kind of reductive moral solipsism. It is only the satirist, in this case Martial, as moral and social critic, who can say, if he were to speak out of character, what constitutes his true, unmasked, unpretended moral vision. Which brings up the fundamental question, namely, whether the entertainment value of satire is not in fact its main objective. In which case, Martial's claim that it is all about laughs turns out to be the truest explanation of his motives for writing the epigrams that he writes. The goal is mockery for the sake of laughter. Or to put it another way, laughter is the thing. Which is why appeals to moral seriousness of a satirist like Martial ultimately prove quite unsustainable. Those appeals look even more ridiculous when Martial mentions on different occasions that he is writing for his living. For the satirist's moral pose is itself a fabrication, constructed to aid his productions, elicit laughter, so as to provide him an income. If Martial should retort that such a reading misrepresents his poetry, then he had better provide a coherent moral vision to substantiate all his art: which he cannot do.

A completely consistent satirical persona cannot sustain a coherent moral vision. One cannot satirize everything; one cannot be completely cynical. The satirical persona dissolves in its own deeply ingrained moral arrogance or superciliousness. What is more, the inducements that a satirist like Martial provides for his readers and patrons to be contemptible toward others who are the objects of his lampoons and scathing criticisms cannot be defined or redescribed as inducements toward some higher moral objectives. No one would confuse the moral discourses of a Seneca (which have their own self-contradictions with respect to Seneca's political and social life) with the epigrams of Martial or the satires of Statius. Not many Romans would have considered Martial and Statius's poetry as high moral discourses. In some very important ways, they are often nothing more than doggerel. This is not a matter of taste, for they appeal to the basest of human instincts, impulses, emotions, and sentiments. Turning them into some highfalutin moral criticism is simply to misconstrue their most basic aims. When the game is up, the satirist simply has to retreat. Martial learned this the hard way.

One way out of this moral cul-de-sac is for the author or the satirist to include himself in those who are mocked. By self-deprecation the author partly loses his moral righteousness and partly humanizes himself as not all that different in his ridiculousness from those he mocks. Of course, he cannot keep this up if he wishes truly to abuse his targets. It is in this respect that other types of comedy do not have to take on all that is conflicted, disingenuous, and self-contradictory about the satirist who writes in the first person. The ploys and conceits of Martial's satire can be detected in the two types of epigrams that characterize his work: the sexually explicit and obscene epigrams on the one hand, and on the other hand, those epigrams that praise Domitian.

When Martial pleads for mercy from the Caesar, he comes closest to an acknowledgment that some of his epigrams are not harmless fun. They have their targets and they have their victims. So which is the greater miracle: that Caesar's lions may extend mercy to a hare caught in its jaws or that heaven protects an eagle that carries its young in its talons? The former, of course. It is that which Martial presumes or wishes to be true. Without exactly spelling it out, Martial here underscores the real substance and power of Caesar as censor. From this point on he will speak directly to and about Domitian in his epigrams, continuing with the theme of the lion and its prey in 1.14.

> 1.6. ON A LION OF CAESAR'S THAT SPARED A HARE.
> "While through the air of heaven the eagle was carrying the youth, the burden unhurt clung to its anxious talons. From Caesar's lions their own prey now succeeds in obtaining mercy, and the hare plays safe in their huge jaws. Which miracle do you think the greater? The author of each is a supreme being: the one is the work of Caesar; the other, of Jove. Ganymede."

> 1.14: TO DOMITIAN.
> "The pastimes, Caesar, the sports and the play of the lions, we have seen: your arena affords you the additional sight of the captured hare returning often in safety from the kindly tooth and running at large through the open jaws. Whence is it that the greedy lion can spare his captured prey? He is said to be yours: thence it is that he can show mercy."[11]

Is this a sign of fear, or of something else? In a rather macabre epigram on Festus (1.78), Martial writes that Festus's suicide was nobler than Cato's because Domitian was Festus's friend. Why not say "Festus was Domitian's friend?" If one did not know anything about the reign of terror that characterized Domitian's rule, one could easily read into this that Festus's suicide was ordered by Domitian. On the other hand, if you were a contemporary of Martial, you would have no doubts as to what Martial means by saying not that Festus was Domitian's friend but that Domitian was Festus's fiend. Whether Festus pretended to be a friend and schemed against Domitian or Domitian was not a friend at all, either way the blame appears to be on Festus. The praise that he died a nobler death than Cato reads then partly as a denunciation of Festus by Martial, who does his best to disparage Cato's presumed nobility and virtue in this first book of Epigrams.

I may be badly mistaken here. But I have read this as a political suicide disguised as a result of an illness. William Fitzgerald asserts that Festus's suicide was not political. Fitzgerald takes Martial at face value when he says that Festus chose to commit suicide because he was suffering from a wasting disease. But who was this Festus?[12] The idea of dying from an "unoffending throat" suggests someone who speaks properly or does not offend Caesar. The contrast with Cato raises it to the level of the political.

> 1.78. ON FESTUS, WHO STABBED HIMSELF.
> "When a devouring malady attacked his unoffending throat, and its black poison extended its ravages over his face, Festus, consoling his weeping friends, while his own eyes were dry, determined to seek the Stygian lake. He did not however pollute his pious mouth with secret poison, or aggravate his sad fate by lingering famine, but ended his pure life by a death befitting a Roman and freed his spirit in a nobler way. This death fame may place above that of the great Cato; for Domitian was Festus' friend."[13]

MARTIAL'S FABLE: THE LION AND THE HARE AND THOSE WHO FEAR

> 1.104. ON A SPECTACLE IN THE ARENA.
> "When we see the leopard bear upon his spotted neck a light and easy yoke, and the furious tigers endure with patience the blows of the whip; the stags champ the golden curbs; the Libyan bears tamed by the bit; a boar, huge as that which Calydon is said to have produced, obey the purple muzzle; the ugly buffaloes drag chariots, and the elephant, when ordered to dance nimbly, pay prompt obedience to his swarthy leader; who would not imagine such things a spectacle given by the gods? These, however, any one disregards as of inferior attraction who sees the condescension of the lions, which the swift-footed timorous hares fatigue in the chase. They let go the little animals, catch them again, and caress them when caught, and the latter are safer in their captors' mouths than elsewhere; since the lions delight in granting them free passage

through their open jaws, and in holding their teeth as with fear, for they are ashamed to crush the tender prey, after having just come from slaying bulls. This clemency (*clementia*) does not proceed from art; the lions know whom they serve."[14]

Martial assures himself that the lion (the Caesar) is not after the hare. If that is so, this is a terrifically dangerous sport. In Martial's description it is the lion who fears. Yet, it is only the lion who seems to know that it will not devour the hare. What clemency is this? Whom exactly does the lion serve? Certainly it is the Caesar who gives the games. If the lion has been taught not to devour the hare, then it will not. But the hare still fears and has reason to fear. If it lacks any fear, it is something of an accident. For it ought not to expect it. Who is that Dacian boy who should not fear Caesar? Still more, who is entitled not to fear Caesar?

> 1.22. TO A HARE.
> Why, silly hare, are you fleeing from the fierce jaws of the lion now grown tame? They have not learned to crush such tiny animals. Those talons, which you fear, are reserved for mighty necks, nor does a thirst so great delight in so small a draught of blood. The hare is the prey of hounds; it does not fill large mouths: the Dacian boy should not fear Caesar.[15]

The opening book of epigrams tactfully and carefully circles around the problem of Caesar's overwhelming might and his power of life and death over the poet. The Dacian boy should not fear Caeser, so says Martial. But if the Dacian boy is in Rome, he is probably there because a prisoner of war, a recent captive of Domitian's Dacian wars. He has everything to fear, and so do others in Rome, if Caesar has informants. There is an undercurrent of fear that can be detected in some of these epigrams. They shine a backlight to Martial's endless adulation of Domitian. That sense of fear also amplifies Martial's language when it turns abusive, caustic, or brutish against his victims or the objects of his witticisms.

For most of Martial's readers who had any sense of the recent past, the mention of mercy or clemency would bring to mind one of the most interesting philosophical texts of first-century Rome, namely Seneca's *De clementia*. It naturally also conjures up the image of Emperor Nero and of Seneca's relationship to him; which in turn brings to mind Nero's cruelty and Seneca's suicide by order of Nero; and of the fateful irony that *De clementia* was written for and dedicated to the young Nero, who in the final analysis did not show any mercy to Seneca his teacher and counselor. All of this evokes the social, political, and philosophical discourses about the differences between a tyrant and a king, and what constitutes the proper conditions for clemency, what absolves a ruler from abuses of power, and so on and so forth.

When Martial arrived in Rome, probably in 64 CE, he was following the path of any number of provincials from Spain (Hispania Tarraconensis) who had succeeded in their careers in the city. These included the rhetorician Quintilian and most notably the family of the philosopher Seneca (Seneca the Younger), his father Lucius Annaeus Seneca (Seneca the Elder), his brother Annaeus Mela, and the poet Lucan (39–65 CE), Marcus Anneaus Lucanus, the son of Mela. In 64 CE the fortunes of the Senecas seemed the most propitious, though the philosopher had retired from public life two years before. However, within a year or so after Martial's arrival, the fortunes of the philosopher and those of his circle dimmed calamitously. Many of them died in 65 CE, committing suicide on the orders of the Emperor Nero in connection with the Pisonian conspiracy that implicated Seneca and others of his circle and the very wealthy and influential Senator Gaius Calpurnius Piso, who was expected to replace Nero if the plot has succeeded.

There is no denying Martial's links to the Seneca family by virtue of their provincial attachments and by social interaction in Rome. One early epigram (1.61) has a line about two Senecas, one Lucan: "Silver-tongued Cordoba speaks of two Senecas and one Lucan." Expressed in a context where Martial celebrates various regions and their contributions to the world of famed poets, the reference to Lucan was meant to memorialize the poet who died so young on the orders of Nero.[16] In Epigram 4.40 Martial mentions the Senecas and Piso as potential patrons, placing him very close to those who lost their lives in 65 CE trying to overthrow Nero.

Given Martial's own personal links with Seneca, it is almost impossible that he did not have Seneca or his *De clementia* in mind when he put pen to paper or stylus to wax tablet when he wrote about the lion and hare, of Caesar's lions, and the mercy shown by the tamed lion toward the puny and "silly" hare that plays in its open jaws at the spectacles. In writing about mercy Seneca also wrote about fear: fear of what one has little or no control over, the fear of tyrants, the fear of the irascible, etc.

Martial shows in "The Lion and the Hare" that there were undercurrents. Then in Book 5 he writes to and about Domitian that the first four books are racy but not this one. But the claim is false. Book 4 had no such verses. Books 1–3 also had verses dedicated to Domitian, so he was not doing something entirely new in Book 5. So, why the pretense, and all of this in 90 CE? As Sullivan notes, Book 5 is a very political work.[17] The mood is confident and buoyant. By the time Martial gets to Book 8, much changes. Here we can sense Martial's own fear.

Book 6 was published in 91 CE (probably in December for the Saturnalia);[18] Book 7 in December 93 CE; and Book 8 in early 94 CE. Book 6.58 has Martial sending the book to his friend Julius Martialis in the hopes that it will get to Emperor Domitian. In Book 7 Martial elaborates on his hopes for an enduring reputation (7.28, 29, 42, 44).[19] Book 8 is all about Domitian. But how is this different from his earlier pieces on Domitian in Books 1–4; or in Book 5 in particular, where he is very political?

If we look at the preface to Book 8, we can sense a change in the mood, and something else. Martial's adulation now incorporates an element of self-censorship that belies the character and tone of some of his earlier verses and also shows him as somewhat anxious. Even when he mentions that Domitian's patronage or readership will grant his works wider circulation, there is a sense in which it sounds plastic and contrived, if his very early claim that he is read the world over has any validity. In short, the words of Martial's preface to Book 8 suggest a state of unease and perhaps tangible fear about the state of things in Domitian's Rome in early 94 CE. Here is the passage with which Martial begins Book 8.

> All my little books, Lord, to which you have given fame, which is to say life, are your petitioners, and will be read, I suppose, for that reason. But this one, entitled the eighth of my works, enjoys more frequent opportunities of showing its devotion. So there was less need to labor with invention, since matter had taken its place. However, from time to time I have tried to vary the same by some admixture of jest, lest every line heap its praises upon your celestial modesty, praises which might more easily weary you than satiate us. Furthermore, although epigrams appearing to aim at the verbal license of mime have been written even by men of the strictest morals and the highest station, I have not allowed these here to talk as wantonly as is their custom. Since the greater and better part of the book is bound up with the majesty of your sacred name, let it remember that only persons purified by religious lustration should approach temples. So that prospective readers may know that I shall observe this principle, I have thought proper to announce it on the very threshold of this little book in the briefest of epigrams.[20]

Martial does not have to mention the changed circumstances in Domitian's Rome between 93 and 94 CE. His readers know instinctively what he feels and may have felt the same thing themselves. Compare this to the beginning of Book 5.

> This I send you, Caesar, whether you tarry on Alba's hills, viewing Trivia on the one hand and Thetis on the other, or whether the truth-telling sisters learn your responses, where on the town's edge sleeps the level surface of the sea, or whether Aeneas' nurse please you, or the daughter of the Sun, or gleaming Anxur with her healthgiving waters, o blest protector and savior of the world, whose safety assures us of Jove's gratitude. Only accept it. I shall believe you have read it and proudly enjoy a Gallic credulity.
>
> Matrons and boys and maidens, to you my page is dedicated. You, sir, who are overmuch delighted by bolder naughtinesses and jests unveiled, read my four wanton little books. The fifth jokes with our Lord, for Germanicus to read without a blush in the presence of the Cecropian maid.[21]

If it is not too much trouble and burden, Muses, please request your friend Parthenius as follows: "So may a late and happy old age one day end you while Caesar lives, so may you be fortunate and Envy wish you well, so may Burrus soon appreciate his father—admit this timid, slender volume within the threshold of the more sacred palace. You know the times when Jove is serene, when he shines with his own gentle countenance wherewith he is wont to deny nothing to suppliants. You need have no fear of exorbitant petitions. The page, adorned with cedar oil and purple, that has grown between its black bosses never asks large, troublesome favors. And do not present the book, hold it as though you were offering nothing, doing nothing. If I know the Lord of the Nine Sisters, he will ask for the little purple volume of his own accord. [22]

BOOK 10, 11, AND 12 IN CONTEXT

Martial does not describe much of his own sense of apprehension during Domitian's reign. In fact, if we take his adulation of Domitian at face value and simply ignore the fact that this was a time that his contemporaries described as fearful, dangerous, treacherous, and so on; when one had to be on your guard because there were informers (*delatores*) everywhere, we might say that Martial experienced none of these things. Here and there in the epigrams there is an allusion to an informer, and then to what dangers attend people as dinner guests (my cups will not make you a defendant), and so on, as I have mentioned before. But on the whole Martial avoids any allusions to the dangerous conditions under which most of the senatorial class lived, to say nothing of others like philosophers and poets.

Given what he knew about the Neronian times, and about how Lucan had suffered on account of Nero's jealousy, and of Lucan's death, Martial's own efforts at literary production in the later years of Domitian's reign seem almost surreal. Did he never imagine that Domitian might turn against him? Had he never contemplated what might happen when Domitian was no longer emperor? Did he simply assume that he would live through his years without suffering any consequences for the praises he had heaped on Domitian in his epigrams? Or, that his contemporaries, many of whom refused to write, might not be forgiving if circumstances changed?

One area where he lifts the lid off the pot, so to speak, is in his epigrams about his books. Here we find occasional references to how the books are being received or the kinds of reception he fears for his books. Here we come into an environment where the books express anxiety about their fate. While Martial is uncompromising in often dismissing some of his readers as censorious, he lets through his anxieties about the books falling not into the wrong hands who censor his poetry for some of their racy content, but the right hands, people who are in a position to affect the fortunes of the books, and so of his own. We see this in the later books. Whereas he is confident about the reception of his poems in the earlier books, in the later books he shows some concerns, even anxieties about whether they will be granted an audience: to Parthenius; to Domitian; to others, and so on. The most dramatic instance is his self-censorship in Book 8 about which I have already given comment.

J. P. Sullivan tries to save Martial, even when he acknowledges that Martial's attempt to present a new image of himself did not work. On the proliferation of obscene material in Book 11, a book supposedly meant to curry favor with Emperor Nerva, Sullivan offers the following explanation:

> A major theme is Saturnalian licence and the sexual frankness it endorses for the epigrammatist. This serves as a defence against the possible charge that the book contains more obscene poems than any other book. The preponderance of obscene epigrams may be explained not only by the dearth of the usual Domitianic material, but also by Martial's belief in the tolerance of Nerva, himself a writer of erotic elegy (8.70; Plin. Ep. 5.3.5). Martial openly admits this predilection several times, adding the usual tongue-in-cheek apologies and warnings (11.2; 6; 15; 17; 20). There are, however, strong political elements in the book, not least in the first six epigrams, although the new regime in Nerva, shaky at best, did not inspire enough confidence in Martial for a complete volte face.[23]

This is peculiar: first Martial resorts to producing more obscene material because he is at a loss because Domitian is dead and he can no longer write poems of praise for Domitian. To this we might suggest that Martial offered his strange apology in Book 8 about excluding the obscene to save Domitain the censor acting against him. However, in earlier books he does not suggest that because there is too much to say about Domitian that is why he included less of the obscene material. If his later attitude is consistent, then writing about the emperor, any emperor should have been enough to prevent him precluding that kind of material.

Certainly, his claim that Nerva liked such poetry seems to support the view that he felt the license then to include more of them. But if that is the case, and he included them to appeal to Nerva, then upon what basis does Sullivan claim that Martial did not undertake a complete volte-face because he knew how shaky Nerva's regime was. What more evidence do we need than Martial's claim that Domitian's reign was oppressive to him? Elsewhere Sullivan writes about his sincerity about the praise he gave Domitian. If he was now willing to recant that praise, is that not a volte-face?

When Sullivan adds that Martial "was still identified in the public mind with the old court poetry, while the new regime was professing a different attitude to imperial power,"[24] he conflates two very different things. Martial's problem as far as the public was concerned was twofold. First that he had praised Domitian excessively at a time when so many others found him odious. Second, that now that Domitian's memory and his regime suffered *damnatio*, he was willing to join the new chorus. It was not a contest between

Martial as court poet and the new imperial politics. If anything, Martial continued to write in the same mode as he had before, except this time around he wanted to praise Nerva, and then Trajan, in the hopes of rehabilitating his image.

Sullivan concedes some such reality when he subsequently notes that "all the same, the book signaled Martial's new, if guarded, loyalty."[25] This is a strange route to arrive at what seems very straightforward. To the point Sullivan adds: "It was fortunate that Martial had earlier addressed friendly compliments to Nerva himself (8.70; 9.26) and that Parthenius had been a long-time friend and patron since at least 88. But none of this would help Martial regain his position as an accepted court poet under the new rulers."[26] But it was not for lack of trying; and it was certainly not because the new regime was too shaky to elicit from Martial a complete recantation of his past. He attempted the recantation, he issued them in the first six epigrams of Book 11. They were simply not compelling in any of the forms in which he presented them.

The second edition of Book 10 that appeared in 98 CE, about two years after Book 11, continued the project. As Sullivan himself notes, part of Martial's strategy in Book 10 was to dissociate himself from Domitian and from his own past.[27] That did not work either. It is in this context that he starts laying the foundations for his return to Bilbilis in Spain. Sullivan calls this a "somewhat ambiguously expressed determination to return to Bilbilis." I would rather suggest that it was like a plea to his detractors. That is, he had now put on record that he was prepared to go back to Bilbilis, almost as a self-imposed exile, if his indirect pleas (or remonstrances) for consideration and *clementia* (there is an element of that) for his past misdeeds in praising Domitian so fulsomely were not acceptable to his fellow Romans. Book 10 contains a carefully-crafted memorandum seeking understanding and mercy. Martial offers a *deprecatio* in many guises. Shame forced him into exile, because his fellow Romans could no longer abide his presence.

Book 11 begins with an epigram to Parthenius (11.1), who supposedly, now, does not read what is sent to him. This is a clever way to suggest that Parthenius was not after all as attentive to Martial's books as one would suppose in light of how Martial had described him in previous books. This seems part and parcel of Martial's revisionist project.

Nerva is proclaimed in Epigram 11.2. Everyone else, those rigid Catos, are asked to leave their censoriousness behind. We are at liberty under Nerva, so we can do as we like. With this, Martial lets the obscenities fly. It is a sham, of course, that he had not been at liberty to write such obscene poetry. He had been doing so from Book 1. If he claimed reserve in the second version of Book 10, that too was disingenuous, for he had written and included such verses along with others that praised Domitian in previous books. It is only if the reader is unaware or has forgotten what he had done in the previous books of the epigrams that Martial's claims in Books 10 and 11 can survive scrutiny. Then by the third epigram in Book 11 he claims that if he had a Maecenas as Vergil did and did not have to make a living, he could write verses that would be immortal. But the simple fact is that he has managed ten books of verses already. So the complaint is somewhat contrived and doubly self-serving, as if to say that his verses would be much better. If it is not a matter of quantity but quality, then he cannot boast at the same time that he is read the world over, even as far away as Britain. So at the very least he is self-contradictory. What is worse, he has compared himself to Vergil in other contexts (for example, when he mentioned Silius Italicus as a new Vergil while he [Martial] was a new Catullus).

The first three epigrams in Book 11, then, set out Martial's second attempt at rehabilitation; or rather the first before the second version of Book 10, which was published after Book 11. Here are the verses: How much he feared about the state of things under Nerva may be discerned from how he portrays Parthenius as both patron and reader (or nonreader) of his books. Events would soon prove that his fears were justified. Parthenius would be executed in 97 CE for his role in the plot that led to the assassination of Domitian in September 96.

1. To His Book
Whither, my book, whither are you going so much at your ease, clad in a holiday dress of fine linen? Is it to see Parthenius? certainly. Go, then, and return unopened; for he does not read books, but only memorials; nor has he time for the muses, or he would have time for his own. Or do you esteem yourself sufficiently happy, if you fall into hands of less note? In that case, repair to the neighbouring portico of Romulus; that of Pompeius does not contain a more idle crowd, nor does that of Agenor's daughter, or that of the inconstant captain of the first ship. Two or three may be found there who will shake out the worms that infest my trifles; but they will do so only when they are tired of the betting and gossip about Scorpus and Incitatus.

2. To His Readers
You stern brows and severe looks of rigid Catos, you daughters of rustic Fabricii, you mock-modest, you censors of morals, aye, and all you proprieties opposed to the joys of darkness, flee hence! Hark! my verses exclaim, "Io, Saturnalia!" we are at liberty, and, under your rule, Nerva, rejoice. Fastidious readers may con over the rugged verses of Santra. We have nothing in common; the book before you is mine.

3. On His Writings
It is not the idle people of the city only that delight in my Muse, nor is it alone to listless ears that these verses are addressed, but my book is thumbed amid Getic frosts, near martial standards, by the stern centurion; and even Britain is said to sing my verses. Yet of what advantage is it to me? My purse benefits nothing by my reputation. What immortal pages could I not have written and

what wars could I not have sung to the Pierian trumpet, if, when the kind deities gave a second Augustus to the earth, they had likewise given to you, O Rome, a second Maecenas.[28]

Martial cannot let go of Cato: so in Epigram 11.5, written in praise of the new emperor Trajan, he surmises that even Cato, were he to be recalled from the dead, would be Caesar's partisan. Why? Because Trajan "has reverence for justice and equity." How strange, when just three epigrams before he was dismissing "rigid Catos." There is something amiss in all of Martial's posturing or the many guises in which he presents himself. In Book 8 he claimed that because the work was dedicated and sent to Domitian, he would not include any obscene verses. I noted that this seemed at best a pretense, since he had included some such verses in earlier books that also contained praise poems for Domitian and were certainly intended for him to read. Here in Book 11 he claims to have more freedom to indulge in his obscene sallies, because in part Nerva approves. The question is why does he include them, and so profusely, when he now turns to praise Trajan the new emperor?

Here is an answer. He had nothing to fear with Nerva and Trajan except his own past: his sycophantic praise of Domitian. Still, he had something to fear when he wrote Book 8 and dedicated it to Domitian, even if earlier in his career had had not feared Domitian's possible reaction to him. What was the difference? Well, at the time of writing Book 8, as I have mentioned previously, others were being executed for what they had written. So while he does not state explicitly why he chose not to include the obscene material in Book 8, the fact that he did not include any and then commented about his self-censorship was in itself testament to his own fears about what Domitian as *censor perpetuus* might do to him, if he found the new book objectionable.

After Domitian, he had his own past to contend with. Managing that past was the task he set himself in Book 11 and the second edition of Book 10, which he issued after Book 11. We may sense an element of apprehension in his description of Parthenius, his long-standing friend, in the first epigram of Book 11. Although in the past he was the person whom he trusted to get his books to Domitian, now he describes him as someone who has no time to read Martial's poems because all he has time for are *libelli* (legal writs or warrants or summons). There is clearly a deliberate attempt here to distance Martial from Parthenius's active patronage, to make him appear less important to Martial's literary efforts than he actually was. Was this all because Martial suspected what was afoot, and wished to inoculate himself from impending danger? Possibly.

His contradictory attitude toward the memory of Cato of Utica in Book 11 is of a similar hue as what he does with Parthenius. Throughout much of the earlier books, he pours scorn on Cato's memory. Here in Book 11, as I have already noted, he tries to be less harsh about Cato. He considers that he might be in Trajan's corner, although he had begun by dismissing other Catos, for equal measure. But no sooner has he said this about Cato being in Trajan's corner than he turns to mocking Cato in Epigram 11.15. Does he intend surreptitiously to mock Trajan? What gives? Martial cannot help himself. His readers most certainly saw through his disguises. The more one reads Book 11 the more incoherent and schizophrenic it reads. Martial takes more liberties to offend, and if this book does not contain some of his most obscene, it has the prize for containing the most number of obscene epigrams among his twelve books. Was this a parting shot? Or was this in fact the attempt to play to an audience in the hope that he might be spared the exile that he knew was due?

Whether or not he already suspected that after the death of Domitian he would have to leave Rome for exile in Spain is not clear. What we may suspect is that the first version of Book 10 probably did not have the epigrams that mentioned his wish to return to Spain; and that those words were most likely added to the second version which he published after Book 11. Whatever the consequences, he needed to rehabilitate himself. Unfortunately for him no one was buying the new and more obscene Martial of Book 11; if they were, they did not show it.

MARTIAL'S WORLD: LANGUAGE, SATURNALIA, AND THE BATHHOUSE

An interesting question is whether Josephus would have read Martial, given Martial's reputation for lewd poetry. Perhaps along with this question we might also ask if Josephus and other Jews in first-century Rome participated in the Saturnalia. If they did not, given the religious connotations and associations, would a Jewish reader venture to read Martial when Martial claimed to be writing in the spirit of the Saturnalia? Others have evoked the spirit of Saturnalia and written erotic verses without approaching the crudities and obscenities of Martial, which, as Victoria Rimell puts it, "makes us long for euphemism."[29]

That longing for euphemism is another way of saying that the freedom and liberties granted by the Saturnalia cannot account for all of Martial's sexually graphic and obscene verses. For that we need to look at a much broader social reality, which provides the background for so much of what Martial seems to take for granted when he writes his bawdy verses: the Roman bathhouse. The bathhouse is both background for Martial's language and stage setting for his performance as poet: a theater for sexual humor. In a good deal of his ribald verses Martial speaks about bathing, the baths, or both; what is seen and unseen, what is done and not done, etc. The Saturnalia happened once a year in December. Going to the baths was a daily affair for some who worked at the baths themselves or in the precincts in shops attached to the baths or in other establishments near the baths, for others it was a regular routine as patrons and customers in those baths. In an almost literal sense, Martial's erotic poetry suggests a linguistic lexicon that would have been appropriate to a language used at or about what obtained in the baths or was thought to obtain among the patrons, attendants, hangers-on, and anyone who saw and experienced the baths in all their fullness. To put it another way, at its most tolerable, Martial's epigrams exploit "bathhouse" humor. At their worst, they descend into lower depths of meanness and cruelty about the male and female body and their attendant sexual or sexualized functions.

The first chapter of Garrett G. Fagan's *Bathing in Public in the Roman World* is a tour with Martial as guide to the public bath.[30] Martial attests to something more: how the bathhouses frame Roman sexual humor. Mary Beard's works on Pompeii are helpful in this regard.[31] The frescoes of Pompeii that continue to fascinate tourists should give us some idea of things. Those frescoes were painted in rooms adjoining a bathhouse. It would be ludicrous to deny that these sexually explicit frescoes depicting sexual acts were not intended to put people in the mind of such acts. Moreover, some of what took place in the baths involved sex or solicitations for sex. Several of the commentators mention them. There were rooms in some bathhouses that were used for prostitution and sometimes houses nearby functioned as bordellos. Some prostitutes, male and female, paraded the bathhouses soliciting for clients. In short, there is a connection between the bathhouses and the general sexual mores of Romans.

This provides a context for Martial's explicit sexual humor. Not simply by saying that this is to be expected, but to have some idea as to why Martial considered his type of humor so normal and expected them to be received by his readers with aplomb. When we hear Pliny the Younger say that he too composed racy verses, and we have allusions from Martial about Emperor Nerva doing likewise, then it is not just someone like Nero and others who might be deemed to have gone beyond the pale, but that among the educated and powerful in Roman society this was part of a common culture. Pliny the Younger cast his own net wide to include almost all the greats of Latin literature before him (Pliny, Letter 5.3). Still, it is not clear that Pliny would have written as crudely, crassly, and wickedly as Martial did. Or perhaps he would have. After all he was either a reader of Martial's epigrams or fully aware of some of what Martial wrote, otherwise he would not have known that Martial had written about him in his books (Pliny, Letter 3.19). Whether or not he enjoyed Martial's sexually explicit epigrams does not necessarily mean he himself would have written them and published them as Martial did. In commenting on Martial, he does not appear to have said anything censorious that would constitute moral criticism of Martial, although some have seen in his words a devastating critique of Martial.[32]

Back to Martial himself: he seemed to suggest that there were some readers who found some of his poetry objectionable. That he addresses them gives some indication that even among those putative and receptive readers some might still find some of his humor troublesome. But what they could not accuse him of was making sport of sex and sexual activity as such. For on this point, he seemed to be merely expressing some of what was part of the common public culture of Rome. I have in mind the social world of the Roman baths.

In a good many of his sexually explicit epigrams Martial often mentions bathing or going to the baths, or both. Martial sometimes describes what takes place at the baths and how ridiculous the protagonists or subjects of his epigrams look doing what they do at the baths. It is almost as if he plays the role of a writer of mimes who takes the Roman bath as his stage or a backdrop to his craft. To a society that saw nothing wrong going to the theater to watch pantomimes that could be crudely and explicitly sexual, Martial's sometimes coarse and vulgar epigrams seemed none the more objectionable for being so sexually explicit. A censorious reader would turn out to be a self-contradiction if that reader did not see anything objectionable in attending the theater and enjoying mimes. Never mind that Romans also often sneered at those who acted in pantomimes.

As Fitzgerald puts it: "The mixed audience of the mime enjoys erotic performance publicly and innocently, whereas the baths are the place where private secrets are both hidden and exposed; somewhere between the baths and the theater we must locate the virtual mixing of Martial's mixed readership."[33] Martial not only assumes, but adverts, that he has the entire world as his audience. He assumes the common knowledge and tacit assumptions about what is allowed and not allowed in the Roman baths and exploits them as both the backdrop and usable content of his epigrams at their most salacious and obscene. He does not leave it to his audience or readers to make the connection. He insists on it.

So much social life was organized around the baths, if we are to believe Martial himself. He mentions especially dinner guests congregating at the baths before proceeding to dinner. The dinner seemed the most important social moment. A lot of socializing and fraternity took place at table. This is most basic. Hence the constant discussion about who gets invited, what takes place, why it matters, etc.

Now, given how the baths were organized, how could a Jew, a circumcised Jew, participate in the activities of the public baths? It is an old problem going back to the Book of Jubilees (second century BCE), where the question is posed about Jews participating in Greek games (in the gymnasium) which were held in the nude. Martial's epigram about Menophilus doing what he always did, doing his sport or rubbing in the baths with a covering only for it to fall off and reveal to others that he is circumcised, brings to mind the anxieties expressed in the Book of Jubilees. In the period after the conquest of Judaea, those anxieties would have been heightened.

After the conquest of Judaea the Jews of Rome lived with a great sense of shame and humiliation. Josephus's account of the Triumphal Parade in Rome in 71 CE gives some idea of what it must have felt like even for Josephus, who indicated in his preface to the *Jewish War* what it meant to him emotionally and psychologically to recount the events. Whatever else he felt on the day of the Triumphal Parade was probably repeated more than a few times as he wrote the *Jewish War* and also witnessed the various monuments constructed in Rome attesting to the conquest of Judaea. What was worse, he himself lived in Rome with the benefactions of the Flavians, whose rise to power was inextricably linked to the Roman victory in Judaea and the destruction of his beloved Jerusalem.

Josephus, like the rest of the Jews living in Rome, would have witnessed the reclamation of the area that the Emperor Nero had used to build his Golden House after the Fire of July 64 CE. The Temple of Peace, constructed in the aftermath of the conquest of Judaea, and dedicated in 75 CE, already housed implements seized from the Temple in Jerusalem.[34] After almost a decade of construction beginning in 71 CE, the new Flavian Amphitheater (the Colosseum) planned by Vespasian was dedicated by the Emperor Titus in 81 CE. It was intended as much to damn the memory of Nero and erase any traces of his Golden House as to point to the new public splendors constructed by the Flavians. Then there was the Arch of Titus, with its depiction of the Triumphal Parade of 71 CE, completed to celebrate Titus after his death in 81 CE.

In the 70s and 80s, then, the Jews of Rome could not live without these visible reminders of their humiliation, which would have been deeper still if in fact some or most of those employed in the construction of these Flavian monuments had been captives from the War who were now slaves in Rome. It is possible that the circumstances improved with the presence of Agrippa II's sister Berenice in the city in the company of none other than Titus,[35] and yet even this came with the unmistakable reminder that Titus was the one who had conquered Jerusalem and destroyed the Temple. Josephus's attempt to exonerate Titus for this deed in his account in the *Jewish War* would most likely have been treated with contempt by his Jewish readers in Rome.

For the Jews of Rome the sight of Agrippa II, Berenice, or Josephus would have been discomforting at best. The three were, for all intents and purposes, as good as apostate Jews. Never mind that the Herodians had always been known and received in Rome as friends of the Julio-Claudian emperors (Tiberius, Claudius, and Nero). So, perhaps, Agrippa II and Berenice's presence could be tolerated, but probably not Josephus's. Even to non-Jews they were in many ways the embodiment of Jewish humiliation, like the architectural monuments that celebrated the conquest of Judaea. The sight of

Berenice would have intensified the shame of the Jews of Rome and most likely earned their disgust in the years during which Berenice lived in Rome as Titus's consort (75–79 CE).[36] The Jews in the city would also have preferred not to see Agrippa II either, who like Josephus the historian, had fought on the side of the Romans against the people of Judaea and Jerusalem.

Still, none of this tells us how the Jews of Rome interacted socially with non-Jews, especially outside the Jewish Quarter. Nor do we have any documentation of how the first generation after the defeat of 70 CE reimagined themselves as residents of the city or felt as they lived in the capital of the empire that had destroyed their ancestral homeland. They must have been socially ambivalent at the very least. That social ambivalence would have limited some of their personal and intimate interactions with non-Jews.

Josephus himself claims that he was the subject of envy by some of his fellow Jews and that he had to endure aspersions about his character and conduct during the War (*Life* 423–425). It could not have been an ordinary time or easy time to be a Jew in Rome, even if one spent almost all of one's time in the Jewish Quarter in the *Transtiberim*. There were daily reminders of the humiliation of the conquest of Judaea and the destruction of Jerusalem.

Under these circumstances one has to wonder whether the social lives of Jews in the city would have involved as much intermingling with non-Jews outside the Jewish Quarter as might have been the case before the War in Judaea. At a minimum the Jews in the city had to come to terms with the contempt the people of Rome had shown and continued to express toward them in the aftermath of the War and what this meant for their continued presence in city. It is in this sense that we have to try to imagine what it would have been like for Jews to participate in the activities associated with the imperial bathhouses in Rome. Much of the record that we possess of Jewish participation in Roman bathhouses in the period before the War and immediately thereafter comes from Palestine or Roman Judaea. In his study of the Roman bathhouse as a Jewish institution, Yaron Eliav notes:

> There is no evidence substantiating an all-inclusive rejection of the bathhouse, either in the Late Roman Period (also referred to as the mishnaic and talmudic period), or in the hundred years prior to the destruction of the Second Temple, when the Roman bath-house was introduced into Palestine. The opposite is true—peculiar as it may seem to those maintaining the view of "widespread disapproval of the Greco-Roman world." Sources inform us that the bath-house was an inseparable and fully legitimate constituent of Jewish life in those days.[37]

But Rome was not Judaea or Galilee. What was tolerable or acceptable in Judaea or Galilee might not necessarily have been endurable in Rome after the War in the last three decades of the first century. Nor should we read back into first-century Rome a good deal of the record we possess from the second century onward; much of that record is from the Near East. It is not far-fetched to suggest that if the Jews of Rome did not have to use the large and imperial bathhouses in the rest of the city, they would not. They must have preferred the small bathhouses (some private) in the Jewish Quarter.

In his reference to Menophilus, Martial gives the impression that he was surprised to discover how well endowed Menophilus was. The surprise suggests two things. If the reference to a disproportionately large circumcised phallus is meant to be a sign that Menophilus was a Jew, then it means that Martial did not know before Menophilus exposed himself that Menophilus was a Jew, in which case Menophilus had been pretending to be something else. If, on the other hand, the reference has nothing to do with being a Jew, then it is irrelevant to the question, except that Martial's surprise still requires explanation. The only interpretation that makes sense is that indeed Menophilus was circumcised and therefore a Jew, either by birth or by choice as a proselyte. Shaye J. D. Cohen, in *The Beginnings of Jewishness*, wonders whether there is another interpretation that has nothing to do with Jews. But the alternative he proposes is caught up partly in the incongruence just raised.

Add to this the oppressive and humiliating inquiries during the time of Domitian in relation to the *fiscus Judaicus*. If a Jew did not want to experience what Menophilus experienced, they did not have to use the imperial bathhouses in Rome. Garrett Fagan is surely right that as a rule Jews were not barred from the bathhouses and that Rabbinic texts did not altogether object. However, the fact that they were not legally barred from the public or imperial bathhouses does not mean they were not the subject of unwelcome attention. Even without Martial's epigram about Menophilus there is every reason to believe that a "circumcised Jew" in the Roman bathhouse would be the subject of prurient interest. Another thing: Suetonius describes the scene he witnessed as a young boy when a ninety-year-old man was subjected to public inspection to see if he was circumcised. Are we to believe that no one had seen him at the baths, and that for all those years no one knew whether he was circumcised or not? Now read what Martial says about Menophilus, who suffered the indignity of having his covering fall off only to expose himself and his circumcision. There is a possible allusion to the indignities associated with the *fiscus Judaicus* here. At the same time, we need to keep in mind that Menophilus need not even have been a real person. It could all be a fiction created by Martial to make a point. That point is that one should be surprised to find such a circumcised person in the intimate company of Martial in the bathhouse in Rome.

Though the numbers are uncertain, there were apparently many non-imperial baths in the *Transtiberim*, the Jewish quarter, in the double digits, and probably more than fifty.[38] The clientele who used the Jewish baths did not have had to mingle with non-Jews; so if they did not wish to suffer any humiliations, they most certainly would have preferred these baths to others.

It is also not surprising that some synagogues had adjoining gymnasia and baths.

I return now to Martial's justification of his craft and his protestations that he was now freer to be as obscene as he wished, and to highlight that many of his contemporaries were just as obscene in private. The proliferation of crude erotic jokes in Book 11, then, did not amount to much. It merely supplied more of the same kinds of bawdy poetry that Martial's readers had come to expect from him and did not substantiate Martial's claim that he was now more liberated because Domitian's era was over and Nerva and Trajan had brought in a new dawn. The bathhouses had not gone anywhere. Martial's fellow Romans like Pliny the Younger could write without embarrassment in Letter 5.3.2 that he enjoyed comedies and lyric poetry; that he liked to write verses; but showed himself not too keen on criticism of his verses. He could barely tolerate them. What is more, he liked "obscene lampoons," so-called "Sotadics."[39] This is so precise a reference that one cannot even pretend otherwise. Pliny's terminology refers specifically to Sotades, the noted and infamous Alexandrian Greek writer of obscene poetry in the third century BC. Pliny did not have a problem with obscenities. He advertised the fact that he himself wrote Sotadics; it had been a pastime.

Pliny defends himself by saying that all the greats of the past have indulged in this either as readers or composers or both. He belongs, then, to a venerable tradition, and so is not to be censured for his love of these kinds of verses. He is in good company as he lists Vergil, Cicero, Ovid, Catullus, etc.: to which he adds, "I am human." From all appearances, Pliny read and appreciated Martial's poetry.

Pliny belonged to a world socially circumscribed by the types of gathering places that Martial mentions and sometimes celebrates in his epigrams: the bathhouses, the dinners by invitation, the private audiences, the poetry recitals in private homes. Besides, Pliny was not a stranger to Pompeii and its indulgent world. As is well known, his uncle Pliny the Elder, stationed at Misenum in the western part of the Bay of Naples, died in 79 CE during the eruption of Vesuvius that destroyed Pompeii. Pliny the Younger was in Misenum with him. His later account of the events of that fateful day for his friend Cornelius Tacitus is preserved in Letter 6.16.

Martial too justified his bawdy poetry by appealing to past masters in Catullus and others. However, there is no indication that Martial considered any of Pliny's Sotadics worthy of consideration. Although much has been made about Pliny the Younger's letter in which he reported Martial's death and commented about an epigram Martial had written about him, there is something somewhat strange about the links between Martial and Pliny.

I shall explore here what seems to me rather peculiar about Martial and Pliny's supposed friendship: Martial mentions Pliny the Younger only once in his book of epigrams; Pliny also mentions Martial only once in the said letter. In Pliny's case, except for his year as a tribune in Syria (c. 82), he spent most of those two decades in Rome; for Martial he had missed only a year in 87 CE which he spent in the north of Italy. Some of what I present here bears on the state of fear in Domitian's Rome. But to appreciate this, we will need a broader context in which to set Pliny's letter about Martial and Martial's epigram about Pliny.

PLINY AND FRIENDS IN DOMITIAN'S ROME

To his friend Voconius Romanus, Pliny writes as follows (Bk 1.5; dated early 97 CE):

> Did you ever see a man more abject and fawning than Marcus Regulus has been since the death of Domitian? His misdeeds were better concealed during that prince's reign, but they were every bit as bad as they were in the time of Nero. He began to be afraid that I was angry with him and he was not mistaken, for I certainly was annoyed. After doing what he could to help those who were compassing the ruin of Rusticus Arulenus, he had openly exulted at his death, and went so far as to publicly read and then publish a pamphlet in which he violently attacks Rusticus and even calls him "the Stoics' ape," adding that "he is marked with the brand of Vitellius." You recognise, of course, the Regulian style! He tears to pieces Herennius Senecio so savagely that Metius Carus said to him, "What have you to do with my dead men? Did I ever worry your Crassus or Camerinus?"—these being some of Regulus's victims in the days of Nero. Regulus thought I bore him malice for this, and so he did not invite me when he read his pamphlet. Besides, he remembered that he once mortally attacked me in the Court of the Centumviri. I was a witness on behalf of Arionilla, the wife of Timon, at the request of Rusticus Arulenus, and Regulus was conducting the prosecution. We on our side were relying for part of the defence on a decision of Metius Modestus, an excellent man who had been banished by Domitian and was at that moment in exile. This was Regulus's opportunity. "Tell me, Secundus," said he, "what you think of Modestus." You see in what peril I should have placed myself if I had answered that I thought highly of him, and how disgraceful it would have been if I had said that I thought ill of him. I fancy it must have been the gods who came to my rescue. "I will tell you what I think of him," I said, "when the Court has to give a decision on the point." He returned to the charge: "My question is, what do you think of Modestus?" Again I replied: "Witnesses used to be interrogated about persons in the dock, not about those who are already convicted." A third time he asked: "Well, I won't ask you now what you think of Modestus, but what you think of his loyalty." "You ask me," said I, "for my opinion. But I do not think it is in order for you to ask an opinion on what the Court has already passed judgment." He was silenced, while I was congratulated and praised for not having smirched my reputation by giving an answer that might have been discreet but would certainly have been dishonest, and for not having entangled myself in the meshes of such a crafty question.[40]

This was a narrow escape, even for someone so accomplished in the Centumviral courts as Pliny the Younger. Pliny certainly considered himself adept at handling problem dealing with wills and inheritances, with forgers and forged documents, and the like. He was almost caught off guard by "so insidious a question," as he put it, and in an environment where trials were not about treasonable offenses. What had taken place in the Centimviral court between Regulus and Pliny was certainly intended to expose the latter and could well have ended quite horribly for him. If Pliny clearly stood on the other side of the divide and opposed the way in which Rusticus had been treated, then Regulus was right not to have invited Pliny.

It was certainly unfortunate that Pliny had to appropriate the work of someone who had been exiled by Domitian in order to make his case in court and then have to suffer the kind of cross-examination that one endured as a witness and not as an advocate. This allowed Regulus to mount his offensive against Pliny, and he almost got Pliny in trouble for having taken such an approach, as using the views of a condemned man, so to speak, to make his case.

In the remainder of the letter that I have not quoted, Pliny describes two other encounters he had with Regulus and the circumstances under which he eventually learned about why Regulus had behaved toward him as he had. Regulus explained that his motivation was to damage Modestus and not Pliny. But Pliny was not so sure. Regulus asserted that he was angry because Metius Modestus l two-legged creatures" (1.5.14). Pliny shared the views and editorializes that "Modestus had been wholly truthful in penning this." He then adds: "This was virtually the end of our conversation, for I had no wish to take the matter further. I wanted to keep all my options open."

Pliny states that he was well aware that Regulus was a powerful man: "He is wealthy, leader of a faction, well regarded by many, and feared by more, fear being an emotion stronger than affection. It is possible, however, that those supports may be shaken, and collapse, for the popularity of evil men is as fickle as the men themselves." Pliny knew how not to get into trouble in his dealings with such a character. The fear was more than palpable, the sense of foreboding and terror very real. Pliny was keenly aware, as so many members of the Roman Senate were, that the slightest miscalculation could lead to exile or worse death; and then their property would be seized by Domitian to support his many ventures.

Such was the case of Pliny's friend Calestrius Tiro who did all he could, in spite of debilitating illness (from gout), to survive Domitian so as not to suffer the loss of his property. Then as soon as Domitian died, he chose to commit suicide to end his misery (1.12). As he mentioned to Pliny before he died, "I want to survive that brigand, if only for a day" (1.12.8).

Pliny managed to throw off Regulus, but, like many of the other Senators, he was not safe by any means.[41] In a world of unseemly characters where he described one such character as "in general a wicked person who had exploited the era of Domitian like many others" (3.9.31), there were certainly others who were after Pliny. In one letter dealing with ghosts, of all things, Pliny lets it be known that he would have been indicted had Domitian lived longer. A case had already been prepared against him by one Carus, he claims. The docket, so he reveals, was found on Domitian's desk at the time of this death (Letter 7. 27.14).

Little wonder then that Pliny felt it part of his duty to seek some kind of redress for the cruel excesses that had transpired during the reign of Domitian and to indict some of those who had participated in the terror and recriminations. In a remarkable letter that needs to be read in full to appreciate the sense of the times, Pliny took to the floor of the Senate to render an indictment in a virtuoso performance that put all his caginess as an advocate on display. With great courage he exposed himself to a dangerous fate. Yet managed to win the day. He related the events to his friend Quadratus:

> Once Domitian was killed I decided on reflection that this was a truly splendid opportunity for attacking the guilty, avenging the injured, and making oneself known. Moreover, though many crimes had been committed by numerous persons, none seemed so shocking as the violent attack in the Senate-house made by a senator on a fellow senator, by a praetorian acting as judge on a consular who had been brought to trial. I had also been the friend of Helvidius, as far as friendship was possible with one who had been driven through fear of the times to hide his famous name and equally famous virtues in retirement, and the friend of his stepmother Fannia and her mother Arria. But I was not moved to act so much by personal obligations as by the demands of common justice, the enormity of the deed, and the thought of establishing a precedent. Now, in the early days after liberty was restored, everyone had acted for himself, brought his personal enemies to trial (if they were not too powerful), and had them condemned amid the general confusion and chaos. By contrast I believed that the proper course, as well as the more effective, was to deal with this atrocious criminal not through the universal hatred of Domitian's time, but by bringing a specific charge against him at a moment when the first outburst had spent itself and the fury which was daily abating had yielded to justice. So though I was greatly distressed at the time by the recent death of my wife, I sent a message to Anteia (widow of Helvidius) asking her to visit me, as I was kept indoors by my recent bereavement. When she came I told her I had determined not to leave her husband unavenged. "Tell this to Arria and Fannia," I said (for they were back from exile). "Talk it over with them and see whether you wish to be associated with this case. I don't need support, but I am not so jealous for my own glory as to grudge you a share in it." Anteia did as I asked and the women acted promptly.[42]

This is the wonderfully dangerous world in which Pliny made his career. Although a lad when Nero died, Pliny was keenly aware of the impact Nero's reign had on Roman society, so that even three decades after his death he could write with some apprehension about a man who had contributed to some of Nero's crimes.

Rex Winsbury argues that Regulus is like a double for Pliny, and that Pliny's presentation of him could be an act of negative self-presentation.[43] In my language, I might have said that Regulus is a foil, both real and imagined. But I think it is an oversimplification to say that the representation of Regulus is mostly for literary purposes and that there is no correspondence to what Regulus was in fact. Why? Well, Tacitus also makes the same charges. Moreover, there are others who agreed, according to Pliny. Next, we have the simple fact that those whom he is said to have victimized were indeed victimized. It was not a theory that his activities had cost many people their lives and livelihoods. In addition, Pliny himself on a few occasions shows how easily a career in the courts could lead to a good deal of evil. There are times, many times, when he presents himself having to be expedient rather than truthful. It was what lawyers did and still do. However, he believed that Regulus took his too far. Why denounce a man whom you have already succeeded in exiling? In another sense, Pliny understood him well, because he knew all the tricks of the trade, and was just simply aghast, it would seem, that Regulus could use them so well, and to such evil consequences. On Pliny's truthfulness in general Ronald Syme seems too cynical. Since so much depends on dates, I am not sure Pliny could have fabricated all these letters to conform to the image that Syme presents. As Winsbury rightly points out, Pliny had contemporaries who could check him on this, since he published these letters. There is corroboration of his view of Regulus, for example, from Tacitus. When Cassius Dio came to write later on, he pointed out that his father helped him check some of the materials he used. Dio also describes Domitian's reign in ghastly terms; so also Suetonius.

In general it seems best to accord Pliny the benefit of the doubt,[44] since he shows at various points that he too knows how to play the game. Everyone had to learn how to play the game to survive. It was a Roman trait. Juvenal satirizes everyone on this score. So, in the end, it is Juvenal who lets it be known what the character of a Roman is. Book 3 of his Satires is unmistakable in this regard.

Pliny's relationship to Marcus Aquilius Regulus was a complicated one, made more peculiar by the parallel lives they lived both as advocates in the Centumviral courts (the court of the one hundred) that judged cases of inheritance and wills. To say that Regulus is Pliny's alter ego as some suggest is to misrepresent the relationship or even what part Regulus plays in Pliny's correspondence.

In the first place, it should be assumed that the recipients of Pliny's letters containing references to Regulus must have shared Pliny's views about Regulus. The contemporary testimonies of Tacitus (*Histories* 4.42) and Suetonius, both friends of Pliny, support Pliny's representations. While they could be dismissed as the equally biased testimonies of Pliny's friends, the fact that they held those views indicates that Regulus did come across the way Pliny, Tacitus, and Suetonius portrayed him. Martial's sympathetic treatment is almost irrelevant on this account, since he merely points out that Regulus was a recipient of many favors. Given his role as an advocate in the Centumviral courts, how he received those favors, especially when they were made in wills of some of his clients and patrons, raises as many questions about the nature of the favors and how he managed to secure them. In fact, in one letter, Pliny described Regulus's methods as nothing short of fraud.

> But why do I worry myself when I live in a country where villainy and rascality have long been getting not less but far more handsome rewards than modesty and virtue? Look at Regulus, for example, who, from being a pauper and without a shilling, has now become such a rich man by sheer villainy that he once told me that, when he was consulting the omens as to how soon he would be worth sixty millions of sesterces, he found double sets of entrails, which were a token that he would be worth 120 millions. So he will too, if only he goes on, as he has begun, dictating wills which are not their own to the very people who are making their wills, which is about the most disgraceful kind of forgery imaginable. Farewell.[45]

As for the general repute in which Regulus was held by his fellow Romans, here too, Pliny had grave concerns. On the occasion of the death of Regulus's son, Pliny seemed almost beside himself and lacking in sympathy. "Regulus has lost his son," he began a letter to Attius Clemens, continuing that this is the "only misfortune he did not deserve, because I doubt whether he considers it as such" (4.2.1). Pliny wondered what would have become of the young man and his talents, and pointed out that Regulus's excessive show of affection for his son, whom he had released from his parental authority in order to inherit from his mother's estate, had always appeared suspicious to others. "It seems incredible," he added, "but remember that it was Regulus. Yet now that his son is dead, he is mad with grief at his loss." The presumption here is that Regulus had a lot to gain from the boy's death. Pliny then describes an odd extravagance: "The boy had a number of ponies, some in harness and others not broken in, dogs both great and small, nightingales, parrots and blackbirds—all these Regulus slaughtered at his pyre. Yet an act like that was no token of grief; it was but a mere parade of it." Pliny complained:

> It is strange how people are flocking to call upon him. Everyone detests and hates him, yet they run to visit him in shoals as though they both admired and loved him. To put in a nutshell what I mean, people in paying court to Regulus are copying the example he set. He does not move from his gardens across the Tiber, where he has covered an immense quantity of ground with colossal porticos and littered the river bank with his statues, for, though he is the meanest of misers, he flings his money broadcast, and though his name is a

byword, he is forever vaunting his glories. Consequently, in this the most sickly season of the year, he is upsetting every one's arrangements, and thinks it soothes his grief to inconvenience everybody. He says he is desirous of taking a wife, and here again, as in other matters, he shows the perversity of his nature. You will hear soon that the mourner is married, that the old man has taken a wife, displaying unseemly haste as the former and undue delay as the latter. If you ask what makes me think he will take this step, I reply that it is not because he says he will—for there is no greater liar than he—but because it is quite certain that Regulus will do what he ought not to do. Farewell.[46]

In another letter, this time to his friend Catius Lepidus, on the subject of Regulus mourning his son, Pliny provided still more commentary on the extravagance of Regulus's ways. He also lamented how much good Regulus could have achieved if he had directed his inexhaustible energy towards better ends:

4.7. TO CATIUS LEPIDUS.
I am constantly writing to tell you what energy Regulus possesses. It is wonderful the way he carries through anything which he has set his mind upon. It pleased him to mourn for his son—and never man mourned like him; it pleased him to erect a number of statues and busts to his memory, and the result is that he is keeping all the workshops busy; he is having his boy represented in colours, in wax, in bronze, in silver, in gold, ivory, and marble—always his boy. He himself just lately got together a large audience and read a memoir of his life—of the boy's life; he read it aloud, and yet had a thousand copies written out which he has scattered broadcast over Italy and the provinces. He wrote at large to the decurions and asked them to choose one of their number with the best voice to read the memoir to the people, and it was done. What good he might have effected with this energy of his—or whatever name we should give to such dauntless determination on his part to get his own way—if he had only turned it into a better channel! But then, as you know, good men rarely have this faculty so well developed as bad men; the Greeks say, "Ignorance makes a man bold; calculation gives him pause," and just in the same way modesty cripples the force of an upright mind, while unblushing confidence is a source of strength to a man without conscience. Regulus is a case in point. He has weak lungs, he never looks you straight in the face, he stammers, he has no imaginative power, absolutely no memory, no quality at all, in short, except a wild, frantic genius, and yet, thanks to his effrontery, and even just to this frenzy of his, he has got people to regard him as an orator. Herennius Senecio very neatly turned against him Cato's well-known definition of an orator by saying, "An orator is a bad man who knows nothing of the art of speaking," and I really think that he thereby gave a better definition of Regulus than Cato did of the really true orator.[47]

These are stinging words. But Pliny was not done. He returned to the subject of the biography that Regulus had written of his dead son: "Have you any equivalent to send me for a letter like this? Yes, indeed, you have, if you will write and say whether any one of my friends in your township, or whether you yourself have read this pitiful production of Regulus in the Forum. . . . For it is so absurd that it will make you laugh rather than sigh, and you would think it was written not about a boy but by a boy. Farewell.[48]

Despite the biting criticism, Pliny reveals a side of himself that genuinely seemed to wish that Regulus had been a better man than he was. His indefatigable energy and determination to achieve his objectives clearly impressed Pliny. In a moment of wistfulness, he allowed himself some nostalgia for the days gone by when Regulus plied his trade in the courts. He wrote to his friend Arrianus a few years after Regulus's death (c. 106–107):

> During court proceedings, I often keep looking out for Marcus Regulus, though I don't like to say that I miss him. So why do I look out for him? Well, he showed respect for oratory, he would look apprehensive, grow pale, write out his speeches (though he could not memorize them). Then, too, he would paint round one or other of his eyes (the right when about to speak for the plaintiff, the left for the defendant); he would sport a white patch over one eye or transfer it to the other; he would always consult a soothsayer on the outcome of a case. All this arose from an excess of superstition, but also from the great respect he had for oratory. Then again, the advocates speaking with him found two of his procedures quite enjoyable: he would ask for unlimited time, and he would muster an audience to listen. What can be more enjoyable than to speak for as long as you like while someone else gets the brickbats, and to be, so to say, constrained to speak appropriately before an audience gathered by another?[49]

Pliny catches himself drifting into a mild encomium: "But for all that, Regulus did well to die, though he would have done still better had he died sooner; since he might now be alive without any danger to the public in the reign of a prince under whom he could do no mischief. I need not scruple therefore to say I sometimes miss him: for since his death, the custom has grown widely prevalent of not allowing, nor indeed asking, more than an hour or two to plead in, and sometimes not half that time."[50]

Pliny goes on to lament the impatience that characterizes more recent proceedings at court and the fact that speakers now wish to finish as quickly as possible, as if those of the past were dimwits for needing more time to make their case. And so: "Dear Regulus, despite your canvassing, you used to get from all the trust which very few vouchsafe today." Still, it would have been better that he died earlier than he did. Such were the times.

The Emperor Nerva's pronouncement lamented those times. It was the general consensus that Nerva had come to save Rome from the horrible reign of Domitian. Marcus Regulus had not only been feared during the time of Domitian, but he had done some of his most dastardly deeds during the reign of Nero, as Pliny mentions in Letter 1.5; and as Cassius Dio also noted in his *Histories*.

Why go through all of Pliny's reportage about Regulus? It is to suggest that the boundaries of friendship and enmity were very thin, and that people who worked so closely within the same theater, like the law courts, could develop enmities that run deep, even if they still maintained close relationships. Some of what Pliny says about Regulus he learned from personal conversations with him. Yet from the sparring between them in court and elsewhere, their enmity toward each other was only thinly disguised. In an environment full of intrigue, informers, and an inconstant emperor many deemed a despotic tyrant, it made for great anxiety and fear. "Who was next to be delated?" That is the question that would have been on everyone's mind. Marcus Regulus was Pliny's foil in more ways than one. Against him Pliny looked his very best. More than anything else, Pliny had learned the art of survival, a skill that was required of almost every successful Roman senator and politician.

We may compare Pliny's survival skills with those of Martial, who seemed to change his tune as quickly as the winds blew differently. He had courted the Flavians, becoming particularly close to Domitian's court, soliciting his patronage. After Domitian's death he shrewdly recanted his earlier praise of him and turned to Nerva and eventually to praising Trajan's regime. Ultimately, he could not live down his adulation of Domitian. That past could not be erased so easily. For all his faults, Pliny the Younger seems to have behaved better than Martial, and by all indications had served his fellow senators more creditably than Marcus Regulus. To a number of those senators, it was the considered judgment of the times how powerless and inept the Roman Senate had been during Domitian's reign.

For Pliny, the Senate had long been an ineffective and somewhat disreputable institution. Writing almost a decade after the final year of Domitian, he noted to his friend Aristo (Letter 8.14) that the senate was "fearful and speechless, for it was dangerous to express your convictions, and humiliating to repress them." He then asked: "What was it possible to learn at that time, or what point was there in having learnt such things" as the conventions of senatorial procedure, "when the Senate was summoned to be wholly idle or wholly wicked, when it was kept in being to be now a laughing-stock and now ripe for grief" (8.14.8)? This is a an indictment of an institution to which Pliny belonged throughout his entire adult life, so he could not possibly question the viability of the institution without calling attention to his own complicities and his role in its failures. Was he willing to indict himself?

> Once we became senators, for many years we witnessed and endured the same evils in which we then took part, so that our talents were blunted, broken, and bruised by them, affecting even our later days. There has been only a brief

period (for every era of greater happiness is shorter) in which it has been our pleasure to come to know our identity, and to apply that knowledge.[51]

If Pliny were to list the evils in which he took part, we might have a better idea just how far he was willing to accuse himself and to what extent he would have taken responsibility for so much of what transpired during the reign of Domitian, whose assassination was greeted with such elation in the Senate, as if none of its members, at least those present, had done anything wrong during those times.

For those who survived the intrigues, Domitian's fifteen-year reign remained a difficult and deeply regrettable memory. However, it could not be so soon forgotten with so many atrocities that cried out for redress. Nerva's conciliatory posture and Trajan's objection to revisiting those days meant that there were many who believed rightly that they had not received justice. Pliny's attempt to seek some kind of redress, as he described it in Letter 9.13, was only partly successful. In the end Publicius Certus, the subject of his indictment, survived. He was not charged with anything so severe, except that he lost the opportunity to be consul. That was the price he paid for acts that had cost many people their lives and property. He died shortly after Pliny had prosecuted his case in the senate. Pliny would eventually be awarded the consulship that was denied Certus. A cynical reading would suggest that this was what Pliny was after all along. Remember that he himself mentioned that prosecuting Certus might enhance his own fame.[52]

In the course of the proceedings it became quite clear that there were some who would have preferred that the charges were not brought at all. When Pliny began his speech detailing the nature of his indictment, he deliberately did not mention the person against whom it was directed. So as he received the approval of some of his fellow senators, they soon realized that they could be setting themselves up for a fall, since they did not know as yet which one or which ones among them was being charged. Some demanded to know who was being charged before Pliny could go on. In due course many guessed that it was Publicius Certus. The other senators managed to reduce the nature of the charge, and in so doing divested the indictment of its more damning elements. Pliny got his adulation and received the approval of his fellow senators for his speech and advocacy. But they managed to give less than he could have received. The Senate had not changed that much, and as his later letter to Aristo showed, it still hadn't changed a whole lot almost a decade after Domitian. In one sense, whether the Senate was reputable or not was a matter of degree. For it always contrived to serve the interests of its most powerful, influential, and most feared members.

Pliny had his anxieties. He continued to believe that he had not fully avenged Helvidius or at any rate that there was still more that he owed his widow, Fannia. Remarking about her failing health, his mind went back to the initial prosecution of her husband and the gallant part she had played as a witness in court. Pliny presented her in a way that put Pliny's own "courage" under scrutiny, "for it grieves me to think that of so excellent a women being torn from all of us, who will never, I fear, see her like again."[53] Every characteristic Pliny mentions raised a question about Pliny himself.

> How exceptional her chastity, her sanctity, her dignity, her loyalty! Twice she followed her husband into exile, and was herself banished the third time on her husband's account. For when Senecio was put on his trial for having written a Life of Helvidius, and said, in the course of his defence, that he had been requested to do so by Fannia, Metius Carus with a threatening gesture asked her whether she had made such a request. "I did request him," was the answer. "Did you give him material to write from? he went on." "I did give them." "Did your mother know?" "She did not know." Not a word did she utter to show that she shrank from the perils which threatened her. More than that, though the Senate had passed a decree—under compulsion and owing to the dangers of the times—that the volumes in question should be destroyed, she took care to preserve and keep them after her goods had been confiscated, and she even carried them with her into the exile of which they were the cause.[54]

Compare Pliny's own artful dodge when he was under "cross-examination" by Marcus Regulus. He confessed in one of his letters that I mentioned previously that he felt trapped. He managed to evade Regulus's questioning, but only barely. He wished neither to face death nor exile. Fannia spoke openly, plainly, and without subtlety or ambiguity. She was as resolute as Pliny was cunning in the face of a merciless foe. By his own admission, Pliny was not a man without guile (6.33.7).

Pliny was in no doubt that Fannia stood head and shoulders above him. For in those times, when Pliny and others knew how to survive, knew the kinds of subtleties and ploys to use so as not to be banished, here was Fannia, determined that her husband's biography be written as a record of those times. Fannia was perfectly willing to accept the consequences, when it was discovered that she had commissioned the book. Hers was the deed. She was willing to die, and she accepted exile. After her exile she still impresses.

> Again, what a delightful and charming woman she was, commanding not only deep respect, but love, as but few women can! Will there ever be another whom we can point to as a pattern to our wives? or another from whom even we men can take a lesson in personal courage—one who inspires us when we see and hear her with the admiration we feel for the heroines of history about whom we read?[55]

Pliny may have discharged his services to Fannia and her mother (now deceased) in times of prosperity and in adversity, consoled them when they were banished, and avenged them when they returned, as he stated in this letter. By his own recognizance, he acknowledged that it was not enough. He has not matched his services to them both, and so he wishes Fannia would survive her current illness so that he will have more time to pay his debts to them both.

Pliny and his friends lived fully cognizant of the "fears of the times." This is an important phrase. It is not an accident that all the letters that Pliny the Younger bequeathed to posterity were written after the death of Domitian in late 96 CE. It is impossible to believe that in all his occupations both professional and private that Pliny had not written any letters until after the death of Domitian. He may well have known that one way to survive was to write as little as possible or to make sure that what he wrote before 97 CE was not bequeathed to posterity. So the likely scenario is that Pliny deliberately chose not to preserve anything he had written before 97 CE. In this way too he was able to shape his past, and especially the period that covered a career that depended in part on Domitian's generosity for the number of appointments he held as military tribune in Syria (c. 82), *quaestor Caesaris* (chosen by Domitian, c. 90); as tribune (*tribunus plebis* c. 92); and as Prefect of the military treasury (c. 94–96). He mentions these appointments retrospectively in the letters (7.16) without ever acknowledging that these very appointments made him as much a person of privilege during Domitian's regime as anyone else.

At the same time, it needs to be acknowledged that taking up the defense of the younger Helvidius when the latter was being prosecuted for treason was a dangerous thing to do under the circumstances. Knowing Pliny, it is likely that he conducted himself in such a way that whichever way the verdict went, he would not come out the worse for it. He was far too shrewd and calculating in his choices as an advocate to have ventured into that hornets' nest of senatorial prosecutions with its suits, countersuits, and intrigues without considering the consequences and implications to his own life. By his own testimony he and his faction, if we may call it that, were outwitted by those they wished to shame. As he tells the story, they had planned a suit. But their victim in turn countersued. That is where Pliny was left hanging. Pliny acknowledged the hazards: To Julius Genitor:

> Our friend Artemidorus has so much goodness of heart that he always exaggerates the services his friends render him, and hence, in my case, though it is true that I have done him a good turn, he speaks of it in far too glowing language. When the philosophers were banished from the city I was staying with him in his suburban residence, and the visit was the more talked about and the more dangerous to me, because I was praetor at the time.[56]

This means that Pliny risked exposing himself to potential charges for showing sympathy for someone who had been banished.

> Moreover, as he stood in need of a considerable sum of money to discharge some debts which he had incurred for the most honourable of reasons, I borrowed the sum and gave it to him as a free gift, when certain of his powerful and rich friends held aloof. I did so in spite of the fact that seven of my friends had been put to death or banished; Senecio, Rusticus, and Helvidius having suffered the former, and Mauricus, Gratilla, Arria, and Fannia the latter punishment. With all these thunderbolts falling round me, I felt scorched, and there were certain clear indications that a like fate was hanging over my head, but I do not on that account think I deserve the splendid credit which Artemidorus assigns me—I only claim to have avoided the disgrace of deserting my friends.[57]

I recalled earlier that elsewhere he mentions that a docket had been prepared against him, and had Domitian lived longer he would certainly have been indicted. So how did he manage? How did he explain it to himself? "I do not think that I have deserved the outstanding reputation such as Artemidorus proclaims; it is merely that I avoided disgrace." It is in the last line: how he managed to avoid disgrace. But could he maintain his equanimity in the face of Martial's friendship to Regulus and his sycophancy toward Domitian, who had murdered some of his closest friends?

PLINY'S LETTER ON MARTIAL'S DEATH

Against this backdrop Pliny's friendship with Martial looks particularly strange. In fact, we might ask exactly what sort of friendship it was. Here is the letter on Martial. To his friend Cornelius Priscus:

> I hear that Valerius Martial is dead, and I am much troubled at the news. He was a man of genius, witty and caustic, yet one who in his writings showed as much candour as he did biting wit and ability to sting. When he left Rome I made him a present to help to defray his travelling expenses, as a tribute to the friendship I bore him and to the verses he had composed about me. It was the custom in the old days to reward with offices of distinction or money grants those who had composed eulogies of private individuals or cities, but in our day this custom, like many other honourable and excellent practices, was one of the first to fall into disuse. For when we cease to do deeds worthy of praise, we think it is folly to be praised.[58]

So for Pliny it was: He quotes the verses. Then he concludes:

> Was I not right to take a most friendly farewell of a man who wrote a poem like that about me, and do I do wrong if I now bewail his death as that of a bosom-friend? For he gave me the best he could, and would have given me more if he had had it in his power. And yet what more can be given to a man than glory and praise and immortality? But you may say that Martial's poems

will not live forever. Well, perhaps not, yet at least he wrote them in the hope that they would. Farewell.[59]

Pliny appears as Martial's patron. Had Pliny forgiven him for being a sycophant? Possibly. When did he write the epigram praising Pliny, before or after Domitian? Was Pliny less harsh and conciliatory because Martial had paid him the ultimate compliment? Maybe. Was this why he seemed to suggest that his friend C. Priscus might not agree with his estimation of Martial committing him to immortality? I suspect. But it need not be. Is there an act of desperation here? It is not so easy to discern. How should we read Pliny's "You will respond that his writings will not be immortal. Perhaps they will not, but he wrote them thinking they would be. Farewell"? How did Priscus read it?

Marc Kleijwegt, in his introduction to *Martial: Selected Epigrams*, suggests that Pliny's comments on Martial could be translated as follows: "he [Martial] was a smart-ass, a schemer, and a bitterly cruel man. In his writing he injected a lack of respect and hatefulness, all wrapped in frankness."[60] He adds that "it is an appropriate response to an epigram (10.20) that comically misrepresents Pliny on essential points, and it is a tribute of which Martial would have been proud."[61] That Martial would have been proud of such a putdown seems highly questionable for one who was at great pains to excoriate the supposed and imagined critics of his poetry. That aside, everything that Kleijwegt says in his translation of Pliny on Martial could be true of Martial's poetry. However, it extends Pliny's words beyond what Pliny seems to have had in mind. Besides, if all Pliny meant to do was point out that Martial's poetry could be bitter and full of gall, he would not be saying anything that Martial himself does not acknowledge about his epigrams. Kleijwegt draws attention to this much when he mentions Epigram 7.25, for example, as an acknowledgment that his poetry can be acerbic, *fel* (bitter, gall), and *acer* (sharp, stinging).

Surely the Ciceronian language in Pliny's description of Martial as *ingeniosus* (ingenious, clever), *acutus* (sharp, keen), and *acer* (stinging, pointed) are terms that can be used in rather ironic ways to devastating effect to mean too clever, scheming, and ruthless. If that is what Pliny has in mind, then Pliny must be deemed rather disingenuous. After all, for being so scheming, clever, and ruthless, Pliny found it worthy of his name and fame to have been immortalized in verse by Martial. Pliny cannot present so devastating a critique of Martial's poetry and then accept Martial's praise at the same time as worthy of comment and repetition.

Another issue here that is not far removed from the surface is between Pliny and his friend Cornelius Priscus, to whom he sent Letter 3.21. Pliny clearly reflects on a difference of opinion between Priscus and himself concerning the value of Martial's poetry; or between two schools of thought regarding Martial's reputation. Apparently, Priscus did not think it was worthy of posterity. Pliny did not wish to press the point, hence his retort to the riposte that he imagined Priscus or someone else could give to his claim that Martial had immortalized him. "Perhaps, he will not be immortal, but he wrote believing he would be:" which implies that Pliny also receives the praise believing that Martial would be immortal. That is to say, Pliny was willing to hedge his bets, and not only that, he too was willing to leave a record of his support and benefaction to the poet (3.21.4). Here is Pliny in character: the lover of praise, when it is merited (in his own words); and the man with an incessant quest for immortality in the writings of others. Notice his repeated comments to Tacitus about being in his writings, his comments about his acclaim as a writer, and so on.

Pliny interestingly picks out the second half of Martial's Epigram 10.20 celebrating him. He leaves out the first half of the epigram by editing out the part that ostensibly does not concern him, but which in every way comments about the world in which both he and Martial live. It is a world full of readers and critics, coteries and patrons. It is not entirely a beautiful portraiture of life.

Pliny's letter on Martial's death actually can be read far more critically that it is often done. Pliny offers faint approval. Pliny's words are couched in somewhat apologetic language. It is almost as if Pliny has to defend himself about his approval of Martial. The larger issues in Martial's poetry concerning his excessive adulation of Domitian are left untouched. Sullivan draws attention to this fact, but does not provide an explanation. So the question is this: why does Pliny condemn Domitian and his reign on so many occasions, but passes over in silence Martial's egregious and indecent adulation of Domitian in his epigrams? Why is it that it was Pliny who had to provide the resources for Martial to make his journey back to Spain? The two issues seem connected somehow. Pliny's words suggest they are inextricably linked. "When he was retiring from Rome," Pliny writes. There is a sense of permanence attached to it, an end to a long sojourn in Rome. He was leaving never to return to Rome, and I suspect Pliny and his links to Trajan the new emperor may have had something to do with the finality of it all, but I cannot prove it. Something else provides the connection that is easier to establish because Pliny mentions it: Pliny's vanity and desire for praise.

Pliny states unapologetically that he acted as a friend to Martial for the praise he offered to him in his epigrams. This memorializing and bequest to history is mostly what motivated Pliny to act as he did. It allows Pliny to overlook Martial's desultory behavior; in the same way that Pliny could feel some nostalgia for his nemesis Regulus, whom he excoriated on numerous occasions in his letters; the same Regulus who was a friend of Martial's, and to whom Martial addressed a few of his epigrams. Pliny overlooked Martial's links with Regulus just as he did his links with Domitian's court. In the end, what mattered for Pliny was that he be praised. Nothing more nothing less, and he was quite prepared to pay even for that, after the fact. This too Pliny acknowledged in his letter.

Pliny's words about Martial, then, should not be read as a straightforward endorsement of Martial's supposedly "good character," if we may even use that phrase. Martial's insistence in Book 1 of the epigrams that he was a better man than his verses is perhaps one of his most peculiar if not pretentious claims in all of his writing. Exactly what that "better" looked like to Pliny and other contemporaries is hard to say. If as Sullivan describes him, he was hypocritical, self-righteous, obscene, obsequious, cruel, mean-spirited, a misogynist, etc., then what is it that constitutes Martial's good character? At a later point Sullivan will try to save Martial by speaking of his ambivalent attitudes. Notice that Pliny says almost nothing about Martial's character; only his intelligence and his wit. This may not be incidental from someone as cagey and particular about his representations and his reputation as Pliny.

If Pliny did not intend to present this silence as an indirect comment on Martial's character, other letters in Book 3 contain details that compel comparisons between Martial and others. This is the same Pliny who writes to his friend Julius Genitro in Letter 3.11 about Artemidorus, the son-in-law of Musonius Rufus the respected Stoic philosopher, and describes what kind of character he admires and commends to others. The characteristics mentioned about Artemidorus are so far removed from Martial that if Pliny had praised Martial's character one would have to consider him by turns disingenuous, duplicitous, or patently dishonest. So it should not be surprising that Pliny should pass over Martial's character in silence. To comment would have placed him in an awkward position since, after all, he wished to be remembered for Martial's attempt at immortalizing him. Elsewhere Pliny shows how shrewd he could be in getting out of difficult circumstances by his choice of words or his silences. Recall his encounter with Regulus that he relates, and keep in mind that Regulus appears to have been one of Martial's friends.

Significantly, Pliny had helped Artemidorus financially in somewhat similar circumstances as Martial found himself. Is this a coincidence, that in both cases he was helping someone who was going into exile, or that in both cases, the individuals are singing Pliny's praises? One after the fact, and the other before the fact? With Artemidorus it was someone he admired for his intelligence, integrity, truthfulness, and his model as a human being and philosopher. In the case of Martial, well, it was someone whose attributes lay in his intelligence and scathing wit, but who praised Pliny for his studies. The two have to be read together.

Pliny was close to Musonius Rufus and the Stoics who got banished or killed by Domitian. Martial excoriates the Stoics in his epigrams and, as

Sullivan says, his sympathies or sensibilities are Epicurean. So here is the incongruity. What Pliny respects is what Martial despises. Let us keep in mind that in spite of appearances Martial does not quite go about things like Seneca, who was also from Spain. Pliny's so-called friendship with Martial seems occasional, if I can use that phrase, or rather, tentative or tenuous at best. It all has to do with the praise that Martial offers in his epigrams. But it is not a sign of any real amity or closeness between them.

Martial, in close relationship with the likes of Regulus and the courtier Parthenius, was among those who clearly thought themselves safe from Domitian's terror. He makes no references in his epigrams to the executions and banishments under Domitian or to anything concerning Pliny's friends. However, in the end Martial too goes into an exile that is undeclared but which Pliny knew to be a fact. It might have escaped comment only because he was returning to his native Spain and to his hometown. Yet, for someone who called Rome his home, that was an exile without any decree from the emperor. We may suspect that Trajan had a hand in compelling Martial to see this through. I am inclined to think that Pliny was part of the effort to get Martial to leave Rome.

It is not for me to discuss or judge Martial's character. It is for his contemporaries to do so. Pliny provides some comparisons. First, we can compare how Pliny speaks about Martial in 3.21, the letter that ends Book 3; and 3.11, the letter in which he discusses his friend Artemidorus. We can then compare his comments about Martial also against another letter, 3.7, in which he mentions the death of Silius Italicus, much the same way he mentions Martial's death in 3.21. In both of these comparisons, Martial comes off the worse for it.

If you compare the two letters, 3.21 and 3.11, you cannot help but see the differences between Pliny calling Artemidorus his friend (3.11) and calling Martial also a friend (3.21). They are worlds apart. Artemidorus was not banished at the time of Pliny's visit to him when Pliny was *praetor*. It was that the philosophers had been banished and seven of his close friends had either been executed or sent into exile. The danger for Pliny, then, was that he was associating with someone related to a known philosopher, Musonius Rufus (30–102/4 CE), who had earlier been banished by Nero (in 65 CE), banished again by Vespasian, but returned under Titus. There is no hint that Domitian tried to exile Musonius again. However, Domitian made it difficult for other philosophers to remain in Rome when he banished them from the city and in all of Italy in 95 CE.[62] Musonius seems to have retired at that time.

If you then compare the two letters, 3.7 and 3.11 you are brought up to see how in many ways Martial's retirement from Rome was an exile that reveals much about Martial's inability to rehabilitate himself the way Silius

Italicus (c. 26–103 CE) was able to. Martial mentions Silius Italicus at 11.48 and 11.49.

> Silius, who possesses the lands that once belonged to the eloquent Cicero, celebrates funeral obsequies at the tomb of the great Virgil. There is no one that either Virgil or Cicero would have preferred for his heir, or as guardian of his tomb and lands.

> There remained but one man, and he a poor one, to honour the nearly deserted ashes, and revered name, of Virgil. Silius determined to succour the cherished shade; Silius, a poet, not inferior to Virgil himself, consecrated the glory of the bard.[63]

So the revised Book 10 appears to have taken on the project of presenting a Martial who now longed for his native Bilbilis. There are jests without gall, he writes in Epigram 10.48: a freedom not to be dreaded the next morning; no word you would wish unsaid; my cups do not make anyone a defendant. Martial's words describe a world in which people feared that their private albeit social talk could turn them into defendants. A dinner party, the most common of social events, could be your ruin. That is what is implied.

Epigram 10.72 is in praise of Trajan and in criticism of Domitian. Martial protests that he will not address any man as lord and god (*domini deusque*), an allusion to what Domitian demanded of his addressees. Suetonius mentions this too. Martial worries about flatterers; then he turns into one. Is this an admission that he had been a flatterer and so now wishes to speak in a way different from of old? Is he saying that they were all flatterers, but now they can be something different? Martial appears to speak as if acknowledging that everyone did as was required. Now that they have a better man for an emperor, a better Senate, there is no need to keep to the old ways. But is this really a defense of his own poetry? Hardly. The epigrams he wrote were not merely because he felt compelled to flatter. He argued against the image of Cato. He contended against Stoics and their pretenses. He could have flattered Domitian even in moderation. But he did something more. He did stand out in his adulation of Domitian; and not all because he was compelled to do so because he was a starving and shivering poet (Epigram 10.74).

He turns cruel about a doctor (Epigram 10.77): He wished he would die from the disease about which he was deemed an expert and a specialist. He seems to think this is only fair. That Martial could engage in such verbal cruelty ostensibly for a laugh in a book of epigrams at a historical time characterized by political violence should be considered troubling, but not surprising given what he had written in the past.

Elsewhere in Book 10.98 he has references to voluptuous male servants and the pretentious morals of some philosophers. He complains about a plagiarist who combines his verses with Martial's in Epigram 10.100, and quickly indicts one Avitus for writing nothing and still claiming the mantle of a poet (10.103). The acerbic tone of these epigrams leading up to the historically framed Epigram 10.103 in which he discusses his wish to return to his native Bilbilis suggests a deep regret about the entire prospect of leaving Rome. There is a hint of anger in the preceding epigrams, which may be indication that he did not want to return to Spain and would have preferred not to go if he did not have to. And so Epigram 10.103, written to his famous townsman in Bilbilis, Salo: "30th season and 4 harvests: if you greet me with kindness, as it were, all will be well. I come to you; if churlish, I can go back. I am your glory and repute; and your fame; I am like Catullus was to Verona; I am not less."[64]

Some commentators suggest that this reference is about the jealousy he felt from his countrymen, but this seems to impose a reading that has almost no historical merit. This is all self-presentation. Martial demands to be respected and celebrated as Catullus. But why does Martial demand to be respected as a new Catullus? Is he not already celebrated in Rome? His protestation could be read as a sign that he was no longer nearly as beloved in Rome as he had been. Who needs the praises of Bilbilis when Rome adores you? Martial's longing for his native Salo has all the attributes of a sentiment contrived to give the impression of normalcy.

Epigram 10.96: To Avitus, who must wonder that although Martial has grown old in Latius he speaks of faraway lands; his native Salo. He has a longing for his native Salo where he could dwell in his cottage surrounded by fields. This is rather awkward, and especially in Book 10, in its second version. The nostalgia seems feigned. He speaks about money, how much it costs to live in Rome. It does not cost that much to live in Bilbilis, he says. Fine. So why did he not go back sooner? Why did he continue to pine after patrons and to seek a livelihood in Rome? At the end, what exactly is he commending to Avitus? That he should leave Rome for less expensive places? Not spend his life seeking patrons when there is a place that offers him what every protector refuses him? If this is advice he is giving someone else, this is advice he should have heeded. Is he speaking to himself in this guise? It is all so belated. In a coda, he speaks of his book going further to Spain, to Bilbilis, to Salo:

> Go, my little book, go; accompany my Flaccus across the wide, but propitious, waters of the deep, and with unobstructed course, and favoring winds, reach the towers of Hispania Tarragona. Thence a chariot will take you, and, carried swiftly along, you will see the lofty Bilbilis, and your dear Salo, after the fifth change of carriages. Do you ask what are my commissions for you? That, the moment you arrive, you offer my respects to a few but old friends, whom I have not seen for thirty-four years, and that you then request my friend Flaccus to procure me a retreat, pleasant and commodious, at a moderate price; a retreat in which your author may enjoy his ease. That is all; now the master of

the vessel is bawling loudly, and chiding your delay, and a fair wind favors the way out of the harbor. Farewell, my book. A single passenger, as I suppose you know, must not keep a vessel waiting.[65]

In its current form Book 10 announces that he is leaving for Spain. If he regrets having stayed in Rome so long and wishes that he had taken the advice he gave Avitus, then he should have been less pretentious about it. As far as we know, he did not visit his native Bilbilis at any time during his stay in Rome. For any number of reasons, he could not. Now that he announces his departure, he does not mention here that he is suffering hard times and cannot afford to pay his way back. We learn that from Pliny the Younger. It is also in this very Book 10 that he mentioned Pliny (Epigram 10.9). The epigram makes plain that Book 10 was sent to Pliny. It has all the appearance of an appeal, not a great remonstrance, rather an attempt to seek favor, or a pardon, of some sort. Pliny would have known all along how close Martial was to Regulus with whom Pliny had had a long rivalry in the Senate and in the courts. He also would have known how much Martial had plied his trade in praise of Domitian and sought his favors. Pliny knew as surely as he knew anything about the palatine staff that Parthenius, the court chamberlain, to whom Martial often sent his books to pass them on to Domitian, was a good friend of Martial's. Pliny also would most likely have known all that was known about Parthenius's complicity in the plot to assassinate Domitian.

To court Pliny at this time was deliberate and tactical. Once Domitian was dead, and his memory damned, Martial needed and wished for some kind of mercy, pardon, forgiveness, or clemency from his contemporaries in Rome.[66] It appears they were not willing to give it, at least not in the form he wished. The best they could do was to afford him an elected, if forced exile, back to Bilbilis in Spain. It was still an act of clemency.

Martial had not mentioned Pliny in any of his books prior to this, and he would not be mentioned again. It was a singular event that stands apart from his references to a number of luminaries, friends, and patrons, among them Regulus, Sillius Italicus, even Nerva, before he became emperor.

Sullivan refers to Pliny as an old patron.[67] This seems to go beyond the evidence. Actually he was not; he was one of the new patrons Martial tried to acquire. He was not mentioned in any previous book as a patron when Martial was mentioning others left and right.[68] If the compliments of Nerva and Trajan got him nothing, it was because his supposed change or his revisionist view of his activities was not acceptable to his contemporaries. They did not accept the view that Sullivan puts forth that what Martial did was what every poet was supposed to do. Statius definitely did so, and perhaps that is why it looks as if every poet did it. Sullivan repeats the notion that Pliny, himself a writer of a *Panegyricus* on Trajan, did not criticize Martial's sincere adulation of Domitian.[69] Sullivan still asks what difference exists between Pliny's

Panegyricus for Trajan and Martial's praise of Domitian.[70] Sullivan wants equivalence, and yet there is a world of difference. It is easier to do what Pliny does if Trajan has not been executing his fellow senators. That is not a small difference. The likes of Pliny and Tacitus did not write much during the difficult years of Domitian. Martial wrote, and he had to write. He did not have another way to make a living, to put it crassly. The question is whether he had to write in precisely those terms in which he chose to write about Domitian. If, as Sullivan supposes, his praise of Domitian was sincere, why did Martial retract it and pour scorn on it? If, as Sullivan also says, it was expected,[71] then why did it have to be sincere? Sullivan seems too determined to find any and every way for Pliny to support Martial's complicities. He completely overlooks the point I made earlier that Pliny deliberately does not discuss Martial's character, though he discusses Artemidorus's.

The impression Sullivan and others create is false. Pliny was not a patron of Martial for most of Martial's career in Rome. To repeat: Martial had not mentioned him once in any of his books prior to Book 10. It is conceivable that he may not have mentioned him in the first edition of Book 10. The current Book 10 that was sent to Pliny (10.19) was a calculated risk in some ways on Martial's part. Pliny could easily have reacted to it as a belated attempt to seek his help and patronage. But he did not. For knowing all that he knew of Martial's associations and his profligacy in writing obsequious poetry for Domitian, Pliny was rather cordial and receptive. Martial knew what he was doing. He played on one of Pliny's well-known traits, nothing peculiar to him; a trait nonetheless that he shared with his fellow Romans: his love of praise. Pliny never shied from mentioning this. He sometimes even demanded it. Martial adroitly appealed to Pliny's vanity. For precisely this offering of praise, Pliny was willing to forgive all of Martial's indiscretions during the reign of Domitian. It is highly doubtful if Pliny the Younger would have been so magnanimous toward Martial if Martial had not immortalized Pliny in Book 10. Pliny all but acknowledged this fact. It is also likely that Martial knew of the cordial relationship that already existed between Pliny the Younger and the new emperor Trajan. Martial may very well have sought Pliny's help to ease his own fears of what might befall him under Trajan. It worked, but only to a point that Pliny helped Martial make his return to Spain. The manner of Martial's departure, his rather unceremonious retreat from Rome, suggests that there was pressure put upon him to do just that, and very likely that the conduit through which that pressure came was Pliny, who also provided the money to make the retreat possible.

The very human Pliny the Younger and his peers had not abandoned all of life in spite of the difficulties they claimed to have endured under Domitian. Pliny, along with a few of his friends like Tacitus, managed to climb the ladder of preferment in the Roman system. In time we will see how they explained those years once Domitian was gone. For now, it remains to show that what emerges in the single letter about Martial that survives in Pliny's corpus and the sole epigram that Martial dedicated to Pliny the Younger in all his writings reveal a far more complicated reality than appears at first sight. Much of that complication has a lot to do with the "fear of the times," as Pliny puts it in one of his letters. It is this fear of the times too that Josephus never even hints at.

MARTIAL, PLINY, AND THE SURREAL IN LATE-FIRST-CENTURY ROME

The relationship between Pliny the Younger and Martial is somewhat feigned. It seems almost artificial. It attests in no small way to the fearful nature of the times in which they lived. It is clear from Book 12 that Priscus was Martial's true patron, as he puts it in 12.1, 2, 4. Priscus is his Maecenas. It is intriguing, in this respect, that we do not have a letter from Martial in Spain to Pliny the Younger. If there was one, it is not extant. But I am sure that if there was such a letter Pliny, would have preserved it. But we have at least one epigram by Martial from Spain directed at Priscus. So with Priscus Martial did not need a patron after all, in spite of his posturing.

As I wrote previously, the satirist writing in the first person always risks self-parody in the best of circumstances. At various times Martial also uses the epistolary or pseudo-epistolary form to comment on his epigrams and to address his readers, hearers, critics, and sympathizers, as well as some of the intended recipients of his books. In doing so, Martial always implied that he had not dropped his satirical gaze. He could get away with it. Now, still playing the part of a satirist, almost unwilling to drop his gaze or unable to, the thin line he treaded before with his epistolary interjections in his epigrams is completely erased.

His letter to Priscus (preface to Book 12) is revealing for this reason. It is not Martial the satirist but Martial and his epistolary self that cannot be mispresented or hidden behind any contrivances. In a sense, this was the only mode of writing left to him to communicate with his friends, patrons, and readers in Rome. He seemed to struggle to come to terms with it, as he continued to write epigrams for a readership that was no longer receptive, it would seem. Martial the letter writer is unable to achieve his intended effects. There is only one persona available to him: his very self. Behind that there was no hiding his true self. Martial in his current predicament would have appeared even more intolerable to his Roman readers who had tired of his posturing. He seemed to be making a mockery of himself, apparently without realizing it. He still seemed to think that he was master of his art.

One question remains, though, in connection to his return to Bilbilis and Pliny's role in providing funds for that undertaking—actually, a series of questions. If Priscus was his patron and had always been, even when he had the likes of Piso and the Senecas as potential patrons, as he claimed in writing back from Bilbilis, why did he need Pliny's help? Had Martial concealed that fact from Priscus? Or did Priscus know that Pliny had provided that help? If he did, how would or should he have read Martial's adulation? Or was this all about the past, which had nothing to do with the most immediate circumstances that had led to his return to Spain? But even so, why praise Priscus at this time, when in fact the one who had made the return possible was Pliny?

Epigram 11.5 is to Nerva. It assumes he is alive; Martial speaks of the tenth and eleventh books. However, 12.6 is a eulogy to Nerva, but it also reads as if Nerva still lives: may you have this ruler, and may he live for evermore. "For even under a severe prince and in bad times you had the courage to be good."[72] This is partly to acknowledge that others were not so commendable.

Epigram 12.8 praises Trajan; and 12.9 also praises him indirectly by praising one of his appointees, a governor to Spain. Epigram 12.11 turns to Parthenius, as the Muses entreat him to show Martial's poems to the emperor. This time it is Trajan and not Domitian. Yet shortly, Parthenius, this friend of Martial's and the Muses, will be executed by Trajan for the part he played in the assassination of Domitian. Parthenius is to recommend the book to Trajan by telling him that this is what Rome reads.

Wasn't Parthenius already dead by the time Martial went to Spain? If he is issuing this book, this little book from Spain, then there is something odd with representing Parthenius in the service of Trajan.

Sullivan puts Martial's return to Spain in 99 CE. Parthenius was killed in late 97. Nerva died in January 98. If that is the case, Book 12, which was written from Spain must be after 99 CE. Sullivan puts Book 12 (first edition) at 101; and (second edition) at 104. So Martial had the opportunity to see how things were developing under Trajan.

The oddities about Book 12 demand some kind of explanation. First, it was sent to Priscus from Spain. Then it has a valedictory for Nerva, written as if Nerva is still alive and commends the Romans for having such a prince, while wishing that he would have more years, and the Romans will have more rulers like him. The poet laments the times of Domitian. Second, it then has praise poems for Trajan. These also assume that Trajan is now Caesar, and the epigrams speak of Trajan's justice and equity for which the Romans are most grateful. Third, there is an epigram to Parthenius too. This is strange. For if he was put to death before Martial returned to Spain, he should not be writing an epigram for him. From these three examples it is clear that something peculiar obtains in Book 12.

One explanation, suggested by Sullivan and supported by others, is that someone else put the book together after Martial's death, and so the book contains a number of leftovers. But if that is the case, how does one explain the first epigram to Priscus? That epigram is a historical piece and appears to be sent for the purpose of informing Priscus of Martial's current condition. If it was sent after his death, it is meaningless and useless. A way out of this is to say that there was a previous Book 12 that Martial himself put together that included the first poem to Priscus, and that another person compiled a second edition of Book 12 and included some of the dated material, which is why it has poems to Parthenius and to Nerva, even though both of them had died by the time Martial returned to Spain.

A question remains, however. Even if the dated material was added to a second edition of Book 12 after Martial's death, the dated material still provides a portrait of Martial that is full of contradictions and pretenses. Significantly, these poems show him engaged in the task of rehabilitation. In fact, the poem to Priscus, which opens Book 12, continues the project of re-representing Martial to his Roman audience. Much of what obtains in Book 12 fits that description. That project had not persuaded anyone when he previously tried it in Book 11 and the second version of Book 10; which is why he continued to try to improve on it.

Ker was at a loss to explain why Martial had to leave and offers two or three possibilities: That he realized that the new regime under Nerva or Trajan was not conducive to "adulation of emperors." Or that he wearied of city life, or that he longed for his native country, or some combination of the two and so returned to Spain (x–xi). That he did so after thirty-five years seems odd on so many grounds, especially as Ker also acknowledges that after three years in Spain, he complained bitterly about how much he missed Rome, and yet did not even hint that he could return to Rome. Martial's protestations suggest that if he could have he would have returned to Rome.

MARTIAL TO HIS FRIEND PRISCUS.
I know that I owe some apology for my obstinate three years' indolence; though, indeed, it could by no apology have been excused, even amid the engagements or the city, engagements in which we more easily succeed in making ourselves appear troublesome than serviceable to our friends, and much less is it defensible in this country solitude, where, unless a person studies even to excess, his retreat is at once without consolation and without excuse. Listen then to my reasons; among which the first and principal is this, that I miss the audience to which I had grown accustomed at Rome, and seem like an advocate pleading in a strange court; for if there be anything pleasing in my books it is due to my auditors. That penetration of judgment, that fertility of invention, the libraries, the theatres, the social meetings, in which pleasure does not perceive that it is studying; everything, in a word, which we left behind us in satiety, we regret as though utterly deserted. Add to this the backbiting of the provincials, envy usurping the place of criticism, and one or two ill-disposed persons, who, in a small society, are a host; circumstances under which it is difficult to be always in the best of humours. Do not wonder

> then that I have abandoned in disgust occupations in which I used to employ myself with delight. Not to meet you, however, with a refusal on your arrival from town, and when you ask me for what I have done (you, towards whom I should not show a proper feeling of gratitude, if I did not exert myself for you to the utmost of my power), I have forced myself to do that which I was once in the habit of doing with pleasure, and have set apart a few days for study, in order to regale your friendly ears with the repast suited to them after their journey. Be pleased to weigh considerately the offering, which is entrusted without apprehension to you, and do not think it too much labour to examine it; and, what you may find most difficult, judge of my trifles without scrupulous regard to elegance, lest, if you are too exacting, I send you to Rome a book not merely written in Spain, but in Spanish.[73]

Why then did he leave? I have already provided an explanation. However, we may do better, still, if we consider the other parts of Ker's *apologia* for Martial.

> During his thirty-five years' sojourn he led the ordinary life of the needy client dependent on rich patrons, and he never ceases to complain of the weariness of levees to be attended, complimentary duties to be discharged at unreasonable hours and in all weathers and of the insolence and stinginess of wealthy men. Yet he was not without compensations. Domitian rejected his petition for a sum of money, but he received from Titus the *jus trium liberorum*, a right confirmed by Domitian, and the *tribunatus semestrix*, a kind of honorary tribuneship carrying with it the title of a knight. Moreover, he mixed in the best society in the capital, numbering among his friends Quintilian, the poets Silius and Valerius Flaccus, the younger Pliny, and Juvenal. That Martial was capable of a very sincere and lasting friendship is shown by many of his epigrams. It is curious that he never mentions Statius, nor is he mentioned by him.[74]

This does not read like the vita of a man who would have left Rome if he did not have to. No one so well connected would have left Rome without reason. He claims in the letter to Priscus that he was satiated. It is a very thin argument for this departure. It does not account for the reality. He does not even mention old age as an excuse or pretext. So in spite of appearances, Martial himself does not provide a credible reason for his departure, nor, does Pliny the Younger, who gave him the money to make his return journey to Spain. If he was that desperate and needed Pliny's help to return, then the notion that he was simply satiated is deliberately misleading. Besides, who are the "we" who were satiated and so had to leave Rome? Even Juvenal's Umbricius of his third Satire gave detailed reasons why he was leaving Rome; in comparison Martial provides next to nothing.

A TIME TO WRITE: TACITUS'S *AGRICOLA* AND PLINY'S *PANEGYRICUS*

For what it is worth, there are various passages from Tacitus's *Agricola* that should give us some idea about all those who might have left Rome of their own accord and those who did leave because they had to or were compelled to. While there is no doubt that Tacitus wishes to praise his father-in-law, his testimony cannot be discounted as mere filial piety or partisanship. Tacitus describes Agricola's difficulties and how he overcame them, or rather, how he mollified Domitian.

> Not once only during those days was he accused to Domitian behind his back, and behind his back acquitted. There was no indictment to account for his danger, no complaint from any victim of wrongdoing: merely an Emperor unfriendly to high qualities: merely the glory of the man, and those worst of enemies, the people who praise you. There followed in fact national vicissitudes, such as did not permit Agricola to be ignored: numerous armies in Moesia, Dacia, Germany, and Pannonia lost by the rashness or supineness of their generals; numerous officers with numerous battalions stormed and captured. Anxiety hinged already not on the river's bank which was the Empire's frontier, but on the possession of the legions' winter quarters. Accordingly, when loss was added to loss, and every year was signalised with death and disaster, the voice of the people began to ask for Agricola's generalship: every one compared his firmness, energy, and experience with the lethargy and panic of the rest. All of which gossip, it is certain, beat upon the ears of Domitian no less than of other men, the best of his freedmen seeking from love and loyalty, the worst from malice and jealousy, to stir the emotions of a master who leaned ever to the worst side. Thus was Agricola pushed headlong even up the steep hill of glory both by his own qualities and by the defects of others.
> The year was now at hand for him to draw lots between the governorship of Africa and Asia; but Civica had just been executed, and Agricola's discretion was as ready as the Emperor's precedents. He was approached by certain confidants of the Imperial mind, who were to ask of their own motion whether he would take a province. (Their first step showed some finesse.) They extolled peace and quiet: a little while and they were offering their own services to second- his excuse: finally, forgoing further mystery, they dragged him to Domitian with mingled advice and warning. The Emperor with ready hypocrisy assumed a pompous air, listened to the petition "to be excused," granted it, and permitted himself to be thanked therefore: the sinister favour brought him no blushes. As for the salary, however, usually offered to a proconsul of consular rank, and in some cases conceded by the Emperor's personal intervention, he did not give it to Agricola: either he was offended that it was not asked for, or he was selfconscious, and did not wish it to appear that he had purchased the decision, which was really due to his own prohibition.
> It is a principle of human nature to hate those whom you have injured: nevertheless Domitian, though by nature of a violent temper and unrelenting in proportion to his secretiveness, was pacified by the moderation and discretion

of Agricola, in whom was no insurgency, no fatuous parade of independence, to invite tattle and tragedy. Let those whose way it is to admire only things forbidden learn from him that great men can live even under bad rulers; and that submission and moderation, if animation and energy go with them, reach the same pinnacle of fame, whither more often men have climbed, with no profit to the state, by the steep path of a pretentious death.[75]

Tacitus tells the story of his father-in-law Agricola to praise the life of a good man who was able to live under a bad ruler. Agricola was not an obscure character. So this was a showpiece of political discourse and moral argument. Tacitus also mentioned toward the end that it was in many ways Agricola's good fortune to have lived and died before the worst of Domitian's atrocities. This puts into question whether Tacitus's argument was not somewhat flawed. After all, if he did not live to see the worst of Domitian, then it was fate that made it seem as if a good man could live under a bad ruler. Who was to say if Agricola would have survived Domitian's worst crimes?

What is more, Tacitus also mentions a rumor to the effect that the illness that eventually led to Agricola's death may have been precipitated by poisoning by none other than the agents of the emperor. In a curious assertion Tacitus states that he is not able to confirm or deny such a report. However, he does mention that the traffic between the imperial household and Agricola's bedside and the sorts of characters who visited him, apparently on Domitian's behalf, gave the impression that they were there to spy or to gather information about the condition of the patient; and that they had great interest in the details of his case.

Earlier Tacitus claimed that Agricola had not been the subject of any previous attempts to defame him before Domitian. But if Domitian and his agents had a hand in Agricola's death, then, in the end Agricola did suffer a fate meted out by the bad ruler, Domitian, and this, in spite of his good character. Agricola's good character may not have saved him from potential poisoning; but fate or fortune did save him, according to Tacitus. What about those like Tacitus and Pliny the Younger who were coming into their own during the fifteen-year reign of Domitian? How did they manage to survive, when a man of Agricola's good character and military accomplishment had to be deemed happy for having died prematurely, as Tacitus put it? Not with good character, but rather something else. It probably involved some combination of luck, fortune, and a shrewd sense of how to manage the competing interests and dangerous factions during those times. Many of them, by their very wish to survive, became complicit in the atrocities of the times, as Tacitus explained: we were guilty.

> For though it would have suited him to survive to the light of this happy age, and to see Trajan ruling—a consummation which he prognosticated in our hearing alike in prayer and prophecy—yet he reaped a great compensation for

his premature death, in escaping those last days wherein Domitian no longer fitfully and with breathing spaces, but with one continuous and, so to speak, single blow, poured forth the life-blood of the state. It was not his fate to see the Senate-house besieged, the Senate surrounded by armed men, and in the same reign of terror so many consulars butchered, the flight and exile of so many honourable women. Metius Carus was still rated at one victory only; Messalinus' rasping voice was confined to the Alban council-chamber; and Baebius Massa was at that time in prison. A little while and our hands it was which dragged Helvidius to his dungeon; we it was who put asunder Mauricus and Rusticus; Senecio bathed us in his unoffending blood. Nero after all withdrew his eyes, nor contemplated the crimes he authorised. Under Domitian it was no small part of our sufferings that we saw him and were seen of him that our sighs were counted in his books; that not a pale cheek of all that company escaped those brutal eyes, that crimson face which flushed continually lest shame should unawares surprise it. Happy your fate, Agricola! happy not only in the lustre of your life, but in a timely death.[76]

Then Tacitus turns to relay the settled opinion of his contemporaries: "As they tell the tale who heard your latest utterance, you met your doom steadily and cheerfully; as though, so far as in you lay, to offer to your Emperor the balm of innocence."[77] The Emperor Domitian was not innocent: so Tacitus charges.

Pliny tells the story of his friends who were executed and banished in 93 CE. He picks up where Tacitus leaves off. Recalling these times, when at some risk to himself he visited Artemidorus the son-in-law of Musonius Rufus, the famed Stoic philosopher, Pliny the Younger wrote in Letter 3.11 that seven of his friends had either been executed or banished: Senecio, Rusticus, and Helvidius were executed; and Mauricus, Gratilla, Arria, and Fannia suffered exile. "Scorched as I was with all these bolts of lightning hurled around me, certain sure signs made me prophesy that the same fate overhung me."[78] In the event, Pliny was relieved his prophecy did not come true. All the executions took place in 93 CE (Suetonius, *Domitian* 10.3ff.; Tacitus, *Agricola* 2).

If these events did not instill fear in Pliny and other senators who may not have counted the three aforementioned who were executed as friends, another event most certainly sent shivers down the spines of most Romans. It seemed an unheard-of cruelty. Here is how Pliny relates it by way of another one of his peers who also suffered exile (Letter 4.11):

To Cornelius Minicianus:
Have you heard that Valerius Licinianus is teaching rhetoric in Sicily? I do not think you can have done, for the news is quite fresh. He is of praetorian rank, and he used at one time to be considered one of our most eloquent pleaders at the bar, but now he has fallen so low that he is an exile instead of being a senator, and a mere teacher of rhetoric instead of being a prominent advocate. Consequently in his opening remarks he exclaimed, sorrowfully and solemnly:

"O Fortune, what sport you make to amuse yourself! For you turn senators into professors, and professors into senators." There is so much gall and bitterness in that expression that it seems to me that he became a professor merely to have the opportunity of uttering it. Again, when he entered the hall wearing a Greek pallium—for those who have been banished with the fire-and-water formula are not allowed to wear the toga—he first pulled himself together and then, glancing at his dress, he said, "I shall speak my declamations in Latin." *You will say that this is all very sad and pitiful, but that a man who defiled his profession of letters by the guilt of incest deserves to suffer. It is true that he confessed his guilt, but it is an open question whether he did so because he was guilty or because he feared an even heavier punishment if he denied it.* For Domitian was in a great rage and was boiling over with fury because his witnesses had left him in the lurch. His mind was set upon burying alive Cornelia, the chief of the Vestal Virgins, as he thought to make his age memorable by such an example of severity, and, using his authority as Chief Pontiff, or rather exercising the cruelty of a tyrant and the wanton caprice of a ruler, he summoned the rest of the pontiffs not to the Palace but to his Villa at Alba. *There, with a wickedness just as monstrous as the crime which he pretended to be punishing, he declared her guilty of incest, without summoning her before him and giving her a hearing, though he himself had not only committed incest with his brother's daughter but had even caused her death, for she died of abortion during her widowhood.* He immediately despatched some of the pontiffs to see that his victim was buried alive and put to death. Cornelia invoked in turns the aid of Vesta and of the rest of the deities, and amid her many cries this was repeated most frequently: "How can Caesar think me guilty of incest, when he has conquered and triumphed after my hands have performed the sacred rites?"

Pliny continued:

It is not known whether her purpose was to soften Caesar's heart or to deride him, whether she spoke the words to show her confidence in herself or her contempt of the Emperor. Yet she continued to utter them until she was led to the place of execution, and whether she was innocent or not, she certainly appeared to be so. Nay, even when she was being let down into the dreadful pit and her dress caught as she was being lowered, she turned and readjusted it, and when the executioner offered her his hand she declined it and drew back, as though she put away from her with horror the idea of having her chaste and pure body defiled by his loathsome touch. Thus she preserved her sanctity to the last and displayed all the tokens of a chaste woman, like Hecuba, "taking care that she might fall in seemly wise." Moreover, when Celer, the Roman knight who was accused of having intrigued with Cornelia, was being scourged with rods in the Forum, he did nothing but cry out, "What have I done? I have done nothing." Consequently Domitian's evil reputation for cruelty and injustice blazed up on all hands. He fastened upon Licinianus for hiding a freedwoman of Cornelia on one of his farms. *Licinianus was advised by his friends who interested themselves on his behalf to take refuge in making a confession and beg for pardon, if he wished to escape being flogged in the*

Forum, and he did so. Herennius Senecio spoke for him in his absence very much in the words of Homer, "Patroclus is fallen," for he said, "Instead of being an advocate, I am the bearer of news: Licinianus has removed himself." This so pleased Domitian that he allowed his gratification to betray him into exclaiming, "Licinianus has cleared us." *He even went on to say that it would not do to press a man who admitted his fault too hard, and gave him permission to get together what he could of his belongings before his goods were confiscated, and granted him a pleasant place of exile as a reward for his consideration.* Subsequently, by the clemency of the Emperor Nerva, he was removed to Sicily, where he now is a Professor of Rhetoric and takes his revenge upon Fortune in his prefatory remarks.[79]

Pliny had offered the sequence of events, as if writing contemporary history for his friend, for as he put it, common gossip merely recounted the fact that Licinianus had been "relegated for sexual depravity," but not the order of events; and certainly not the details as Pliny provides them here. Licinianus's confession was to admit to sexual immorality with the freedwoman of Cornelia, and in doing so to seek the emperor's clemency, whether or not he was actually guilty as charged. I have quoted most of the letter because a mere summary cannot do justice to the sense of dread that Pliny and his contemporaries must have experienced under Domitian as these events unfolded among them.

While Pliny's commentary leaves no room for any other interpretation of Domitian than as a maniacal tyrant, the facts of the matter do not elicit a sympathetic reading under any circumstances. There was not much Pliny could have done to exaggerate about those ordered to be buried alive for what appeared to some if not most as trumped-up charges. Even if the particular punishment meted out to the Vestal Virgins was not one that Domitian invented, it was still not so commonly pronounced and effected as to be not shocking. Plutarch seemed to have been puzzled and shocked by it as to include it in his *Roman Questions* (#96): why Vestal Virgins who are deemed to have violated their vows of purity are buried alive. He gives a couple of explanations as to why, and in the process suggests that what is said to have happened during Domitian's reign was not a form of punishment that Domitian devised. It was a long-standing view that he merely enacted. What appears to have troubled those who knew of this ancient custom was probably that it was visited upon the said accomplices of the condemned Vestals in question.

Pliny's friend Herennius Senecio was unfortunately put in the position of having to defend his fellow senator Licinianus, and may well have unwittingly brought himself the kind of unwelcome publicity or notoriety that attracted Domitian's suspicions. Pliny says that Domitian was impressed by Senecio's defense of Licinianus. Ironically, it was the same "impressed" Domitian who will eventually order Senecio's execution a couple of years hence (93/94).

Did any of this matter to Josephus? Apparently not. One would not be able to guess that Pliny, Tacitus, and friends shared with Josephus this terrifying world in Rome ruled over by Domitian. About all this, Josephus says nothing. Finishing his *Antiquities* in 93/94, the year when these massacres took place, Josephus only speaks of the privileges he continued to receive from Domitian. Yet, he could not have been ignorant about any of this, for whatever happened to senators were certainly matters of public record. Whatever befell the Vestal Virgins was public knowledge in Rome. It would have taken a great feat of resolute indifference for Josephus to miss any of this.

While Martial mocked the "circumcised poet," and turned to obscene phallic imagery to ridicule Jews for having to pay a tribute to Rome for burning down Jerusalem, Josephus boasted that Domitian exempted him from paying taxes on his properties in Judaea (some of which had been given to him by Poppaea Sabina, Nero's wife; the rest of which he acquired after the service he provided to the Romans after his surrender to them in Galilee. Vespasian in fact had given him some of the property). The level of Josephus's insensitivity here is astonishing, and in many ways appalling. Elsewhere in the *Life* he speaks about others being jealous of him because of his special circumstances, privileges, and current station in life. Josephus does not necessarily engender sympathy or kindness by seeming to rub the noses of his fellow Jews in the dirt. They suffer the humiliations and degradations associated with paying the *fiscus Judaicus* while Josephus brags about being tax-exempt in Judaea as he heralds the benefactions he continued to receive from Emperor Domitian and his wife Domitia.

Although he remained silent about Domitian's atrocities and the executions and banishment of senators, he did not fail to mention that he himself had been under suspicion for quite some time. He mentions that during the reign of Titus he was often the subject of accusations, but Titus never put much store in them. It would be interesting to know who Josephus's accusers were, the specific nature of the accusations they often brought against Josephus, and whether they had to do with his past dealings in Judaea or his current circumstances in Rome or both. That he mentions that during the time of Domitian he had accusations made against him by people in Judaea suggests that his past was still something to reckon with. In fact, the motivation behind writing the autobiography had everything to do with that past. So the *Life* served in part to answer his accusers about his conduct during the Jewish War and in particular the circumstances of his command in Galilee.

He also mentions that during the time of Domitian a eunuch, a slave who was also tutor to this son, made accusations against him. Josephus writes that Domitian had the slave punished (*kolasthenai*). The connotation here may be closer to exacting some form of vengeance, if that makes any sense (the Loeb translation has "disciplined"). Exactly what the charges were is unclear, nor the nature of the said punishment meted out to the slave. Josephus, however, uses the same language in speaking about his accusers in Judaea who were punished (*ekolasen*) by Domitian. Is the word, "punished," here Josephus's euphemism for torture, imprisonment, or execution? He seems in any case to have accepted that Domitian acted justly on his behalf, the same way that his brother Titus and his father Vespasian before him had done in dealing with his accusers.

A slave who betrayed his master could face a capital charge. Pliny mentions in a few of his letters the general state of anxiety in which people lived in relation to their slaves and what the latter were capable of doing, including murdering their masters.[80] Seneca wrote about how the cruelty meted out to slaves made them all the more likely to commit horrible deeds.

In one instance Pliny described to his friend Acilius the case of Larcius Macedo, a praetorian who was assaulted by some of his slaves at the baths (3.14). It seemed like a well-planned assault. He survived the assault thanks to some of his other "more trusty" slaves, but only long enough to identify his attackers and exact his vengeance upon them before he finally succumbed to the injuries he had sustained in the initial attack. "You realize to what dangers and insults and derision we are exposed. No man can remain untroubled because he is relaxed and gentle, for masters are murdered through wickedness rather than considered judgement" (3.14.5).

Pliny prided himself on treating his slaves well. But he could not assume that the slaves he acquired came well disposed toward him. As Pliny acknowledged or lamented to his friend Plinius Paternus, "All joking apart, I think that the slaves that I bought on your recommendation are suitable. Their honesty is still in question, for so far as slaves go, our judgement rests on hearsay rather than our eyes" (1.21). In one letter he recounted not one but two harrowing tales about people he knew who were most likely murdered by their slaves and had not been heard from (6.25). In the most recent case, the son of the missing man (the disappeared) was still looking for his father.

> To his friend Hispanus:
> You write that Robustus, a distinguished Roman knight, journeyed with my friend Atilius Scaurus as far as Ocriculum, but has not been seen anywhere since. You beg me to ask Scaurus to come, and to put us, if he can, on any track in the investigation. He will come, but I fear that it will be of no avail. For my suspicion is that something untoward has befallen Robustus, as happened to my fellow townsman Metilius Crispus some time ago. I had secured the rank of centurion for him, and as he was leaving I also presented him with 40,000 sesterces with which to kit himself out and to smarten himself up. But thereafter I received no letters from him, nor any message that he had died. It is not clear whether he had been ambushed by his slaves or together with them; what is sure is that neither he nor any of his slaves has been seen again, and the slaves of Robustus likewise. However, we must make the attempt, and sum-

mon Scaurus. We must make the gesture in response to the praiseworthy pleas of both yourself and that most honourable young man who with impressive devotion and also impressive intelligence is searching for his father. May the gods favour him in finding his father, as he has already found the identity of his travelling-companion! Farewell.[81]

Pliny also knew well enough not to take the good behavior of his slaves for granted. He treated them well.

A slave who was a *paidagogos*, a teacher to Josephus's son, would have been among the most privileged of slaves, closer to a freedman than to other slaves. From a *paidagogos* much was expected, but not betrayal. That the slave brought an accusation against Josephus may also be an indication of his perceived sense of right and immunity before Domitian and of Josephus's vulnerability at the time. That the slave was also a eunuch would have probably incensed Domitian, who had passed a law barring people becoming eunuchs. Martial praised Domitian for this ban in one of his epigrams (2.60).[82] Josephus's language suggests the possibility of the slave being executed by Domitian. Josephus does not express any complaints about the punishment the slave received. He also leaves unstated whether the slave was his own personal slave or one that was provided for him by Domitian, his brother Titus, or their father Vespasian.

Josephus elsewhere mentions how Vespasian handled accusations brought against him by one Jonathan, a weaver, of Cyrene (*Life* 424–425; *Jewish War* 7.437–53). In the end, Vespasian ordered Jonathan to be burned alive, although Catullus the proconsul of Cyrene and Crete who appears to have been at the center of the libel against Josephus, did not suffer much for it either from Vespasian or those who followed him. Josephus mentions him not suffering from "the emperors." Josephus, however, saw in his death divine retribution for his deeds, since he appears to have lost his mind and suffered from a wasting disease. No stranger to cruelty and the horrors of war about which he writes in gruesome detail, Josephus, however, reports the death of Jonathan so routinely as to suggest nothing exceptional in such a cruel and horrific death ordered by Vespasian.

Josephus had promised in the opening paragraphs of his *Jewish War* that he would not spare any of the horrific and gruesome details, nor his own suffering and miseries. Whether this meant that Josephus had become cauterized to violence, cruelty, and the horrors he experienced and reported is an open question. Still, his seeming indifference to the sufferings of some of his contemporaries in Rome under the Flavians, in particular those who met their cruel ends during the time of Domitian, gives the impression that he had little or no sympathy for those victims of his patrons, whether senators, philosophers, or notable writers. He says almost nothing about them. Even Martial, for all his sycophantic praise of Domitian, could manage on rare occasions to intimate that all was not well. I have mentioned previously how his fable of the Lion and the Hare intimated certain undercurrents in Domitian's Rome; and also pointed out how in one epigram he berated an informer.

Pliny the Younger described how it felt to live in a world of informers in his *Panegyricus*. Josephus may not have been alive to hear of Pliny's speech that he delivered in the Roman Senate in September 100 CE. He may not have been alive when Trajan did to the informers of Domitian's era what Pliny describes. "The sight was unforgettable," Pliny begins his account.

> A whole fleet of informers (*deletorum*) thrown on the mercy of every wind, forced to spread sail before the tempests, driven by the fury of the waves on to the rocks in their course. What joy for us to watch the ships scattered as soon as they left harbour, and on the very water's edge to render thanks to our ruler who in his unfailing mercy had preferred to entrust vengeance over men on earth to the gods of the sea! Then indeed we knew how times had changed; the real criminals were nailed to the very rocks which had been the cross of many an innocent man; the islands where senators were exiled were crowded with the informers (*delatorum*) whose power you had broken for all time, not merely for a day, held fast as they were in the meshes of punishments untold. They set out to rob other men of money: now let them lose their own. They sought to evict men from their homes: let them be homeless too. Let them stop presenting a brazen and unblushing front, unmarked by any disgrace, stop laughing off all reproaches. Now they can expect losses in proportion to their rewards and know apprehension to match their former hopes; now they can feel the fear they once inspired.[83]

This crowd of informers and the world they helped to create in the time of Domitian is nowhere to be found in anything that Josephus wrote. Yet, if we are to believe Tacitus, Pliny the Younger, Juvenal, and others, this is the world in which Josephus lived, and among such dastardly characters in the time of Domitian, as Pliny describes in his *Panegyric*. "Now they can feel the fear they once inspired." The sight must have been something to behold indeed: to see the informers who had made life so unbearable for many in Rome being sent off to their doom.

How often Pliny adverts to fear; how often he uses the language of dread, anxiety, and terror in describing the times under Domitian in his *Panegyricus* is a testament to what it must have felt for him and other senators. What should not also be missed is that as much as Pliny assailed the dreadful and calamitous deeds of the informers (*delatores*) he was equally condemning of the Senate for its complicities during Domitian's reign. That he pronounced such judgment on the Senate to whom he was addressing, and that he was speaking on behalf of the same Senate, should make clear that he was far from absolving that august institution of the crimes of the recent past.

> Could any spot remain ignorant of the lamentable spirit of adulation in the country, when tribute to the emperors was paid in the form of shows and riotous entertainment, where dancing and wailing ran through every kind of buffoonery and effeminacy, expressed in rhythmic antics and shrieks? But the scandal was that everything was approved in the Senate as well as on the stage, through consul and actor alike.[84]

What Pliny says next may be a comment on writers like Martial and Statius, and perhaps even Josephus, when he mentions those who, for a moment's publicity, do the things they do.

> You [Trajan] cut out all these stage performances from honours paid to you. Thus serious poetry and the everlasting glory of our historic past pay you tribute in place of a moment's disgraceful publicity; furthermore, the whole theatre-audience will rise to show its respect with all the more unanimity now that the stage is to say less of you. But why confine my admiration to this, when the other honours we offer you are always so sparingly accepted or else refused? Hitherto, anyone called on to speak in the Senate, on any subject however slight and trivial, had to prolong his speech with adulation of the emperor. We debated the increase in number of gladiators or the founding of a workers' union; the boundaries of empire might have been extended as we discussed colossal arches and inscriptions too long for temple architraves, or else the months, when more than one were to take the names of the Caesars. For their part, the emperors suffered this and even enjoyed it, believing it their due. But which of us today spends the proper time for his speech on praising the emperor as if forgetful of the subject of debate? The credit here is due to moderation on your part, not self-restraint on ours; it is in obedience to your wishes that we assemble in the House not to compete in flattery but to practise and render justice, and to pay tribute to your open-hearted sincerity through our confidence that your likes and dislikes are genuinely what you say they are. We start and finish at a point where neither was possible when another was in power; for though there have been others who refused most of the honours offered them, no one was great enough before for us to believe that he did not want them offered. This, I think, is more splendid than any inscription, since your name is engraved not on beams of wood or blocks of stone but in the records of imperishable glory.[85]

This is one more contrast that Pliny draws between the new order under Trajan and what obtained under Domitian. The Senate is not spared its embarrassments. Josephus was not a senator and perhaps not even a friend of senators. But he lived in a world where they dominated affairs in Rome. The axis of power and political life run through the Senate and the imperial court. If you were close to one, you had to have been informed and knowledgeable about the other. Josephus owed his presence and livelihood in Rome to the Flavians. For his own good and for his survival, it was always in his interest to know how the political winds blew in Rome. He would not have been ignorant about the state of things in the Senate.

Pliny offers yet another contrast, this time, on how the new emperor Trajan conducted himself in his role as consul in the senate compared to Domitian. Pliny had a particular interest in this since he had been involved in trials in the senate presided over by Domitian as consul.

> It was in accordance with the best traditions of the consulate that the Senate should continue in a three-day sitting, following your own example of patience, and that during that time you acted solely in your capacity as presiding consul. Each senator when called on for his opinion spoke as he thought fit; he was free to disagree, to vote in opposition, and to give the State the benefit of his views. We were all consulted and even reckoned with, and the sentence which carried the day was the better one, and not merely the first proposed. Contrast the previous reign: who dared then to open his mouth or say a word except the poor wretches called on for the first speech? The rest, too terrified to move, endured the forced necessity of giving assent in silence, without rising from their seats, their mental anguish as painful as their physical fears. A solitary senator expressed a single view for all to follow, though none approved, and least of all the speaker. (People detest nothing so much as measures which pretend to be the general will.) Maybe the Emperor put on an attitude of respect for the Senate in its presence, but once out of the House he was emperor again, throwing off all his consular obligations with careless contempt. But Caesar [Trajan] has conducted himself as if he were only consul, thinking nothing beneath him unless it were beneath a consul too.[86]

Fear, terror, mental anguish, silence, forced necessity—that was how senators behaved. Domitian for his part pretended to consult, treated the Senate with contempt, ruled with absolute power. They dared not open their mouths.

On a personal level, Pliny the Younger also had some explaining to do in terms of how he had survived Domitian's reign and how he could present himself as one of the aggrieved when he seems to have advanced in his career through those years.

> To you, Conscript Fathers, my debt is great, and this is published in the official records. You it was who paid me tribute according to the best traditions, for my orderly conduct as tribune, my moderation as praetor, my integrity and determination in carrying out the requests you made of my professional services for the protection of our allies. More recently, you hailed my designation as future consul with such acclamation that I am well aware that I must redouble my efforts if I am to receive your continued approval, and retain and increase it day by day; I do not forget that the truest judgement on whether a man merits an office or not is passed at the moment of his assuming it. All I ask is your support in my present undertaking and your belief in what I say.[87]

How well he could be trusted depended on how he explained his career to his fellow senators, who knew him so well. It appears they accepted his account as true:

> If then it is true that I advanced in my career under that most treacherous of emperors before he admitted his hatred for honest men, but was halted in it once he did so, preferring a longer route when I saw what the short cuts were which opened the way to office; that in bad times I was one of those who lived with grief and fear, and can be counted among the serene and happy now that better days have come; that, finally, I love the best of princes as much as I was hated by the worst: then I shall act not as if I consider myself consul today and ex-consul tomorrow, but as if I were still a candidate for the consulate, and in this way shall minister at all times to the reverence which is due to you all.[88]

What more could be asked of him, except for his *recusatio*, his counter-argument or retort about his fear and grief under Domitian against anyone who would accuse him of complicity; and of his serenity and happiness under Trajan? To his credit, Pliny speaks often about these fears throughout the *Panegyricus* in a manner that is completely absent from anything written by Josephus. If we take Josephus's writings of the 90s as a guide, we might be tempted to think he lived in an entirely different city other than the one Tacitus, Pliny, Martial, and friends inhabited. While Tacitus, Pliny, and friends write about the world around them and how they managed to cope under Domitian, often alluding to or mentioning their complicities, Josephus appears untroubled by that world. He sometimes writes as if the world Pliny and Tacitus and others like them describe does not even exist.

Josephus's writings inhabit a world indifferent to the one in which he actually lived as a resident of Rome during the years of Domitian's reign. He is at variance with Dio of Prusa and Plutarch, both of whom as outsiders described their experiences of Domitian's terror in Rome and beyond in ways that substantiate the descriptions and recriminations of Pliny, Tacitus, and their friends. Whatever their literary merits, whatever their apologetic intentions, the parts of Josephus's *Antiquities*, *Life*, and *Against Apion* that deal with the last decades of the first century are as silent about the state of anxiety and fear that obtained in Rome in the 80s and 90s as they are about the Jews of Rome. They are also silent, indifferent, or unaware of the Christians of Rome who produced First Clement. Whatever motivated Josephus possible ignorance, palpable silences, and omissions place him in a category all his own.

NOTES

1. Plutarch, *On Being a Busybody* 522 (LCL 337, 513).
2. Dio Chrysostom, *Oration* 13.1–2 (LCL 339, 91).
3. Dio Chrysostom, *Oration* 45.1–2 (LCL 376, 209–11).
4. Dio Chrysostom, *Oration* 13.2–3 (LCL 339, 91–93).
5. Dio Chrysostom, *Oration* 13.9 (LCL 339, 97).
6. Dio Chrysostom, *Oration* 13.11 (LCL 339, 99).
7. Martial, Epigram 11.66 (Bohn translation).

8. Martial, Epigrams Book 1, Preface (Bohn translation).
9. Martial, Epigram 1.1 (Bohn translation).
10. Martial, Epigrams 1.4–5 (Bohn translation).
11. Martial, Epigrams 1.14–15 (Bohn translation).
12. William Fitzgerald, *Martial: The World of the Epigram* (Chicago: University of Chicago Press, 2007), 80–81.
13. Martial, Epigram 1.78 (Bohn translation).
14. Martial, Epigram 1.104 (Bohn translation).
15. Martial, Epigram 1.22 (Bohn translation).
16. Tacitus, *Annals* 15.49 & 70; Suetonius, *Lives of Illustrious Men*, Lucan (LCL 38, 483–85).
17. J. P. Sullivan, *Martial: The Unexpected Classic* (Cambridge: Cambridge University Press, 1991), 35.
18. I am following the dates provided by J. P. Sullivan, *Martial: The Unexpected Classic*, 37.
19. Cf. Ibid., 40.
20. Martial, Epigrams Book 8, Preface (Bohn translation).
21. Martial, Epigrams 5.1–2 (Bohn translation).
22. Martial, Epigram 5.6 (Bohn translation).
23. Sullivan, *Martial: The Unexpected Classic*, 47.
24. Ibid.
25. Ibid.
26. Ibid., 87.
27. Ibid., 48.
28. Martial, Epigrams 11.1–3 (Bohn translation).
29. Victoria Rimell, *Martial's Rome: Empire and the Ideology of Epigram* (Cambridge: Cambridge University Press, 2009), 177.
30. Garrett G. Fagan's *Bathing in Public in the Roman World* (Ann Arbor: University of Michigan Press, 1999), 12–39.
31. Mary Beard, *The Fires of Vesuvius: Pompeii Lost and Found* (London: Profile Books, 2008).
32. See, *Martial: Selected Epigrams*, translated with notes by Susan McLean, with an introduction by Marc Kleijwegt (Madison: University of Wisconsin Press, 2014) for Kleijwegt's argument.
33. Fitzgerald, *Martial: The World of the Epigram*, 148.
34. Cassius Dio, *Roman History* 66.15.1.
35. Tacitus, *Histories* 2.2–4.
36. Cassius Dio, *Roman History* 64.15.3–5.
37. Yaron Z. Eliav, "The Roman Bathhouse as a Jewish Institution: Another Look at the Encounter between Judaism and the Greco-Roman Culture," *Journal for the Study of Judaism* 31/1–4 (2000), 416–54. The reference is to 422.
38. Fagan (*Bathing in Public in the Roman World*, p. 358) gives a figure of eighty-six, though it is uncertain given the nature of the sources used to calculate the figure. I have deliberately taken half of eighty-six and rounded it off.
39. *Pliny the Younger: Complete Letters*. A New Translation by P. G. Walsh (New York: Oxford University Press, 2006 [henceforth, Walsh translation]), 110.
40. Pliny, Letter 1.5.1–7 (Firth translation).
41. See Shadi Bartsch, *Actors in the Audience: Theatricality and Doublespeak from Nero to Hadrian* (Cambridge, MA: Harvard University Press, 1994), 63–64, on the manners of Roman Senators in a world of theatricality and doublespeak. Cf. Carlin A. Barton and Daniel Boyarin, *Imagine No Religion: How Modern Anxieties Hide Ancient Realities* (New York: Fordham University Press, 2106), 178–99, for the studied ambiguity in Josephus's writings, which is not quite the same thing as the caution required by the likes of Tacitus, Pliny the Younger, and their fellow senators who were the subject of intrigue, rumor, and the damning words of informants.
42. Pliny the Younger, Letter 9.13.2–5 (LCL 59, 99–101).

43. Rex Winsbury, *Pliny the Younger: A Life in Roman Letters* (London: Bloomsbury Academic 2014), 7–9.
44. Cf. Winsbury, *Pliny the Younger*, 105.
45. Pliny the Younger, Letter 2.20.12–14 (Firth translation).
46. Pliny the Younger, Letter 4.2.3–8 (Firth translation).
47. Pliny the Younger, Letter 4.7.1–5 (Firth translation).
48. Pliny the Younger, Letter 4.7.6–7 (Firth translation).
49. Pliny the Younger, Letter 6.2.1–3. Pliny Letters (New York: Macmillan, 1905), 441–43.
50. Pliny the Younger, Letter 6.2.4–5. Pliny Letters (New York: Macmillan, 1905), 443–45.
51. Pliny the Younger, Letter 8.14.9–10 (Walsh translation, 199–200).
52. Winsbury, *Pliny the Younger*, 106–17.
53. Pliny the Younger, Letter 7.19.4 (Firth translation).
54. Pliny the Younger, Letter 7.19.4–6 (Firth translation [amended]).
55. Pliny the Younger, Letter 7.19.7 (Firth translation).
56. Pliny the Younger, Letter 3.11.1–2 (Firth translation).
57. Pliny the Younger, Letter 3.11.2–3 (Firth translation).
58. Pliny the Younger, Letter 3.21.1–3 (Firth translation).
59. Pliny the Younger, Letter 3.21.6 (Firth translation).
60. Kleijwegt, in his introduction to *Martial: Selected Epigrams*, xlii.
61. Ibid., xliii.
62. Suetonius, *Life of Domitian* 10.3; Tacitus, *Agricola* 2.
63. Martial, Epigrams 11.48–49 (Bohn translation).
64. Martial, Epigrams 10.103 (Bohn translation).
65. Martial, Epigram 10.104 (Bohn translation; slightly altered).
66. See Susanna Braund's Commentary on Seneca's *De clementia* (Oxford: Oxford University Press, 2009) for the many different ways in which the Romans thought about clemency.
67. Sullivan, *Martial: The Unexpected Classic*, 49.
68. Cf. ibid., 52.
69. Ibid., 75.
70. Ibid., 128.
71. Ibid., 52.
72. Martial, Epigram 12.6 (Bohn translation).
73. Martial, Epigrams, Book 12. Preface (Bohn translation.).
74. Martial, Epigrams (Ker's LCL translation, Volume 1 [1919], x).
75. Tacitus, *Agricola* 41–42 (LCL 35, 103–5).
76. Tacitus, *Agricola* 44–45 (LCL 35, 109–11).
77. Tacitus, *Agricola* 45 (LCL 35, 248–50).
78. Pliny, Letter 3.11.3 (Walsh translation, 71).
79. Pliny the Younger, Letter 4.11.1–14 (Firth translation, [italics mine]).
80. On the fear of slaves, see, for example, Richard Gamauf, "Fear of Slaves and Roman Law," in Anastasin Serghidou, *Fear of Slaves, Fear of Enslavement in Ancient Mediterranean* (Besançon: Presses Univ. Franche-Comte, 2007), 145–64.
81. Pliny, Letter 6.25 (Walsh translation, p. 153).
82. Sullivan, *Martial: The Unexpected Classic*, 145. Cf. 38–39.
83. Pliny the Younger, *Panegyricus* 35.1–3 (LCL 59, 397–99).
84. Pliny the Younger, *Panegyricus* 54.1–2 (LCL 59, 445).
85. Pliny the Younger, *Panegyricus* 54.2–7 (LCL 59, 445–47).
86. Pliny the Younger, *Panegyricus* 76 (LCL 59, 501–3).
87. Pliny the Younger, *Panegyricus* 95.1–3 (LCL 59, 545).
88. Pliny the Younger, *Panegyricus* 95.3–5 (LCL 59, 545–47).

Chapter Five

Paul, the Jewish Past, and the Roman Contexts of First Clement

Tacitus's *Agricola* is an important benchmark, marking the revitalizing of literary culture in the period immediately following the demise of Domitian and the reign of the Emperor Nerva. It bears witness to both the life of his father-in-law Agricola and the times under Domitian.

> For the term of fifteen years, a large space in human life, chance and change have been cutting off many among us; others, and the most energetic, have perished [due to] the Emperor's ferocity; while the few who remain have outlived not merely their neighbours but, so to say, themselves; for out of their prime have been blotted fifteen years, during which mature men reached old age and old men the very bounds almost of decrepitude, and all without opening their lips.[1]

In his preface, Tacitus had summed up the moral laxity of his contemporaries with a pithy, "so harsh is the spirit of our age, so cynical towards virtue."[2] In slightly different tones First Clement 60.3 offers a prayer: "Rescue us from those who hate us without cause." Could First Clement and Tacitus be speaking about the same things?

The bend of the River Tiber as it meandered its way through Rome marked off a region on its right bank from the rest of the city. The southern end of this region was known in antiquity as the *Transtiberim* (the region across or on the other side of the Tiber). The geography and physical layout of the city were such that a lot could take place in the *Transtiberim* that would not be known to those who were not resident there. Much could happen in the Jewish Quarter, located in the *Transtiberim*, that would not be known elsewhere. If the Christians of Rome in the first century were largely domiciled in or near the Jewish Quarter,[3] it would have been possible for such a small community to escape notice and scrutiny, except for the fact that the previous history of the Christians of Rome during the time of Nero was public knowledge. This is what is implied, if we are to believe Tacitus's later account (*Annals* 15.44); Suetonius's comment that the Christians were persecuted by Nero (*Life of Nero* 16.2); Juvenal's reference or allusion to Nero's henchman, his praetorian prefect Tigellinus, making human torches of the condemned (Satire 1.155); and Pliny the Younger's statement in relation to the Christians in Bithynia-Pontus that he had not previously witnessed a trial of Christians presumably in Rome where he had spent most of his career (Letter 10.96).

JEWS AND CHRISTIANS IN FLAVIAN ROME

Even so, one would assume that most of the Christians of Rome did not escape the persecutions mentioned by Suetonius and Tacitus, and in any case, those who did not perish in the aftermath of the Fire of 64 CE would not have remained in the city. However, First Clement provides testimony that by the end of the first century, a little over a generation later, a vibrant community had emerged once again, self-assured enough to be consulted about matters of internal strife among the Christians in faraway Corinth in Achaia.

We must assume that such channels of communication already existed between the Christians of Corinth and the Christians of Rome to create the conditions that made possible the response generated by the church or assembly of God (*ekklēsia tou theou*) in Rome. Furthermore, this connectedness was not merely a historical precedent linked to the apostle Paul that had only recently been revived. Rather, all indications are that the church in Rome and the church in Corinth had always been in communion, a testament to what is clearly indicated at the very end of Paul's Letter to the Romans, that the person who delivered that letter to the Romans was none other than the woman Phoebe, a leader of the church in Cenchrea, the port city near Corinth. If the Christians of Rome were unknown to most residents in the city, they were nevertheless known to their fellow Christians in Corinth. Their main line of communication would also have followed the pattern of shipping traffic between Corinth and Rome.

The *Transtiberim*, as is well known, contained the main terminal in Rome for the shipping that brought people and goods from the port of Ostia at the mouth of the Tiber. So it was also not possible to have what took place in the *Transtiberim* completely sealed off from the rest of Rome, since it served as the main artery of the commercial heart of the city. The rest of Rome could not and would not be unaffected by what was public in the *Transtiberim*. Martial's Epigrams allude to this.

The Christians of Rome, such as were their numbers after the persecutions under Nero, lived in this environment: the public nature of the port and the wharves along the Tiber; the comings and goings in the *Transtiberim*; the memory of the Christian past in the aftermath of the Fire of 64 CE; and the likelihood of a small reconstituted community of Christians in the years after the destruction of Jerusalem. Anything was possible. First Clement provides the answer to what was possible and did in fact materialize.

As we have already seen from the previous two chapters, the excesses of the Emperor Domitian put a damper on literary production, so we are left with what emerged after his death. For this reason, we can only imagine what was lost because few dared to write anything historical or contemporary for fear of recriminations. This is what must condition our reading of the extant sources. But even more fundamentally, most of the writers on whom we are dependent routinely do not comment on so much else that was common knowledge or unquestionable around them. Of Jewish life in Rome and life in the Jewish Quarter in the decades after the War in Judaea there is little to no attestation. It is one important piece of the puzzle. It is as if it is non-existent, if we have only the writers of this period to depend upon. There are traces of their presence in Martial, and in Juvenal, almost nothing in Statius, hardly a word in Pliny the Younger, important notices in Suetonius, and then the ethnographic material in Tacitus. Yet, the Jews of Rome had not gone anywhere. They were still there. Their numbers may well have increased with the addition of captives from the War. Josephus was one of them.

What do we make of these silences? First, we have no evidence that Jews in Rome stopped participating in their synagogues as they had before. Perhaps they did even more of it than before. Philo mentions the existence of many prayer houses (*proseuche* = house of prayer = synagogue) in the *Transtiberim* in his *Legatio ad Gaium*. Those synagogues had not disappeared during Josephus's long residence in the city. You would not know any of this from Josephus, who never mentions in any of his writings a single synagogue or anything associated with a synagogue in Rome in all his time there, even though he writes about synagogues in other places in his works.

Second, Pliny the Younger had interactions with people in the Jewish Quarter at one point in his career in Rome, because as overseer of the Tiber, tasked with dealing with the periodic flooding that needed to be controlled, he could not avoid coming into contact with the residents of that district. Once again, you would not know any of this from Pliny the Younger, who lived in the same environment as the poet Martial and was personally responsible for providing funds for Martial when the latter was leaving Rome to return to his native Bilbilis in Spain. There is hardly a reference to Jews or Jewish life in the letters of Pliny the Younger, one of the most important sources of our knowledge of the period. Yet there had always been a sizable community of Jews living in Rome long before Pliny the Younger and all the way through his lifetime. His uncle Pliny the Elder wrote about Jews and Judaea in his *Natural Histories* and at one point commented about the destruction of Masada, saying that Masada, like Jerusalem, was a heap of ashes (*Natural Histories* 5.73); a clear reference to the Jewish War. Thirdly, even Tacitus, who writes about Jews in his *Histories* 5.2–5, does it in a somewhat detached way as if he did not know any contemporary Jews in Rome. Curiously, although writing in the early second-century (c. 100–110 CE), Tacitus's ethnography of Jews or Judaeans gives no hint that he was acquainted with Josephus's *Antiquities* or *Against Apion*. If he knew either work, then his description of Jewish customs and religious ways had not been affected by Josephus's writings. The garbled and somewhat dismissive and contemptuous nature of Tacitus's ethnography raises the question as to how he could have lived in full view of life in the Jewish Quarter in one of the most well-defined districts of Rome and not have better and more accurate knowledge of Jewish ways than he provides in his write-up. Did the likes of Tacitus and Pliny the Younger and those of their circle care to know what Jewish ways consisted of or did they settle for impressions formed from a distance?

What seems evident is that a number of the writers of the extant sources for the last three decades of the first century tend in general not to tell us a whole lot about the world around them in Rome that they took for granted, especially as it related to Jews or Judaeans. So if Tacitus says nothing about contemporary Jews living in Rome, we should not take this as a sign that there was no such community in Rome. Similarly, if Tacitus writes in one instance about Christians during the time of Nero but says nothing about Christians in the later decades of the first century, it is not proof that he did not know of any Christians in Rome in the time of Domitian. The much later testimony of Cassius Dio's *Roman History* 67.14 about the consul Flavius Clemens and his wife Flavia Domitilla provides something of a cautionary tale about what some of the contemporary sources do not reveal about the influence or presence of Jewish life within the inner circles of the Roman elites. Cassius Dio's account gives the impression that there were many who found themselves entrapped in this way (there is an extensive literature on Flavius Clemens and Flavia Domitilla).

> Domitian slew, along with many others, Flavius Clemens the consul, although he was a cousin and had to wife Flavia Domitilla, who was also a relative of the emperor's. The charge brought against them both was that of atheism (*atheotetos*), a charge on which many others who drifted into Jewish ways (*ton Ioudaion ethe*) were condemned. Some of these were put to death, and the rest were at least deprived of their property. Domitilla was merely banished to Pandateria.[4]

The accusation of atheism brought against them conjoined with the disapproval of those who had drifted into Jewish ways in the particular way in which Cassius Dio juxtaposes them is intriguing. Tacitus, for example, does not describe Jewish monotheism as atheism, though he implies it and is very clear that it opposes all the gods (Tacitus, *Histories* 5.5). At the same time, Dio's words sound suspiciously close to what Tacitus and Pliny the Younger allege with respect to Christians insofar as the Christians were understood to have originated in Judaea. Suetonius (*Domitian* 17) mentions "a slight suspicion" as the basis of the downfall of Flavius Clemens, but he does not name the charge.

Suetonius himself, who names Josephus as the origin of a prophecy concerning Vespasian, says very little specifically about Jewish life in the city of Rome in the last three decades of the first century, though he is otherwise not reticent about Jews elsewhere and in other time periods. His keen sense of the special burden of the *fiscus Judaicus* on Jews and those suspected to be Jews (or had adopted Jewish ways) in the days of Domitian is particularly noteworthy; and so we must presume extensive knowledge of Jews and Jewish life on Suetonius's part. This fits into the pattern of basic silences that Tacitus and Pliny the Younger attest to about Jewish life in Rome and about someone like Josephus, who was resident among them, well known, and yet is completely unattested, in the extant writings of either Tacitus or Pliny. It is conceivable, in the case of Tacitus, that the missing (or nonextant) parts of the *Histories* (after chapter 26 of Book 5) that dealt with the rest of the year 70 CE through the end of the reign of Domitian may have contained details about the Jewish presence in Rome. What he wrote about the days of Domitian in his *Agricola* (98 CE) gives reason to believe he would have said a great deal about those times in the lost parts of the *Histories*. We shall have to keep all this in mind as we approach First Clement and the Christians of Rome at the end of the first century and of Josephus's possible ignorance or deliberate silence about them.

The earlier comment from Tacitus's *Agricola* describes how the fifteen-year reign of Domitian affected the lives of the residents of Rome. Fifteen years is a long time, laments Tacitus, as he describes how mature men grew old beyond their years and old men tottered on destitution in almost abject silence. No one dared to speak; fewer still dared to write.

In the previous chapter I described the state of anxiety, fear, and terror that characterized life in Rome in the era of Domitian, and especially the years immediately preceding his assassination in September 96 CE. I indicated how Tacitus and Pliny in particular described the ways in which they had to conduct themselves and the traps they had to avoid in order to survive those years. From Tacitus's *Agricola* to Pliny's *Panegyricus* we gained a sense of what the death of Domitian meant and must have meant to the citizens of Rome both near and far, including the likes of Dio Chrysostom

(Dio of Prusa) and Plutarch. Tacitus, Suetonius, and Pliny the Younger do not mention the existence of Christians in Rome in the last three decades of the first century. So as Tacitus and Pliny lament the horrid state of affairs in Domitian's Rome, it is easy to assume that none of this had anything to do with Christians, because there were no Christians in Rome. Josephus, who lived in Rome during most of this period, also says nothing about them, and in his own way aids in this sense of their absence or nonexistence. Josephus also says nothing about the reign of Domitian to suggest that the likes of Martial, Statius, Tacitus, Suetonius, and Pliny the Younger lived the kinds of lives they came to write about after the death of Domitian. Josephus's silences about all things Roman during Domitian's reign was nearly total, even though he was a living witness to all of it. In this respect his ignorance or silence about Christians in Rome in the last decades of the first century is not unrelated to all his other silences about his fellow residents of Rome in those years.

Yet, as we shall see, there were Christians in Rome who endured and survived the years of Domitian. After Domitian's death they too found it an occasion to write, and it is from them that we have the work that has come down to us as First Clement. Everything about First Clement engenders questions about Josephus's ignorance or silence about Paul, the Christian Jews of Judaea, and the Christians of Rome against him.

So, in this chapter, I focus on the very Christians of Flavian Rome who produced First Clement. They, like Tacitus and Pliny the Younger, also describe a state of affairs that prevented them from writing for a while to the church of Corinth that had solicited their assistance. From all indications they took to writing First Clement shortly after Domitian's death. It is against the fear and terror described by Martial, Tacitus, Pliny, and friends, but never mentioned by Josephus, that we have to read First Clement, without which we would never have suspected that a vibrant community of Christians endured the years of Domitian to see the day when he was no more. We would be remiss to think that the Christians of Flavian Rome knew nothing of the enforced silence that Tacitus mentions in *Agricola*. There are more than a few hints in First Clement that speak of irrational hatred, imprisonment, and perhaps something more directed at the Christians of Rome. That they survived the fifteen years that Tacitus laments may be some indication of how much they tried not to attract too much attention in the same way that Tacitus, Pliny the Younger, and their friends and neighbors (as Tacitus mentions) managed to do in coping with Domitian and his band of informers and enforcers, who made life very difficult for most of the inhabitants of Rome.

I speak of the "Christians of Rome" and First Clement interchangeably for the simple reason that the letter addresses itself to "the church of God" in Corinth from "the church of God" in Rome without qualification. I shall also speak of the writer often in the singular and sometimes in the plural (as representing a collective authorship). The work speaks in the voice of the entire community of Christians or followers of Jesus Christ in Rome to the community in Corinth. It knows no other way of describing the senders and recipients except "those who have been called and made holy by the will of God through our Lord Jesus Christ."[5] While the word "Christians" (*christianoi*) does not appear in the letter, it would be preposterous to suggest that First Clement has no conception of it or what it means to be "Christian." Like the letters of Paul, its preferred lexeme for being Christian is the phrase "in Christ" (*en Christo*). And it uses all kinds of ways of describing what it is to be "a Christian" without actually using the words "Christian" (*christianos*), "Christians" (*christianoi*), or "Christianity" (*christianismos*). First Clement also does not use the word *Ioudaismos*, that is, "Judaism" or "Jewish ways."

Importantly, First Clement has almost no sense of being Christian as something unhinged from and unrelated to the Hebrew or Jewish Scriptures and its traditions. In fact, it presumes that to be "in Christ" is to belong to the Hebrew past and the Jewish scriptures. It turns to the heroes of the Jewish past as the "ancestors" (17–19) of Christians. It is, however, deeply conscious of "those who are ignorant, unlearned, foolish, and uneducated" (*aphrones, asynetoi, mōroi, apaideutoi*), who are contemptuous of Christians (39.1). This is the wider world in which the Christians live among their fellow Romans: who "mock and ridicule us" (*chleuazousin hemas kai muktērizousin*).

Equally significantly, First Clement was written at about the same time that Josephus completed *Against Apion*, written after Josephus had already published the *Antiquities* and its supplement, his *Life*, or autobiography. If any of the Christians of First Clement had read the later chapters of Josephus's *Antiquities*, they would have been surprised that, in dealing with matters in first-century Judaea in the years during the High Priesthood of Caiaphas, Josephus mentions almost nothing about Jesus of Nazareth and his followers, or that when he came to write about Jewish sects active in the first century, he excluded the Christian Jews. They would have been intrigued, and surprised again, and perhaps even confused as to why Josephus would acknowledge their existence in his *Antiquities* when he referred to James the brother of Jesus, who was thought to be the Christ (*Antiquities* 20.197–203), but did not acknowledge their social presence by the simple fact that they were a known group in Jerusalem with a recognized leader in James the brother of Jesus for almost thirty years before he was murdered at the instigation of the High Priest Ananus son of Ananus, himself a relative of Caiaphas.

The Christians behind First Clement would also have been puzzled about Josephus's claims to be writing in defense of Judaism, the Jewish Constitution, and Jewishness against those who continued to culminate Jews, Jewishness, and Jewish religious life when he himself had been for all intents and purposes an apostate from Jewish life when he took the name Flavius Josephus and joined cause with the Romans. They may well have wondered exactly what Jewishness Josephus wished to rehabilitate or defend in *Against Apion* by his idealized representations when in fact he did not present a single character from the past as the exemplary figure or representative of the Judaism or Jewishness he sought to propagate, except to defend Moses as a legitimate lawgiver who provided a constitution better than what Greeks and Romans possessed. There are no moral exemplars in *Against Apion*, and against his own practices of retelling the lives of biblical characters in the *Antiquities*, Josephus presents no one or no living community of Jews as the representation of the Judaism or Jewishness that he sought to promote in *Against Apion*. There is nothing like what Philo does when he presents various characters from the Hebrew Scriptures as worthy representations of Greek virtues, for example.[6]

Josephus dared not even write against any contemporary Romans but instead turned his criticism against Greeks and Alexandrians, as well as historians of the past, and the deceased first-century Alexandrian grammarian Apion. All of which turns his claims to contemporary relevance in the last years of the first century into something of a fiction. His interlocutors have no currency or contemporary resonance in the last decade of the first century in Rome; and even less so in the immediate aftermath of Domitian's assassination. There is nothing in *Against Apion* that speaks to the social realities and political verities of the period immediately after the death of Domitian when Josephus wrote it. As I argued in chapter 3, it was a work intended to justify Josephus himself after the death of Domitian.

First Clement, on the other hand, claims the entire Jewish past as its inheritance. It describes the personalities of the Hebrew Scriptures as the ancestors of all Christians (Jews and non-Jews), and engages with the contemporary Roman discourses about life and immortality in a way Josephus's *Against Apion* barely touches upon. Compared to *Against Apion*, it is First Clement that presents the faith, beliefs, and religious lives of the ancestors of Israel and the Hebrews as the answers that both Greeks and Romans have long been bereft of.

At every turn, First Clement insists that the apostles of Jesus Christ, primarily in the persons of Paul and Peter, bequeathed to the church of Rome and to the church of Corinth an inheritance for all ages. First Clement presents the memory of Paul and the legacies of his apostolic mission as the indispensable bequest for both the present and future life of the church of God in Jesus Christ. First Clement can no more conceive of a Christian inheritance without Paul than it can imagine a Christian inheritance without the Hebrew Scriptures and the ancestors of the Jews. To this end, First Clement makes a claim that Paul and the earliest Christian Jews constitute one of the most important documented traditions in the archives of first-century Jewish life, contrary to Josephus's exclusion of the Christian Jews from his description of Jewish groups in the first century in final books of his *Antiquities*.

In what follows I shall describe in what ways First Clement does what Josephus does not do; and will point out a few contemporary resonances and the extent to which First Clement engages fellow Romans in the immediate aftermath of the death of Domitian. The contrived and supposedly contemporary polemic that is *Against Apion* makes for poor comparison with First Clement, even though First Clement does not style itself as such as a polemic against Roman ways in the way Josephus presents *Against Apion*.

THE PHOENIX: A CIPHER

To begin with, there is an interesting detail in First Clement that links the letter/treatise somewhat indirectly to the company of Tacitus, Suetonius, and Pliny the Younger. It devolves on contemporary sentiment and interpretations about the legend of the Phoenix. It bears comparison with the legend as it is reported by Tacitus in *Annals* 6.28.

In reporting what he considers full of doubt and exaggeration, Tacitus harks to traditions going as far back as Hesiod (Fragment 50), and Herodotus (Histories 2.73).[7] More importantly he claims that the bird has made a recent appearance c. 32–37 CE. Here is his version of the tale.

> During the consulship of Paulus Fabius and Lucius Vitellius, the bird called the phoenix, after a long succession of ages, appeared in Egypt and furnished the most learned men of that country and of Greece with abundant matter for the discussion of the marvelous phenomenon. It is my wish to make known all on which they agree with several things, questionable enough indeed, but not too absurd to be noticed. That it is a creature sacred to the sun, differing from all other birds in its beak and in the tints of its plumage, is held unanimously by those who have described its nature. As to the number of years it lives, there are various accounts. The general tradition says five hundred years. Some maintain that it is seen at intervals of fourteen hundred and sixty-one years, and that the former birds flew into the city called Heliopolis successively in the reigns of Sesostris, Amasis, and Ptolemy, the third king of the Macedonian dynasty, with a multitude of companion birds marvelling at the novelty of the appearance. But all antiquity is of course obscure. From Ptolemy to Tiberius was a period of less than five hundred years. Consequently, some have supposed that this was a spurious phoenix, not from the regions of Arabia, and with none of the instincts which ancient tradition has attributed to the bird. For when the number of years is completed and death is near, the phoenix, it is said, builds a nest in the land of its birth and infuses into it a germ of life from which an offspring arises, whose first care, when fledged, is to bury its father. This is not rashly done, but taking up a load of myrrh and having tried its strength by a long flight, as soon as it is equal to the burden and to the journey, it carries its father's body, bears it to the altar of the Sun, and leaves it

to the flames. All this is full of doubt and legendary exaggeration. Still, there is no question that the bird is occasionally seen in Egypt.[8]

Tacitus may have had Pliny the Elder's *Natural History* as the most proximate source of the legend. However, there are some details of his account that differ somewhat from Pliny's. The Christians of Rome also appear to have made up their minds about the Phoenix. First Clement provides the following commentary on the tale.

> Let us consider the incredible sign that occurs in the eastern climes, that is, in the regions near Arabia. For there is a bird called the phoenix. This unique creature lives five hundred years. And when at last it approaches its dissolution through death, it makes a tomb for itself out of frankincense, myrrh, and other spices. Then, when the time has been fulfilled, it enters into the tomb and dies. But when its flesh rots, a worm is born. And nourished by the secretions of the dead creature, it sprouts wings. Then when it becomes strong, it takes the tomb containing the bones of its predecessor and bears these from Arabia to Egypt, to the city called Heliopolis. In the daytime, while all are watching, it flies onto the altar of the sun and deposits these things, and so hastens back. Then the priests examine the records of the times and discover that it has come after five hundred years have elapsed. (First Clement, 25.1–5)[9]

Some of the details of the story in First Clement clearly differ from the version in Tacitus. Clement's version seems closer to the tale as told in Pliny's *Natural History* 10.2, but also seems to conflate both accounts. Pliny himself credits Manilius the Roman senator for the source of his account. Where Tacitus has the phoenix with a load of myrrh, Pliny the Elder has the phoenix constructing a nest of wild cinnamon and frankincense; and First Clement has a nest made of "myrrh, frankincense, and other spices." Tacitus's account gives 500 years, just as Ovid's *Metamorphoses* 15, while Pliny mentions 540 years. First Clement follows the traditions in Ovid and Tacitus. Like Tacitus and Pliny, First Clement has the bird traveling from Arabia to Egypt.

First Clement does not raise the issue of "legendary exaggeration" as Tacitus does. However, like Tacitus, it is not in doubt that the bird does appear in Egypt. Then comes Clement's argument, which reads in part like a response to the tale as mentioned in Seneca's *Epistle* 42.1 and Ovid's *Metamorphoses*, as well as a riposte to Tacitus before the fact (Martial's *Epigrams* merely allude to the treasures and scented perfumes of the phoenix's nest). Although not insisting that the Christian belief in the resurrection of Jesus is symbolized by what this unusual bird does, Clement uses the tale to argue for the resurrection of all those who have believed in Jesus's death and resurrection; and not only those who now believe, but those who believed the God of the Jews long before the coming of Jesus. In so doing First Clement also joins a tradition of thought found in Plato and others that saw the phoenix as a symbol of the soul in its many lives,[10] except for First Clement as opposed to Plato's *Phaedrus* 248e–249b, the soul does not require so many cycles of birth and rebirth before it finally escapes the cycles of birth and achieves its liberation; ten cycles of a thousand years each as Plato has it in the *Phaedrus*.

> Do we then think that it is so great and marvelous that the Creator of all things will raise everyone who has served him in a holy way with the confidence of good faith, when he shows us the magnificence of his promise even through a bird? . . . Let our souls, therefore, be bound by this hope to the one who is faithful in his promises and upright in his judgments. The one who commanded us not to lie, how much more will he not lie? For nothing is impossible with God, except lying. Let his faithfulness be rekindled within us and let us realize that all things are near to him. (First Clement 26.1; 27.1–3)[11]

The critical difference here is this: souls bound by a hope in the one who is faithful to his promises and upright in his judgments; the one who commands us not to lie, and who is incapable of lying, the Creator of all things, the God of the Jews. There is no ambiguity or confusion in the thought and language of First Clement. In the days of Domitian, as we have already seen, such expressions would have been tantamount to treason and sacrilege. As we shall see shortly, First Clement and the Roman poets were writing at cross purposes and in opposition to each other.

STATIUS, DOMITIAN, AND THE WORLDS OF FIRST CLEMENT

In the previous two chapters I considered a number of contemporaries, among them Martial, Pliny the Younger, Josephus, Tacitus, Suetonius, Dio Chrysostom, and Plutarch. One member of this group I have yet to consider: the poet Statius. Like Martial, Statius wrote while Domitian was alive and counted the emperor as one of his readers.

The prologue or preface to Book 4 of Statius's *Silvae* has much to commend it in laying out Statius's intentions. Composed in 94 or 95 CE when Statius had resettled in Naples after a short tenure in Rome (c. 92–94), Statius made sure to celebrate aspects of life in Rome that still held him sway, and of course, the emperor who had done much to adorn the city in its recent past. It is tempting to think that he may have run into Plutarch when the latter took to the lecture circuit in Rome c. 92. Unlike Plutarch, who seems to have picked up on the shady underbelly of life in the imperial capital, Statius seemed to see nothing that intimated or insinuated the dreadful conditions of fear and distress that his younger contemporaries Pliny the Younger, Tacitus, and Suetonius describe in their writings about this period of time. To his friend Marcellus, Statius explains:

> STATIUS TO HIS FRIEND MARCELLUS GREETINGS
> I have found a book, dearest Marcellus, that I can dedicate to your loyal affection. I think indeed that I have never begun any little work of mine without invoking the divinity of our great Emperor [Domitian]; but *this* book has three * * * than that the fourth is by way of honoring you. First, I have acclaimed the seventeenth consulship of our Germanicus. Second, I have given thanks for the honor of his most sacred banquet. Third, I have admired the Domitian Way, by which he has eliminated a very irksome delay due to the sands. Thanks to him you will receive my letter more expeditiously, which I am writing to you from Naples in this volume. Next comes an ode to young Septimius Severus, one of the most distinguished members of the second Order, as you know, and a classmate of yours too, but a very close friend of mine apart from this relationship.... So why are there more items in the fourth book of my *Extempore Poems* than in its forerunners? Because I don't want those who, as I am told, criticized my publishing this kind of composition to think that their strictures have had any effect. First, it is a waste of time to argue against a *fait accompli.* Second, I had already presented many of these items to our lord Caesar—and how much more is that than publication! Is there a law against practicing in fun? "Privately, no," they say. But ball games and fencing matches admit spectators. Finally, whoever reads something of mine with reluctance, let him at once declare himself my adversary; so why should I take his advice? In sum, I am the one under fire; let him hold his tongue and be thankful. As for this book, however, you will defend it, Marcellus, if you think fit; and so much for that. If not, I shall live with the censure. Farewell.[12]

Did Statius truly mean what he said that anyone who reads him reluctantly should consider himself an adversary? If so, did his friend Marcellus have a choice in the matter, when he implores him to either defend the book or remain silent? Would Marcellus's silence mean that he has rejected it?

Ostensibly, Statius presented the poems concerning the emperor to Domitian prior to sending them out to a general readership. So the first poem celebrating Domitian's seventeenth consulship must have received Domitian's approval before Statius included it with the second, in which he gave thanks for being invited to a sacred banquet with the emperor, and the third, about the Via Domitiana which has made traveling from Naples to Rome a less tiresome event. We should assume that the subsequent pieces dealing with Domitian had received imperial approval. There is no hint in any of them that Statius had any qualms about the troublesome and fearful aspects of Domitian's reign. To the contrary: Rome is to rejoice for having so laurelled a Caesar. Statius's calm stands in such awkward and dizzying juxtaposition to the words of Tacitus, Pliny the Younger, Plutarch, and Dio Chrysostom that we have already encountered.

> THE SEVENTEENTH CONSULSHIP OF EMPEROR AUGUSTUS GERMANICUS
> Joyfully does Caesar's purple join the twice eight entries in the Calendar and Germanicus inaugurate a banner year. He rises with the new sun and the stars in their grandeur, himself shining more brilliantly than they, greater than Eous. Let Latium's laws exult, rejoice, ye curule chairs, and more proudly let Rome knock at the sky with her Seven Hills; above all the other summits let Evander's hill triumph. New rods [the standards of the lictors] have entered the Palace, and see, the twelvefold honor returns. Its prayers heard, the Senate House rejoices to have vanquished Caesar's modesty.[13]

For Statius, peace and concord join the Senate's prayers for Domitian the reluctant ruler. What obtained the year before, and what was to come? Domitian's seventeenth consulship began in January 93. It would be a traumatic year for the Senate whose prayers are evoked here. A few of its notable members would be executed. Statius could not possibly have foreseen this eventuality. What he did know was that Domitian had given some indication of his disapproval of some aspects of Roman life in his role as censor and had shown a capacity for resorting to cruel punishment. The infamous case of the Vestal Virgins was of the most immediate past. Suetonius, no fan of Domitian, mentions that while Vespasian and Titus overlooked the infractions of the Vestals, Domitian punished them severely (Suetonius, *Domitian* 8.3–4). Some of those implicated were from the Senate, notably one Valerius Lucinianus about whom Pliny the Younger devotes Letter 4.11. None of this mattered to Statius, it seems. It is all encomia.

> Janus himself, greatest renewer of measureless time, raises his head and gives thanks from either threshold; you have tied his hands with his neighbor Peace and bidden him lay aside all warfare and swear fealty to the laws of the new Forum. See, he raises upturned hands on this side and on that, and thus with his two voices speaks: "Hail, great Father of the world, who make ready with me to renew the ages! Your Rome desires ever to see you thus in my month: thus, 'tis meet that times be born, thus that the years make entrance. Give joys continual to the Calendar. Let the fold surround these your shoulders with plenteous purple, and the bordered gown from your own Minerva's hastening hands. See you how a new gleam is in the temples, how the flame mounts higher on the altars, and how the very stars of my midwinter grow warm for you, matching your manners? Knights and tribes and purple-clad Fathers rejoice, every office draws luster from our Consul. Did any former year, I pray you, have the like?"[14]

Indeed: has any former time seen the likes of this? Is that not always the question with a panegyric: have we seen anything like this? Is this just like the former times? How much better have things become? So follow Statius's rehearsal of Domitian's achievements; nothing trivial, not even those that are equal to the past; but only those that show him surpassing the past. Only these will he recount.

> Come, tell me, mighty Rome, and long Antiquity, count with me the annals, nor rehearse petty examples but only those that my Caesar would deign to surpass. Thrice and ten times as the years rolled by did Augustus bear the Latin rods, but 'twas long before he began to deserve them: you were young when you outdid grandsires. And how much you refuse, how much you forbid! Yet you will be prevailed upon and will often promise this day to the Senate's prayers. A longer series remains beyond, and thrice and four times shall fortunate Rome bestow as many curule chairs upon you.[15]

What then will Rome not yield to this Lord and master? Which nations within his far-flung empire would not agree to his rule? All the gods promise long years, Statius assures his readers.

> With me you shall found a second century and for you the altar of ancient Tarentus shall be renewed. You shall bear a thousand trophies, only permit the triumphs. Bactra and Babylon have still to be curbed with new tributes, not yet are Indian laurels *in* Jove's bosom, not yet do Arabs and Seres make petition, not yet does all the year have its honor, ten months still crave your name. So Janus, and gladly withdrew behind his closed portal. Then all the gods opened wide and gave signs in a joyful heaven, and Jupiter accorded you, great leader, a long youth and promised years as many as his own.[16]

Silvae Book 4.2 is the most revealing. Not merely as panegyric, but a self-portrait as well of the poet. Statius, the person, is as much a subject as Emperor Domitian. If we join his self-portrait with his preface, we cannot deny his confidence in his artistry and his riposte to his critics near and far. As he notes in the preface, if they cannot tolerate his art, they should let it perish.

> THANKSGIVING TO EMPEROR AUGUSTUS GERMANICUS DOMITIANUS
> [Vergil] He that brought great Aeneas to the fields of Laurentum extols the royal feast of Sidonian Elissa, and [Homer] he that wore out returning Ulysses with much seafaring portrays Alcinous' repast in immortal verse. But I, now that for the first time Caesar has granted me novel joy of his sacred banquet, granted me to attain to his imperial board, with what lyre am I to celebrate my answered prayers, what thanks shall I avail to render? Not though Smyrna and Mantua both were to bind holy laurel on my happy head should I find fitting utterance. Me seems I recline with Jupiter among the stars and take immortal liquor proffered by Ilian hand. Barren are the years behind me. This is the first day of my span, here is the threshold of my life. Do I behold you as I recline, sovereign of the lands, great parent of a world subdued, you, hope of mankind, you, care of the gods? Is it granted me indeed to gaze at this face from nearby amid wine and tables, and lawful for me not to rise?[17]

"Great parent," "conqueror," "sovereign of the world," "dear to the gods," "hope of all mankind." Yet these were the times in which men like Helvidius, Senecio, and Rusticus lived and died: the blood of senators spilled by Domitian. There is no hint of any of this madness in Statius. Instead he revels at an invitation to a heavenly banquet with the emperor. In the rest of the poem he celebrates the august building in which the banquet was held, almost as if to bear witness to what Suetonius will write later about Domitian's architectural accomplishments and his lavish entertainments. At the end he prays for Domitian's continued rule. At the same time, the finale pays tribute to Statius himself, as he recalls receiving the prize for a poetry contest from Domitian. He relives his previous triumph, when he wrote in praise of Domitian's Dacian campaign and his German war.

> May the gods (for 'tis said they often give ear to lesser souls) grant that you pass twice and thrice the limits of your father's field. May you send established deities skyward, give temples—and live in your home. Often may you throw open the yearly threshold, often greet Janus with new lictors, often repeat the quinquennial festival with wreathed lustrations. The day you gave me the auspicious banquet and the rites of your table, such it came to me as that day long ago when under Trojan Alba's hills your hand invested me with Pallas' gold [Minerva's Crown] as I sang now of German battles, now of Dacian.[18]

Notice the differences between this prayer and the one that is found in First Clement. At the very end of First Clement the writing turns into an extended prayer from 59.3–61.3. A little past its halfway point it reads (60.3): "Yes, Master, make your face shine on us in peace, for our own good, that we may be protected by your powerful hand and rescued from our every sin by your exalted arm. *And rescue us from those who hate us without cause*" (*misounton hemas adikos*).[19]

For much of First Clement there is very little if any reference to a world outside of the church that posed a threat to the Christians in Rome; and there is no hint that the church in Corinth needed to be rescued from some such distress. What follows gives an idea of what is implied.

> Give harmony and peace both to us and to all those who inhabit the earth, just as you gave to our ancestors when they called upon you in a holy way, in faith and truth; and allow us to be obedient to your all-powerful and all-virtuous name, and to those who rule and lead us here on earth. (First Clement 60.4–61.3)[20]

No one would miss the reference to temporal order and the world of potentates who rule the earth. The Roman Empire and its emperor are clearly in view here.

> You have given them, O Master, the authority to rule through your magnificent and indescribable power, that we may both recognize the glory and honor you have given them and subject ourselves to them, *resisting nothing that conforms to your will*. Give to them, O Lord, health, peace, harmony, and stability, so that without faltering they may administer *the rule that you have given to them*. For you, O Master, Heavenly King forever, give humans glory, honor, and authority over the creatures of the earth. O Lord, *make their plan conform with what is good and acceptable before you*, that when they administer with piety the authority you have given them, in peace and meekness, *they may attain your mercy*. You who alone can do these things for us, and do what is more abundantly good, we praise you through the high priest and benefactor of our souls, Jesus Christ, through whom the glory and majesty be yours both now and for all generations and forever. Amen. (First Clement 61.1–3)[21]

To make them conform to what is good and acceptable to the God of the Christians is to demand a different political order. To resist nothing that conforms to God's will also means that one is in the right when one resists whatever does not conform to that will. First Clement does not simply underwrite the order of things in the Roman Empire.

> This is the path, loved ones, in which we have found our salvation—Jesus Christ, the high priest of our offerings, the benefactor who helps us in our weaknesses. Through this one we gaze into the heights of the heavens; through this one we see the reflection of his perfect and superior countenance; through this one our foolish and darkened understanding springs up into the light; through this one the Master has washed us to taste the knowledge of immortality. He is the radiance of his magnificence, as superior to the angels as he has inherited a more excellent name. For so it is written: "The one who makes his angels spirits and his ministers tongues of fire." But the Master says this about his Son: "You are truly my Son; today I have given you birth. Ask from me, and I will give you the nations as your inheritance, and the ends of the earth as your possession." And again he says to him, "Sit at my right hand, until I make your enemies a footstool for your feet." Who then are the enemies? Those who are evil and oppose his will. (First Clement 36.1–5)[22]

To speak of making one's enemies (*echthroi*) a footstool (*hypopodium*) is to presume conflict and to promise and predict conquest. We shall have to compare First Clement with the expressions of imperial power in Pliny the Younger's *Panegyricus*.

It is a fairly good guess that if any of Domitian's informants (*delatores*) had gotten hold of a work like First Clement, they could easily have brought charges of "*maiestas*," or treason against the leaders of the church in Rome who had written this letter. At the very minimum First Clement constitutes a provocation so daring that the leaders of the church in Rome would have had to be interrogated for the views expressed here. Notice that others who were well-placed had been found guilty of "*maiestas*" for following "Jewish ways." The writer or writers of First Clement could easily be charged with the same crime, "attending to Jewish ways," since so much of the letter is suffused with the Jewish Scriptures in Greek (the LXX or Septuagint). Any Christian associated with First Clement, to say nothing of each of the three emissaries who were the only ones named in the letter, would have had no way to exonerate him- or herself except to recant his or her Christian beliefs and their Jewish origins.

If it is true that there were people in Rome who "hated the Christians without cause," then we have reason to believe that the church in Rome that issued this letter lived in distress under some kind of threat. In which case, the church would not have written what we call First Clement until the threat had disappeared or at least subsided substantially. They would not have exposed themselves in such a telltale fashion and would in all probability have written only after Domitian's death in September 96. To have composed and sent it while Domitian reigned supreme would have been extremely risky, if not suicidal. Recall the words of Tacitus. Mature men grew prematurely old, and older men became decrepit, while living in silence, in fear of what might befall them if they dared to speak. Recall the words of Pliny. Many authors either refused to write or did not make public what they wrote for fear of what might befall them.

Statius's *encomia* for Domitian portend a different order than First Clement's prayer for those who rule. They present sharply divergent and antithetical views about the order of things. They cannot be reconciled in the language of First Clement's favorites: "peace" and "concord," at least not on Statius's or Domitian's terms. The difference for First Clement is that "high priest and benefactor of our souls, Jesus Christ."

The world viewed by Statius and represented by his *Silvae* looked dramatically different from the one that Pliny the Younger and his friends described in their writings about the years of Domitian. First Clement suggests a world similar to the one presented by Pliny the Younger and Tacitus.

Tacitus is emphatic. He states at the beginning of his *Agricola* that the account he provides about his fellow senators, who were murdered, is matter of public record. So this is not simply oral history. There are public records to attest to the facts. He must surely have in mind the archives of the Roman Senate. He emphasizes not only that the convicted senators were executed but that their books (the memories of them) were put to the flames. It has taken the new emperor Nerva to restore liberty, which now continues in the reign of Trajan. Tacitus writes of persecution, censorship, inquisitors, informers, etc.

> It is recorded that when Rusticus Arulenus extolled Thrasea Paetus, when Herennius Senecio extolled Helvidius Priscus, their praise became a capital offence, so that persecution fell not merely on the authors themselves but on

the very books: to the public hangman, in fact, was given the task of burning in the courtyard of the Forum the memorials of our noblest characters. They imagined, no doubt, that in those flames disappeared the voice of the people, the liberty of the Senate, the conscience of mankind; especially as the votaries of Philosophy also were expelled, and all liberal culture exiled, in order that nowhere might anything of good report present itself to men's eyes. Assuredly we have furnished a signal proof of our submissiveness; and even as former generations witnessed the utmost excesses of liberty, so have we the extremes of slavery; wherein our "Inquisitors" [or informers, (*delatores*)] have deprived us even of the give and take of conversation. *We should have lost memory itself as well as voice, had forgetfulness been as easy as silence.* Now at last heart is coming back to us: from the first, from the very outset of this happy age, Nerva has united things long incompatible, Empire and liberty; Trajan is increasing daily the happiness of the times; and public confidence has not merely learned to hope and pray but has received security for the fulfillment of its prayers and even the substance thereof.[23]

The list of recriminations is a long one. Domitian executed senators, burned the books written about them, expelled philosophers, subdued the Senate. They lived in servitude (or slavery) but now live in a happier age where empire and liberty, two things long thought incompatible, have been united. He does not reflect on the fact that to achieve its empire Rome wages wars, deprives other peoples of their sovereignty, or even reduces them to a form of servitude by imposing tributes on conquered people.

Tacitus continues about Domitian's ferocity and the fifteen years that have been lost to people's lives. He wants to make amends. He could not have written about his father-in-law during those times, he seems to suggest. So now that he has liberty he will extol his virtues, it is the first installment of his writing the history of those times. His generation has been fearful and indolent, but now they are slowly recovering from their diseases. There is an interesting question: what positions did he hold during those fifteen years? He was *quaestor Augusti* (c. 81?); *tribunus plebis* (85?), *praetor* in 88; and *consul* in 97; he published *Agricola* and *Germania* (98). Like Pliny the Younger, he too rose through the ladders of the *cursus honorum*. His success probably accounts for why he acknowledges that even as he speaks about the past that he wishes to memorialize he does so with stammering lips; and that somehow in giving an account of his father-in-law Agricola he would like to perform a kind of expiation for his complicities, if at all possible: "After all I shall not regret the task of recording our former slavery and testifying to our present blessings, albeit with unpractised and stammering tongue. As an installment of that work this book is dedicated to the vindication of my father-in-law Agricola: its plea of filial duty will commend or, at least, excuse it."[24]

If men like Tacitus and Pliny the Younger, at the very centers of power and vested with much authority, found themselves incapable of speech, conversation, and lived in fear of informers, we can only imagine how ordinary Romans would have felt. Yet Tacitus, Pliny, and friends continued to participate in social activities that exposed them to possible censure, recrimination, prosecution, or death. They continued in their public lives in association with Domitian's court and survived his reign. Fortunately, as Tacitus remarks, forgetfulness is not as easy as silence. They did not forget what they had endured.

SUETONIUS'S *DOMITIAN* AND THE DATING OF FIRST CLEMENT

Suetonius came of age at a time when his older contemporaries and elders had damned the memory of Emperor Domitian. He witnessed monuments that had been dedicated by Domitian to himself being defaced, and he witnessed a general disposition among his fellow Romans that suggested that they lived in a better and more glorious age than the one that had just recently ended.

Suetonius, a younger contemporary and friend to both Tacitus and Pliny, had the good fortune of not having to advance in his career during the time of Domitian. He was too young for that. He also has the benefit of hindsight and some distance from which to assess Domitian's regime. He in particular of the three was puzzled by what he recognized as a change in Domitian from the period of his early reign characterized by a certain semblance of peace to the end of his reign characterized by extreme and unpredictable cruelty. Whereas Pliny compares the bad Domitian to the good Trajan, Suetonius, who dutifully did not write about Trajan, compares Domitian to himself: the cruel Domitian against the less cruel ("good") Domitian. What he then records or recounts of the deeds of the cruel Domitian leads one to believe just how terrified the people of Rome would have been under Domitian; and why First Clement's language about "sudden and repeated misfortunes" is as good a piece of social commentary for the times as any, given the random character of Domitian's cruelties, the general unpredictable nature of the charges brought against his victims, and the anxiety and fear as to who his next victim might be.

First Clement begins: "The church of God that temporarily resides in Rome to the church of God that temporarily resides in Corinth. To those who have been called and made holy by the will of God through Jesus Christ. May Grace and Peace be increased among you, from the all-powerful God, through Jesus Christ."[25] The greeting alone contains a well-formulated theological view of things: "Called," "Made Holy," "Through Jesus Christ." It is a long letter, certainly a treatise. The letter ends at chapter 65 as follows: "But send back to us quickly our envoys: three of them: Claudius Ephebus,

Vaterius Bito, along with Fortunatus, in peace and with joy, that they may inform us without delay about the peace and harmony that we have prayed and desired for you. Then we will rejoice more quickly in your stability."[26] Rejoicing in the stability of the Corinthians was also partly reflexive. Without a sense of their own stability, the church of Rome could not speak thus.

The notion of being temporarily resident in both Rome and Corinth frames the entire letter in the language of eschatology and perhaps of temporal indifference to the lived circumstances of both Christian communities. The theme also underscores for both senders and hearers that they belonged historically and eschatologically to a different kingdom, polis, society, or commonwealth, which differed in its origins and destiny from the one that currently claimed them as citizens. Might the language of temporal residence also not allude to the idea that whatever their present troubles or the misfortunes of the recent past, they were not bound by them?

When was the letter written? I have already given indication that it must have been after the death of Domitian in September 96 CE. Philip Schaff offered the following assessment.

> The date of this Epistle has been the subject of considerable controversy. It is clear from the writing itself that it was composed soon after some persecution (chap. i.) which the Roman Church had endured; and the only question is, whether we are to fix upon the persecution under Nero or Domitian. If the former, the date will be about the year 68; if the latter, we must place it towards the close of the first century or the beginning of the second. We possess no external aid to the settlement of this question. The lists of early Roman bishops are in hopeless confusion, some making Clement the immediate successor of St. Peter, others placing Linus, and others still Linus and Anacletus, between him and the apostle. The internal evidence, again, leaves the matter doubtful, though it has been strongly pressed on both sides. The probability seems, on the whole, to be in favour of the Domitian period, so that the Epistle may be dated about a.d. 97.[27]

It is not too far off Kirsopp Lake's construal:

> The date of I. Clement is fixed by the following considerations. It appears from chapter 5 to be later than the persecution in the time of Nero, and from chapters 42–44 it is clear that the age of the apostles is regarded as past. It can therefore scarcely be older than 75–80 a.d. On the other hand chapter 44 speaks of presbyters who were appointed by the apostles and were still alive, and there is no trace of any of the controversies or persecutions of the second century. It is therefore probably not much later than 100 a.d. If it be assumed that chapter 1, which speaks of trouble and perhaps of persecution, refers to the time of Domitian, it can probably be dated as c. 96 a.d.; but we know very little about the alleged persecution in the time of Domitian, and it would not be prudent to decide that the epistle cannot be another ten or fifteen years later. It is safest to say that it must be dated between 75 and 110 a.d.; but within these

limits there is a general agreement among critics to regard as most probable the last decade of the first century.[28]

The old consensus captured here by Philip Schaff and Kirsopp Lake is not far from J. B. Lightfoot's view expressed in his work on the apostolic fathers published at the end of the nineteenth century.[29] For Lightfoot, the internal references within First Clement tend to set it to about 95 or 96 CE. However, the language upon which that assessment is based is not without controversy.

The writer speaks of "sudden and repeated misfortunes and setbacks we have experienced."[30] He does not necessarily say that they have ended. Since the text also mentions that the leaders of the churches who were appointed by the apostles have now passed on, it means the writer belongs to the generation after them. So on the normal assumption that Paul and Peter did not live past 64/65 CE, the next generation, in the normal sense in which the ancients accorded a generation as thirty years (according to Heraclitus) or at most thirty-three years (a Hesiodian generation according to the scholiast on Homer's *Iliad* 6.101), we would be up to 95 CE or so. This coincides with Domitian's reign that ended with his assassination in September 96. It has seemed natural then to assume as so many interpreters do that this also means that the Christians suffered persecution under Domitian. The inference makes sense, but it is probably a mistake if we mean by persecution a well-defined program directed by the emperor with the objective of destroying or exterminating Christians in Rome. J. B. Lightfoot, however, believed and argued that there was a concerted effort at persecuting Christians in the time of Domitian tied to the story of the consul Flavius Clemens and his wife Domitilla.[31]

In his attempt to pinpoint the time of composition of First Clement, Allen Brent finds useful the coincidences with some of what we learn later in the correspondence between Pliny the Younger and Trajan about the Christians in Bithynia. Some of those who were interrogated, according to Pliny, claimed to have given up on their Christian beliefs some twenty years before, which will put their recantation to c. 92 CE. For Brent, this is another piece of evidence of Domitian's persecution of Christians. The conclusion may be premature though. That something happened in Bithynia-Pontus may not necessarily mean that it happened everywhere else in the empire, and still less in Rome, if we have no evidence of it in the imperial capital. Furthermore, the interpretation of the language of "sudden and repeated misfortunes and setbacks" that we find in First Clement does not have to mean a well-defined pattern of persecution or even a systematic attempt to harry Christians in the way that Pliny the Younger's letter suggests about what obtained in Bithynia-Pontus.

As we saw in the previous chapter, there was a general state of fear and terror during Domitian's reign. About this there is no dispute. However, many interpreters of the reference to "sudden and repeated misfortunes and setbacks" simply ignore this context, even though Tacitus, Pliny the Younger, and Suetonius all attest to it. We have as well the testimonies of Plutarch and Dio Chrysostom, to mention two outsiders.[32] The catalog of Domitian's atrocities as recounted by his contemporaries is wrenching.[33] For a society fed on ritualized violence of games and spectacles and so used to tolerating other forms of domesticated violence under the law and on the estates of the great families, the sense of shock and affront expressed by the citizens of Rome toward Domitian is revealing. They were used to or had historical memory of wicked emperors like Gaius Caligula and Nero. For most of them the only comparison they could draw for Domitian's cruelties were those recounted or alleged about Nero. That they found themselves shocked and outraged by Domitian's cruelties says a great deal.

Suetonius, who lists many of Domitian's atrocities in his *Lives of the Caesars*, does not present him in an entirely negative light. In fact, he makes the point that in many ways Domitian made great benefactions in the way of public works, if only to demand that all those things be named after him. As is Suetonius's style in the various portraits of the Caesars, he tells the story of Domitian by beginning with Domitian's benefactions before addressing his unusual cruelty, noting at the turning point in the narrative that Domitian turned from acts of mercy in his earlier period more speedily toward cruelty than to avarice (*Domitian* 10.1). Suetonius would soon add, after providing some details of the unusual cruelties, that "his savage cruelty was not only excessive but also sudden" (*Domitian* 11.1).

More than two generations after Domitian, Cassius Dio (c. 154–229 CE), still marveled at the cruelty of Domitian. Dio seems to tire in recounting Domitian's cruelties. It was something of a relief even from a historian's standpoint, and certainly for the reader of Dio's history, to move from Domitian to the deeds of Nerva's short reign. But for Dio and for any historian, one cannot quite get away from Domitian when speaking about Nerva, nor could anyone for that matter who had lived at that time. It is Domitian who makes Nerva's brief reign such a hopeful and promising respite for the Romans, including Jews and Christians.

> After Domitian, the Romans appointed Nerva Cocceius emperor. Because of the hatred felt for Domitian, his images, many of which were of silver and many of gold, were melted down; and from this source large amounts of money were obtained. The arches, too, of which a very great number were being erected to this one man, were torn down. Nerva also released all who were on trial for *maiestas* and restored the exiles; moreover, he put to death all the slaves and the freedmen who had conspired against their masters and allowed that class of persons to lodge no complaint whatever against their masters; and no persons were permitted to accuse anybody of *maiestas* or of adopting the Jewish mode of life. Many of those who had been informed

[upon] were condemned to death, among others Seras, the philosopher. When, now, no little commotion was occasioned by the fact that everybody was accusing everybody else, Fronto, the consul, is said to have remarked that it was bad to have an emperor under whom nobody was permitted to do anything, but worse to have one under whom everybody was permitted to do everything; and Nerva, on hearing this, ordered that this condition of affairs should cease for the future.[34]

Given all that transpired during the reign of Domitian, from the murder of the members of the Stoic party, to the prosecution of members of the Senate, to the new measures attached to the *fiscus Judaicus*, and those within the imperial household who were under suspicion for Jewish sympathies, it would not have taken much for the Christians in Rome to feel that they lived in a period of "sudden and repeated misfortunes."

Some Christians may well have died on account of Domitian's direct actions, but it would not have been solely because they were Christian, but because they were perceived to have contributed to some plots against him or were associated with those who were deemed his adversaries or enemies. Pliny the Younger was well aware of this possibility that his own associations, even those whom he chose to defend in court, could lead to his doom, either going into exile or being executed. One simply did not know upon what basis an indictment could be made. Kirsopp Lake, Lightfoot, and others were right to doubt the claims that the Flavian household itself had members who had been persecuted for being Christian. Lightfoot reviews the evidence in exhaustive detail before coming to this conclusion. Nevertheless, he seemed to have been misled about First Clement's language. "Sudden and repeated misfortunes" has all too easily been translated into an idea of persecution supposedly on the pattern of what was assumed to have occurred under Nero. But it need not be.

There are indications in First Clement that indeed some Christians in Rome did suffer for being Christian. In addition to First Clement's use of the Letter to the Hebrews, one of his most interesting features is his use of the Book of Job. First Clement juxtaposes Job to Abraham, who is described as "Friend of God" (17.1–3). Job is described as a man with a good reputation who gazed upon God with a humble heart, because he realized that he was but dust and ashes (quoting Job 1:1). One of its most extensive quotations from Job comes in the context of an important section in 39.1ff., to which I have already alluded.

> Senseless and stupid and foolish and ignorant people jeer and mock us, wishing to exalt themselves in their own imaginations. For what can a mortal do? Or what strength does an earthborn creature have? For it is written: "There was no form before my eyes; I heard only a breath and a voice. What then? Shall a mortal be clean in the presence of the Lord? Or shall a man be blameless for

his deeds, seeing that he does not trust his servants and has found some fault against his angels? Not even heaven is clean in his sight, much less we who dwell in houses of clay, the very same clay of which we ourselves are made. He crushed them like a moth, and between morning and evening they cease to exist. Because they could not help themselves, they perished. He breathed upon them and they died, because they had no wisdom. But call out, if some one should obey you, or if you should see one of his holy angels. For wrath kills the foolish person, and envy slays one who has gone astray. And I have seen fools putting down roots, but suddenly their house was consumed. May their children fair from safety. May they be mocked at the doors of lesser men, and there will be none to deliver them. For the things prepared for them, the righteous shall eat; but they themselves will not be delivered from evil." (First Clement 39.1–9)[35]

The paragraph is a pastiche of passages from Job 4:16–5:5 and 15:15. Elsewhere First Clement also quotes Job 14:4–5 (First Clement 17.4), 38:11 (20.7), 19:26 (26.3), 11:2–3 (30.4–5), and 5:17–26 (First Clement 56.6–15), another extensive quotation from Job.

Here First Clement presents an argument against those who mock and ridicule "us," who set themselves above everything that exists and who think they are like God. Hence the question: what can a mere mortal accomplish? First Clement picks up the variegated discourse found in Job about the fragility and worthlessness of human beings as mere dust and ashes, and compares it to the immensity and incomprehensibility of God. That First Clement appropriates this tradition to answer those who scoff at the Christians is intriguing and highly perceptive of its sense of theological propriety. Then, immediately following this, it turns to narrate the handing down of an authoritative tradition from Jesus to the apostles and to the church and its faithful overseers (39.1–42.1). At 43.1 it compares the apostles to Moses. At 46.1 it admonishes and implores the Corinthians that they should cling to these examples.

In addition to describing those "who mock and ridicule us," First Clement also mentions other stresses. This time it is not in the form of an argument but in the prayer that comes at the end of the letter. Given the liturgical nature of the ending, most interpreters barely comment on the currency and timeliness of some of the contents in the prayers. Take 59.4. I shall list them in verse:

> We ask you, Master, to be our helper and protector
> Save those among us who are in distress
> Have mercy on the humble
> Raise up the fallen
> Show yourself to those in need
> Heal the sick
> Turn back those of your people who wander

> Feed the hungry
> Ransom our prisoners
> Raise up the weak
> Comfort the discouraged
> Let all the nations know that you are the only God, that Jesus Christ is your servant, and that we are the people and the sheep of your pasture.[36]

The petitions speak of current and prevailing circumstances. They are not merely formulaic. Attention should be drawn to "those among us who are going astray" and those who need to be ransomed. Specifically it pleads: "rescue those among us who are in prison." The earlier part of the prayer reads:

> Grant us, Lord, to hope on your name, which is the primal source of all creation, and open the eyes of our hearts that we may know you, who alone are highest among the high; you are holy, abiding among the holy. You humble the pride of the proud; you destroy the plans of nations; you exalt the humble and humble the exalted; you make rich and make poor; you kill and make alive. You alone are the benefactor of spirits and the God of all flesh, looking into the depths, scanning the works of humans; the helper of those who are in peril, the savior of those in despair; the creator and guardian of every spirit. You multiply the nations upon the earth, and from among all of them you have chosen those who love you through Jesus Christ, your beloved servant, through whom you instructed us, sanctified us, honored us. (First Clement 59.3)[37]

First Clement has internalized the theology of Job, the Psalms, and much of the Wisdom tradition in the Hebrew Scriptures. It has also internalized the theology of Paul's letters, Hebrews, and the Gospels about Jesus as the Christ, the Messiah, and the perfect sacrifice for human redemption (Hebrews).

If we connect the dots from the early reference to the "sudden and repeated misfortunes" in First Clement 1.1 to the ignorant who mock us (39.1ff.), to those who hate us without reason (60.3), and those of us in prison (59.4), we should be able to appreciate the kind of distress under which the church in Rome lived prior to the writing of First Clement. There is a connection between mockery and hating someone without cause or reason. The consequences are usually very grave for the object of that hatred. Notice that the phrasing of 59.4 (ransom those of us in prison) is very similar to 60.3 (deliver us from those who hate us without cause) even if different words are used: *lytrosai* (ransom/redeem) and *rhuosai* (deliver). It does not require great imagination to appreciate this, nor does it demand some notion of "great persecution" to make intelligible that this was a community derided and that some of their members were in prison on account of the contempt they endured from their fellow Romans.

Recall Dio Chrysostom's words about people being hauled together with those who were being executed because they happened to be associated with those under indictment. What everyone had to take for granted was that the threat of an indictment was an ever-present possibility and one could not anticipate in advance where it would come from, who would initiate it, and what type of charge would be brought against you. Basically, as long as you lived among informers, you did not need a public declaration of any sort to be in fear. So the "sudden and repeated misfortunes" of the church in Rome need not be a reference to a persecution that was formerly declared that targeted the Christians.

Like everyone else, the Christians in Rome lived under threat, and there were other aspects of their lives that could draw undue attention. Because First Clement does not spell out comprehensively but only allusively the extent of the misfortunes endured by the Christians of Rome, it is difficult to say exactly how their distress expressed itself in full or from which parts of Roman society the distress emanated. What we can say with confidence is that the misfortunes abated enough for the church at Rome to recover its bearings and write to the Christians in Corinth in the province of Achaea, and to send along three emissaries to deliver the letter. All indications are that this period coincided with the accession of Nerva in late 96 CE, and that the leaders of the church in Rome felt something of the relief that Tacitus expresses in *Agricola*, Dio Chrysostom in his *Orations*, Suetonius later in his *Lives of the Caesars* (*Domitian*), and Pliny the Younger in his letters and his *Panegyric* written in 100 CE.

THE TRADITIONS OF FIRST CLEMENT

What, else, can we learn from this letter about Christianity in Rome in the last decade of the first century? What self-understanding does the letter embody and express about the nature of Christianity? What it is, who belongs to it, why it matters, etc.? Fundamentally, First Clement is founded on the idea of tradition (*paradosis*) or traditions.

> We write these things, dear friends, not only to admonish you but also to remind ourselves. For we are in the same arena, and the same contest awaits us. Therefore let us abandon empty and futile thoughts, and let us conform to the glorious and holy rule of our tradition (*paradosis*); indeed, let us note what is good and what is pleasing and what is acceptable in the sight of the one who made us. Let us fix our eyes on the blood of Christ and understand how previous it is to his Father, because, being poured out for our salvation, it won for the whole world the grace of repentance. Let us review all the generations in turn, and learn that from generation to generation the Master has given an opportunity for repentance to those who desire to turn to him. (First Clement 7.1–5)[38]

"Clement" speaks of this *paradosis* that also provides a way back through repentance. He uses *paradosis* here in a way similar to Paul's use of it in Galatians 1:14, and in First Corinthians. In these two uses Paul also establishes two points: first, with respect to Galatians 1:14 that this is about received tradition as authoritative; and in relation to First Corinthians it is also a source for examples for the present. With regard to the first, First Clement underwrites its own authority by appealing to its inextricable links with Paul and Peter as apostles who founded the churches of Rome and Corinth. With respect to the second, First Clement wishes to imitate Paul's understanding of the Old Testament as an exemplary text, with narratives that provide object lessons for the present.

Much depends on the idyllic description of the Corinthians that "Clement" presents in the preamble (or peroration). That portrait does not correspond to what the Corinthians are at the time he is writing to them, otherwise they would not be needing the help they have requested from the church in Rome. To what reality then does that point? Is it to the historical past or something closer to First Clement's own time? Do we have anyway of knowing? If it is to a historical past, how far back does it go? Does it go to the time of Paul and the Corinthian letters?

One possibility is that it goes to the historical past and to the relationship of Paul to the Corinthians. If so, then that idyllic portrait must have some connection to what we learn about the Corinthians from Paul's letter(s). From First and Second Corinthians we know that Paul wrote more than two letters to the Corinthians. But if we have to pick which one of the two extant letters comes closest to sustaining the idyllic portrait, it cannot be First Corinthians. There it is all strife and contention. However, in Second Corinthians much has been resolved and one gets the sense of a church renewed and invigorated to live out its true calling. Paul's Second Letter to the Corinthians could serve as a backdrop for the kind of encomium that "Clement" provides in his opening words. It is an apostrophe to the Church of Corinth, all as a prelude to offering the kind of instruction and reproof that the church in Rome proposes. There are, however, elements in Second Corinthians that do not speak of an idyllic situation in Corinth. Not after everything that preceded it.

His repeated references to the strife and dissension that obtained when the Corinthians were distinguishing themselves as belonging to Paul, Cephas, and Apollos stand in some contrast to the idyll that he portrays in the early chapter of First Clement. He leaves no doubt that the letter he wishes them to take and read is the one that discusses those issues: it is self-explanatory.

> Take up the epistle of the blessed Paul that apostle. What did he first write in the beginning of the gospel? In truth, he sent you a letter in the manner of the Spirit about himself, Cephas, and Apollos, because at that time you created

dissensions. But that dissension brought you a lesser sin, for you took the part of the attested apostles and of a man approved among them. (First Clement 47.1–4)[39]

In other words, your factionalism was about preferring one approved person over two others who were apostles, none of whom were at fault. But the current circumstances are much different.

> It is shameful, indeed, very shameful, and things unworthy of your conduct in Christ to hear of the very solid and ancient church of the Corinthians because one or two persons are fomenting rebellion against the presbyters. And this report has reached not only us, but others who differ from us, so that blasphemies against the Lord's name are piled on because of your folly. And it is producing danger for you. (First Clement 47.6–7)[40]

First Clement derives its ideal of the church from the Letter to Titus. It alludes to Titus 3:1 in First Clement 2.7. But that is not all there is to its appropriation of Titus. In fact, much of the description it provides of a church at peace in First Clement 1.2–2.8 is patterned mostly on the kind of church that is described in Titus and also in First and Second Timothy, the so-called Pastorals.

> For who, when they visited you, did not approve your faith, so firm and full of virtue? Who could fail to be amazed at your wise and gentle piety in Christ? Who did not proclaim the magnificence of your hospitality and not bless your perfect and secure knowledge? You have conducted yourselves in every way without favoritism, and you have walked in God's commands by being subject to your leaders and rendering fitting honor to the presbyters among you. You have enjoined the young to think on moderate and solemn things. The women you have commanded to conduct all their affairs in a blameless, devout, and pure conscience, each loving her own husband appropriately. You have taught them to work at home devoutly by the rule of submission, always acting wisely. You all were of a humble mind without boasting, being submissive rather than dominating, giving gladly rather than receiving. By being satisfied with Christ's provisions and by heeding his words, you embraced them in your inner hearts with his sufferings before your eyes. (First Clement 1.2–2.1)[41]

First Clement establishes its authority along several axes. First, it appeals directly and indirectly to Paul's memory, his relationship to the Corinthians, and to his letters to them. Second, it assumes that the Corinthians have at least one of Paul's letters to which they can refer. In which case, it is not necessary for the writer to quote any of Paul's letters known to the Corinthians. This is a fact that has baffled interpreters, who cannot fathom why the writer does not explicitly quote Paul's letters to invoke Paul's authority. He does not have to. It is foundational to everything he does.

First Clement also presumes on an existing bond between the Church of Corinth and the Church of Rome. The presumption is implied in the appeal that the Corinthians themselves make to the Romans to come and help them resolve their difficulties. (From a Roman administrative standpoint, Achaia was a province much prized, for that is what they understood to be Greece proper: consider Pliny's remarks to his friend Maximus in Letter 8.24 when the latter was to take up the governorship of Achaia.) Some of this can be discerned from Paul's Letter to the Romans. At the end of that letter he mentions a few individuals from Achaia who had been instrumental in the proclamation of the gospel. He recommends them to the church at Rome as stalwarts for the work that lay ahead of them. The Letter to the Romans itself was composed either at Corinth or nearby in Cenchrea (Romans 16).

First Corinthians 7 also provides a template that may well have influenced First Clement. The scheme is not an accident:

1 Corinthians 7:10	I give this command (not I, but the Lord)
1 Corinthians 7:12	I say this (I, not the Lord / saying of the Lord)
1 Corinthians 7:25	I have no command from the Lord
	I give a judgment as one who by the Lord's mercy is trustworthy
1 Corinthians 7:37	In my judgment . . . and I think that I too have the Spirit of God

Earlier in the letter (chapters 1 and 2) Paul speaks about the gospel he preaches and what has been revealed to him by the Spirit. If there is a command from the Lord or a saying of the Lord, he puts it forth (v. 10); where there are no sayings of the Lord, he puts forth his own saying, so to speak (v. 12); verses 25–37 expand on what he can and cannot say.

He speaks of his judgment as someone who by the Lord's mercy is trustworthy; and also because he has the Spirit of God. Paul does not claim any exclusive rights to exercise judgment. It is for everyone. But the one who exercises judgment needs the Spirit of God and needs to be trustworthy. This is most critical when there are no explicit commands from the Lord (sayings of Jesus) that speak to the issue. By extension we might say that the same applies if there are no biblical texts that speak directly to the issue. A good proportion of his recommendations in First Corinthians fit this last category of providing teaching and instruction in areas where there are no sayings or teachings from Jesus. This kind of activity invariably becomes inscripturated when they end up in Paul's letter and are passed on to the church. But it is not like the revelation that he claims to have received about the gospel that he preaches and other things related to it.

For Paul, then, much of what underwrites teaching in the church belongs to this category of a trustworthy teacher who has the Spirit of God and is able to exercise good judgment. It is this that underwrites First Clements repeated references to what he is able to do through the Spirit of God. It shapes the teaching and rhetoric of the whole letter from the Romans to the Corinthians.

First Clement approaches the Hebrew Scriptures as a treasure trove of moral *exempla*. The author appears to be following Paul in this respect. The writer applies the texts or passages to the current state of dissension and discord in Corinth and he reminds his audience to remember Paul's letters to them. In fact, his style seems to be in imitation of how Paul uses some Old Testament passages for moral instruction in the Corinthian correspondence. Paul uses the story of Exodus to say that just as the Israelites were under a cloud but did such-and-such, so the Corinthians must understand it to mean so and so. Likewise, First Clement uses a lot of stories from the Hebrew Scriptures for moral exemplarism. At times the exegesis seems forced, as he seeks to appropriate the lives, acts, and characteristics of various individuals and incidents in the Hebrew Scriptures to make his case about humility, peace, concord, self-sacrifice, etc. But all is in the service of pressing home the fundamental point that the Corinthians need to be as one body working together to exemplify the image of Christ in them. At one point he adopts the example of Roman military efficiency and togetherness to describe what he has in mind and parallels that with the body and its various parts working together. The body metaphor seems to appropriate Paul's own use of that metaphor in First Corinthians 12:12–3; the military imagery seems to be all his own:

> Brothers, let us live as soldiers with all zeal in [following] his faultless orders. Let us consider those who fight for our leaders, how orderly, how obediently, how submissively they accomplish their orders. Not all are commanders, commanders of thousands, of hundreds, of fifty, etc. Each in his own order completes those things ordered by the king and his leaders. The great cannot exist without the small, nor the small without the great. There is a certain intermingling in every respect and benefit in these [orders]. Let us take our body [as an example]. The head is nothing without the feet nor the feet without the head. The least important members off our body are necessary and useful for the whole body. Rather, all work together and employ a united obedience so that the whole body can be healthy [saved]. (First Clement 37.1–5)[42]

Yet, even as the writer of First Clement commands the Corinthians to take up Paul's letter and even imitates Paul's method, he does not always repeat exactly what Paul does. Paul uses the terms *typoi* and *typikos* (types) in 1 Corinthians 10:6 and 10:11 respectively for the examples he appeals to from the Hebrew Scriptures. First Clement, however, does not use *tupoi* or *tupikos* though he means to represent the same idea. It is a cautionary tale, because if the writer did not tell us that he knew First Corinthians, we would be inclined to say that because he does not use *tupoi* and *tupikos* but chooses instead *hupodeigmata* (5.1; 6.1; 46.1; 63.1; 55.1), when he means examples or types, he probably did not have First Corinthians. After all, he was writing on the same subject, and also imitating Paul in other ways. Yet, here we are with a choice of vocabulary that stands apart from the very source that he claims to have. Instead of repeating Paul's lexical choices, First Clement's use of *hypodeigmata* is similar to how Old Testament exemplars are used in Hebrews 11.[43]

The command to take up Paul's letter presupposes the authority of Paul. So, without saying it, First Clement assumes that the words of Paul are sacrosanct. Whether this leads invariably to a conception of Paul's letters as scripture is in one sense a matter of definition and nomenclature. It also reflects on exactly how one conceives of the relationship between "scripture" and authoritative tradition or teaching, and whether the latter entails a conception of scripture even before it is made explicit or formalized. The distinction may be a matter of indifference to First Clement.

FIRST CLEMENT'S CONCEPTION OF SCRIPTURE

So what exactly is Clement's conception of scripture, if he has one? First things first: Clement uses scripture profusely. Some are exact quotations that match the LXX and the canonical New Testament. Some are inexact. Here it is not always clear whether they are allusions or paraphrases. In the case of the former there is a wide spectrum of uses or appropriations that can qualify as allusions. But in almost all cases the ideas or some of the ideas entailed in the antecedent text are implied in the allusions. Paraphrases are more difficult to pin down, because it is possible for a paraphrase to use words that do not even appear in the antecedent text and yet be able to capture the meaning or some of the meanings implied in the prior text. First Clement's uses cover the entire spectrum. This also attaches to the words or circumlocutions or signals that he uses to indicate his appropriations. The most common place to look is his use of the word "scripture" (*graphe*) and its corollary, the phrase, "it is written" (*gegraptai*). He uses others like, "it says" (*legei*), *eipen, phesi,* etc., or "a saying" (*logos*), to indicate God speaking or the speech or words of some prophet or biblical character.

So, for example, at 23.3 it has "this scripture where it says" (*he graphe aute hopou legei*), then he cites a passage that is not attested in any known scripture: New Testament, Old Testament, or Apocrypha. Again at 23.3 he has "as the scripture also testifies" (*kai tes graphes*); at 23.3–4 where he writes, "may this scripture be far removed from us that says. . . ." At 28.2, he has "for the scripture somewhere says" (referring to Ps 139: 7–8); at 29.2, "for it is written" (Deut 2:8–9); at 29.3, "and in another place it says" (Deut 4:34; 14:2; Num 18:27); at 34.6: "for the scripture says" (*legei gar he graphe*); at 35.7: "for the scripture says" (*legei gar he graphe*); at 42.5: "for the scripture says" (*legei gar he graphe*); at 45.1–3, "the sacred scriptures" (*tas hieras grapsas*); at 44.6, "*graphe*" (scriptures); and at 46.2, "*gegraptai gar*" (for it is written). As we can see, First Clement is constantly referring to scripture: "somewhere it says," "it is written," "God said," "for he said," "for he himself calls us through the Holy Spirit" (referring to Jesus and then quoting Psalm 34:11–17, 19 at 22.1–7).

First Clement makes the case for the Jewish origins or Jewishness of being Christian. It lays out in great detail how Christian belief and practice originate from the Hebrew Scriptures. It speaks implicitly about the authority of the Hebrew Scriptures and stakes its own claim to authority for being an epistle sent from the church of Rome whose lineage includes Peter and Paul. In chapter 2 it states that "the commandments and righteous demands of the Lord were inscribed upon the tablets of your hearts" (8). This alludes to the Hebrew Scriptures, the giving of the Law on tablets, to Paul's own language in the Corinthian correspondences, and so on, and so on (including Proverbs 7:3). The writer of First Clement uses much of the scriptures at his disposal; and in his use of both the Hebrew Scriptures and what we will come to know as the New Testament, and a few passages in the apocrypha, he actually attests to the authority of the New Testament sources that he uses as of the same nature as the sources from the Hebrew Scriptures. The apocryphal sources, he considers authoritative too.

First Clement also mentions as scripture passages that we have not been able to locate: at 17.6 (presumably attributed to Moses or from Exodus). Whether this derives from an oral tradition or textual traditions of obscure origins is not clear. Whatever the case may be, First Clement attests to a notion of scriptural authority that is both implicit and explicit. It is explicit in its references to scripture—"what is written," "it says," etc.—and it is implicit in how it presents Christian belief and teaching. It links Christian thought with the traditions associated with Paul and Peter and originating in Jesus. It makes plain that the Letters of Paul (at least one of them to the Corinthians) have the status of being authoritative texts along the same lines as the teachings of Jesus. So without actually setting out any list of books as the authoritative collection of the Church in Rome, First Clement, an authoritative letter from the Romans to the Corinthians, leaves little doubt as to what underwrites its authority and the authoritative traditions that are foundational to the Christian community.

Citing or alluding to unknown sources is of a different order than quoting what has come to be known as apocrypha. Still, the use of material from the apocrypha poses its own problems. This may complicate matters, and perhaps put in doubt whether the writer of First Clement was not confused about "scripture," because it quotes or alludes a few times to sources that are not to be found in the canonical Old Testament (by which I mean the Hebrew Scriptures in the Greek or LXX version) or the canonical New Testament. But this is in a way a problem of our own historical distance and making.

If we understand the derivative nature of the notion of scripture for the early followers of Jesus Christ, it may be less problematic. It derives from contemporary Jewish communities around them. Those in Judaea and Galilee would have been most conversant with the scriptural sources used in the synagogues of Palestine. Those in the early Christian circles beyond Judaea and Galilee would be exposed to whatever the earliest Christian missionaries, including Paul, took as scripture. So the use of noncanonical Old Testament sources by First Clement does not pose the kind of problem that it does, as some assume. Rather it shows how the very idea of the apocrypha came to be construed later on.

First Clement's idea of scripture, then, begins with Paul and with whatever was understood as scripture by contemporary Jews with whom the earliest Christians (most of whom were Jews) were in contact constituted the notion and scope of scripture for these Christians. The upshot of this is that if they found themselves among Jews who appropriated a said book as scripture they could not object to that designation. They had to accept it as such. Of course, in Paul's case, he quotes almost entirely from the Septuagint. Although there were books belonging to the Septuagint that were later considered noncanonical, he could easily have quoted them.

In the case of First Clement, if the writer uses a text or passage from a work that is not found among the texts of the canonical Old Testament, and he cites it as scripture, he does so almost certainly because he assumes or believes that those works are accepted as scripture among the Jews of the first century that he knows or knows about. It would not make any sense otherwise, since it is not his prerogative to determine what counts or does not count as Jewish scripture. The assumptions of the Christians of Rome may turn out to be wrong, but it does not invalidate their hermeneutical principle. So, if First Clement claims a source as scripture and it turns out to be an "error" or a false attribution, it is likely not one of its own making. It is a structural error, predicated on the implicit relationship between the conception of Jewish scriptures held in the first century and the notion of scripture that the early Christians came to formulate. As long as the concept remains fluid within the Jewish tradition up until the first or early second century, it remains the same for the earliest Christians who are dependent on Jewish scripture(s).

To put it another way: the earliest Christians, almost all of them Jews, derived their notion of scriptural authority first from the Jewish or Hebrew Scriptures as known to them. If they were reading it in Greek, then it was the Septuagint. Paul's conception of scripture, as outlined in his letters, assumes this much. Those who follow after him, both Jews and non-Jews, assume the same. So if they find themselves in a situation where a group of Jews use a text as scripture, they assume that text is scripture. They do not themselves have the grounds on which to determine which Jewish texts are scripture or not. The only safeguard is that Paul usually quotes from the Septuagint or LXX. So, invariably, the LXX is scripture for the earliest Christians, both Jews and non-Jews. If anyone should say to them such and such a text is scripture among us Jews, they have no way of objecting to that. If the writer of First Clement understands that a particular source he is using is thought of as scripture among his Jewish contemporaries he will likely cite those sources as such.

First Clement quotes profusely from the sources. Of the Hebrew Scriptures alone or the Old Testament, W. Wrede noted that there were more than 70 citations and 20 reminiscences, as he puts it. Adolf von Harnack put it at 120 Old Testament quotations and allusions.[44] As for the canonical New Testament, it proves difficult to give an exact estimate given the richly allusive nature of First Clement's language about the gospel, Jesus Christ, and Christian belief and practice.[45] It could be as high as 250 given how one counts, that would be on the conservative end. This would then put its total count of both Old Testament and putatively New Testament quotations and allusions to close to 350, using Wrede and Harnack's figures for the Old Testament. One estimate suggests that First Clement has as close to 400 quotations and allusions to scripture. That is on the high end, but it may not be that far off.

This also puts in perspective the significance of First Clement's quotations or allusions from the apocrypha. If there are nearly 250 scriptural quotations and allusions in First Clement in the letter, to find even 10 such references (4 percent or less) to apocryphal sources may not be that remarkable. If there are 400 quotations the figure drops to 2.5 percent. At the same time, it bears pointing out that the number of references becomes even less significant if the passages in question do not contribute in any way toward establishing any major views or ideas presented in the work, and function mostly for illustrative purposes. In which case, they are mostly superfluous or at best decorative. Still, they are there and need to be accounted for in terms of how First Clement construes authoritative traditions and scripture.

What about First Clement's use of material from sources related to the Gospels or traditions about Jesus that are not to be found in the canonical Gospels or elsewhere in extant material? Michael F. Bird has a way of dealing with the two sayings of a Gospel nature that First Clement mentions but that cannot be found in any sayings source or other Gospel.[46] They are found in 1 Clement 13.1–2 and 46.7–8:

> Most of all, let us remember the words of the Lord Jesus, which he spoke as he taught gentleness and patience. For he said this: "Show mercy, so that you may receive mercy; forgive, so that you may be forgiven. As you do, so shall it be done to you. As you give, so shall it be given to you. As you judge, so shall you be judged. As you show kindness, so shall kindness be shown to you. With the measure you use it will be measured to you. (First Clement 13.1–2)[47]

The second reads as follows:

> Remember the words of Jesus our Lord, for he said: "Woe to that person! Rather than cause one of my elect to sin, it would have been good for that one not to have been born. It would have been better for that person to have been tied to a millstone and cast into the sea, rather than pervert one of my elect." (First Clement 46.7–8)[48]

Bird argues that "the appeals to 'remember' might be all the more pertinent for sayings such as this one not found in the Gospels (i.e., the *agrapha*) since there is no written deposit that we know of containing it, so it could only be preserved in corporate memory."[49] It is an interesting argument, but it comes with some baggage. Isn't First Clement then testament in its own right that this is a saying of Jesus, and therefore a witness independent of other sayings? But more importantly, anyone who is familiar with the four canonical Gospels, and especially with the Sermon of the Mount, can easily make out the similarities between these sayings in 13.1–2 and some of the sayings in the canonical Gospels.

This is indeed as it should be, for when he says "let us remember," in 13.1–2, he is assuming something that is common knowledge among the church in Rome and in Corinth. He appears then to be paraphrasing from a source that they all know. One does not have to seek another source other than that. That is what is presumed. Bird himself mentions in relation to First Clement 13.1–2 that the author "introduces an agraphon that is analogous to Matt 5:7; 6:14; 7:1–2, 12 and Luke 6:31, 36–38."[50] It is just as well to suggest that the agraphon is in fact nothing more than a version of the sayings of which it is analogous that has been repeated among them or has been crafted by the writer at just this moment. It does not have to be more than that, so as to constitute an entirely unknown source. As for the second passage, that too appears to be made of paraphrases from different passages in the canonical Gospels.

So there is no need to posit a collective "corporate memory" for this, an idea that presumes that the saying remained in oral tradition. Or, to put it another way, First Clement does not make any claims here that it is presenting a saying from Jesus that is not to be found in any form in any of the canonical Gospels. Putting the saying or the statements in quotation marks gives the impression that together the words constitute a distinct saying that must have a source in which the words appear just as they appear here in First Clement. But even the prefatory, "the words of Jesus our Lord, for he said," is not necessarily a claim to exact quotation. Moreover, even if it was an oral tradition, the mere fact that it is a shared tradition between the church of Rome and the church of Corinth means that it was as good as "written."

Here is a basic question: how did First Clement manage all the scriptural citations and allusions if the writer did not have the texts and sources readily available or at hand? What would the nature of the sources have been? Scrolls, codices, other forms? We do not know. Did he have a compendium? Did he go to any of the synagogues in Rome? Or did the church in Rome at this time already have its own versions of the Hebrew Scriptures? Did they possess copies of scrolls of the LXX or fragments or some compilations from which he quotes?

Given that Paul modeled his initial activities on synagogue practices (Acts confirms this), in terms of teaching and instruction (like the *haftarah* he uses), did they follow synagogue practice and have copies of Old Testament texts made? Most likely. Otherwise, they would not have had a basis for the teaching Paul and others did. First Clement's profuse use of Hebrew Scriptures bears witness to this reality. So he has an Old Testament textual tradition available to him.

From the Pentateuch or Torah, First Clement quotes from Genesis, Exodus, Numbers, Deuteronomy, but not Leviticus. First Clement uses or alludes to passages from the Prophetical books of Isaiah, Jeremiah, and Ezekiel. He also uses Psalms, Job, Wisdom, Jonah, Proverbs, Daniel, and First Samuel. For the NT he uses a lot of Hebrews, and passages from First Corinthians, Mark, Luke, and Matthew. There are references to Acts, James, First Peter, and Ephesians, though no references to the Gospel of John.[51]

First Clement uses the stories of many Old Testament characters for moral instruction and highlights them: Cain and Abel (four), Jacob and Esau, Joseph, Abraham, Enoch, Elijah, Elisha, Ezekiel, Rahab, Moses, David, the Levites, Esther, etc. It would be interesting to compare these vignettes with Josephus's treatment of these characters. Needless to say, First Clement appears to have knowledge of Biblical traditions that Josephus also attests in his *Antiquities*. If it is not too out of place to say it, First Clement knows traditions analogous to "Josephus's Bible," if I may use such an expression, and a few other sources to which Josephus does not bear witness.

THE CHURCH OF CORINTH AND THE MEMORY AND LEGACY OF PAUL IN ROME

Some scholars have taken the lack of explicit quotations from Paul's letters as a sign that First Clement is somehow indifferent to Paul's authority and even ignorant of Paul's letters. This is pure fiction. However, it is repeated with regularity to prove that Paul's letters were nowhere in sight in the later decades of the first century and even in the first half of the second century prior to Marcion's supposed creation of the New Testament. For now it should be stated without ambiguity that First Clement does not make any sense without Paul's authority and without some understanding that that authority is linked to his writings, some of which were well known to the church in Roman and in Corinth. First Clement assumes that without Paul there would be no relationship or connection between the two communities.

By asking them to read Paul's letter (or letters), First Clement signals that it is quoting the entire letter to them. What I mean is this: if it were practicable, the writer(s) of First Clement would have quoted the entirety of First Corinthians. So we should assume that as the foundation upon which it constructs whatever it presents to them. The lack of explicit quotations from Paul's letters, then, means something quite different from what scholars usually make of it. It is not an indication that the writer is indifferent to Paul. That would be absurd. It is that once he signals that Paul is the foundation of the church in Corinth, and that his writings should be picked up and read, there is no need for him to quote all of that material to them. The authority of Paul is the foundation upon which the authority of the church of Rome stands; and it is upon that same authority that it writes First Clement. It is that simple. This may also explain why First Clement mimics the patterns in First Corinthians by using the Old Testament writings as exemplary texts for Christian moral instruction. It learns from Paul. That is the primary mode in which it speaks. The letter is in this fundamental sense an expression or articulation of Paul's legacy, to the Corinthians (first) and then to the Romans.

Historically, Paul established the church in Corinth before he went to Rome; and his Letter to the Romans pays homage to the church in Corinth, since it was written either at Corinth or Cenchrea, the port for Corinth six miles away. To which then can be added other ancient traditions it mines.

Telling the Christians of Corinth to go and read Paul's earlier letter or letters to them saves the writer of First Clement from having to quote extensively from those correspondences. Everything presented in First Clement, then, ought to be understood as a supplement to what the Corinthians already possess from Paul.

My point is this: if they already have First Corinthians, First Clement does not have to quote it to them. He merely has to allude to it, because he has already pointed to them that they should go and look at First Corinthians, and he also says there are other scriptures from which they have been taught. This seems to suggest that they have other Pauline texts too. However, that is not the case with the Old Testament or any Jewish scriptures. In this respect, and from a historical standpoint, it is remarkable and also revealing that

Eusebius preserves a section of a letter from Dionysius, bishop of Corinth in the later half of the second century (c. 170 CE), to Soter the bishop of Rome that has a reference to First Clement written more than seven decades before. In the letter Dionysius mentions that the Roman Letter to the Corinthians (First Clement) is read in the church of Corinth regularly (Eusebius, *HE* 4.23.9, 11). The Corinthians had not lost the memory of that past and continued to see themselves in a special relationship with the church of Rome. It does not sound as if the practice was a recent one either. It seemed long-standing.

First Clement establishes a link between the church in Rome in Italy and the church in Corinth in Achaia/Achaea; and speaks in such a way as to claim a strong sense of a shared history; and of belonging to something universal. The significance of this Roman Letter to the Corinthians cannot be overestimated. It stands with the Letter to the Hebrews as a testament to how others besides Paul the apostle to the Gentiles understood the teaching of Paul and the gospel of Jesus before the end of the first century. These were not incompetent individuals who did not know what they were writing about. They speak or write with clarity, sophistication, and insight. They are like the two sides of a diptych: Clement from what might be called a Roman viewpoint that is both Jewish and non-Jewish (given the makeup of the church in Rome), and the Letter to the Hebrews, from a specifically Jewish standpoint, or at least, with a deep knowledge of Jewish religious life. Both use the Hebrew Scriptures profusely but to slightly different ends. You cannot have these two texts and say that the Christians of Rome did not know what it is they believed. If you compare these two with the second-century Gnostic-inspired writings, you have a clear sign of just what is unusual and strange about the second-century texts.

While the attribution to the said Clement is reasonable, it is not a fact, although if he was the bishop of Rome at the time, or the titular head of the churches in Rome, then it is likely that he was involved in writing the letter. As for the various stories about his lineage, we don't need any of it to make sense of what the letter represents. Lightfoot goes into exhaustive detail. So there is no need to revisit it.

For my part, the important emphasis should be on how well the letter captures the mood of Christianity in Rome and Corinth after the Pauline epistles, and the extent to which it shows acquaintance with some of the other texts that form the canon of the New Testament, especially the Letter to the Hebrews, which led some to suggest as early as the second century that he may have written it. That is, that the person who wrote the letter to the Corinthians from the Church of Rome was probably the author of Hebrews as well. The better and most likely possibility is that the writer of First Clement knew Hebrews, and so used and alluded to a lot of its themes. As a simple exercise, if you read Hebrews before reading First Clement you can hear Hebrews resounding in your ears as you read some sections of First Clement. Likewise, if you have some knowledge of the Pauline epistles, you can detect resonances in First Clement, even without his explicit citations of Paul. This goes a long way to discounting the earnest efforts of those who say there is no reference or mention of Paul's letters anywhere prior to Marcion in the second century. The beginning of First Clement opens like one of Paul's letter, with the "grace and peace to you all," etc.

Back to the *Didache* and First Clement: Here the ecclesiology is similar. For the *Didache* we have a collection of churches that lie behind the work, with a collective sense of their belonging to one shared religious outlook. The writer of First Clement assumes some such reality when he writes to the Corinthians, a sensibility that is also reflected in the fact that the Corinthians asked for the help of the Christians in Rome in the first place. From the very beginning, then, the Corinthians and the Romans see themselves as belonging to a collective, universal reality that links various churches in various towns and cities, all following the gospel or teachings of Jesus Christ.

The ecclesiology of First Clement has attracted a lot of comment. It is not a surprise. Its view of leadership seems clearly in line with a collegial model of presbyters. It speaks in this sense about the leadership of the church in Corinth, and it assumes some such pattern with the church in Rome, when it adopts the third person plural in some sections of the work. It should be added, however, that the use of a collective "we" does not in itself imply a college of elders. But in this case it seems to imply it.

We have a hybrid model. A lot depends on local circumstances: how large the community is, where they are able to meet, what is the local political order and pattern of representation, etc. In other words, it is possible to have in some small towns or villages just one person who heads the community of Christians; this will give then a conception of a single presbyter (i.e., as bishop). Whereas in places where there are a number of people who are identified as the leaders of the community, it would seem very natural to speak of a group of presbyters and perhaps one bishop or presbyter who oversees all. Yet even in the case of a very diffuse sense of leadership, one person or a still small group of maybe two or three will be considered the putative leaders of the community. So in many ways we are dealing with a sociological fact. No matter how it begins, eventually one person will be identified as the putative leader among a collective or in a singular role.

First Clement 42 adopts a historical point of view about what the apostles received as a mandate from the Lord Jesus Christ. In spelling out that mandate, it reaches back to the Hebrew Scriptures to point out that it was ordained that wherever they went in their preaching, after establishing churches, they should appoint bishops and deacons over them. First Clement cites the LXX of Isaiah 60:17: "I will appoint their bishops in righteousness and their deacons in faith." It could be argued that this is the pattern that is assumed to be the norm that should obtain in the life of the church. It is a theological norm derived from Israel's historical past, but it is not a current sociological fact. That reality is pointed out in chapter 44 where the text describes what has actually obtained.

First Clement 44 speaks of the office of the bishop and then later of the presbyters who have gone forth, that is, passed away. In this context, it is also reminding the readers of the presbyters who were appointed by the apostles. As long as the apostles were around, they were the putative heads of the churches. So they had presbyters. There was no need to have bishops as such, unless the idea or title of "bishop" and "presbyter" were at this point interchangeable. It is possible to morph the two realities together by saying that there will be a college or group of presbyters (or elders), and among them one will be designated the bishop, the putative head of the community. In this respect, they will be fulfilling what is said in Isaiah 60.17 (I will appoint their bishops in righteousness and their deacons in faith), while also recognizing the kind of collective leadership that the apostles exemplified and instituted.

Didache 15.1 has the combination of bishops and deacons in the way that it appears in the quotation from Isaiah 60:17 found in First Clement 42, and so states: "elect for yourself bishops and deacons worthy of the Lord." These exemplary men are to exercise the ministry of prophets and teachers, functions that are described in the preceding chapters 11ff. Yet, the *Didache* gives the impression that the bishops are not quite in place, and that much of the current leadership of the churches from which the document emerges devolves on apostles, prophets, and teachers. It appears that the prophets and teachers play the role of bishops.

When we get to the letters of Ignatius of Antioch in the early second century, we encounter an even more intriguing reality. He does not speak of himself as the bishop of Antioch. He is the bishop of Syria. That is a much more expansive notion of a bishop. It is closer to what we will come to know later as a patriarchate. Ignatius in many ways presents himself as the patriarch of Syria. Ignatius claims all of Syria.

However, in his Letter to the Magnesians, Ignatius describes a church order that blends the role of bishop and presbyter in the way that I intimated a short while back. In Magnesians 13.1 he describes a leadership made up of a bishop, presbyters, and deacons. If this is descriptive of the Magnesians, then it means there is presumably one bishop, several presbyters (who constitute a council of elders), and deacons.[52] This model could be used in different ways as befitting particular circumstances, I imagine. For even in Ignatius's own case, if he is the bishop of Syria (the entire province), he would not be bishop over one church but all the churches of Syria. In which case, each local congregation would either have to be headed by just a council of elders, or by bishops who were deemed auxiliaries to Ignatius, who holds the preeminent position. Similarly, if one's jurisdiction covered an entire city with more than one congregation, then there could be either only councils of presbyters overseeing the respective congregations or bishops who were auxiliary bishops in relation to the one pre-eminent bishop in the city. First Clement does not preclude the possibility of different congregations within the city of Rome, even as it speaks in the singular about both the church of Rome and the church of Corinth. That sense of the singular, as in one community of Christians, pilgrims and strangers in the world, who may be found in Rome and in Corinth, is in imitation of a conception of the people of God in the Hebrew Scriptures upon which First Clement is so dependent. First Clement appropriates the Hebrew Scriptures in a way that Josephus would have recognized, since he rewrites much of the Hebrew Bible himself; but also in way that Josephus would have repudiated or at least refuses to acknowledge.

JOSEPHUS, HEBREWS, THE TEMPLE, AND FIRST CLEMENT: BEFORE AND AFTER 70 CE

In the *Antiquities* and in *Against Apion* Josephus writes about the sacrificial system of Jewish religious cult in the historical present. He is not the only Jewish author or source that does this. Other sources, including the Mishnah (e.g., tractate Middot), do sometimes write about the sacrifices as if they were a present and ongoing reality.[53] No one who reads any of these sources takes them as historical facts, namely, that the Temple still exists. In fact, the sources in question assume that everyone knows that the Temple does not exist.

Should we then say that in all instances this is what should be assumed? Well, it is not that simple. If we already know the time of composition of the work, then the judgment is easy to make. But if the time of composition of the source is in dispute, then it cannot be determined so easily. So, for example, when we encounter the Letter to the Hebrews, we cannot take it for granted that what it says about the Temple and its sacrifices admit of no difficulty in terms of determining the date of the work. If the writer composed his work after 70 CE and writes as if the Temple still exists, then we have a problem.

For now it should be said that it would have been rather pathological to pretend the Temple sacrifices were still being done day-by-day (as the writer puts it) when everyone knows the Temple no longer exists. Why? Here is where both Josephus and Tacitus's testimonies about the oracle that was making the rounds in the East bears on this issue. As was often the case, people in different parts of the Roman world cared about what was going on in other parts of the empire. What the Romans were doing in Syria, Judaea, and Egypt was on everyone's mind. The destruction of the Temple in Jerusalem was in that respect a worldwide event, as far as the Roman Empire was concerned. The Romans made sure of this, built a Triumphal Arch for Titus and commemorated the event in other ways. This was not a minor event in the annals of Rome's imperial might, and all the way to the end of the first century it would be talked about. It was a world historical event for Romans and Jews, and for non-Jews within and beyond the Roman Empire. It was an object lesson. Pliny's *Panegyricus* made sure to disabuse anyone of any doubt.

No one in his right mind could pretend otherwise. So for anyone to write to an audience within the Roman Empire and to pretend that the event had not happened would have been laughable in the extreme. Josephus's own works made sure of this, as his *Jewish War*, which appeared between 75 and 79 CE provided a detailed account of the event. Josephus offered his own memorial of sorts in his writings.

The most unproblematic reading of Hebrews, and especially of its detailed argument in chapters 8 through 10, is that the Temple still stood when these words were written. Otherwise it would have been the height of lunacy to say, for example, at 8:13: "In speaking of a 'new covenant,' he has made the first one obsolete. And what is obsolete and growing old will soon disappear." If the Temple had been destroyed when he wrote this, he should rather have said, "what was obsolete and old had just disappeared." The entire argument of the work presumes the existence of the Temple, the priesthood tied to the temple, and the temple sacrifices. The writer of Hebrews is not writing at a much later time and staging the event as if it were earlier. There is nothing in the work to suggest such a construction.

First Clement too mentions the sacrifices and speaks in the historical present. Now for someone in Rome writing after 70 CE to write as if the Temple and its sacrifices were still being performed would be ludicrous. At worst, the historical present of First Clement is no different from Josephus in Rome writing in the historical present about the sacrifices in his works. In the case of Josephus no one doubts that this must be the case, because he was there when the Temple was destroyed. The historical present of First Clement also assumes what Josephus knows; and what Romans know because they celebrated the event in 71 CE and have monuments commemorating it: The Temple of Peace and the Arch of Titus.

The references from Tacitus and Suetonius about the oracle that was believed in the East about a future messianic ruler provides a clue as to how we should read Hebrews, anonymous work and all. Taictus, Suetonius, and Josephus are in agreement on the widespread nature of the oracle and its interpretations in the East.

When Titus concluded his campaign, he dismissed most of the large cohort of troops he had gathered in Jerusalem. According to Josephus, he kept a small contingent to accompany him in his travels but returned most of the troops to their respective basis, from where they have been called to join the assault on Jerusalem. Each one of those contingents (Josephus mentions some of them) would have carried the news of the destruction of Jerusalem wherever they traveled and to their home bases. Some went as far as Cappadocia and the town of Euphrates in Asia Minor. Others went toward the east.

Once he had dispatched them, Titus himself then proceeded on what was in every way a victory tour north toward Caesarea Maritima and then to Caesarea Philippi, where, according to Josephus, he held games in which 2,500 of the Jewish captives form the campaign in Jerusalem were offered for sport. He would eventually make it to Antioch in Syria and would also receive emissaries from the Parthians. The news had spread. His very presence in Antioch and elsewhere was to make it clear to everyone that he could not be challenged, and that the fate of Jerusalem awaited anyone who dared. The use of the Jewish captives was deliberate. Titus did not have to wait for a triumphal celebration in Rome to prove the point.

At Antioch the non-Jewish residents appealed to him to expel the Jews from the city. Without any sense of contradiction Titus responded that the Jews of Antioch would not have anywhere to go since Jerusalem, which would have been the place for them, lay in ruins. What irony? The man who had just destroyed the city and had Jewish captives in tow felt sympathy for the Jews of Antioch. Was this not a display of magnanimity? Perhaps, for, after all, he could say that, unlike the other Jews in Galilee and in Jerusalem, the Jews of Antioch had not revolted. Consequently, they needed to be treated differently, even if their non-Jewish neighbors were keen to exploit the fate of the Jews in Jerusalem for their own purposes at this time.

Josephus makes no mention of Christians in Antioch, though we might guess that there should have been Christians there given what we learn from Paul's Letter to the Galatians. Or was it rather that most of the Christians of Antioch could not be distinguished or separated from the Jews of Antioch because most of them were Jewish, God-fearers, or proselytes? This also raises an interesting question, not so much for the Christians in Antioch, whether Jewish or Gentile, but Christians who may have been in Galilee and Judaea at the beginning of the revolt: Did they join? Did they flee? Were they allowed to flee?

If, as Josephus reports, the rebels (the Zealots and the Sicarii) did everything they could to prevent people from fleeing Jerusalem, then we may have to assume that whatever Christian population existed in Jerusalem probably met the same lot as everyone else. In any case, it is far more likely that most of the Christians of Jerusalem left the city after the judicial murder of James the brother of Jesus in 62 CE, so there were probably no Christians left when the revolt began in 66 CE.

But what about places like Galilee, over which Josephus had exercised general command? We simply do not know. However, Eusebius of Caesarea states in his *Ecclesiastical History* that the Christians of Judaea and Jerusalem fled to Pella, east of Samaria on the Jordan river, during the war. Whatever the truth of this claim, it should be clear that after the suppression of the revolt in Galilee and the devastation and depredations of Jerusalem whatever Christian population existed in Judaea would have been next to nothing.

Caesarea Maritima, Caesarea Philippi, and other towns that had not been subject to any Roman military action, and above all Antioch, stood the best chance of having any Christian populations even if Josephus makes no mention of them. If there were any such Christian groups, they would certainly be in no doubt as to who the Romans and every one of their neighbors thought ruled the world.

If, as it seems the case, many in that period had come to believe that there were oracles that had foretold of a kingly or messianic figure arising from the east, as Tacitus, Josephus, and Suetonius claimed, this would have put the Christian-Jewish proclamation of Jesus as the Messiah in a most interesting and peculiar light. For as both Tacitus and Suetonius contend, the unfolding of events in Judaea made it abundantly clear that the prophecies or omens pointed to none other than Vespasian. Josephus also chimed in with his own personal insertion into this story, claiming to have predicted that much, a story Suetonius repeats.

In such an environment, the Christians would stand out as the most impish and recalcitrant of the lot, who, in spite of Vespasian and Titus's triumph, would have the audacity to proclaim otherwise. But did they have such audacity? Or had most of their texts that spoke about Jesus as the Messiah already been written before 70 CE? Notice that there is not a single reference to any Christian writer whose works were deemed to undermine this new imperial theology that Tacitus, Suetonius, and Josephus all preached about Vespasian. At the same time, we should not overlook the trauma of this event for Jews and even for Gentiles in the area of Syria, Galilee, and east of the Jordan.

Part of Josephus's impulse for writing the *Jewish War* was to commit the trauma of the destruction of Jerusalem, the Temple, and much of the Jewish population present in the city at the time to historical memory: initially for those who spoke and read Aramaic and subsequently for those who spoke or read Greek. That initial impulse to write in Aramaic was a reflex that serves an important critical function and should not go unappreciated. The choice of Aramaic for the first version of the *Jewish War* is tied to Josephus's claim that he wrote it for the Jews of the inner-lands or the up-country in Mesopotamia to apprise them about what had actually and truly taken place, over and against current reports or versions of the story that were circulating. He had an initial sense of this duty when emissaries from the Parthians made their way toward Titus during his travels soon after the destruction of Jerusalem. Josephus himself had also witnessed the capture of members of the royal house of Adiabene in northern Mesopotamia, then resident in Jerusalem, who had provided support for the rebellion against the Romans.

FAULTLINES: PLINY'S *PANEGYRICUS*, FIRST CLEMENT, AND THE CRIME OF *MAIESTAS*

In the previous chapter I quoted Pliny the Younger's *Panegyricus* to underline the state of fear that existed in Domitian's Rome. I used a few passages from the *Panegyricus* where Pliny contrasts Domitian with Trajan, setting out and comparing what they did in particular situations. When he makes such comparisons, Pliny settles on acts and deeds and so it is difficult to criticize him for being a biased reporter. Still, some historians quibble. Brian W. Jones, for example, claims Pliny is simply biased and in that sense cannot be fully relied upon, even though Pliny made those comparisons to his fellow senators and among his fellow Romans who knew those facts.[54] When Pliny turns to praising Trajan, however, we might say that all bets are off. He can easily be criticized for doing the very thing he decries among his generation in the time of Domitian. But is that in fact the case?

In his letters Pliny discusses more than once that there is nothing wrong with praise when it is merited, and he in particular does not disdain it when it is offered to him. In fact, he loves to be praised when it is merited. So it is not the matter of being praised or praising something that is at issue. The important differential is what one is praised for. His objections are about those who praise for the wrong reasons and those who praise what is not praiseworthy. In his particular role as panegyrist he opens himself to such scrutiny. Panegyric always invites questions about truth and representation. Both types of questions reflect on the sincerity of the panegyrist. It is one of the most obvious objections made against the value of any praise poem. Can a praise poem be credible and/or truthful? Are the words expressed by a praise poet or functionary to be believed?

In a recent volume on Latin Panegyric, Shadi Bartsch draws attention to the problem of sincerity, the bane of the genre,[55] by examining Pliny's *Panegyricus*. She seems indifferent to some of the historical context and literary framework of the *Panegyricus*. Her argument does not consider the role of biography and history in this particular panegyric. She questions Pliny's description of the times under Domitian and the fact that Pliny climbed the ladder of preferment at this time and still lamented the times. Interestingly, she does mention that the Emperor Trajan himself, who was the subject of the panegyric, was part of that very group of people who had prospered in their careers, like Pliny, during Domitian's reign. If Pliny was both ungrateful and insincere, then the same could be said of Trajan or anyone who managed to advance in their careers during the time of Domitian.

If it is one's responsibility to praise, and it is a duty imposed on you by the Senate, there is no way out of it. It is a tradition. The critical issue is how one carries on the task responsibly or without losing one's reputation, whatever that reputation may be. Whatever the faults of Pliny's *Panegyricus*, it is clear that its author, Pliny, puts a lot of emphasis on biography, and makes a claim to be venturing into the writing of history. It is not simply a literary memorial or apostrophe comparing Domitian and Trajan. That is the obvious comparison. But it runs deeper. It is about reading, or better yet, writing the history of the so-called good prince or ruler, if you like.

Pliny alludes to Nero, Claudius, Vespasian, and the most recently deceased emperor Nerva. So it is a discourse about *imperium*; which is why the themes about the Senate, its role in Roman society, the populace, the Temples, the gods, etc., are all attended to. I would not call it ideological. I would simply say that it presents a theory and enactment of the good prince, for the lack of a better word. Others have noted this too.

But I insist that the only way Pliny can save himself from sycophancy, given that this is partly implicit in the demand to praise, is to attend to Trajan's life and Pliny's biography of Trajan as presented in the *Panegyricus*. Pliny made specific references to the life that Trajan had actually lived, the details of which were known to his audience. By focusing attention of Trajan's biography, Pliny set certain constraints on himself. There was only so much he could have exaggerated. On Trajan's biography, he is largely correct. Those aspects too are the ones that lead me to my commentary, and so sustain Pliny's criticism of the recent past. If Trajan did not have the biography he had, he would not have been recommended to Nerva as the man for the times. This is one of Pliny's most important claims, whatever else we think of Pliny.

In a context where the responsibility of the panegyrists is also a social, political, and oratorical demand, our questions multiply as to how truly the image of the subject presented in the panegyric reflects the reality of the subject in fact. In one respect, this misses the point. If there is no element of praise, then a panegyric would be nothing more than a résumé of some sort that simply lists the accomplishments of the subject in a way not different from a basic biographical narrative. To present a panegyric or to offer any composition in the register of praise is to go beyond the subject as such, as he exists in fact, to venture an example for commendation and imitation. The *commendatio* depends on comparisons with other accepted or acceptable models and ideals of exemplarity. In the case of the Romans it often demands a comparison with the gods.

It is in its comparisons and idealizations that the praise poem establishes its effectiveness as a truly panegyric work. At its most fundamental the panegyric is dependent on historical and biographical facts, details, or attestations in venturing its many comparisons and idealizations. The salient issue is not whether the poet is sincere. That may be hard to prove in any case. The poet's protestations of his innocence, his defenses of his sincerity, only complicate matters. It does so without necessarily resolving the problem. We may be justified in saying that any and every panegyrist practices an art of "sincere fiction." He is required to describe his subject in idealized terms that everyone knows are not true to fact. At best the panegyric captures hopes and aspirations. We may even be tempted to say that this involves the poet in a certain amount of sanctioned hypocrisy. In this particular case involving Pliny the Younger it may be described as "statutory hypocrisy," because it is required by an act of the Senate that the suffect consul offer praise on his own behalf and on behalf of the Senate. There are limits, however. No one is truly deceived into believing that the poet speaks entirely without being constrained to speak as he does. He is not at liberty not to praise; and his hearers are at liberty to believe only as much of it as they wish to believe.

In Pliny's case this takes on special significance since he goes to some lengths to comment on just what kind of *libertas* he and his fellow Roman possess: what was once lost to him and his contemporaries under Domitian in the recent past and has been restored by Trajan. Pliny's claims about his *libertas* and whether it is true or genuine are among the most interesting aspects of his panegyric. On the face of it, it appears to be a piece of blatant self-contradiction to speak about the liberty of citizens and senators in relation to an emperor who possesses *imperium*. One way of coming to terms with it is simply to accept that for Pliny there is no such thing as an absolute liberty. He does not claim any such notion, nor does he present it even as an ideal. Instead, he situates his conception of *libertas* within the framework of the obedience (*obsequius*) to the laws and to the gods of Rome. Within this framework he speaks to both the "conscript fathers" of the Senate and to the emperor as both subject to the laws and the gods. This idea is fundamental to his view of empire, of the proper expression of Roman power and dominion over other peoples, and so on.

If Pliny is not at liberty not to praise, then the only way to avoid "sincere fictions" about the emperor is not to speak at all. He had practiced this art with exceptional success during the time of Domitian. Presumably, he could have continued to do the same under Trajan, if he had not been so honored by Trajan as suffect consul. Since he was under obligation to speak not only for himself, but also for the entire Senate, his panegyric had to bear some relation to the world as viewed by his fellow senators.

The critical question, as I have already noted, is whether the historical and biographical facts claimed by Pliny the panegyrist are credible and substantiated. It is from that standpoint that we can assess how far and how usefully the panegyrist appropriated his sources or his knowledge of his subject and his times. Would his fellow senators, who were witnesses with him of the most recent past, have questioned his descriptions and interpretations of the past? Was he speaking for them as well in his account of the present? Did they agree with him in his idealizations of Trajan, and what difference would it have made if they did not? The fact that the *Panegyricus* was published answers some of these questions. In an important sense, Pliny's published *Panegyricus* is an authorized, semi-official historical document. The published version rests on the approval or endorsement of the oral version that was presented in the Senate. The version of the *Panegyricus* that he delivered received the fate of previous acts of the senate that he called attention to at *Panegyrius* 75.1: all that the senators "decided to save from oblivion by publishing in the official records and inscribing in bronze." He adds that "hitherto, only the speeches of the emperors were made safe for all time by records of this kind, while our acclamations went no farther that the walls of the senate-house."[56] This new era promises more, and Pliny lays out the contours of that promised future.

He does not sign off without one more salute to Trajan for making him a consul at a time when being a consul did not incur fear and terror (which could be extended to say that an official appointment at the time of Domitian was a dangerous honor as much to be feared as to be desired):

> There is still something which demands praise beyond all else: the fact that when you have made consuls you allow them to act without interference, by which I mean that there are no fears nor perils as regards the Emperor to weaken and destroy their spirit; the consuls will not have to listen to anything against their will nor have decisions forced on them. Our office retains and will retain the respect due to it, and in exercising our authority we need lose none of our peace of mind. Moreover, if the high dignity of the consulate should chance to be diminished, the fault will not be found in the times we live in but in ourselves. So far as rests with our prince, the consuls are free to fill their role as they did before the days of emperors. Is there any proper return we can make you, to match all you have done for us?[57]

In the opening lines of the *Panegyricus* Pliny also laid out a conception of Roman society situated between its reverence for the gods and Jupiter and its devotion to its laws. He celebrated a prince who did not rule without laws and who, though among the gods, did not pretend to be a god: all references intended to show the contrast between Trajan and Domitian.

> For what gift of the gods could be greater and more glorious than a prince whose purity and virtue make him their own equal? If it were still in doubt whether the rulers of the earth were given us by the hazards of chance or by some heavenly power, it would be evident that our emperor at least was divinely chosen for his task; for it was no blind act of fate but Jupiter himself who chose and revealed him in the sight and hearing of us all, among the many altars of the Capitol, in the very place where the god makes his presence as clearly felt as in the heavens and stars. Wherefore, mighty Jupiter, once the

founder and now the preserver of our realm, it is my right and proper duty to address my prayers to you: grant, I pray you, that my speech prove worthy of consul, Senate and prince, that independence, truth, and sincerity mark my every word, and my vote of thanks be as far removed from a semblance of flattery as it is from constraint.[58]

Pliny's words merely extend the imperial theology and ideology of conquest articulated by the Flavians and enshrined in the Temple of Peace, built by Vespasian after the conquest of Jerusalem and Judaea. Pliny's final prayer at the end of the *Panegyricus* implores the gods on behalf of the empire and its prince:

To end my speech, I call on the gods, the guardians and defenders of our empire, speaking as consul on behalf of all humanity: and to you in particular, Capitoline Jupiter, I address my prayer that you shall continue your benefits, and augment the great gifts you have bestowed by making them perpetual. You heard our prayers under a bad prince; now give ear to our wishes on behalf of his opposite. We are not burdening you with vows—we do not pray for peace, concord, and serenity, nor for wealth and honours: our desire is simple, all-embracing, and unanimous: the safety of our prince. This is no new concern we ask of you, for it was you who took him under your protection when you snatched him from the jaws of that monster of rapacity; for at the time when all the peaks were tottering to their fall, no one could have stood high above them all and remained untouched except by your intervention. So he escaped the notice of the worst of emperors [Domitian], though he could not remain unnoticed by the best [Nerva]. It was you too who gave him clear signs of your interest as he set out to join his army, when you yielded to him your own name and glory; and you who spoke your opinion through the voice of the Emperor [Nerva], when you chose a son for him, a father for us, a Chief Pontiff for yourself. It is therefore with increased confidence, using the same form of vow that he asked to be made on his behalf, that I make this my earnest prayer: "If he rules the State well and in the interests of all," first preserve him for our grandsons and great-grandsons, then grant him one day a successor born of him and formed by him in the image of the adopted son he is, or if fate denies him this, guide and direct his choice to someone worthy to be adopted in your temple on the Capitol.[59]

First Clement could well have offered this prayer on behalf of Trajan, but it would have been disingenuous. The invocation, of course, would have been significantly different. Not to Capitoline Jupiter but to the God of Jesus Christ, of Abraham and the Hebrew prophets. First Clement had other ideas too that are not at all consonant with the rhetoric of the divine or divinized emperor that Pliny presents in his panegyric. First Clement does not share the same ancestors as Pliny. When First Clement speaks of ancestors, it has the Hebrew Scriptures in view and the most recent attestation of the Hebrew tradition in Paul and the gospel of Jesus Christ. For Pliny, the ancestors belong to the Roman past.

First Clement represented an alternative and downright subversive order to the world as conceived by the Roman Senate and as described in Pliny's *Panegyricus*. It is important in this respect not to read back into First Clement's posture at the end of the first century the standpoint of Christian writers in the second century. Its consciousness as a people or kingdom in pilgrimage, sojourning in this temporal order, stands in sharp contrast to the empire that Pliny prays to protect and to endure in perpetuity. I am insisting here that we take seriously the conflicting and incommensurable claims of First Clement and Pliny's *Panegyricus*. Even after the demise of Domitian, the church in Rome could not necessarily take it for granted that it would continue untroubled—hence its prayer to be rescued from those in Rome "who hate us without cause." It was not a prayer meant to evoke the times of Domitian when a document like First Clement could easily have prompted charges of *maiestas*, as I noted previously. It is a prayer for the present (c. 98 CE).

POSTSCRIPT

Against those who still insist that First Clement could not be speaking about some kind of "persecution" in its own time but only those of the past, it is good to recall First Clement 5 and link it to what is currently going on: those in prison in the later chapter.

> But to pass from the examples of ancient times, let us come to those champions who lived nearest to our time. Let us consider the noble examples that belong to our own generation. Because of jealousy and envy the greatest and most righteous pillars were persecuted and fought to the death. Let us set before our eyes the good apostles. There was Peter, who because of unrighteous jealousy endured not one or two but many trials, and thus haven given his testimony went to his appointed place of glory. Because of jealousy and strife Paul showed the way to the prize for patient endurance. After he had been seven times in chains, had been driven into exile, had been stoned, and had preached in the east and in the west, he won the genuine glory for his faith, having taught righteousness to the whole world and having reached the farthest limits of the west. Finally, when he had given his testimony before the rulers, he thus departed from the world and went to the holy place, having become an outstanding example of patient endurance.[60]

Now: "rescue those who are in prison." There is clearly a shared tradition between the church of Rome and the church of Corinth about how Peter and Paul met their end: they were like athletes in the arena. The expressions are not precise enough for our later ears. But to the contemporaries who read or heard these words, they would have understood exactly what First Clement had in mind. Besides, the Christians in Rome seemed to be in no doubt about what precisely this was. They belonged to the generation after those who were appointed by the apostles to lead them. The insinuation is that both Peter and Paul were martyred. But no further details are provided.

The point I wish to emphasize here is that Josephus's writings should be read in relation to what lies behind First Clement. Although much of First Clement is about exhortation, calling upon the Christians of Corinth to live in harmony and peace, much of what it contains in its background about Rome and the exigencies of the times are essential to understanding Josephus as well. Another way of saying this is to say that Josephus's presentation of Judaism and Jewish difference or uniqueness in the *Antiquities*, his *Life*, and in *Against Apion* has to be read not only against Roman objections and criticism of Judaism per se, but also against the appropriation of Jewish traditions found in First Clement, with its profuse use of Hebrew or Jewish Scriptures. First Clement reads and appropriates Jewish Scriptures and the Hebrew past in ways Josephus does not.

If we did not have First Clement, we should almost all be convinced that there were no Christians in Rome in the last two decades of the first century. Josephus's silence about Christians would be considered decisive as far as extant records go. Even with First Clement, some historians write as if there were no Christians in Rome in those two decades, and even if there were, they were probably so obscure that Josephus did not have to pay them any heed. But that is to fall for Josephus's stratagem.

The community that produced First Clement was not a deprived community lacking in self-confidence what it believed or how it understood itself. It was clearly well-established enough for them to be sought after to address problems afflicting the church in faraway Corinth in Achaia/Achaea. Peculiarly, the church in Corinth had apparently not consulted churches in Asia Minor across the Aegean or Ionian Seas to help resolve their difficulties. They sought out the church in Rome. There are two things involved. First, the possibility that the church in Corinth understood itself rightly or wrongly as the leading church in Macedonia and Achaea, and perhaps among the leading churches of all that Paul had founded. There is nothing in Paul's letters to detract from such a view, and still nothing in the Acts of the Apostles to undermine such a notion. (The later jurisdictional authority and pastoral oversight expressed by Dionysius of Corinth in the second half of the second century suggests some such view of its oversight and influence.) Second, the Corinthians also understood that the church in Rome had some kind of informal and unstated status as preserving the memory of Peter, Paul, and the apostolic generation. This is assumed and articulated in First Clement. The Corinthian appeal to the church in Rome, then, attests to the viability, relevance, and importance of the church of Rome for Christians everywhere.[61] A third factor is simply that Corinth was by foundation a Roman colony, and so maintained strong historical, social, cultural, political, and economic bonds with Rome itself, since the refounding of Corinth in 44 BCE.

As for Josephus's knowledge of the Christians of Rome who produced First Clement, this much should be clear. Rome was not so large a metropolis that Josephus could live there and not know a good deal of what transpired in the city. As I mentioned earlier, the entire city was about four times the size of Central Park in New York. The *Transtiberim*, on the right bank of the Tiber, which housed the Jewish Quarter, would have been home to some of the Christians of Rome. It is only if Josephus shunned the *Transtiberim* in all his years living in Rome would he have been completely ignorant of some of Rome's Jews and perhaps of Rome's Christians. Even the poet Martial, for all his anti-Jewish sentiment, did not exactly ignore that section of the city. He seems to have known its environs well.

Josephus's native Jerusalem was even smaller by comparison to the city of Rome. The old city of David was not more than 0.36 square mile; all in all about one-sixteenth the size of Rome. I should like to think that Josephus knew at least one Christian Jew in Jerusalem. If the reference to James the brother of Jesus in the *Antiquities* is authentic, then he knew a whole lot more than one Christian named James, and his brother Jesus who initiated the movement. He knew this in 62 CE when James was murdered. This was before Josephus was asked to lead a delegation to Rome to secure the release of some priests from Jerusalem. As I have already discussed, it was that visit to Rome that placed him in the city or its environs in July 64 when a fire destroyed much of the city, an event that was associated with the Christians in some quarters. If Josephus knew of the murder of James the brother of Jesus in 62 CE, he would hardly have been an uninterested spectator to events in Rome in 64 CE that engendered strong sentiments and reactions against the Christians of Rome. He could not pretend, even if he wanted to, that he knew nothing of Christians: not in 62 CE in Judaea, nor in 64 CE in Rome. He could not claim complete indifference toward them when, as a resident of Rome from 71 CE to the end of the first century, he was writing his *Jewish War*, *Antiquities*, *Life*, and *Against Apion*.

If Domitian's reign had not been so censorious and so dangerous for writers and for historians in particular, there may well have been more documentation about what obtained in the last two decades of the first century, and with it, better accounting of how the community that wrote First Clement came into its own from the days of the Neronian Fire of 64 CE, survived Nero, and lived through the 70s, 80s, and 90s in the time of the Flavians to whom Josephus owed so much. That we lack this documentation, on the other hand, is not proof that such a historical reality did not exist, only that the living witnesses were too afraid to write about them.[62] All the same, we have First Clement itself, Tacitus's *Agricola*, Plutarch's reminiscences, Dio

Chrysostom's *Orations*, Pliny the Younger's Letters, and his *Panegyricus* especially, to bear witness to the times. In spite of themselves, the poets Martial and Statius also attest to the anxieties and fears of those years.

If we keep this framework in mind, then some of what emerges in the early second century, even in Pliny the Younger's interaction with Christians in Bithynia-Pontus, or Justin Martyr's claims about Christianity and his own personal history, may not seem so out of the ordinary, if the church in Rome and the church in Corinth already had some sense of belonging to a single, unbroken tradition linked to the apostles Peter and Paul. This self-understanding alone presumes a historical and social sense of being Christian (*christianos*) that is essentially Jewish that is found in the *Didache* and in Paul's letters. It establishes a historical consciousness about what I have called "Christian Judaism" over and against Josephus's silences about Paul and about the Christians of Judaea, Galilee, and Rome in the first century. As I have argued about Josephus's *Against Apion*, the very conception of Jewish life (with words like *Ioudaikos, nomos, thrēskeia* in his other writings) that Josephus presents in that work (with *nomos, politeia, politeuma, theokratia*)[63] can be read as a contestation of the kind of Christian Judaism found in First Clement, even if Josephus never says a word about Christians in *Against Apion*. To reiterate: Josephus wrote *Against Apion* in Rome in the last years of the first century living in the same world that produced First Clement, with its profound sense of the Jewishness of being Christian. While Josephus's *Against Apion* defends Judaism, as he construes it, by imagining its possible future, First Clement attests to a living community founded on the Jewish past founded on the apostles Peter and Paul that Josephus barely acknowledges in *his Antiquities*, as if his silences would be enough to erase it from the Jewish archives of the first century. But as Josephus himself claimed, historians always have their reasons for their most blatant omissions.

NOTES

1. Tacitus, *Agricola* (LCL 35, 171).
2. Tacitus, *Agricola*, Preface (LCL 35).
3. See Peter Lampe, *Christians at Rome in the First Two Centuries: From Paul to Valentinus* (Minneapolis, MN: Fortress Press, 2003), 38–40; 65.
4. Cassius Dio, *Roman History* 67.14.1–2 (LCL 176, 349).
5. Bart Ehrman, *The New Testament and Other Early Christian Writings: A Reader* (New York: Oxford University Press, 2004 [2nd Edition]), 303.
6. See, for example, Philo, *On the Virtues* (LCL 341).
7. On the cultural trajectories and uses of the Phoenix, see now, Joseph Nigg, *The Phoenix: An Unnatural Biography of a Mythic Beast* (Chicago: University of Chicago Press, 2016).
8. Tacitus, *Annals* 6.28 (LCL 312, 201–3).
9. Ehrman, *Reader*, 310.
10. See here the major work by R. Van Den Broek, *The Myth of the Phoenix in Antiquity: According to Classical and Early Christian Traditions* (Leiden: Brill, 1971).

11. Ehrman, *Reader*, 310.
12. Statius, *Silvae*, Preface (LCL 206, 225–27).
13. Statius, *Silvae*, 4.1 (LCL 206, 229).
14. Statius, *Silvae* 4.1 (LCL 206, 299–31).
15. Statius, *Silvae* 4.1 (LCL 206, 231–33).
16. Statius, *Silvae* 4.1 (LCL 206, 233).
17. Statius, *Silvae* 4.2 (LCL 206, 233–35).
18. Statius, *Silvae* 4.2 (LCL 206, 239).
19. Ehrman, *Reader*, 319 (italics mine).
20. Ibid.
21. LCL 24, 145–47 (italics mine).
22. LCL 24, 99–101.
23. Tacitus, *Agricola* 2 (LCL 35, 170–71 [italics mine]).
24. Tacitus, *Agricola* 3 (LCL 35, 173).
25. LCL 24, 35.
26. LCL 24, 151.
27. Philip Schaff, *ANF 01: The Apostolic Fathers with Justin Martyr and Irenaeus* (Peabody: Hendrickson, 1996), 6.
28. LCL 24 (1913), 4–5.
29. J. B. Lightfoot, *Apostolic Fathers, Part 1, Volume 1: S. Clement of Rome* (New York: Macmillan and Co., 1890), 346–58.
30. LCL 24, 35.
31. Lightfoot, *Apostolic Fathers: S. Clement*, 39–42; 81.
32. Odd Magne Bakke, *Concord and Peace: A Rhetorical Analysis of the First Lettter of Clement* (Tübingen: Mohr Siebeck, 2001) argues that the reference is to internal strife. This seems mistaken. For it to be credible, it would have to be describing internal strife within the church in Rome and not the church in Corinth. Yet the discussion of strife throughout much of First Clement and the plea for concord and peace is all about the Christians of Corinth who sought the help of the church in Rome in the first place. Compare John Granger Cook, *Roman Attitudes towards Christians: From Claudius to Hadrian* (Tübingen: Mohr Siebeck, 2010), 112–34, who finds Bakke inconclusive, and perhaps even tendentious.
33. Likewise, efforts by some historians and scholars to classify the reportage on Domitian's cruelties as mere political propaganda and defamation. For a complicated assessment see, for example, Brian W. Jones, *The Emperor Domitian* (London: Routledge, 1992). Incidentally, while Jones discusses terror in relation to Domitian's court, the word "cruelty" does not appear in his work. See as well, Pat Southern, *Domitian: Tragic Tyrant* (London: Routledge, 1997). See also L. L. Thompson, *The Book of Revelation: Apocalypse and Empire* (New York: Oxford University Press, 1990); alternatively, Miriam Griffin, "The Flavians," *Cambridge Ancient History, volume 11* (Cambridge: Cambridge University Press, 2000), 81–82. And G. K. Beale, *The Book of Revelation* (Grand Rapids, MI: Eerdmans, 1999), 5–7.
34. Cassius Dio, *Epitome* 68.1:1–3 (LCL 176, 361).
35. Michael W. Holmes (ed.), *The Apostolic Fathers in English* (Grand Rapids, MI: Baker Academic, 2006), 60.
36. Ibid., 70.
37. Ibid., 69–70.
38. Michael W. Holmes, *The Apostolic Fathers: Greek Text and English Translations*, 3rd edition (Grand Rapids, MI: Baker Academic, 2007), 53–55.
39. Kenneth J. Howell, *Clement of Rome and the Didache: A New Translation and Theological Commentary* (Zanesville, OH: CHResources, 2012), 120.
40. Ibid., 120.
41. Ibid., 80–81.
42. Ibid., 110–11.
43. Donald A. Hagner, *The Use of the Old Testament and New Testament in Clement of Rome* (Leiden: Brill, 1997), 126–27.
44. Ibid., 22n3.
45. Ibid., 21–24; 353–55.

46. Michael F. Bird, *The Gospel of the Lord* (Grand Rapids, MI: Eerdmans, 2014), 102–3.
47. Holmes, *The Apostolic Fathers: Greek Text and English Translations*, 61–63.
48. Ibid., 107–9.
49. Bird, *The Gospel of the Lord*, 103.
50. Ibid., 246n96.
51. For extensive discussion see Hagner, *The Use of the Old Testament and the New Testament in Clement of Rome*; with corrections from C. Breytenbach and L. L. Welborn (eds.), *Encounters with Hellenism: Studies on the First Letter of Clement* (Leiden: Brill, 2004).
52. See here Allen Brent, *The Imperial Cult and the Development of Church Order* (Leiden: Brill, 1999), 140–63; and *A Political History of Early Christianity* (London: Bloomsbury T&T Clark, 2009), 175–208.
53. See Naftali S. Cohn, *The Memory of the Temple and the Making of the Rabbis* (Philadelphia: University of Pennsylvania Press, 2012), 1–15.
54. Brian W. Jones, *The Emperor Domitian*.
55. Shadi Bartsch, "The Art of Sincerity: Pliny's Panegyricus," in Roger Rees (ed.), *Latin Panegyric* (New York: Oxford University Press, 2012), 148–93.
56. Pliny the Younger, *Panegyricus* 75.1–2 (LCL 59, 499). Cf. *Panegyricus* 95.1.
57. Pliny the Younger, *Panegyricus* 93.1–3 (LCL 59, 539).
58. Pliny the Younger, *Panegyricus* 1 (LCL 59, 323–25).
59. Pliny the Younger, *Panegyricus* 94 (LCL 59, 543–45).
60. Holmes, *The Apostolic Fathers: Greek Text and English Translations*, 51–53.
61. See Lampe, *Christians at Rome in the First Two Centuries*.
62. My point about documentation is not meant to be an assertion that the Christians in Rome had increased in such numbers by the end of the century, only that they were not as obscure as some historians and sociologist of the period seem to think. See Rodney Stark's estimates of the growth of Christianity in *The Rise of Christianity: A Sociologist Reconsiders History* (Princeton: Princeton University Press, 1996). Cf. Ramsay MacMullen, *Christianizing the Roman Empire* (New Haven: Yale University Press, 1984).
63. See Carlin A. Barton and Daniel Boyarin, *Imagine No Religion: How Modern Anxieties Hide Ancient Realities* (New York: Fordham University Press, 2016), 135–99. Cf. Daniel Boyarin, "An Isogloss in First Century Palestinian Jewry: Josephus and Mark on the Purpose of the Law," in *The Faces of the Torah: Studies in the Texts and Contexts of Ancient Judaism in Honor of Steven Fraade*, edited by Michal Bar-Asher Siegel, Tsvi Novick, and Christine Hayes (Göttingen: Vandenhoeck and Ruprecht, 2107), 63–80.

Epilogue

In his highly influential book, *The Christians as the Romans Saw Them*, Robert Wilken writes in the preface that his principal motivation was to tell the story of the early Christians from the standpoint of their non-Christian neighbors.[1] Wilken's work, which begins in the second century, helps us to appreciate how the Christians were perceived rightly or wrongly in the wider world of the Roman Empire. I have sought here to push Wilken's initiative back into the first century and not only to inquire as to how the Romans saw the earliest Christians but also to assess how one particular Roman, in this case, the Jewish historian Flavius Josephus, our most important witness to so much of Jewish life in the first century, saw or did not see the Christians both in his native Judaea and in Rome, where he lived for almost three decades after the Jewish War with the Romans. The preceding can be described, following Wilken, as: Paul and the early Christians as Flavius Josephus and his Roman contemporaries saw (and did not see) them.

I have had as much to say about what Josephus and his contemporaries do not say as I have said about what they actually say. In the process I have offered comment about what Josephus and his contemporaries must have known also about each other; what they said and did not say about what they knew; and how their respective silences should be read.

We have seen over the course of these five preceding chapters that Josephus manages to be silent about a great deal to which he was a witness. Not only about the early Christians in Jerusalem about whom he knew certain details surrounding their community and the leadership of James the brother of Jesus. But also that, in spite of his knowledge of these Christians and perhaps because of it, he was silent about bearing witness to anything concerning the Fire of 64 in Rome and Nero's accusation that the Christians of the city had set the fire. Again, in spite of what he knew about James's judicial murder and the harrying of the Christians of Jerusalem in 62 CE, Josephus says nothing about the persecution and murder of Christians by Nero and his prefect Tigellinus in 64 CE even though he was almost certainly in Rome or nearby when it happened.

As if by design and with intentionality, Josephus also remained manifestly silent about most of his contemporaries in Rome during the nearly three decades he lived there, and never once engages any of the literary figures of Rome in any of his writings; not even the poet Martial, who castigated and wrote derisively and contemptuously about Jews, Jerusalem, and the destruction of the Temple in Jerusalem. More broadly, if we were to depend on Josephus for some evidence of his Roman contemporaries, we would know next to nothing.

At the same time, while his living contemporaries explained the difficulties they endured and suffered during the reign of Domitian, Josephus pretended as if there was nothing to worry about, and instead wrote his *Against Apion*, styled as a defense of Judaism to a readership that would have poured scorn on the very apologia that Josephus claimed to be writing. The artificiality of Josephus's last extant work reveals the extent to which he went to avoid the social and political realities of his day even as he sought to rehabilitate himself after the end of the Flavian dynasty. As he pursued his self-justifications and his apologia for a Judaism he had long since abandoned as a resident of Rome, the Christians of Rome celebrated in First Clement the Jewish past as their very inheritance, making plain that their way of life (call it Christianity) was nothing more than "Christian Judaism." There is not a hint of "anti-Judaism" of any sort in First Clement. The relevance of this for our understanding, interpretation, and conceptualization of Jewish-Christian relations in the first century has largely been overlooked by historians and scholars.

Unlike Josephus, First Clement adverts to a living history that links the believers of the Hebrew/Jewish past with the current members of the churches or assemblies of God of Rome and Corinth. It claims the memory of Paul the apostle as foundational to the very life and existence of the Christian communities in Rome and Corinth. Against First Clement, Josephus's silences about the Christians of Rome during the reign of Nero (attested by Tacitus and Suetonius) and during his own long stay in the city, prove him to be as a historian of a particular kind, whose silences may say as much or perhaps more about his credibility as his articulations. They are also of a similar nature as his silences about the High Priest Caiaphas and about Gamaliel the Elder, the great leader of the Pharisees.

Instead of silence, Josephus could have provided a history of the early Christian movement as part of his cycle on religious or revolutionary leaders from Galilee and compared Jesus of Nazareth (the brother of James, the leader of the Christians of Jerusalem) to Judas of Galilee and others about whom he writes. He could have presented a fuller portrait of James the brother of Jesus and others of the nascent Christian community including Paul the former Pharisee, and he could have added his own personal reminiscences of what the Christians did in relation to other Jews during the period from his birth to the beginning of the War with the Romans. That comparison would have been most apposite in relation to the conversion of Adiabene royals.

From that point on it would have been commonplace to speak of the Christians (and of Christianity) as one of the "schools" of Judaism in the first century, using Josephus's nomenclature. This characterization would most certainly have greatly shaped the self-consciousness of Christian and non-Christian Jews as well as the self-understanding and historical consciousness of Gentiles who became Christians. This is what could have been. This would probably have made it extremely difficult though not impossible for Christian Gentiles to think of themselves in any other way than as adopted Jews practicing a form of Judaism. Likewise, non-Christian Jews would have to think of Christian Gentiles as like proselytes to non-Christian Judaism. The consequences would have been unmistakable. The later conceptualization, if not the history, of Christianity and of Judaism would probably have been markedly different from what it became.

Let us imagine, for a moment, another contemporary of Josephus who might have attempted a description of the Christian Jews and the early Christian movement without Josephus's sentiments and antipathies. He could easily have described them as the fifth philosophy, placing them in a natural historical sequence after Judas of Gamala (in Galilee) and his movement, which Josephus describes as the fourth philosophy. It would go something like this:

After Judas of Gamala who inaugurated the movement called the Zealots, there came another man claiming to be the messiah of the Jews named Jesus from another town in Galilee called Nazareth. Unlike Judas of Gamla and the other messianic imposters who preached a political kingdom in open defiance of Roman rule, this Jesus of Nazareth appeared to teach something different. He is believed to have received baptism from John the Baptizer, whom so many Judaeans regarded so well for his teaching on repentance. John encouraged many Jews to be ritually and morally cleansed to live rightly before God. Jesus of Nazareth also had followers like John. But his followers believed he was the Messiah and even attributed some of that belief to John's baptism of Jesus as a sign of Jesus's messiahship. In time he became a problem to both the leading men of Judaea and the Roman authorities, and he was arrested and suffered the most horrible death by being crucified during the governorship of Pontius Pilate. The High Priest Josephus Caiaphas approved of his death.

After his crucifixion his disciples put out a story that he had risen from the dead and proceeded to say that this was proof of what he had taught before he died. His followers continue to this day, although many Jews or Judaeans are not sure whether their teachings should be given any credence; or whether they should be treated like the Samaritans who broke away from us so long ago. Some, however, believe that the followers of the Nazarene have the truth and follow them in their belief in resurrection. In this they are like the Pharisees who also believe in resurrection. Indeed one of their most prominent leaders is a man named Paul who was taught by Rabbi Gamaliel in Jerusalem and for a period was also sympathetic to the views of the High Priest Caiaphas before he himself changed to become a follower of the Nazarene.

Paul preached to many outside Judaea, creating numerous assemblies of both Jews and Gentiles who are followers of the Nazarene. This proved to be a problem for some of the Jews in these assemblies, since they could not quite understand whether without becoming circumcised such Gentiles should be admitted as Jews or that such Jews who had fellowship with uncircumcised Gentiles should be considered truly to be living in accordance with the laws and customs of their fathers. There were other Jews like the High Priest Ananus son of Ananus (a relative of Caiaphas) who was also ill-disposed toward the Christians. In his short reign as the high priest he succeeded in masterminding the murder of James the brother of Jesus, who was thought to be the Messiah.

When Josephus visited Rome a year or so after the murder of James the brother of Jesus of Nazareth, he learned about the Christians of Rome. In the year of the great fire of 64, they were blamed for it by Nero. During the time that Josephus lived in Rome after the War, there was a community of Christians who were so devoted to the Scriptures that it was difficult to distinguish them from other Jews in their love of the patriarchs and the Prophets of old. Most Romans had long known that the Christians had their origins in Judaea. But Josephus and others tried to point out to some of them that the Christians, while originating in Judaea, did not properly or truly represent Judaism, but were only one sect among the few that were to be found among us before the War.

Some such description would have captured some of what went on in the early Christian movement in Jerusalem, Judaea, and in Galilee about which Josephus says nothing; and about the Christians who lived in Rome during the time of Nero and later years when Josephus lived in retirement there. If Josephus had offered a rendition like this in the words of this fictional contemporary that I am imagining, it would commit him to nothing about the Christian movement. He would merely be reporting what it is they represented and what a peculiarity the Christians were to some Jews who could not quite understand how uncircumcised Gentiles could be considered full partakers of the Jewish inheritance in Abraham. But it would commit Josephus to saying that, despite certain misgivings, the Christian Jews were part of the Jewish fold. Such an appreciation of the Christian Jews may have been too much for Josephus to tolerate. Just in case we are wondering, this fictional witness could have been Herod Agrippa II.

The account I have imagined, of course, sidesteps the question as to how the categories of God-fearers and proselytes were understood by Jews in general. The difference is that for Paul the Christian Gentiles did not have to become Jewish proselytes first nor did they have to remain proselytes or God-fearers as such. They could become fully and completely the children of Abraham by believing the gospel of Jesus Christ that Paul preached. Paul's teaching appropriated to the fullest the missionary impulse within Judaism and claimed it almost as an exclusive right. He spelled out its inner logic as to make the story of the conversion of the Adiabene royals dated even as Josephus narrated it in his writings. For "as many of you as were baptized in Christ have clothed yourselves in Christ. There is no longer Jew or Greek, there is no longer slave or free, there is no longer male or female; for all of you are one in Christ Jesus. And if you belong to Christ, then you are Abraham's offspring, heirs according to the promise" (Galatians 3:2–9 [NRSV]).

More pointedly, if Josephus had mentioned the Christian Jews as one of the schools within Judaism, like the Pharisees, Sadducees, and Essenes, he would have made it impossible for the rabbis and the later Rabbinic tradition to treat the followers of Jesus of Nazareth, the Nazarenes, as minim or heretics.

At its core, First Clement affirms that being Christian is to be a partaker of the ancient inheritance of the Jews; and that there is no other way of conceptualizing Christianity both historically and theologically than as "Christian Judaism." First Clement, therefore, attests to a different fate of early Christianity than can be surmised from the writings of Flavius Josephus.

NOTE

1. Robert L. Wilken, *The Christians as the Romans Saw Them* (New Haven: Yale University Press, 1984).

Bibliography

Alexander, Philip S. "What Happened to the Jewish Priesthood after 70?" In *A Wandering Galilean: Essays in Honour of Seán Freyne*, edited by Zuleika Rodgers, with Margaret Daly-Denton and Anne Fitzpatrick McKinley, 5–33. JSJSup 132. Leiden: Brill, 2009.
Alon, Gedaliah. *Jews, Judaism, and the Classical World*. Translated by Israel Abrahams. Jerusalem: Magnes Press, 1977.
Altshuler, David. "On the Classification of Judaic Laws in the *Antiquities* of Josephus and the Temple Scroll of Qumran." *AJSR* 7–8 (1982–83): 1–14.
Appelbaum, Alan. "'The Idumeans' in Josephus' *The Jewish War*." *JSJ* 40.1 (2009): 1–22.
Atkinson, Kenneth, and Jodi Magness. "Josephus's Essenes and the Qumran Community." *JBL* 129.2 (2010): 317–42.
Attridge, Harold W. *The Interpretation of Biblical History in the "Antiquitates Judaicae" of Flavius Josephus*. Harvard Dissertations in Religion 7. Missoula, MT: Scholars Press, 1976.
———. "Josephus and His Works." In *Jewish Writings of the Second Temple Period: Apocrypha, Pseudepigrapha, Qumran Sectarian Writings, Philo, Josephus*, edited by Michael Stone, 185–232. CRINT II.2. Assen: Van Gorcum, 1984.
Avery-Peck, Alan J., and Jacob Neusner, eds. *Judaism in Late Antiquity*. Pt. 4. *Death, Life-after-Death, Resurrection and the World-to-Come in the Judaisms of Late Antiquity*. Leiden: Brill, 1999.
Bakhos, Carol, ed. *Ancient Judaism in Its Hellenistic Contexts*. Leiden: Brill, 2004.
Bakke, Odd Magne. *Concord and Peace: A Rhetorical Analysis of the First Lettter of Clement*. Tubingen: Mohr Siebeck, 2001.
Barclay, John M. G. *Against Apion: Translation and Commentary*. Edited by Steve Mason. BJP 10. Leiden: Brill, 2007.
———. "Constructing Judean Identity after 70 CE: A Study of Josephus's *Against Apion*." In *Identity and Interaction in the Ancient Mediterranean: Jews, Christians, and Others: Essays in Honour of Stephen G. Wilson*, edited by Zeba A. Crook and Philip A. Harland, 99–112. Sheffield, England: Sheffield Phoenix Press, 2007.
———. *Jews in the Mediterranean Diaspora: From Alexander to Trajan, 323 BCE–117 CE*. Berkeley: University of California Press, 1999.
Baron, Salo Wittmayer. *A Social and Religious History of the Jews*. 16 vols. New York: Columbia University Press, 1952–1983.
Barton, Carlin A., and Daniel Boyarin. *Imagine No Religion: How Modern Abstractions Hide Ancient Realities*. New York: Fordham University Press, 2016.
Baumbach, Günther. "The Sadducees in Josephus." In *Josephus, the Bible, and History*, edited by Louis H. Feldman and Gohei Hata, 173–95. Detroit: Wayne State University Press, 1989.

Baumgarten, Albert I. "But Touch the Law and the Sect Will Split: Legal Dispute as the Cause of Sectarian Schism." *Review of Rabbinic Judaism* 5.3 (2002): 301–15.

———. *The Flourishing of Jewish Sects in the Maccabean Era: An Interpretation.* Leiden: Brill, 1997.

———. "Josephus and Hippolytus on the Pharisees." *HUCA* 55 (1984): 1–25.

———. "Josephus on Essene Sacrifice." *JJS* 45.2 (1994): 169–83.

———. "The Pharisaic *Paradosis.*" *HTR* 80.1 (1987): 63–77.

———. "Who Cares and Why Does It Matter? Qumran and the Essenes, Once Again!" *DSD* 11.2 (2004): 174–90.

———. "The Zadokite Priests at Qumran: A Reconsideration." *DSD* 4.2 (1997): 137–56.

Baumgarten, Joseph M. "Sadducean Elements in Qumran Law." In *The Community of the Renewed Covenant: The Notre Dame Symposium on the Dead Sea Scrolls*, edited by Eugene Ulrich and James VanderKam, 27–36. Notre Dame, IN: University of Notre Dame Press, 1994.

———. *Studies in Qumran Law.* SJLA 24. Leiden: Brill, 1977.

Beale, G. K. *The Book of Revelation.* Grand Rapids: Eerdmans, NIGTC, 1999.

Beall, Todd S. *Josephus' Description of the Essenes Illustrated by the Dead Sea Scrolls.* Society for New Testament Studies Monograph Series 58. Cambridge: Cambridge University Press, 1988.

Beer, Moshe. "The Destruction of the Second Temple in Early Jewish Thought." In *The Jews in the Hellenistic-Roman World: Studies in Memory of Menahem Stern*, edited by Isaiah M. Gafni, Aharon Oppenheimer, and Daniel R. Schwartz, 437–51. Jerusalem: Zalman Shazar Center for Jewish History, 1996.

Begg, Christopher T. "The Gedaliah Episode and Its Sequels in Josephus." *Journal for the Study of the Pseudepigrapha* 6.12 (1994): 21–46.

———. "'Josephus's Portrayal of the Disappearances of Enoch, Elijah, and Moses': Some Observations." *JBL* 109.4 (1990): 690–93.

———. *Judean Antiquities 5–7.* Edited by Steve Mason. BJP 4. Leiden: Brill, 2001.

———. "The Massacre of the Priests of Nob in Josephus and Pseudo-Philo." *Estudios Biblicos* 55 (1977): 171–98.

———. "Ruler or God? The Demolition of Herod's Eagle." In *The New Testament and Early Christian Literature in Greco-Roman Context: Studies in Honor of David E. Aune*, edited by John Fotopoulos, 257–86. Leiden: Brill, 2006.

Begg, Christopher T., and Paul Spilsbury. *Judean Antiquities 8–10.* Edited by Steve Mason. BJP 5. Leiden: Brill, 2005.

Bergmeier, Roland. "Die drei jüdischen Schulrichtungen nach Josephus und Hippolyt von Rom: Zu den Paralleltexten Josephus, *B.J.* 2,119–166 und Hippolyt, *Haer.* IX 18,2–29,4." *JSJ* 34.4 (2003): 443–70.

Bernstein, Moshe J., and Shlomo A. Koyfman. "The Interpretation of Biblical Law in the Dead Sea Scrolls: Forms and Methods." In *Biblical Interpretation at Qumran*, edited by Matthias Henze, 61–87. Grand Rapids, MI: Eerdmans, 2005.

Biale, David, ed. *Cultures of the Jews: Volume 1. Mediterranean Origins.* New York: Shocken Books, 2002.

Bickerman, E. J. *Studies in Jewish and Christian History: A New Edition in English Including "The God of the Maccabees."* 2 vols. Edited by Amram Tropper. With an introduction by Martin Hengel. Ancient Judaism and Early Christianity 68. Leiden: Brill, 2007.

Bilde, Per. "Josephus and Jewish Apocalypticism." In *Understanding Josephus: Seven Perspectives*, edited by Steve Mason, 35–61. JSPSup 32. Sheffield, England: Sheffield Academic Press, 1998.

Bird, Michael F. *The Gospel of the Lord.* Grand Rapids: Eerdmans, 2014.

Boccaccini, Gabriele. *Beyond the Essene Hypothesis: The Parting of the Ways between Qumran and Enochic Judaism.* Grand Rapids, MI: Eerdmans, 1998.

———. *Middle Judaism: Jewish Thought 300 BCE to 200 CE.* With a foreword by James H. Charlesworth. Minneapolis: Fortress, 1991.

———. *Roots of Rabbinic Judaism: An Intellectual History, from Ezekiel to Daniel.* Grand Rapids, MI: Eerdmans, 2002.

Boda, Mark J., Daniel K. Falk, and Rodney A. Werline, eds. *Seeking the Favor of God*. Vol. 1. *The Origins of Penitential Prayer in Second Temple Judaism*. EJL 21. Atlanta: Society of Biblical Literature, 2006.

———. *Seeking the Favor of God*. Vol. 2. *The Development of Penitential Prayer in Second Temple Judaism*. EJL 22. Atlanta: Society of Biblical Literature, 2007.

Bond, Helen K. *Caiaphas: Friend of Rome and Judge of Jesus?* Louisville, KY: Westminster John Knox, 2004.

———. "New Currents in Josephus Research." *Currents in Research: Biblical Studies* 8 (2000): 162–90.

Bowersock, Glen W. *Martyrdom and Rome*. Cambridge: Cambridge University Press, 1995.

Boyarin, Daniel. *Border Lines: The Partition of Judaeo-Christianity*. Philadelphia: University of Pennsylvania Press, 2004.

———. *Dying for God: Martyrdom and the Making of Christianity and Judaism*. Stanford: Stanford University Press, 1999.

Boyle, Anthony, and William Dominik, eds. *Flavian Rome: Culture, Image, Text*. Leiden: Brill, 2003.

Braund, Susanna M. *Seneca, De Clementia, Edited with Text, Translation, and Commentary*. New York: Oxford University Press, 2009.

Brent, Allen. *The Imperial Cult and the Development of Church Order*. Leiden: Brill, 1999.

———. *A Political History of Early Christianity*. Edinburgh: Bloomsbury T&T Clark, 2009.

Breytenbach, C., and L. L. Welborn, eds. *Encounters with Hellenism: Studies on the First Letter of Clement*. Leiden: Brill, 2004.

Brighton, Mark Andrew. *The Sicarii in Josephus's "Judean War": Rhetorical Analysis and Historical Observations*. EJL 27. Atlanta: Society of Biblical Literature, 2009.

Capes, David B., April D. DeConick, Helen K. Bond, and Troy A. Miller, eds. *Israel's God and Rebecca's Children: Christology and Community in Early Judaism and Christianity, Essays in Honor of Larry W. Hurtado and Alan F. Segal*. Waco, TX: Baylor University Press, 2007.

Cavallin, Hans Clemens Caesarius. *Life after Death: Paul's Argument for the Resurrection of the Dead in I Cor 15*. Coniectanea biblica: New Testament Series 7. Lund: Gleerup, 1974.

Chapman, Honora Howell. "Masada in the 1st and 21st Centuries." In *Making History: Josephus and Historical Method*, edited by Zuleika Rodgers, 82–102. JSJSup 110. Leiden: Brill, 2007.

Chapman, Honora Howell, and Zuleika Rogers, eds. *A Companion to Josephus*. West Sussex: John Wiley & Sons, 2016.

Charlesworth, James. ed. *Jesus and Temple: Textual and Archaeological Explorations*. Fortress Press, 2014.

Cohen, Gerson D. *Studies in the Variety of Rabbinic Cultures*. JPS Scholars of Distinction Series. Philadelphia: Jewish Publication Society, 1991.

Cohen, Shaye J. D. "Alexander and Jaddus according to Josephus." *AJSR* 7–8 (1982–83): 41–68.

———. *The Beginnings of Jewishness: Boundaries, Varieties, Uncertainties*. Berkeley: University of California Press, 1999.

———. "The Destruction: From Scripture to Midrash." *Prooftexts* 2.1 (1982): 18–39.

———. "History and Historiography in the Against Apion of Josephus." *History and Theory* 27.4 (1988): 1–11.

———. "Jacob Neusner, Mishnah, and Counter-Rabbinics: A Review Essay." *Conservative Judaism* 37.1 (1983): 48–63.

———. *Josephus in Galilee and Rome*. Columbia Studies in the Classical Tradition 8. Leiden: Brill, 1979.

———. "Josephus, Jeremiah, and Polybius." *History and Theory* 21.3 (1982): 366–81.

———. "Masada: Literary Tradition, Archaeological Remains, and the Credibility of Josephus." *JJS* 33.1–2 (1982): 385–405.

———. *The Significance of Javneh and Other Essays in Jewish Hellenism*. Tubingen: Mohr Siebeck, 2010.

———. "The Significance of Yavneh: Pharisees, Rabbis, and the End of Jewish Sectarianism." *HUCA* 55 (1984): 27–53.

———. "The Temple and the Synagogue." In *The Cambridge History of Judaism*. Vol. 3. *The Early Roman Period*, edited by William Horbury, W. D. Davies, and John Sturdy, 298–325. Cambridge: Cambridge University Press, 1999.

Collins, John J. *Apocalypticism in the Dead Sea Scrolls*. London: Routledge, 1997.

———. *Beyond the Qumran Community: The Sectarian Movement of the Dead Sea Scrolls*. Grand Rapids, MI: Eerdmans, 2010.

———. "The Essenes and the Afterlife." In *From 4QMMT to Resurrection: Mélanges qumraniens en homage à Émile Puech*, edited by Florentino García Martínez, Annette Steudel, and Eibert Tigchelaar, 35–53. STDJ 61. Leiden: Brill, 2006.

———. "The Sibylline Oracles, Book 4." In *The Old Testament Pseudepigrapha*, edited by James H. Charlesworth, 2 vols., 1:381–89. Garden City, NY: Doubleday, 1983.

Colson, F. H., and G. H. Whitaker, eds. and trans. *Philo of Alexandria*. 10 vols., with 2 supp. volumes translated by Ralph Marcus. LCL. Cambridge, MA: Harvard University Press, 1929–62.

Coogan, Michael D., ed., with Marc Z. Brettler and Pheme Perkins, associate eds. *The New Oxford Annotated Bible, New Revised Standard Version with Apocrypha: Fully Revised Fourth Edition*. New York: Oxford University Press, 2010.

Cook, John Cranger. *Roman Attitudes towards Christians: From Claudius to Hadrian*. Tubingen: Mohr Siebeck, 2010.

Costa, Tony. "Is Saul of Tarsus Also among the Prophets? Paul's Calling as Prophetic Divine Commission." In *Christian Origins and Hellenistic Judaism: Social and Literary Contexts for the New Testament*, edited by Stanley E. Porter and Andrew W. Pitts. Brill, 2013.

Crenshaw, James L. *Ecclesiastes: A Commentary*. Old Testament Library. Philadelphia: Westminster, 1987.

———. "Gold Dust or Nuggets? A Brief Response to J. Kenneth Kuntz." *CBR* 1.2 (2003): 155–58.

———. "Method in Determining Wisdom Influence upon 'Historical' Literature." *JBL* 88.2 (1969): 129–42.

———. *Old Testament Wisdom: An Introduction*. 3rd ed. Louisville, KY: Westminster John Knox, 2010.

———. "The Problem of Theodicy in Sirach: On Human Bondage." *JBL* 94.1 (1975): 47–64.

———. "Wisdom Psalms?" *Currents in Research: Biblical Studies* 8 (2000): 9–17.

Cross, Frank Moore. *The Ancient Library of Qumran*. 3rd ed. Minneapolis: Fortress, 1995.

———. *Canaanite Myth and Hebrew Epic: Essays in the History of the Religion of Israel*. Cambridge, MA: Harvard University Press, 1973.

Damon, Cynthia. "Pliny on Apion." In *Pliny the Elder: Themes and Contexts*, edited by Roy Gibson and Ruth Morello, 131–45. Leiden: Brill, 2011.

Danby, Herbert. *The Mishnah: Translated from the Hebrew with Introduction and Brief Explanatory Notes*. Oxford: Oxford University Press, 1933.

Daube, David. "Typology in Josephus." *JJS* 31.1 (1980): 18–36.

David, Joseph E., Martin Goodman, and Corinna R. Kaiser, *Toleration within Judaism*. Oxford: Littman Library of Jewish Civilization, 2013.

Den Hollander, William. *Josephus, the Emperors, and the City of Rome: From Hostage to Historian*. Leiden: Brill, 2014.

Dexinger, Ferdinand. "Samaritan Eschatology." In *The Samaritans*, edited by Alan D. Crown, 266–92. Tübingen: Mohr Siebeck, 1989.

Di Lella, Alexander A. "Conservative and Progressive Theology: Sirach and Wisdom." *CBQ* 28.2 (1966): 139–53.

Dillon, John. *The Middle Platonists: 80 B.C. to A.D. 220*. Rev. ed. with a new afterword. Ithaca, NY: Cornell University Press, 1996.

———. "Plutarch and Second Century Platonism." In *Classical Mediterranean Spirituality: Egyptian, Greek, Roman*, edited by Arthur Hilary Armstrong, 214–29. World Spirituality 15. New York: Crossroad, 1987.

Dimant, Devorah. *Qumran Cave 4, XXVI: Parabiblical Texts*. Pt. 4. *Pseudo-Prophetic Texts*. Partially based on earlier transcriptions by John Strugnell. DJD 30. Oxford: Clarendon, 2001.
Draper, Jonathan A. "Christian Self-Definition against the Hypocrites of Didache VIII." In *The Didache in Modern Research*, edited by Jonathan A. Draper, 233–43. Leiden, Brill, 1996
———, ed. *The Didache in Modern Research*. Leiden: Brill, 1996.
Draper, Jonathan A., and Clayton N. Jefford, eds. *The Didache: A Missing Piece of the Puzzle in Early Christianity*. Atlanta, GA: SBL, 2015.
Droge, Arthur J., and James D. Tabor. *A Noble Death: Suicide and Martyrdom among Christians and Jews in Antiquity*. New York: HarperSanFrancisco, 1992.
Eckstein, A. "Josephus and Polybius: A Reconsideration." *Classical Antiquity* 9 (1990): 175–208.
Edmondson, Jonathan, Steve Mason, and James Rives (eds.). *Flavius Josephus and Flavian Rome*. Oxford: Oxford University Press, 2005.
Edwards, Mark, David Goodman, Simon Price in association with Christopher Rowland, eds. *Apologetics in the Roman Empire*. Oxford University Press, 1999.
Ehrenkrook, Jason von. *Sculpting Idolatry in Flavian Rome: (An)iconic Rhetoric in the Writings of Flavius Josephus*. EJL 33. Atlanta: Society of Biblical Literature, 2011.
Ehrman, Bart. *The New Testament and Other Early Christian Writings: A Reader*. Oxford: Oxford University Press, 2004 (2nd Edition).
Elbogen, Ismar. *Jewish Liturgy: A Comprehensive History*. 1931. Reprint, Translated by Raymond P. Scheindlin. Philadelphia: Jewish Publication Society, 1993.
Eliav, Yaron Z. "The Roman Bathhouse as a Jewish Institution: Another Look at the Encounter between Judaism and the Greco-Roman Culture." *Journal for the Study of Judaism* 31/1–4 (2000): 416–54.
Elior, Rachel. *Memory and Oblivion: The Mystery of the Dead Sea Scrolls* [Hebrew]. Jerusalem: Van Leer Institute, 2009.
Epstein, Jacob N. *Introduction to the Text of the Mishnah* [Hebrew]. 2 vols. 2nd ed. Jerusalem: Magnes Press, 1964.
Eshel, Hanan. *The Dead Sea Scrolls and the Hasmonean State*. Translated by David Louvish and Aryeh Amihay. Grand Rapids, MI: Eerdmans, 2008.
———. "Josephus' View on Judaism without the Temple in Light of the Discoveries at Masada and Murabba'at." In *Gemeinde ohne Tempel: Zur Substituierung und Transformation des Jerusalemer Tempels und seines Kults im Alten Testament, antiken Judentum und frühen Christentum*, edited by Beate Ego, Armin Lange, and Peter Pilhofer, in cooperation with Kathrin Ehlers, 229–238. WUNT 1, 118. Tübingen: Mohr Siebeck 1999.
Fagan, Garrett G. *Bathing in Public in the Roman World*. Ann Arbor: University of Michigan Press, 1999.
Feldman, Louis H. "The Identity of Pollio, the Pharisee, in Josephus." *JQR* 49.1 (1958): 53–62.
———. *Jew and Gentile in the Ancient World: Attitudes and Interactions from Alexander to Justinian*. Princeton: Princeton University Press, 1993.
———. *Josephus's Interpretation of the Bible*. Hellenistic Culture and Society 27. Berkeley: University of California Press, 1998.
———. *Judaism and Hellenism Reconsidered*. Leiden: Brill, 2006.
———. *Judean Antiquities 1–4: Translation and Commentary*. Edited by Steve Mason. BJP 3. Leiden: Brill, 2000.
———. "A Select Critical Bibliography of Josephus." In *Josephus, the Bible, and History*, edited by Louis H. Feldman and Gohei Hata, 330–448. Detroit: Wayne State University Press, 1989.
———. *Studies in Josephus' Rewritten Bible*. JSJSup 58. Leiden: Brill, 1998.
———. "Torah and Greek Culture in Josephus." *Torah U-Madda Journal* 7 (1997): 47–87.
Feldman, Louis H., and Gohei Hata, eds. *Josephus, Judaism, and Christianity*. Detroit: Wayne State University Press, 1987.
———. *Josephus, the Bible, and History*. Detroit: Wayne State University Press, 1989.
Feldman, Louis H., and J. R. Levison. *Josephus's Contra Apionem: Studies in Its Character and Context*. Leiden: Brill, 1996.

Fine, Steven. "A Note on Ossuary Burial and the Resurrection of the Dead in First-Century Judaism." *JJS* 51.1 (2000): 69–76.
Finkelstein, Louis. *The Pharisees: The Sociological Background of Their Faith*. 3rd ed. With supp. 2 vols. Philadelphia: Jewish Publication Society, 1962.
———, ed. *Sifre on Deuteronomy* [Hebrew]. 1939. Reprint. New York: Jewish Theological Seminary, 1993.
Fitzgerald, William. *Martial: The World of the Epigram*. Chicago: University of Chicago Press, 2007.
Fleischer, Ezra. "On the Beginnings of Obligatory Jewish Prayer" [Hebrew]. *Tarbiz* 59.3–4 (1990): 397–441.
Flusser, David. "Josephus on the Sadducees and Menander." *Immanuel* 7 (1977): 61–67.
———. *The Josippon [Josephus Gorionides]: Edited with an Introduction, Commentary and Notes*. Vol. 1. *Text and Commentary* [Hebrew]. 2nd corrected ed. Jerusalem: Bialik Institute, 1981.
———. "*Josippon*, a Medieval Hebrew Version of Josephus." In *Josephus, Judaism and Christianity*, edited by Louis H. Feldman and Gohei Hata, 386–397. Detroit: Wayne State University Press, 1987.
———. *Judaism and the Origins of Christianity*. Jerusalem: Magnes Press, 1988.
———. *Judaism of the Second Temple Period*. Vol. 1. *Qumran and Apocalypticism*. Edited by Serge Ruzer. Translated by Azzan Yadin. Jerusalem: Magnes Press, 2007.
———. *Judaism of the Second Temple Period*. Vol. 2. *The Jewish Sages and Their Literature*. Edited by Serge Ruzer. Translated by Azzan Yadin. Grand Rapids, MI: Eerdmans; Jerusalem: Magnes Press, 2009.
———. "The Pharisees and the Stoic Sages according to Josephus" [Hebrew]. *Iyyun* 14 (1963): 318–29 (English summary 366–67). English translation in Flusser, *Judaism of the Second Temple Period*, vol. 2, *The Jewish Sages and Their Literature*, edited by Serge Ruzer and translated by Azzan Yadin, 221–31. Jerusalem: Magnes Press, 2009.
Fox, Michael V. *A Time to Tear Down and a Time to Build Up: A Rereading of Ecclesiastes*. Grand Rapids, MI: Eerdmans, 1999.
Fraade, Steven D. *Legal Fictions: Studies of Law and Narrative in the Discursive Worlds of Ancient Jewish Sectarians and Sages*. JSJSup 147. Leiden: Brill, 2011.
Freeman, Charles. *A New History of Early Christianity*. New Haven: Yale University Press, 2009.
Fuks, Gideon. "Josephus on Herod's Attitude towards Jewish Religion: The Darker Side." *JJS* 53.3 (2002): 238–45.
Gafni, Isaiah. "Historical Background." In *Jewish Writings of the Second Temple Period: Apocrypha, Pseudepigrapha, Qumran Sectarian Writings, Philo, Josephus*, edited by Michael Stone, 1–31. CRINT II.2. Assen: Van Gorcum, 1984.
———. "Josephus and I Maccabees." In *Josephus, the Bible, and History*, edited by Louis H. Feldman and Gohei Hata, 116–31. Detroit: Wayne State University Press, 1989.
Gager, John. *The Origins of Anti-Semitism: Attitudes toward Judaism in Pagan and Christian Antiquity*. Oxford: Oxford University Press, 1985.
———. *Who Made Early Christianity? The Jewish Lives of the Apostle Paul*. New York: Columbia University Press, 2015.
Garrow, Alan. *The Gospel of Matthew's Dependence on the Didache*. London: Bloomsbury, 2004.
Goldenberg, Robert. "The Broken Axis: Rabbinic Judaism and the Fall of Jerusalem." *JAAR* 45.3 supp. (1977): F 869–82.
———. "The Destruction of the Jerusalem Temple: Its Meanings and Its Consequences." In *The Cambridge History of Judaism*, vol. 4, *The Late Roman-Rabbinic Period*, edited by Steven T. Katz, 191–205. Cambridge: Cambridge University Press, 2006.
Goodman, Martin. *A History of Judaism*. Penguin Books, 2017.
———. *Judaism in the Roman World: Collected Essays*. Leiden: Brill, 2006.
———. *Mission and Conversion: Proselytizing in the Religious History of the Roman Empire*. Oxford: Clarendon Press, 1995.

———. "Religious Variety and the Temple in the Late Second Temple Period and Its Aftermath." *JJS* 60.2 (2009): 202–13.

———. *The Roman World: 44 BC–AD 180*. New York: Routledge, 2012 (2nd Edition).

———. *Rome and Jerusalem: The Clash of Ancient Civilizations*. New York: Knopf, 2007.

———. *Rome and Jerusalem: The Clash of Ancient Civilizations*. New York: Vintage Books, 2008.

———. *The Ruling Class of Judaea: The Origins of the Jewish Revolt against Rome A.D. 66–70*. Cambridge: Cambridge University Press, 1987.

———. "Sadducees and Essenes after 70 CE." In *Crossing the Boundaries: Essays in Biblical Interpretation in Honour of Michael D. Goulder*, edited by S. E. Porter, P. Joyce, and D. E. Orton, 347–56. Leiden: Brill, 1994.

———. *State and Society in Roman Galilee: A.D. 132–212*. Totowa, NJ: Rowman and Allanheld, 1998.

Grabbe, Lester L. *Judaic Religion in the Second Temple Period: Belief and Practice from the Exile to Yavneh*. London: Routledge, 2000.

———. "The Law, the Prophets, and the Rest: The State of the Bible in Pre-Maccabean Times." *DSD* 13.3 (2006): 319–38.

———. "The Pharisees: A Response to Steve Mason." In *Judaism in Late Antiquity*, pt. 3, vol. 3, *Where We Stand: Issues and Debates in Ancient Judaism*, edited by Jacob Neusner and Alan J. Avery-Peck, 35–47. Leiden: Brill, 2000.

Gray, Rebecca. *Prophetic Figures in Late Second Temple Palestine: The Evidence from Josephus*. New York: Oxford University Press, 1993.

Green, Bernard. *Christianity in Ancient Rome: The First Three Centuries*. London: Bloomsbury T&T Clark, 2010.

Griffin, Miriam. "The Flavians," 1–82. *Cambridge Ancient History, Volume 11*. Cambridge: Cambridge University Press, 2000.

Grossman, Maxine, L. "Priesthood as Authority: Interpretive Competition in First-Century Judaism and Christianity." In *The Dead Sea Scrolls as Background to (319) Postbiblical Judaism and Early Christianity: Papers from an International Conference at St. Andrews in 2001*, edited by James R. Davila, 117–31. Leiden: Brill, 2003.

———. "Reading *4QMMT*: Genre and History." *RevQ* 77/20.1 (2001): 3–22.

———, ed. *Rediscovering the Dead Sea Scrolls: An Assessment of Old and New Approaches and Methods*. Grand Rapids, MI: Eerdmans, 2010.

Gruen, Erich S. *The Construction of Identity in Hellenistic Judaism: Essays in Early Jewish Literature and History*. Berlin & Boston: De Gruyter, 2016.

———. *Diaspora: Jews Amidst Greeks and Romans*. Cambridge: Harvard University Press, 2002.

———. *Heritage and Hellenism: The Reinvention of Jewish Tradition*. Berkeley: University of California Press, 1998.

———. *Rethinking the Other in Antiquity*. Princeton: Princeton University Press, 2010.

Haaland, Gunnar. "Josephus and the Philosophers of Rome: Does *Contra Apionem* Mirror Domitian's Crushing of the 'Stoic Opposition'?" In *Josephus and Jewish History in Flavian Rome and Beyond*, edited by Joseph Sievers and Gaia Lembi, 297–316. JSJSup 104. Leiden: Brill, 2005.

———. "What Difference Does Philosophy Make? The Three Schools as a Rhetorical Device in Josephus." In *Making History: Josephus and Historical Method*, edited by Zuleika Rodgers, 262–88. JSJSup 110. Leiden: Brill, 2007.

Hadas, Moses. *The Third and Fourth Books of Maccabees: Edited and Translated*. Jewish Apocryphal Literature. New York: Harper (for Philadelphia: Dropsie College), 1953.

Hagner, Donald A. *The Use of the Old Testament and New Testament in Clement of Rome*. Leiden: Brill, 1997.

Halivni, David Weiss. *Breaking the Tablets: Jewish Theology after the Shoah*. Edited and with an introduction by Peter Ochs. Lanham, MD: Rowman & Littlefield, 2007.

———. *Midrash, Mishnah, and Gemara: The Jewish Predilection for Justified Law*. Cambridge, MA: Harvard University Press, 1986.

Hardwick, Michael E. *Josephus as an Historical Source in Patristic Literature through Eusebius.* BJS 128. Atlanta: Scholars Press, 1989.
Harrison, Stephen, ed. *Blackwell: A Companion to Latin Literature.* Oxford: Blackwell, 2005.
Hata, Gohei. "Is the Greek Version of Josephus' 'Jewish War' a Translation or a Rewriting of the First Version?" *JQR* 66.2 (1975): 89–108.
Hayes, Christine E. *Gentile Impurities and Jewish Identities: Intermarriage and Conversion from the Bible to the Talmud.* New York: Oxford University Press, 2002.
Hayward, Robert. "The Jewish Temple at Leontopolis: A Reconsideration." *JJS* 33.1–2 (1982): 429–43.
Hengel, Martin. *Judaism and Hellenism: Studies in Their Encounter in Palestine during the Early Hellenistic Period.* Translated by John Bowden. Minneapolis: Fortress, 1974.
———. *The Zealots: Investigations into the Jewish Freedom Movement in the Period from Herod I until 70 A.D.* Translated by David Smith. Edinburgh: T&T Clark, 1989.
Hengel, Martin, with Christoph Markshies. *The "Hellenization" of Judaea in the First Century after Christ.* London: SCM Press, 1989.
Holmes, Michael W. *The Apostolic Fathers: Greek Text and English Translations.* 3rd edition. Grand Rapids, MI: Baker Academic, 2007.
———, ed. *The Apostolic Fathers in English.* Grand Rapids, MI: Baker Academic, 2006.
Horbury, William. "The Christian Use and the Jewish Origins of the Wisdom of Solomon." In *Wisdom in Ancient Israel: Essays in Honour of J. A. Emerton,* edited by John Day, Robert P. Gordon, and H. G. M. Williamson, 182–96. Cambridge: Cambridge University Press, 1995.
———. *Messianism among Jews and Christians: Biblical and Historical Studies.* London: Bloomsbury T&T Clark, 2016 [2nd Edition].
Howell, Kenneth J. *Clement of Rome and the Didache: A New Translation and Theological Commentary.* Zanesville, OH: CHResources, 2012.
Huitink, Luuk, and Jan Willem van Henten. "The Publication of Flavius Josephus' Works and Their Audiences." *Zutot* 6.1 (2009): 49–60.
Inowlocki, Sabrina. "Did Josephus Ascribe the Fall of Jerusalem to the Murder of James, Brother of Jesus?" *Revue des études juives* 170.1–2 (2011): 21–49.
———. "'Neither Adding nor Omitting Anything': Josephus' Promise Not to Modify the Scriptures in Greek and Latin Context." *JJS* 56.1 (2005): 48–65.
Isaac, Benjamin *The Invention of Racism in Classical Antiquity.* Princeton: Princeton University Press, 2004.
Jefford, Clayton. "Locating the Didache." *Forum,* Third Series 3.1 (Spring 2014): 39–68.
———, ed. *The Didache in Context: Essays on Its Text, History, and Transmission.* Leiden: Brill, 1995.
Jones, Brian W. *The Emperor Domitian.* New York: Routledge, 1992.
Jones, Kenneth R. *Jewish Reactions to the Destruction of Jerusalem in A.D. 70: Apocalypses and Related Pseudepigrapha.* JSJSup 151. Leiden: Brill, 2011.
Kalimi, Isaac. "Murder in Jerusalem Temple, the Chronicler's Story of Zechariah: Literary and Theological Features, Historical Credibility, and Impact." *RB* 117.2 (2010): 200–209.
———. "The Murder of the Prophet Zechariah in the Gospels." *RB* 116.2 (2009): 246–61.
———. "The Murders of the Messengers: Stephen versus Zechariah and the Ethical Values of the 'New' versus 'Old' Testament." *Australian Biblical Review* 56 (2008): 67–73.
Kalms, J. U., ed. *Internationales Josephus-Kolloquium, Aarhus 1999.* Munster: Lit, 2000.
Keener, Craig. *Acts: An Exegetical Commentary, Volume 4: 24:1–28:31.* Baker Academic, 2015.
Kelley, Nicole. "The Cosmopolitan Expression of Josephus's Prophetic Perspective in the 'Jewish War.'" *HTR* 97.3 (2004): 257–74.
Klawans, Jonathan. *Impurity and Sin in Ancient Judaism.* New York: Oxford University Press, 2000.
———. "Josephus, the Rabbis, and Responses to Catastrophes Ancient and Modern." *JQR* 100.2 (2010): 278–309.
———. "Sadducees, Zadokites, and the Wisdom of Ben Sira." In *Israel's God and Rebecca's Children: Christology and Community in Early Judaism and Christianity, Essays in Honor*

of Larry W. Hurtado and Alan F. Segal, edited by David B. Capes, April D. DeConick, Helen K. Bond, and Troy A. Miller, 261–76. Waco, TX: Baylor University Press, 2007.

Kraft, Robert. *Barnabas and the Didache*. New York: Thomas Nelson and Sons, 1965.

Krause, Andrew R. *Synagogues in the Works of Flavius Josephus: Rhetoric, Spatiality, and First-Century Jewish Institutions*. Leiden: Brill, 2017.

Ladouceur, David J. "Josephus and Masada." In *Josephus, Judaism and Christianity*, edited by Louis H. Feldman and Gohei Hata, 95–113. Detroit: Wayne State University Press, 1987.

———. "Masada: A Consideration of the Literary Evidence." *Greek, Roman, and Byzantine Studies* 21.3 (1980): 245–60.

Lampe, Peter. *Christians at Rome in the First Two Centuries: From Paul to Valentinus*. Minneapolis: Fortress Press, 2003.

Lembi, Gaia., and Joseph Sievers, eds. *Josephus and Jewish History in Flavian Rome and Beyond*. Brill, 2005.

Leoni, Tommaso. "The Text of Josephus's Works: An Overview." *JSJ* 40.2 (2009): 149–84.

———. "Translations and Adaptations of Josephus's Writings in Antiquity and the Middle Ages." *Ostraka: Rivista di antichità* 16.2 (2007): 481–92.

Levenson, Jon D. *Resurrection and the Restoration of Israel: The Ultimate Victory of the God of Life*. New Haven: Yale University Press, 2006.

Levine, Lee I. *Judaism and Hellenism in Antiquity: Conflict or Confluence?* Seattle: University of Washington Press, 1998.

Lichtenberger, Herman. "Zion and the Destruction of the Temple in 4 Ezra 9–10." In *Gemeinde ohne Tempel: Zur Substituierung und Transformation des Jerusalemer Tempels und seines Kults im Alten Testament, antiken Judentum und frühen Christentum*, edited by Beate Ego, Armin Lange, and Peter Pilhofer, in cooperation with Kathrin Ehlers, 239–49. WUNT 1, 118. Tübingen: Mohr Siebeck, 1999.

MacMullen, Ramsay. *Christianizing the Roman Empire*. New Haven: Yale University Press, 1984.

Magness, Jodi. "The Arch of Titus at Rome and the Fate of the God of Israel." *JJS* 59.2 (2008): 201–17.

Mandel, Paul. "Scriptural Exegesis and the Pharisees in Josephus." *JJS* 58.1 (2007): 19–32.

Marcus, Ralph. "The Pharisees in the Light of Modern Scholarship." *Journal of Religion* 32.3 (1952): 153–64.

Martial. *Martial: Epigrams*. Selected and translated by James Michie. Introduction by Shadi Bartsch. New York: Modern Library, 2002.

———. *Martial: Selected Epigrams*. Translated with notes by Susan McLean, with an introduction by Marc Kleijwegt. Madison: University of Wisconsin Press, 2014.

Mason, Steve. *Flavius Josephus on the Pharisees*. SPB 39. Leiden: Brill, 1991.

———. Introduction to *Judean Antiquities 1–4*, by Louis Feldman, xii–xxxvi. BJP 3. Leiden: Brill, 2000.

———. *Josephus and the New Testament*. 2nd ed. Peabody, MA: Hendrickson, 2003.

———. "Josephus, Daniel, and the Flavian House." In *Josephus and the History of the Greco-Roman Period: Essays in Memory of Morton Smith*, edited by Fausto Parente and Joseph Sievers, 161–91. SPB 41. Leiden: Brill, 1994.

———. *Josephus, Judea, and Christian Origins: Methods and Categories*. Peabody, MA: Hendrickson, 2009.

———. *Life of Josephus: Translation and Commentary*. BJP 9. Leiden: Brill, 2001.

———. "Pharisaic Dominance before 70 CE and the Gospels' Hypocrisy Charge (Matt 23:2–3)." *HTR* 83.4 (1990): 363–81.

———. "Revisiting Josephus's Pharisees." In *Judaism in Late Antiquity*, pt. 3, vol. 2, *Where We Stand: Issues and Debates in Ancient Judaism*, edited by Jacob Neusner and Alan J. Avery-Peck, 23–56. Leiden: Brill, 1999.

———. *Understanding Josephus: Seven Perspectives*. JSPSup 32. Sheffield, England: Sheffield Academic Press, 1998.

———. "What Josephus Says about the Essenes in His *Judean War*." In *Text and Artifact in the Religions of Mediterranean Antiquity: Essays in Honour of Peter Richardson*, edited by

Stephen G. Wilson and Michel Desjardins, 423–55. Studies in Christianity and Judaism 9. Waterloo, Canada: Wilfrid Laurier University Press, 2000.
Mason, Steve, with Honora Chapman. *Judean War 2: Translation and Commentary*. BJP 1b. Leiden: Brill, 2008.
McLaren, James S. "Ananus, James, and Earliest Christianity: Josephus' Account of the Death of James." *Journal of Theological Studies* 52 (2001): 1–25.
———. *Turbulent Times? Josephus and Scholarship on Judaea in the First Century CE*. JSPSup 29. Sheffield, England: Sheffield Academic Press, 1998.
Meyer, John. "Jewish Culture in Greco-Roman Palestine." In *Cultures of the Jews: Volume 1. Mediterranean Origins,* edited by David Biale, 149–57. New York: Shocken Books, 2002.
Meyers, Eric M. *Jewish Ossuaries: Reburial and Rebirth, Secondary Burials in Their Ancient Near Eastern Setting*. Biblica et orientalia 24. Rome: Biblical Institute Press, 1971.
Milavec, Aaron. *The Didache: Hope, Faith, and Life of Earliest Christian Communities, 50–70 C.E.* Mahwah, NJ: Paulist Press, 2003.
———. *The Didache: Text, Translation, Analysis, and Commentary*. Minnesota: Liturgical Press, 2003.
Milikowsky, Chaim. "Notions of Exile, Subjugation and Return in Rabbinic Literature." In *Exile: Old Testament, Jewish, and Christian Conceptions,* edited by J. M. Scott, 265–96. JSJSup 56. Leiden: Brill, 1997.
Millar, Fergus. *The Roman Near East: 31 BC–AD 337*. Cambridge: Harvard University Press, 1995.
Momigliano, Arnaldo. *Essays on Ancient and Modern Judaism*. Edited with an introduction by Sylvia Berth. Translated by Maura Masella Gayley. Chicago: University of Chicago Press, 1994.
Nauta, Ruurd R. *Poetry for Patrons: Literary Communication in the Age of Domitian*. Leiden: Brill, 2002.
Netzer, Ehud, with Rachel Laureys-Chachy. *The Architecture of Herod the Great Builder*. Tübingen: Mohr Siebeck, 2006.
Neusner, Jacob. "The Conversion of Adiabene to Christianity." *Numen* (13:2) 1966: 144–50.
———. "Emergent Rabbinic Judaism in a Time of Crisis: Four Responses to the Destruction of the Second Temple." *Judaism* 21.3 (1972): 313–27.
———. "From History to Religion." In *The Craft of Religious Studies,* edited by Jon R. Stone, 98–116. New York: Palgrave, 2000.
———. *From Politics to Piety: The Emergence of Pharisaic Judaism*. New York: Ktav, 1979.
———. *How Important Was the Destruction of the Second Temple in the Formation of Rabbinic Judaism?* Lanham, MD: University Press of America, 2006.
———. "In Quest of the Historical Rabban Yohanan Ben Zakkai." *HTR* (1966): 391–413.
———. *Introduction to Rabbinic Literature*. New York: Doubleday, 1994.
———. *Israel after Calamity: The Book of Lamentations*. Valley Forge, PA: Trinity Press International, 1995.
———. *Judaism: The Evidence of the Mishnah*. Chicago: University of Chicago Press, 1979.
———. *The Mishnah: A New Translation*. New Haven: Yale University Press, 1988.
———. *Rabbinic Judaism: Structure and System*. Minneapolis: Fortress, 1995.
———. *The Rabbinic Traditions about the Pharisees before 70*. 3 vols. Leiden: Brill, 1971.
Neusner, Jacob, and Alan J. Avery-Peck, eds. *Judaism in Late Antiquity*. Pt. 3, vol. 1. *Where We Stand: Issues and Debates in Ancient Judaism*. Leiden: Brill, 1999.
Neusner, Jacob, and Bruce D. Chilton, eds. *In Quest of the Historical Pharisees*. Waco, TX: Baylor University Press, 2007.
Newell, Raymond R. "Forms and Historical Value of Josephus' Suicide Accounts." In *Josephus, the Bible, and History,* edited by Louis H. Feldman and Gohei Hata, 278–294. Detroit: Wayne State University Press, 1989.
Nickelsburg, George W. E. *Resurrection, Immortality, and Eternal Life in Intertestamental Judaism and Early Christianity* (1972). Expanded ed. Harvard Theological Studies 56. Cambridge, MA: Harvard University Press, 2006.
Niditch, Susan. *War in the Hebrew Bible: A Study in the Ethics of Violence*. New York: Oxford University Press, 1993.

Nigg, Joseph. *The Phoenix: An Unnatural Biography of a Mythic Beast*. Chicago: University of Chicago Press, 2016.
Novenson, Matthew V. *The Grammar of Messianism: An Ancient Jewish Political Idiom and Its Users*. Oxford: Oxford University Press, 2017.
Olson, Ryan S. *Tragedy, Authority, and Trickery: The Poetics of Embedded Letters in Josephus*. Hellenic Studies 42. Washington, DC: Center for Hellenic Studies, 2010.
Olyan, Saul B. "Ben Sira's Relationship to the Priesthood." *HTR* 80.3 (1987): 261–86.
———. "Zadok's Origins and the Tribal Politics of David." *JBL* 101.2 (1982): 177–93.
Paget, Carleton J. "Some Observations on Josephus and Christianity." *Journal of Theological Studies* N.S. 52:2 (2001): 539–624.
Pardee, Nancy. *The Genre and Development of the Didache: A Text-Linguistic Analysis*. Tubingen: Mohr Siebeck, 2012.
Pastor, Jack, Pnina Stern, and Menahem Mor, eds. *Flavius Josephus: Interpretation and History*. Leiden: Brill, 2011.
Penner, Ken. "The Fate of Josephus's *Antiquitates Judaicae* 13.171–73: Ancient Jewish Philosophy in Context." *Journal of Biblical Studies* 1.4 (n.d.): 1–26.
Popović, Mladen. "Bones, Bodies, and Resurrection in the Dead Sea Scrolls." In *The Human Body in Death and Resurrection*, edited by Tobias Nicklas, Friedrich V. Reiterer, and Joseph Verheyden, in collaboration with Heike Braun, 221–42. Deuterocanonical and Cognate Literature Yearbook. Berlin: de Gruyter, 2009.
Porton, Gary G. "Sadducees." In *Anchor Bible Dictionary*, edited by David Noel Freedman, 6 vols., 5:892–95. New York: Doubleday, 1992.
Price, Jonathan J. "Josephus and the Dialogue on the Destruction of Jerusalem." In *Josephus und das Neue Testament: Weshselseitige Wahrnehmungen: II. Internationales Symposium zum Corpus Judaeo-Hellenisticum, 25.–28. Mai 2006*, edited by Chistfried Böttrich and Jens Herzer, with the assistance of Torsten Reiprich, 181–94. WUNT 1, 209. Tübingen: Mohr Siebeck, 2007.
———. "The Provincial Historian in Rome." In *Josephus and Jewish History in Flavian Rome and Beyond*, edited by Joseph Sievers and Gaia Lembi, 101–18. JSJSup 104. Leiden: Brill, 2005.
———. "Some Aspects of Josephus' Theological Interpretation of the Jewish War." In *"The Words of a Wise Man's Mouth Are Gracious" (Qoh 10,12): Festschrift for Günter Stemberger on the Occasion of his 65th Birthday*, edited by Mauro Perani, 109–19. SJ 32. Berlin: de Gruyter, 2005.
Rajak, Tessa. *The Jewish Dialogue with Greece and Rome: Studies in Cultural and Social Interaction*. Leiden: Brill, 2002.
———. "Josephus and Justus of Tiberias." In *Josephus, Judaism and Christianity*, edited by Louis H. Feldman and Gohei Hata, 81–94. Detroit: Wayne State University Press, 1987.
———. *Josephus: The Historian and His Society* (1983). 2nd ed. London: Duckworth, 2002.
Raviv, Rivka. "The Talmudic Formulation of the Prophecies of the Four Kingdoms in the Book of Daniel" [Hebrew]. *Jewish Studies: An Internet Journal* 5 (2006): 1–20.
Rees, Roger, ed. *Latin Panegyric*. Oxford: Oxford University Press, 2012.
Regev, Eyal. "Herod's Jewish Ideology Facing Romanization: On Intermarriage, Ritual Baths, and Speeches." *JQR* 100.2 (2010): 197–222.
———. "Sadducees." In *New Interpreters Bible Dictionary*, edited by Katharine Doob Sakenfeld, 5 vols., 5:32–36. Nashville, TN: Abingdon Press, 2009.
———. *The Sadducees and Their Halakhah: Religion and Society in the Second Temple Period* [Hebrew]. Jerusalem: Yad Ben-Zvi, 2005.
Regev, Eyal, and David Nakman. "Josephus and the Halakhah of the Pharisees, the Sadducees, and Qumran" [Hebrew]. *Zion* 67.4 (2002): 401–33 (English summary, xxxii).
Reinhartz, Adele. *Caiaphas the High Priest*. Minneapolis: Fortress Press, 2013.
Rengstorf, Karl Heinrich, ed. *A Complete Concordance to Flavius Josephus*. 1969–83. Study Edition in Two Volumes, Including Supplement 1: *Namenwörterbuch zu Flavius Josephus*, by Abraham Schalit. Leiden: Brill, 2002.
Revel, Bernard. "Some Anti-traditional Laws in Josephus." *JQR* 14.3 (1924): 293–301.

Richardson, Peter. *Building Jewish in the Roman East*. Waco, TX: Baylor University Press, 2004.

———. *Herod: King of the Jews and Friend of the Romans*. Columbia: University of South Carolina Press, 1996.

Rimell, Victoria E. *Martial's Rome: Empire and the Ideology of Epigram*. Cambridge: Cambridge University Press, 2009.

Rodgers, Zuleika, ed. *Making History: Josephus and Historical Method*. Brill, 2006.

Rubenstein, Jeffrey L. *Talmudic Stories: Narrative Art, Composition, and Culture*. Baltimore: Johns Hopkins University Press, 1999.

Rubenstein, Richard L. "The Fall of Jerusalem and the Birth of Holocaust Theology." In *Go and Study: Essays and Studies in Honor of Alfred Jospe*, edited by Raphael Jospe and Samuel Z. Fishman, 223–40. Washington, DC: B'nai B'rith Hillel Foundations, 1980.

Safrai, Shmuel, ed. *The Literature of the Sages, First Part: Oral Torah, Halakha, Mishna, Tosefta, Talmud, External Tractates*. CRINT II.3.1. Assen: Van Gorcum, 1987.

Saldarini, Anthony J. *Pharisees, Scribes and Sadducees in Palestinian Society: A Sociological Approach*. Wilmington, DE: Michael Glazier, 1988.

Sanders, E. P. "The Dead Sea Sect and Other Jews: Commonalities, Overlaps, and Differences." In *The Dead Sea Scrolls in Their Historical Context*, edited by Timothy H. Lim, with Larry W. Hurtado, A. Graeme Auld, and Alison Jack, 7–43. London: T & T Clark, 2004.

———. *Jewish Law from Jesus to the Mishnah: Five Studies*. London: SCM Press, 1990.

———. *Judaism: Practice and Belief, 63 BCE–66 CE*. London: SCM Press, 1992.

———. *Paul and Palestinian Judaism: A Comparison of Patterns of Religion*. Minneapolis: Fortress, 1977.

Schäfer, Peter. "Bar Kokhba and the Rabbis." In *The Bar Kokhba War: New Perspectives on the Second Jewish Revolt against Rome*, edited by Peter Schäfer, 1–22. TSAJ 100. Tübingen: Mohr Siebeck 2003.

———. *Judeophobia: Attitudes toward the Jews in the Ancient World*. Cambridge: Harvard University Press, 1998.

Schaff, Philip. *ANF 01: The Apostolic Fathers with Justin Martyr and Irenaeus*. Peabody: Hendrickson, 1996.

Schiffman, Lawrence H. *From Text to Tradition: A History of Second Temple and Rabbinic Judaism*. Hoboken, NJ: Ktav, 1991.

———. *Qumran and Jerusalem: Studies in the Dead Sea Scrolls and the History of Judaism*. Grand Rapids, MI: Eerdmans, 2010.

Schofield, Alison, and James C. VanderKam. "Were the Hasmoneans Zadokites?" *JBL* 124.1 (2005): 73–87.

Schreckenberg, Heinz. "Josephus in Early Christian Literature and Medieval Christian Art." In *Jewish Historiography and Iconography in Early and Medieval Christianity*, by Heinz Schreckenberg and Kurt Schubert, 1–138. CRINT III.1. Assen: Van Gorcum 1992.

Schremer, Adiel. "'The Lord Has Forsaken the Land': Radical Explanations of the Military and Political Defeat of the Jews in Tannaitic Times." *JJS* 59.2 (2008): 183–200.

———. "'[T]he[y] Did Not Read in the Sealed Book': Qumran Halakhic Revolution and the Emergence of Torah Study in Second Temple Judaism." In *Historical Perspectives: From the Hasmoneans to Bar Kokhba in Light of the Dead Sea Scrolls; Proceedings of the Fourth International Symposium of the Orion Center for the Study of the Dead Sea Scrolls and Associated Literature, 27–31 January, 1999*, edited by David Goodblatt, Avital Pinnick, and Daniel R. Schwartz, 105–26. STDJ 37. Leiden: Brill, 2001.

Schuller, Eileen. "Petitionary Prayer and the Religion of Qumran." In *Religion in the Dead Sea Scrolls*, edited by John J. Collins and Robert A. Kugler, 29–45. Grand Rapids, MI: Eerdmans, 2000.

Schürer, Emil. *The History of the Jewish People in the Age of Jesus Christ*. Revised and edited by Geza Vermes, Fergus Millar, and Matthew Black. 4 vols. Edinburgh: T & T Clark, 1973–1987.

Schwartz, Daniel R. "Josephus on the Jewish Constitutions and Community." *Scripta Classica Israelica* 7 (1983): 30–52.

———. "KATA TOYTON TON KAIPON: Josephus' Source on Agrippa II." *JQR* 72.4 (1982): 241–68.

———. "Law and Truth: On Qumranic-Sadducean and Rabbinic Views of Law." In *The Dead Sea Scrolls: Forty Years of Research*, edited by Devorah Dimant and Uriel Rappaport, 229–40. STDJ 10. Leiden: Brill, 1992.

———. "On Abraham Schalit, Herod, Josephus, the Holocaust, Horst R. Moehring, and the Study of Ancient Jewish History." *Jewish History* 2.2 (1987): 9–28.

———. *Reading the First Century: On Reading Josephus and Studying Jewish History of the First Century.* Tubingen: Mohr Siebeck, 2013.

———. Review of *Jewish Martyrs in the Pagan and Christian Worlds*, by Shmuel Shepkaru. *Review of Biblical Literature*, 2/2007.

———. *Studies in the Jewish Background of Christianity.* WUNT 1, 60. Tübingen: Mohr Siebeck, 1992.

———. *2 Maccabees.* Commentaries on Early Jewish Literature. Berlin: de Gruyter, 2008.

Schwartz, Seth. "The Composition and Publication of Josephus's *Bellum Iudaicum* Book 7." *HTR* 79.4 (1986): 373–86.

———. *Imperialism and Jewish Society, 200 B.C.E. to 640 C.E.* Princeton: Princeton University Press, 2001.

———. *Josephus and Judaean Politics.* Columbia Studies in the Classical Tradition 18. Leiden: Brill, 1990.

———. *Were the Jews a Mediterranean Society? Reciprocity and Solidarity in Ancient Judaism.* Princeton: Princeton University Press, 2010.

Segal, Alan F. *Paul the Convert: The Apostolate and Apostasy of Saul the Pharisee.* New Haven: Yale University Press, 1990.

———. *Rebecca's Children: Judaism and Christianity in the Roman World.* Cambridge, MA: Harvard University Press, 1986.

Seneca, Lucius Annaeus. *Moral and Political Essays.* Cambridge: Cambridge University Press, 1995.

Serghidou, Anastasin. *Fear of Slaves, Fear of Enslavement in Ancient Mediterranean.* Franche-Comte: Presses Univ. Franche-Comte, 2007.

Shapiro, Schubert. "In Defense of the Defenders of Masada." *Tradition* 11.1 (1970): 31–43.

Sharples, R. W. "Alexander of Aphrodisias, *De Fato*: Some Parallels." *Classical Quarterly* 28.2 (1978): 243–66.

Sievers, Joseph. "Josephus and the Afterlife." In *Understanding Josephus: Seven Perspectives*, edited by Steve Mason, 20–34. JSPSup 32. Sheffield, England: Sheffield Academic Press, 1998.

———. "Josephus, First Maccabees, Sparta, the Three *Haireseis*—and Cicero." *JSJ* 32.3 (2001): 241–51.

———. *Synopsis of the Greek Sources for the Study of the Hasmonean Period: 1–2 Maccabees and Josephus, "War "1 and "Antiquities," 12–14.* Subsidia biblica 20. Rome: Pontifical Biblical Institute, 2001.

———. "Who Were the Pharisees?" In *Hillel and Jesus: Comparisons of Two Major Religious Leaders*, edited by James H. Charlesworth and Loren L. Johns, 137–55. Minneapolis: Fortress Press, 1997.

Sievers, Joseph, and Gaia Lembi, eds. *Josephus and Jewish History in Flavian Rome and Beyond.* Leiden: Brill, 2005.

Simon, Marcel. *Jewish Sects at the Time of Jesus.* Philadelphia: Fortress, 1967.

Singer, Isidore, et al., eds. *The Jewish Encyclopedia.* 12 vols. New York: Funk and Wagnall's, 1901–1906.

Smallwood, E. Mary. *The Jews under Roman Rule: From Pompey to Diocletian.* Leiden: Brill, 1976.

Smith, Morton. "The Dead Sea Sect in Relation to Ancient Judaism." *New Testament Studies* 7 (1961): 347–60.

———. "The Description of the Essenes in the Josephus and the Philosophumena." *HUCA* 29 (1958): 273–313.

Southern, Pat. *Domitian: Tragic Tyrant.* New York: Routledge, 1997.

Spilsbury, Paul. "*Contra Apionem* and *Antiquitates Judaicae:* Points of Contact." In *Josephus' "Contra Apionem": Studies in Its Character and Context with a Latin Concordance to the Portion Missing in Greek*, edited by Louis H. Feldman and John R. Levison, 348–68. AGJU 34. Leiden: Brill, 1996.
———. "Flavius Josephus on the Rise and Fall of the Roman Empire." *JTS* 54.1 (2003): 1–24.
———. "God and Israel in Josephus: A Patron-Client Relationship." In *Understanding Josephus: Seven Perspectives*, edited by Steve Mason, 172–91. JSPSup 32. Sheffield, England: Sheffield Academic Press, 1998.
———. "Josephus on the Burning of the Temple, the Flavian Triumph, and the Providence of God." *Society of Biblical Literature Seminar Papers* 41 (2002): 306–27.
Stark, Rodney. *The Rise of Christianity: A Sociologist Reconsiders History*. Princeton: Princeton University Press, 1996.
Stemberger, Günter. *Jewish Contemporaries of Jesus: Pharisees, Sadducees, Essenes*. Translated by Allan W. Mahnke. Minneapolis: Fortress, 1995.
———. "The Sadducees—Their History and Doctrines." In *The Cambridge History of Judaism*, Vol. 3, *The Early Roman Period*, edited by William Horbury, W. D. Davies, and John Sturdy, 428–43. Cambridge: Cambridge University Press, 1999.
Sterling, Gregory. "Explaining Defeat: Polybius and Josephus on the Wars with Rome." In *Internationales Josephus-Kolloquium, Aarhus* 1999, edited by J. U. Kalms, 135–51. Munster: Lit, 2000.
Stern, Menahem. *Greek and Latin Authors on Jews and Judaism: Edited with Introductions, Translations, and Commentary*. 3 vols. Jerusalem: Israel Academy of Sciences and Humanities, 1976–1984.
———. "Josephus and the Roman Empire as Reflected in *The Jewish War*." In *Josephus, Judaism and Christianity*, edited by Louis H. Feldman and Gohei Hata, 71–80. Detroit: Wayne State University Press, 1987.
Stern, Pnina. "*Life of Josephus:* The Autobiography of Flavius Josephus." *JSJ* 41.1 (2010): 63–93.
Stone, Michael, ed. *Jewish Writings of the Second Temple Period: Apocrypha, Pseudepigrapha, Qumran Sectarian Writings, Philo, Josephus*. CRINT II.2. Assen: Van Gorcum, 1984.
Stroumsa, Guy G. "From Anti-Judaism to Antisemitism in Ancient Christianity?" In *Contra Iudaeos: Ancient and Medieval Polemics between Christians and Jews* (p.336), edited by Ora Limor and Guy G. Stroumsa, 1–26. Texts and Studies in Medieval and Early Modern Judaism 10. Tübingen, Mohr Siebeck, 1996.
Sullivan, J. P. "Martial's Sexual Attitudes." *Philologus-Zeitschrift fur antike literature und ihre Rezeption*. Volume 123.1–2 (1979): 288–302.
———. *Martial: The Unexpected Classic*. Cambridge: Cambridge University Press, 1991.
Taylor, Joan E. "Philo of Alexandria on the Essenes: A Case Study on the Use of Classical Sources in Discussions of the Qumran-Essene Hypothesis." *Studia Philonica Annual* 19 (2007): 1–28.
Tcherikover, Victor. *Hellenistic Civilization and the Jews*. Translated by S. Appelbaum. Philadelphia: Jewish Publication Society, 1959.
Thackeray, H. St. John. *Josephus: The Man and the Historian*. With a preface by George Foot Moore. New York: Jewish Institute of Religion, 1929.
Thackeray, H. St. John, Ralph Marcus, Allen Wilkgren, and L. H. Feldman, eds. and trans. *Josephus*. LCL. 9 vols. Cambridge, MA: Harvard University Press, 1926–1965.
Thoma, Clemens. "High Priesthood in the Judgment of Josephus." In *Josephus, the Bible, and History*, edited by Louis H. Feldman and Gohei Hata, 196–215. Detroit: Wayne State University Press, 1989.
Thompson, Leonard L. *The Book of Revelation: Apocalypse and Empire*. Oxford: Oxford University Press, 1990.
Tomes, Roger. "Heroism in 1 and 2 Maccabees." *Biblical Interpretation* 15.2 (2007): 171–99.
Trever, John C. *The Dead Sea Scrolls: A Personal Account*. Rev. ed. Grand Rapids, MI: Eerdmans, 1977.
Tuval, Michael. *From Jerusalem Priest to Roman Jew: Josephus and the Paradigms of Ancient Judaism*. Tubingen: Mohr Siebeck, 2013.

Ulrich, Eugene. *The Dead Sea Scrolls and the Origins of the Bible*. Grand Rapids, MI: Eerdmans, 1999.

Urbach, Ephraim E. *The Sages: Their Concepts and Beliefs*. Translated by Israel Abrahams. Cambridge, MA: Harvard University Press, 1987.

Van den Broek, R. *The Myth of the Phoenix in Antiquity: According to Classical and Early Christian Traditions*. Leiden: Brill, 1971.

VanderKam, James C. *From Joshua to Caiaphas: High Priests after the Exile*. Minneapolis: Fortress, 2004.

VanderKam, James C., and Peter Flint. *The Meaning of the Dead Sea Scrolls: Their Significance for Understanding the Bible, Judaism, Jesus, and Christianity*. New York: HarperSanFrancisco, 2002.

Van de Sandt, Huub, and David Flusser, eds. *The Didache: Its Jewish Sources and Its Place in Early Judaism and Christianity*. Van Gorcum & Fortress Press, 2002.

Van de Sandt, Huub, and Jurgen K. Zangenberg, eds. *Matthew, James and The Didache: Three Related Documents in Their Jewish and Christian Settings*. SBL Press, 2008.

Van Henten, Jan Willem. "Noble Death in Josephus: Just Rhetoric?" In *Making History: Josephus and Historical Method*, edited by Zuleika Rodgers, 195–218. JSJSup 110. Leiden: Brill, 2007.

Vermes, Geza. *The Complete Dead Sea Scrolls in English*. Rev. ed. New York: Penguin, 2004.

———. "A Summary of the Law by Flavius Josephus." *Novum Testamentum* 24.4 (1982): 289–303.

Vermes, Geza, and Marin D. Goodman, eds. *The Essenes: According to the Classical Sources*. Sheffield, England: JSOT Press (for Oxford Centre for Postgraduate Hebrew Study), 1989.

Walbank, Frank W. *Polybius, Rome, and the Hellenistic World: Essays and Reflections*. Cambridge: Cambridge University Press, 2002.

———. "'Treason' and Roman Domination: Two Case-Studies, Polybius and Josephus." In F. W. Walbank ed., *Polybius, Rome, and the Hellenistic World: Essays and Reflections*, 258–76. Cambridge: Cambridge University Press, 2002.

Walsh, P. G. *Pliny the Younger: Complete Letters*. Oxford: Oxford University Press, 2006.

Weitzman, Steven. "Josephus on How to Survive Martyrdom." *JJS* 55.2 (2004) 230–45.

———. *Surviving Sacrilege: Cultural Persistence in Jewish Antiquity*. Cambridge, MA: Harvard University Press, 2005.

Wellhausen, Julius. *The Pharisees and Sadducees*. 1874. Reprint. Translated by Mark E. Biddle. Macon, GA: Mercer University Press, 2001. (338)

Werman, Cana. "Oral Torah vs. Written Torah(s): Competing Claims to Authority." In *Rabbinic Perspectives: Rabbinic Literature and the Dead Sea Scrolls; Proceedings of the Eighth International Symposium of the Orient Center for the Study of the Dead Sea Scrolls and Associated Literature, 7–9 January 2003*, edited by Steven D. Fraade, Aharon Shemesh.

Whiston, William, trans. *The Works of Josephus: Complete and Unabridged*. 1736. Reprint, new updated ed., Peabody, MA: Hendrickson, 1995.

Williams, Michael A. "Higher Providence, Lower Providences and Fate in Gnosticism and Middle Plantonism." In *Neoplatonism and Gnosticism*, edited by Richard T. Wallis and Jay Bregman, 483–507. Albany: State University of New York Press, 1992.

Williamson, H. G. M. "The Historical Value of Josephus' *Jewish Antiquities* XI, 197–301." *JTS* 28.1 (1977): 49–66.

Winsbury, Rex. *Pliny the Younger: A Life in Roman Letters*. New York and London: Bloomsbury Academic, 2014.

Winston, David. *The Ancestral Philosophy: Hellenistic Philosophy in Second Temple Judaism*. BJS 331. Providence: Brown Judaic Studies, 2001.

Winter, Paul. "Ben Sira and the Teaching of 'Two Ways.'" *VT* 5.3 (1955): 315–18.

Wolfson, Harry Austryn. *Philo: Foundations of Religious Philosophy in Judaism, Christianity, and Islam*. 2 vols. Cambridge, MA: Harvard University Press, 1947.

Yonge, Charles Duke, trans. *The Works of Philo Judaeus: The Contemporary of Josephus*. 1854–90. Reprint, new updated version with foreword by David M. Scholer. Peabody, MA: Hendrickson, 2004.

Zeitlin, Solomon. "The Account of the Essenes in Josephus and in the Philosophumena (a reply to M. Smith)." *JQR* 49.4 (1958–59): 292–99.

———. *The Rise and Fall of the Judaean State: A Political, Social and Religious History of the Second Commonwealth*. 3 vols. Philadelphia: Jewish Publication Society, 1962–1978.

Index

Abraham, 33, 100, 101, 103, 104, 285, 298, 311, 322, 323
Abrahamic, 101
Abusch, Ra'anan, 173
Achaia (Achaea), 43, 102, 112, 264, 288, 291, 300, 313
Adiabene, 6, 10, 11, 13, 21, 34, 42, 47, 94, 95, 97, 98, 99, 100, 101, 102, 103, 104, 105, 124, 127n37, 130, 153, 154, 306, 320, 323
adoption, 100
Against Apion (Josephus), 13, 14, 15, 18n21, 19n22, 32, 40, 41, 57, 66, 79, 82, 86, 101, 119, 126n4, 126n5, 130, 132, 136, 141, 144, 156, 159, 172, 173, 174, 175, 176, 177, 178, 179, 180, 181, 182, 183, 184, 185, 186, 187, 188, 189, 190, 191, 194n84, 195n86, 195n90–195n91, 260, 265, 269, 270, 271, 303, 313, 314, 315, 320
Against Flaccus (Philo), 15, 130
Agricola, 138, 161, 162, 249–250, 251, 262n62, 262n75–262n77, 263, 267, 279, 280, 288, 314, 315n1, 315n2, 316n23, 316n24
Agrippa I, Marcus Julius, 8, 10, 68, 75, 76, 190, 191
Agrippa II, 6, 8, 9–10, 11, 13, 18n13, 22, 42, 52, 54, 58, 77, 94, 125, 126, 158, 171, 190, 221, 322
Albinus, 1, 28, 29, 30, 52, 54
Alexander "the Alabarch", 68
Alexander the Great, 62n19, 67, 95, 193n52
Alexander, Tiberius Julius, 48
Alexandria, 15, 47, 48, 52, 68, 75, 96, 106, 124, 130, 131, 132, 147, 148, 157, 177, 185, 187, 188, 192n5
Aliturus, 75, 76, 77, 78
Ananias (Jewish merchant/teacher), 11, 34, 35, 95, 96, 97, 98, 99, 100
Ananus son of Ananus (High Priest), 1, 3, 4, 9, 28, 30, 44, 49, 50, 51, 52, 53, 54, 57, 58, 59, 63n43, 73, 74, 104, 198, 269, 322
Ananias son of Nebedaeus, 57
anti-Jewish, 14, 91, 156, 178, 185, 192n15, 314
anti-Judaism, 320
Antioch, 55, 102, 103, 105, 115, 117, 121, 122, 126, 138, 302, 305, 306
Antiochus the Apostate, 138
Antiochus IV Epiphanes, 21
Antipas, Herod, 99
Antiquities of the Jews (Josephus), 3, 4, 8, 9, 10, 11, 14, 15, 18n21, 21, 22, 25, 26, 29, 31, 32–33, 34, 35, 41, 42, 44, 49, 50, 55, 61n4, 63n46, 66, 68, 69, 74, 77, 79, 81, 82, 83, 84, 87, 89, 90, 92, 94, 101, 103, 119, 126, 130, 131–132, 133–134, 136, 137, 140, 141, 143, 149, 154, 155, 156, 159–160, 174–175, 176,

178–179, 180, 181, 182, 183, 184–185, 186, 188, 189, 190, 198, 254, 260, 265, 269, 270, 298, 303, 313, 314, 315
Apion, 14, 15, 79, 130, 131, 172, 174, 177, 178, 179, 180, 185, 186, 187, 188, 189, 190, 191, 192n8, 194n62, 194n64, 194n74–194n77, 194n81
Appian, 157
Arch of Titus, 150, 153, 155, 164, 221, 303, 304
archives, 1, 41, 279
archives, Jewish, 11, 14, 26, 60, 65, 66, 99, 105, 123, 270, 315
Argonautica (Valerius Flaccus), 150
Augustus, Caesar (Octavian), 75, 170, 216, 275, 276

Babylonian, 117, 151
Babylonian Talmud, 6, 8
Bannus, 5, 75
Bakke, Odd Magne, 316n32
barbarians, 197
Barclay, John M. G., ix, x, 18n21, 32, 186, 188
Bar Kokhba, 336
Barnabas, Epistle of, 111, 119, 121, 122, 128n45
Bartsch, Shadi, 261n41, 307
bathhouses, 219, 222, 223, 224
baths, 169, 170, 204, 218, 219, 220, 223, 255
Baths of Agrippa, 170
Begg, Christopher, ix, 62n38
Berenice, 8, 9, 10, 11, 22, 77, 94, 125, 126, 221
Bilde, Per, ix, 174
Bird, Michael F., 296, 297
Bithynia, 201, 283
Bithynia-Pontus, 263, 283, 315
Bond, Helen, 32, 51
Boyarin, Daniel, x, 33, 128n49, 261n41, 317n63
Braund, Susanna, 262n66
Brent, Allen, 283

Caesar, Julius, 170
Caesarea Maritima, 6, 305
Caiaphas, 1, 2, 3, 9, 44, 55, 56, 57, 58, 59, 60, 62n41, 63n45, 63n46, 68, 269, 320, 321, 322
Caligula (Gaius), 15, 76, 81, 131, 160, 188, 190, 283
Cato the Younger, 205, 209, 215, 216, 217, 230, 241
Cenchrea, 264, 291, 299
Chaeronea, 199
Charlesworth, James H., 63n46
Charax Spasinu, 95, 97, 98, 100
Chrestus, 12, 72, 82, 169
Christianity, 11, 14, 32, 33, 44, 45, 46, 49, 61n1, 61n2, 61n11, 62n20, 62n37, 63n43, 68, 72, 73, 74, 83, 84, 91, 93, 101, 103, 111, 124, 127n8, 127n24, 127n37, 127n39, 128n46, 268, 288, 300, 315, 317n52, 317n62, 320, 321, 323
Christian Jews, 1, 3, 4, 9, 13, 14, 22, 26, 27, 37, 38, 46, 48, 51, 59, 60, 67, 73, 81, 86, 102, 105, 112, 120, 123, 124, 125, 126, 198, 268, 269, 270, 321, 322, 323
Christian Judaism, 17, 35, 46, 315, 320, 321, 323
Christian movement, ix, 4, 10, 11, 12, 22, 36, 38, 40, 44, 45, 48, 67, 68, 69, 73, 74, 82, 83, 85, 86, 87, 88, 95, 105, 112, 124, 126, 130, 143, 320, 321, 322
Christians, 2, 3, 7, 8, 11, 12, 13, 14, 16, 17, 18n8, 25, 27, 28, 31, 37, 38, 40, 42, 45, 46, 47, 49, 51, 52, 53, 54, 55, 60, 61n9, 62n33, 67, 69, 70, 71, 72, 74, 77, 83, 84, 86, 89, 90, 91, 100, 101, 102, 103, 104, 105, 107, 111, 114, 117, 122, 123, 124, 125, 127n16, 130, 139, 140, 143, 159, 198, 260, 263, 264, 265, 266, 267, 268, 269, 270, 272, 277, 278, 279, 283, 284, 285, 286, 288, 295, 299, 300, 301, 302, 305, 306, 312, 313, 314, 315, 315n3, 316n32, 317n61, 317n62, 319, 320, 321, 322, 323n1
Christus, 12, 69, 70, 72, 82, 84
Chronicle of Arbela, 101, 105
Cicero, 129, 130, 141, 192n1, 192n2, 224, 237, 241
circumcision, 13, 34, 35, 96, 97, 98, 100, 103, 115, 174, 175, 223
citizen(s), 5, 15, 22, 23, 24, 29, 39, 59, 72, 75, 78, 130, 141, 149, 150, 153, 183,

185, 189, 191, 202, 267, 282, 283, 309
citizenship, Roman, 75, 148, 157, 187
Claudius (emperor), 9, 10, 48, 72, 77, 95, 102, 104, 221, 281, 308, 316n32
Clement of Rome. *See* First Clement
Cohen, Shaye J. D., ix, 187, 223
Cook, John Granger, 316n32
coins, 164
Corinth, 16, 43, 46, 55, 60, 101, 102, 103, 264, 268, 270, 271, 281, 282, 288, 289, 291, 292, 297, 298, 299, 300, 301, 302, 312, 313, 315, 316n32, 320

Damon, Cynthia, 185
Daniel, prophesy of, 85, 298
David, 83, 89, 101, 105, 118, 123, 124, 298
David, city of, 314
David, God of, 14, 105, 112, 117, 118
Dead Sea Scrolls, 111
De superstitione (Seneca), 141, 142, 192n3
delatores (informers, informants), 203, 213, 257, 278, 279
delegation to Rome (Josephus), 36, 43, 53, 74, 76, 77, 78, 82, 143, 314
demon, 197, 201
Den Hollander, William, 127n18, 136
Didache, 14, 105, 106, 107, 108, 109, 110, 111, 112, 113, 114, 115, 116, 117, 118, 119, 120, 121, 122, 123, 124, 127n38, 127n39, 127n40, 127n41, 127n42, 128n43, 128n44, 128n45, 128n46, 128n47, 128n49, 301, 302, 315, 316n39
Dio, Cassius, 228, 261n34, 261n36, 266, 267, 284, 315n4, 316n34
Dio of Prusa (Dio Chrysostom), 133, 135, 156, 197, 199, 201, 202, 260, 260n2–260n6, 267, 273, 274, 283, 288, 314
Dionysius of Corinth, 299, 313
Domitia, 137, 138, 140, 149, 254
Domitian, 1, 9, 11, 14, 15, 16, 17, 74, 81, 82, 131, 133, 136, 137, 138, 140, 142, 143, 144, 149, 152, 156, 160, 161, 162, 165, 173, 178, 179, 180, 181, 182, 183, 186, 190, 193n16, 193n17, 197, 198, 199, 200, 201, 202, 203, 204, 206, 208, 209, 210, 211, 212, 213, 214, 215, 216, 217, 218, 223, 224, 225, 226, 227, 228, 231, 232, 233, 235, 236, 237, 238, 239, 240, 241, 243, 244, 246, 248, 249, 250, 251, 252, 253, 254, 256, 257, 258, 259, 260, 262n62, 263, 265, 266, 267, 268, 270, 271, 273, 274, 275, 276, 277, 278, 279, 280, 281, 282, 283, 284, 285, 288, 307, 308, 309, 310, 311, 312, 314, 316n33, 317n54, 320
Drusilla, 8, 11, 22, 77, 125, 126

Ecclesiastical History (Eusebius), 106, 299, 305
Egypt, 13, 48, 68, 84, 102, 121, 188, 189, 271, 272, 303
Egyptian, 67, 131, 177, 181, 183, 185, 186, 187
Eleazar (the Galilean), 11, 34, 35, 96, 97, 98, 99, 100, 124
Eliav, Jaron Z., 222
Epaphroditus, 149, 156, 177, 190
Epictetus, 156, 159
Essenes, 37, 105, 175, 323

Fadus, Cuspius, 10
Fagan, Garrett G., 219, 223, 261n38
fear, 16, 96, 98, 100, 137, 140, 154, 160, 180, 182, 191, 198, 203, 209–210, 211, 212, 213, 216, 217, 224, 226, 227, 231, 232, 233, 235, 241, 244, 245, 251, 255, 257, 259, 260, 265, 267, 268, 273, 274, 279, 280, 281, 283, 288, 307, 310, 314
Feldman, Louis H., ix, 21, 26, 27, 41, 42, 83, 173
Felix, Antonius, 6, 25, 28, 75, 77
Festus, Porcius, 25, 28, 30, 52, 54, 77
Fire of Rome (Great Fire), ix, 12, 13, 16, 53, 55, 60, 69, 70–72, 79, 81, 82, 104, 124, 130, 143, 221, 264, 265, 314, 319, 322
First Clement, 11, 16, 17, 40, 43, 46, 60, 101, 140, 199, 260, 263, 264, 265, 267, 268, 269, 270, 271, 272, 273, 277, 278, 279, 281, 283, 285, 286, 287, 288, 289, 290, 291, 292, 293, 294, 295, 296, 297, 298, 299, 300, 301, 302, 303, 304, 307, 311, 312, 313, 314, 315, 316n32, 320, 323
fiscus Judaicus, 142, 143, 164, 169, 178, 223, 254, 267
Fitzgerald, William, 209, 220

Flaccus (proconsul of Asia), 129, 141
Flavian Amphitheater, 221
Fourth Philosophy, 321
Freeman, Charles, 91–94

Gager, John, 32, 171
Gaius (emperor). *See* Caligula
Galatians (Paul's Letter to), 2, 13, 22, 23, 27, 34, 35, 38, 45, 46, 57, 62n25, 86, 87, 88, 93, 97, 100, 102, 103, 104, 105, 112, 114, 115, 122, 126, 289, 305, 323
Galilee, 1, 6, 8, 11, 18n8, 22, 31, 39, 40, 41, 42, 44, 48, 52, 53, 56, 59, 67, 68, 73, 74, 77, 82, 86, 96, 97, 98, 99, 105, 119, 120, 123, 124, 125, 126, 134, 143, 151, 158, 159, 162, 163, 178, 190, 192n11, 222, 254, 295, 305, 306, 315, 320, 321, 322
Gamaliel the Elder, 1, 2, 3, 22, 23, 24, 25, 26, 60, 61n4, 61n7, 320, 322
Gamaliel, Simon son of, 22, 23, 24, 25, 61n4, 61n7
Garrow, Alan, 116, 117, 121, 127n42, 128n43
Gentiles, 2, 10, 11, 13, 34, 35, 38, 46, 86, 87, 88, 89, 93, 100, 102, 103, 104, 106, 112, 115, 116, 119, 124, 130, 173, 178, 300, 306, 321, 322, 323
God of David, 14, 105, 112, 117, 118
God of Jesus Christ, 311
God-fearer(s), 305, 323
Goodman, Martin, ix, x, 7, 27, 66, 76, 178, 179
Green, Bernard, 72, 73
Griffin, Miriam T., 316n33
Gruen, Erich S., 192n15

haftarah, 85, 298
Hagner, Donald A., 317n51
Hasmonaean(s), 38, 125
Helena, Queen of Adiabene, 10, 11, 13, 34, 35, 65, 94, 95, 96, 97, 98, 99, 100, 101, 102, 103, 104, 153, 154
Heraclitus, 283
Herodians, 8, 9, 10, 18n13, 18n16, 68, 125, 158, 221
Herod of Chalcis, 57
Herod the Great, 2, 6, 21, 31, 32, 42, 99
Herodotus, 21, 271

Hesiod, 271, 283
Hillel, 23, 61n7, 336, 337
History of the Church (Eusebius). *See Ecclesiastical History*
Homer, 21, 168, 185, 202, 252, 276, 283
Howell, Peter, 166, 186
Hyrcanus, John, 55, 149

Ignatius of Antioch, 121, 302
Isaiah, 83, 84, 178, 298, 301, 302
Israel, 37, 58, 82, 89, 90, 101, 107, 115, 175, 270, 301
Israelites, 292
Izates, King, 10, 11, 13, 34, 35, 94, 95, 96, 97, 98, 99, 100, 101, 103, 153, 154

Jacob, 298
James (brother of Jesus), 1, 3, 4, 5, 9, 22, 25, 26, 28, 30, 31, 37, 44, 45, 47, 48, 49, 50, 51, 52, 53, 54, 55, 56, 57, 58, 59, 60, 62n42, 63n43, 73, 74, 77, 82, 86, 87, 103, 104, 120, 125, 198, 269, 305, 314, 319, 320, 322
Jerusalem, 1, 2, 3, 4, 5, 6, 7, 8, 9, 10, 11, 13, 14, 18n13, 22, 23, 24, 25, 28, 29, 30, 31, 33, 36, 38, 39, 41, 42, 43, 45, 46, 47, 48, 49, 50, 51, 52, 53, 54, 55, 57, 58, 59, 60, 61n4, 61n12, 65, 66, 67, 68, 73, 74, 75, 76, 77, 78, 82, 86, 87, 88, 96, 97, 99, 100, 101, 102, 103, 104, 105, 119, 120, 122, 125, 126, 126n3, 127n14, 129, 130, 133, 138, 141, 142, 143, 147, 150, 152, 153, 154, 155, 156, 157, 159, 164, 166, 167, 168, 169, 171, 178, 183, 186, 190, 198, 221, 222, 254, 265, 269, 303, 304, 305, 306, 311, 314, 319, 320, 322
Jefford, Clayton, 122, 128n46
Jerusalemite(s), 3, 22, 42, 51, 54, 96
Jesus Christ, 3, 4, 22, 24, 27, 61n8, 72, 89, 90, 111, 115, 117, 122, 123, 268, 270, 278, 279, 281, 287, 295, 296, 301, 311, 323
Jesus (Jesus of Nazareth), 1, 3, 4, 5, 9, 13, 18n8, 22, 25, 26, 27, 28, 30, 31, 33, 35, 37, 44, 45, 46, 47, 48, 49, 50, 52, 53, 54, 55, 56, 57, 58, 59, 60, 62n41, 63n46, 68, 69, 73, 74, 77, 82, 87, 90, 91, 92, 93, 94, 100, 103, 104, 108, 109,

110, 115, 116, 117, 118, 120, 124, 125, 269, 272, 286, 291, 293, 294, 296, 305, 314, 319, 320, 321, 322, 323
Jesus, Lord (our Lord), 297, 301
Jesus, Gospel of, 298, 301, 323
Jesus, Sayings of, 296, 297
Jesus, Traditions of, 286, 291, 294, 296, 297
Jesus the Messiah (Jesus the Christ), 22, 25, 26, 27, 35, 45, 46, 49, 60, 74, 86, 100, 103, 104, 110, 111, 116, 124, 198, 287, 306
Jesus the Nazarene (Jesus the Galilean), 77, 86, 87, 125
Jesus son of Ananias, 26, 28, 29, 30, 31, 49, 50, 51
Jesus son of God, 87, 88
Jesus Seminar, 122
Jewish Christianity, 91
Jewish Quarter (Rome), 17, 75, 77, 79, 124, 139, 155, 170, 222, 223, 263–265, 314
Jewish War, 14, 27, 39, 52, 82, 86, 87, 99, 119, 120, 125, 126, 132, 133, 143, 149, 162, 170, 171, 174, 198, 254, 265, 319
Jewish War (Josephus), 3, 6, 7, 8, 9, 10, 11, 18n1, 18n4, 18n5, 18n10, 18n21, 21, 25, 28, 30, 31, 41, 43, 50, 57, 60, 61n4, 62n17, 66, 68, 78, 79, 82, 84, 91, 94, 101, 119, 126, 126n1, 133, 134, 136, 137, 138, 139, 140, 142, 146, 147, 149, 150, 151, 153, 154, 155, 156, 157, 158, 163, 171, 174, 175, 176, 178, 179, 182, 183, 184, 190, 191, 193n18–193n21, 193n29–193n34, 193n41, 194n61, 221, 256, 304, 306, 314
John the Baptist, 45, 59, 68
John the Baptizer, 44, 59, 68, 124, 198, 321
Jones, Brian W., 307, 316n33
Josephus, Flavius, ix, x, 1, 2, 3, 4, 5, 6, 7, 8, 9, 10, 11, 12, 13, 14, 15, 16, 17, 18n1, 18n2–18n9, 18n11–18n14, 18n17–19n22, 21, 22, 23, 24, 25, 26, 27, 28, 30, 31, 32, 33–37, 38–41, 42–54, 55, 56–58, 59–60, 61n1–61n4, 61n11, 61n16–62n17, 62n26–62n35, 62n37–63n44, 63n46, 65, 66, 67, 68, 72–75, 76–86, 87–88, 89, 90, 91, 93, 94–95, 96, 97, 98–100, 101–103, 104–105, 112, 119, 121, 123, 124, 125–126, 126n1, 126n2, 126n4, 126n5, 127n10–127n12, 127n18, 127n32, 127n33–127n36, 130–131, 132, 133–140, 141, 142–143, 144–151, 152, 153, 154–159, 160, 161–163, 164, 168, 170, 171–172, 173–177, 178–180, 181–184, 185–190, 191, 192n4–192n14, 193n18–193n38, 193n41–193n42, 194n61–194n71, 194n74–194n77, 194n80, 194n84–195n91, 198–199, 200, 202, 218, 221, 222, 244, 254, 256–257, 258, 260, 261n41, 265, 267–268, 269–271, 273, 298, 302–306, 313, 314–315, 317n63, 319–321, 322–323
Jotapata, 39, 145, 146, 147, 163
Judaea, 1, 4, 8, 10, 11, 12, 13, 22, 24–25, 27, 28, 30, 31, 38, 40, 41, 42, 44, 45, 46, 47, 48, 49, 52, 54–56, 58, 59, 60, 66, 67, 68, 69, 72, 73, 76, 77, 78, 82, 84, 88, 89, 97, 98, 100, 102, 103, 104, 105, 120, 123, 126, 129, 130, 136, 137, 138, 139, 143, 148, 149, 151, 153, 154, 155, 157, 158, 164, 167, 171, 178, 183, 189, 190, 198, 220, 221, 222, 254, 265, 267, 268, 269, 295, 303, 305, 306, 311, 314, 315, 319, 321, 322
Judaean(s), 3, 9, 10, 11, 14, 23, 39, 59, 66, 67, 82, 100, 105, 126, 130, 142, 144, 152, 153, 171, 178, 186, 265, 266, 321, 322
Judaean politics (society), 33, 34, 67, 68, 190
Judaean priests, 77, 78
Judaean War, 68
Judaism, 3, 13, 22, 24, 27, 33, 34, 35, 36, 38, 42, 46, 47, 60, 61n4, 85, 86, 90, 91, 93, 96, 97, 100, 103, 104, 111, 112, 122, 123, 124, 141, 142, 154, 156, 157, 159, 164, 171, 172, 173, 175, 178, 179, 181, 182, 186, 268, 269, 313, 315, 320, 321, 322, 323
Judas of Gamala, 125, 321
Justus of Tiberias, 6, 7, 9, 21, 134, 137, 149, 158, 174, 193n28, 335
Juvenal, 141, 157, 164, 171, 185, 198, 228, 248, 257, 263, 265

Kasher, Aryeh, 173
Ker, Walter C. A., 165, 168, 248
Kleijwegt, Marc, 237
Kraft, Robert A., 121, 122

Lake, Kirsopp, 282, 283, 285
Lampe, Peter, 79
Legatio ad Gaium (Philo), 15, 68, 76, 81, 130, 131, 185, 188, 195n92, 265
Levison, John R., 173, 174
Levites, 298
Life (autobiography of Josephus), 5, 6, 8, 9–10, 11, 12, 13–14, 15, 24, 25, 33, 37, 38, 41, 43, 48, 50, 52, 53, 61n4, 66, 74, 79, 81, 82, 84, 86, 87, 91, 103, 119, 131, 132–135, 136, 137, 138, 139–140, 141, 142, 144, 147, 148, 149, 156, 157, 159, 160, 163, 174, 175, 178, 180, 181, 183, 184, 185, 222, 245, 254, 256, 260, 269, 313, 314
Lightfoot, J. B., 283, 285, 300
Luke, 18n15, 68, 122, 297, 298
Luke-Acts, 33, 37
Lysimachus, 177, 189

MacMullen, Ramsay, 317n62
Manetho, 177, 189
Martial, xi, 2, 11, 14, 15, 16, 39, 40, 130, 133, 141, 142, 143, 144, 156, 157, 159, 160, 161, 164, 165–167, 168, 169–170, 171–172, 174, 179, 181, 183, 185, 186, 187, 189, 193n17, 200, 201, 202–206, 207–220, 223, 224, 228, 232, 236–248, 254, 256, 258, 260, 264, 265, 267, 268, 272, 273, 314, 320
Masada, 21, 42, 265
Mason, Steve, ix, 4, 18n21, 35–37, 61n4, 65, 134, 135, 157–158, 172–175, 186, 194n62
Matthias (father of Josephus), 2, 10, 22, 25, 47, 49, 50, 54, 57, 74, 191
Mesopotamia, 6, 13, 34, 41, 47, 94, 97, 99, 100, 101, 103, 154, 306
Meyer, John, 175
minim (heretics), 3, 37, 323
Momigliano, Arnaldo, 84–85, 180
Monobazus (King of Adiabene), 94, 95, 101

Moses, 6, 15, 33, 96, 141, 176, 269, 286, 294, 298

Nanos, Mark, 34
Nazarenes, 59, 125, 323
Nero (emperor), 9, 12, 53, 54, 60, 69–72, 75, 76–77, 79–81, 82, 89, 124, 130, 140, 143, 144, 145, 156, 160, 198, 202, 203, 210, 211, 213, 219, 221, 225, 227, 231, 240, 250, 254, 263, 265, 266, 282, 283, 285, 308, 314, 319, 320, 322
Nerva, Marcus Cocceius (emperor), 202, 203, 204, 214, 215, 216, 217, 219, 224, 231, 232, 233, 243, 246, 247, 252, 263, 279, 284, 288, 308, 311
Neusner, Jacob, 23, 61n7, 105
Nicanor, 78, 144, 146, 147, 156
non-Christian Jews, 27, 73, 114, 119, 321

Octavian. *See* Augustus
oracles. *See* prophecy
Ostia, 264
Ovid (*Metamorphoses*), 272

Paetus, Thrasea, 279
Palestine. *See* Judaea
panegyric, 257, 275, 276, 307, 308–309, 311
Panegyrcus (Pliny the Younger), 15, 243, 249, 257, 260, 267, 278, 288, 303, 307, 308, 309, 310, 311, 312
Pardee, Nancy, 121, 122
Parthia (Parthian), 95, 305, 306
Parthenius, 144, 202, 213, 215, 216, 217, 240, 243, 246
Passover, 55, 56, 58, 154
Paul (apostle), ix, 2–3, 4, 5–6, 8–9, 10, 11, 13, 17, 22, 23, 24–26, 27, 28, 31–38, 41, 42–43, 45, 46–48, 55, 57, 59, 60, 67, 73, 77, 85, 86–94, 100, 102–104, 105, 112, 114–117, 118, 122–123, 124, 125–126, 130, 139, 264, 268, 270, 283, 287, 289, 290–293, 294, 295, 298–300, 305, 311, 312, 313, 315, 319, 320, 322, 323
Pentecost, 58
Persius, 185
Petronius, 164

Index 347

Pharisee(s), 1, 2, 3, 5, 6, 9, 13, 21–24, 26, 27–28, 31, 33, 34–36, 37, 38, 47, 50, 59, 60, 73, 74, 85, 86, 87, 90, 93, 98, 115, 123, 124, 126, 162, 175, 185, 191, 320, 322, 323
Philo of Alexandria, 15, 47–48, 67, 68, 75, 76, 81, 91, 93, 103, 124, 130, 131, 172, 185, 190, 191, 265, 269
Philotheos Bryennios (Archbishop of Nicomedia), 106
Phoenix, 271–272
Pilate, Pontius, 44, 45, 55, 55–56, 59, 68, 69–70, 72, 82, 321
Pliny the Elder, 12, 71, 95, 124, 170–171, 185, 272
Pliny, *Natural History*, 71, 272
Pliny the Younger, xi, 2, 11, 15, 16, 39–40, 67, 81, 133, 135, 137, 139, 141–142, 161, 198, 199, 200, 201, 204, 219, 224–240, 243–245, 248, 250, 251–254, 255–256, 257–260, 263, 265, 267, 268, 271, 273, 274, 275, 278, 279, 280, 281, 283, 285, 288, 291, 303, 307–312, 314–315
Plutarch, 78, 133, 134, 135, 156, 190, 197, 199–200, 253, 260, 267, 273, 274, 283, 314
Polybius, 183
Pompeii, 219, 224
Pompey, Gnaeus, 129, 130
Poppaea (Poppaea Sabina), 76, 79, 80, 81, 82, 127n18, 143, 145, 160, 254
Price, Jonathan, 156, 157
Priscus, Helvidius, 200, 227, 233–234, 235–236, 250, 251, 277, 279
prophecy, 7, 30–31, 82, 85, 113, 146, 250, 251, 267
prophet(s), 26, 30–31, 33, 49, 84–85, 89, 107, 108–109, 112–114, 116, 120, 145, 162, 174, 175, 176, 178, 183, 293, 298, 302, 311, 322
proselyte(s), 13, 34, 35, 97, 100, 223, 305, 321, 323
prostitute(s), 219
prostitution, 219
Ptolemy, 271
punishment, 52, 69, 71, 82, 236, 251, 253, 254, 256, 257, 275

Quintilian, 141–142, 185, 200, 211, 248
Qumran, 83, 84, 111, 178

Rajak, Tessa, ix, 28, 62n42, 136
Rimell, Victoria E., 218
Roman(s), 1, 2, 4, 6, 8, 9, 10, 11, 16, 21, 22, 24, 28, 31, 39–40, 54, 55, 56, 58, 59, 67, 69, 74, 80–81, 82, 84, 86, 119, 130, 141, 144–148, 151–158
Romans, Paul's Letter to, 89–90, 93–94, 100, 102, 112, 116
Rome, ix, 1, 2, 6, 8, 9, 10, 11–13, 14–17, 18n21, 22, 26, 28, 31, 33, 36, 39–40, 42–43, 46, 49, 50, 53, 54–55, 55, 56, 57, 60, 66, 67, 68, 69, 71–73, 74, 75–76, 77–79, 81–82, 84, 85, 89–90, 95, 101, 102–103, 104, 112, 124, 127n18, 129, 130, 132–133, 134, 135–136, 137, 138–140, 141, 142, 143, 144–145, 146, 148, 149, 150, 152, 153–154, 155–156, 157–158, 159–160, 161, 162, 163, 164, 167, 169, 170, 171, 172, 173, 178–179, 181, 183, 185, 186, 188, 190, 191, 197, 198–199, 201, 202, 203, 210–211, 212, 216, 218, 220, 221–222, 223, 224, 225, 231, 236, 238, 240, 241–242, 243, 244–245, 246, 247, 248, 249, 254, 256, 257, 258, 260, 263–268, 270, 272, 273, 274–275, 276, 277, 278–279, 280, 281–282, 283, 285, 287–288, 289, 291, 294, 295, 297–298, 299, 300–301, 302, 303, 304, 305, 307, 309, 312–314, 315, 316n32, 317n62, 319–320, 322
Rufus, Musonius, 200, 202, 239, 240, 251
Rusticus, L. Junius Arulenus, 197, 199–200, 225, 226, 236, 250, 251, 277, 279

Sabbath, 75, 76, 174, 175, 185
sacrifices, 75, 116, 119–120, 152, 303, 304
Sadducees, 27, 37, 50, 175, 323
Samaritan(s), 21, 120, 322
Sanders, E. P., 34
Sanhedrin, 50, 52
satirist (satirical self), 206–208, 245
Schaff, Philip, 282, 283, 316n27
Schwartz, Daniel R., ix, x, 37–38
Schwartz, Seth, ix, 62n42

Scribes, 123
Second Temple Period (Judaism), 42, 83, 84, 175
Segal, Alan F., 38
Sepphoris, 6, 7, 8, 99, 125
Septuagint (LXX), 119, 278, 293, 294, 295, 298, 301
Seneca the Elder, 211, 245
Seneca the Younger, 81, 82, 88, 93, 130, 141–142, 143, 159, 160, 185, 207, 210, 211, 239, 245, 255, 272
sex (sexuality), 91, 149, 165, 166, 204, 208, 214, 218–220, 253
Sicarii, 57, 305
silence(s), ix, 2, 3, 6–8, 10, 11–13, 14, 16–17, 22, 23, 26, 28, 31, 33–34, 36, 38, 40–41, 43, 46, 47–48, 49, 53, 55, 56, 59–60, 66–67, 72–73, 78–79, 81, 82, 83, 84, 85, 94, 95, 99, 102, 105, 112, 121, 123, 124, 125–126, 130, 131, 132, 133, 135, 136, 138, 139–140, 143–144, 147, 159, 164, 174, 178, 197, 198, 199, 225, 238, 239, 259, 260, 265, 267–268, 274, 279, 280, 313, 315, 319, 320
Simon son of Gamaliel. *See* Gamaliel, Simon son of
Simon son of Gioras, 152, 157
slave (slavery), 101, 130, 149, 157, 158, 168, 173, 204, 221, 254–256, 262n80, 279–280, 284, 323
Spain (Hispania), 15, 39, 144, 165, 172, 211, 215, 218, 238, 239, 240, 241, 242–243, 244, 245, 246, 247, 248, 265
Stein, Menahem, 192n8
Stark, Rodney, 317n62
Statius, 39, 156, 159, 161, 162, 176, 248, 258, 265, 267, 273–277, 279, 314
Stoics, 162, 225, 239
Stoicism, 162
Suetonius, 7, 12, 16, 37, 39, 53, 67, 70–72, 80, 81, 89, 102, 124, 139, 142–143, 156, 162–163, 169, 182, 198, 201, 223, 228, 241, 251, 263, 264, 265, 267, 271, 273, 275, 277, 281, 283–284, 288, 304, 306, 320
Sullivan, J. P., 164–165, 166, 211, 214–215, 238, 239, 243, 244, 246

synagogue(s), 17, 77, 84, 85, 115, 223, 265, 295, 298
Syria, 11, 13, 30, 31, 67, 75, 78, 84, 97, 105, 115, 121, 123, 126, 138, 224, 235, 302, 303, 305, 306

Tacitus, Cornelius, 2, 11, 12, 16, 37, 39, 53, 54, 55, 67, 68–70, 71–72, 79, 80, 82, 89, 104, 124, 137, 138, 139, 142, 154, 155, 156, 157, 159, 160, 161, 162–163, 185, 192n15, 198, 199, 201, 224, 228, 237, 243, 244, 249–251, 254, 257, 260, 261n41, 263–264, 265–266, 267, 268, 271–272, 273, 274, 279–280, 281, 283, 288, 303, 304, 306, 314, 320
Talmud, 6, 8
Temple of Peace (Rome), 150, 153, 170–171, 221, 304, 311
Temple of Saturn (Rome), 78
Temple (Jerusalem), 2, 5–6, 7, 9, 10, 13, 29, 42, 55, 57, 58, 59, 65, 68, 74, 75, 77, 82, 87, 96, 101, 104, 119–120, 122, 129, 130, 138, 141, 142, 147, 150–151, 152–153, 155, 156, 163, 167, 171, 177, 178, 186, 188, 190–191, 221, 222, 303–304, 306, 308, 320
Testimonium Flavianum, 26, 27, 45, 68, 83
theocracy, 15, 174
Thucydides, 4
Tiber, 75, 76, 155, 170, 229, 263, 265, 314
Tiberias, 6, 7, 8, 9, 21, 99, 125, 134
Tiberius (emperor), 31, 68, 69, 70, 185, 191, 221, 271
Tiberius Julius Alexander, 48
Tigellinus, 54, 60, 263, 319
Titus (Caesar), 1, 8, 9, 48, 57, 65, 68, 78, 82, 137, 138, 140, 143, 144, 145, 146, 147, 148, 149, 150, 152, 153, 154, 155, 156, 187, 221, 240, 248, 254, 256, 275, 304, 305, 306
Torah, 52, 84, 98, 150, 175, 298
Trajan (emperor), 15, 95, 101, 214, 217, 224, 232, 233, 238, 240, 241, 243, 244, 246, 247, 250, 257, 258–259, 260, 279, 281, 283, 307–308, 309–310, 311
Transtiberim, 75, 76, 79, 124, 139, 155, 170, 222, 223, 263, 264, 265, 314

Valerius Flaccus, 248

Van Henten, Jan Willem, ix, 173
Vergil, 215, 224, 276
Vespasian (emperor), 1, 7, 9, 14, 16, 30, 39, 82, 84, 137, 138, 140, 142, 144, 145–147, 148, 149, 150, 152, 153, 154, 155, 156, 158, 162–163, 170–171, 178, 186, 202, 221, 240, 254, 256, 267, 275, 306, 308, 311
Vitellius (governor of Syria), 31, 55

Wagner, J. Ross, 173, 174
Wilken, Robert, 319, 323n1
Wright, N. T., 33, 34

violence, 27, 51, 52, 60, 150, 241, 256, 283

Yohanan ben Zakkai, 8

Zealots, 125, 305, 321

About the Author

F. B. A. Asiedu was educated at Swarthmore College (BS in engineering), Westminster Theological Seminary (MDiv, ThM), and the University of Pennsylvania (MA, PhD). He has previously taught at the University of Pennsylvania, Villanova University, Middlebury College, and Emory University. He is currently a visiting scholar at Duke University.

www.ingramcontent.com/pod-product-compliance
Ingram Content Group UK Ltd.
Pitfield, Milton Keynes, MK11 3LW, UK
UKHW041011220326
11408UKWH00001B/123